Teaching Ritual

AMERICAN ACADEMY OF RELIGION

TEACHING RELIGIOUS STUDIES SERIES

SERIES EDITOR
Susan Henking, Hobart and William Smith Colleges

A Publication Series of
The American Academy of Religion
and
Oxford University Press

TEACHING LEVI-STRAUSS
Edited by Hans H. Penner

TEACHING ISLAM
Edited by Brannon M. Wheeler

TEACHING FREUD
Edited by Diane Jonte-Pace

TEACHING DURKHEIM
Edited by Terry F. Godlove, Jr.

TEACHING AFRICAN AMERICAN RELIGIONS
Edited by Carolyn M. Jones and Theodore Louis Trost

TEACHING RELIGION AND HEALING
Edited by Linda L. Barnes and Inés Talamantez

TEACHING NEW RELIGIOUS MOVEMENTS
Edited by David G. Bromley

AMERICAN ACADEMY OF RELIGION

Teaching Ritual

EDITED BY CATHERINE BELL

OXFORD

UNIVERSITY PRESS

2007

OXFORD
UNIVERSITY PRESS

Oxford University Press, Inc., publishes works that further
Oxford University's objective of excellence
in research, scholarship, and education.

Oxford   New York
Auckland   Cape Town   Dar es Salaam   Hong Kong   Karachi
Kuala Lumpur   Madrid   Melbourne   Mexico City   Nairobi
New Delhi   Shanghai   Taipei   Toronto

With offices in
Argentina   Austria   Brazil   Chile   Czech Republic   France   Greece
Guatemala   Hungary   Italy   Japan   Poland   Portugal   Singapore
South Korea   Switzerland   Thailand   Turkey   Ukraine   Vietnam

Published by Oxford University Press, Inc.
198 Madison Avenue, New York, New York 10016

www.oup.com

Oxford is a registered trademark of Oxford University Press

Library of Congress Cataloging-in-Publication Data
Teaching ritual / edited by Catherine Bell.
    p. cm.—(AAR teaching religious studies series)
Includes bibliographical references and index.
ISBN 978-0-19-517645-2; 978-0-19-517646-9 (pbk.)
1. Ritual—Study and teaching.   2. Rites and ceremonies—
Study and teaching.   I. Bell, Catherine M., 1953–
BL600.T43 2007
203'.8071—dc22   2006030319

9 8 7 6 5 4 3 2 1

Printed in the United States of America
on acid-free paper

Dedicated to our teachers,

as well as the colleagues and students

who helped to make our teaching

effective and enjoyable.

Preface

I particularly want to thank Susan Henking, editor of the AAR Teaching Religious Studies series, and the staff of Oxford University Press—Cynthia Read, Theodore Calderera, and Linda Donnelly—whose patience and assistance greatly aided this editor at every turn.

Like most edited volumes, this collection has been in preparation for several years. Many of the contributors have been with the project from the very beginning, and they continually buoyed the editor with their enthusiastic conviction about the project's intrinsic value. Those who joined later worked with great efficiency and tolerance of the constraints that time pressed on us all. Now, rereading all of these essays, I hear their voices afresh—wondering and reflecting, explaining and suggesting, as dazzling with their creativity as they are impressive in their expertise. They have been wonderful colleagues, and now they will have the opportunity to help answer a question of which we are so well aware: how can we, with this book, convey ways to teach what is so poorly conveyed by books?

Contents

Contributors

Linda L. Barnes is Associate Professor of Family Medicine and Pediatrics at Boston University School of Medicine (BUSM), a medical anthropologist, historian, and religion scholar who directs the Boston Healing Landscape Project at BUSM. Her publications include *Needles, Herbs, Gods, and Ghosts: China, Healing, and the West to 1848* (2005) and the coedited volume *Religion and Healing in America* (2005).

Catherine Bell is the Bernard J. Hanley Professor of Religious Studies at Santa Clara University. In addition to two books on ritual (*Ritual Theory, Ritual Practice* [1992] and *Ritual: Perspectives and Dimensions* [1997]), she has also written on aspects of Chinese morality books, beliefs, and Falungong practices, among other things. She is currently working on a manuscript on the religious practices of believing.

Linda Ekstrom teaches studio art in the College of Creative Studies at the University of California, Santa Barbara (UCSB). Her sculptures and installation spaces explore a range of issues at the center of religious traditions, especially a number of memorial spaces arising from the Shoah. Ekstrom's work has been in both solo and group exhibitions nationally, including, "Faith: The Impact of Judeo-Christian Religion on Art at the Millennium" at the Aldrich Museum of Contemporary Art. Ekstrom and Richard Hecht developed a course on religion and contemporary art which they have co-taught for ten years in the Department of Religious Studies and the College of Creative Studies at UCSB. They are completing a book manuscript on religion and the cultures of contemporary art.

Richard A. Gardner is currently Dean of the Faculty of Liberal Arts at Sophia University in Tokyo. With a number of publications on Japanese religion, notably Noh, Yasukuni Shrine practices, and Aum Shinrikyô, his more recent work includes "Aum and the Media: Lost in the Cosmos and the Need to Know," in *Religion and Social Crisis in Japan: Understanding Japanese Society through the Aum Affair*, ed. Robert J. Kisala and Mark R. Mullins (2001); "Collective Memory, National Identity: Victims and Victimizers in Japan," in *Quoting God: How Media Shape Ideas about Religion and Culture*, ed. Claire H. Badaracco (2005); and "Humor and Religion: An Overview," *Encyclopedia of Religion*, ed. Lindsay Jones (2005).

Sam Gill is Professor of Religious Studies at the University of Colorado at Boulder and the author of *Storytracking: Texts, Stories, Histories in Central Australia* (1998) and a number of other works on Native American religions, play, and dancing.

Ann Grodzins Gold is Professor in the Departments of Religion and Anthropology at Syracuse University, the William P. Tolley Distinguished Teaching Professor in the Humanities for 2005–2007, and currently Director of Syracuse University's South Asia Center. Her publications include numerous articles and four books: *Fruitful Journeys: The Ways of Rajasthani Pilgrims* (2000); *A Carnival of Parting: The Tales of King Bharthari and King Gopi Chand* (1993); *Listen to the Heron's Words: Reimagining Gender and Kinship in North India*, with Gloria Raheja, (1994); and, most recently, *In the Time of Trees and Sorrows: Nature, Power and Memory in Rajasthan*, with Bhoju Ram Gujar (2002), which was awarded the 2004 Ananda Kentish Coomaraswamy Book Prize from the Association for Asian Studies.

Ronald L. Grimes is Professor of Religion and Culture at Wilfrid Laurier University in Waterloo, Canada, and holds the Chair of Ritual Studies at Radboud University, Nijmegen, in the Netherlands. One of the founding editors of the *Journal of Ritual Studies*, he is the author of several books on ritual, most recently, *Rite Out of Place: Ritual, Media, and the Arts* (2006). Among his other works on ritual are *Deeply into the Bone: Re-Inventing Rites of Passage* (2002) and *Readings in Ritual Studies* (1995).

Richard D. Hecht is Professor of Religious Studies at the University of California, Santa Barbara. Among his most recent publications is *To Rule Jerusalem* (2000) with Roger Friedland. He has also written numerous essays and short stories on the profane politics of sacred places and people caught in the borderlands of urban and national politics. See the entry for Linda Ekstrom for a description of their collaborations.

Lindsay Jones is Associate Professor in the Department of Comparative Studies at Ohio State University. He is author of *Twin City Tales: A Hermeneutical Reassessment of Tula and Chíchén Itzá* (1995) and *The Hermeneutics of Sacred Architecture: Experience, Interpretation, Comparison* (2000), two volumes, as well as editor in chief of the revised second edition of Mircea Eliade's *Encyclopedia of Religion* (2005).

Christopher I. Lehrich is Instructor in the Boston University College of Arts and Sciences Writing Program. He is the author of *The Language of Demons and Angels*, a study of the occult philosophy of Cornelius Agrippa, and has a forthcoming book on method and theory for the study of magic and occultism.

Mary E. McGann, RSCJ, is Associate Professor of Liturgy and Music at the Franciscan School of Theology and the Graduate Theological Union in Berkeley, California. She is author of *A Precious Fountain: Music in the Worship of an African American Catholic Community* (2004) and *Exploring Music as Worship and Theology: Research in Liturgical Practice* (2002).

John Nelson is Professor of East Asian Religions in the Department of Theology and Religious Studies at the University of San Francisco, where he also directs the Asian Studies Program. Among his publications are *Enduring Identities: the Guise of Shinto in Contemporary Japan* (2000), *A Year in the Life of a Shinto Shrine* (1996), and numerous articles related to religion and politics in East Asia. He has recently completed a documentary, *Spirits of the State*, on the controversy over enshrining spirits of the military dead at Yasukuni Shinto shrine.

David Pinault is Associate Professor of Religious Studies at Santa Clara University. Interested in both textual and current popular traditions, he is the author of *Story-Telling Techniques in the Arabian Nights* (1992), *The Shiites: Ritual and Popular Piety in a Muslim Community* (1992), *Horse of Karbala: Muslim Devotional Life in India* (2001), and of articles on topics including the ritual relationships of Muslim and Hindu communities.

Richard Schechner is University Professor at the Tisch School of the Arts, New York University where he teaches Performance Studies. Among Schechner's books are *Between Theater and Anthropology* (1986), *Performance Theory* (1988), and *Performance Studies—An Introduction* (2002; 2006). He has founded several professional theater companies and directed many plays, including *Dionysus in 69*, *The Oresteia*, *Three Sisters*, *Hamlet*, *Yokastas Redux*, and *Timbuktu*.

Susan S. Sered is Senior Research Associate at Suffolk University's Center for Women's Health and Human Rights, formerly director of the 'Religion, Health and Healing Initiative' at Harvard University's Center for the Study of World Religions, and Associate Professor of Anthropology at Bar Ilan University, Israel. Her many books and articles include *Uninsured in America: Life and Death in the Land of Opportunity* (2005), *Priestess, Mother, Sacred Sister: Religions Dominated by Women* (1996), and the coedited volume *Religion and Healing in America* (2004).

Andrew Strathern and Pamela J. Stewart are a husband-and-wife collaborative team who work in anthropology, cultural history, and ritual studies.

Their most recently coauthored books include *Witchcraft, Sorcery, Rumors, and Gossip* (2004) and *Empowering the Past, Confronting the Future* (2004), while their coedited volumes include *Terror and Violence: Imagination and the Unimaginable* (with Neil L. Whitehead, 2006) and *Expressive Genres and Historical Change: Indonesia, Papua New Guinea, and Taiwan* (2005). They jointly edit the Ritual Studies Monograph Series and coedit the *Journal of Ritual Studies*.

Ann Taves is Professor of Religious Studies at the University of California at Santa Barbara and the author of *Fits, Trances, and Visions: Experiencing Religion and Explaining Experience from Wesley to James* (1999), among other books and articles.

Theodore Vial is Associate Professor of Theology at the Iliff School of Theology and author of *Liturgy Wars: Ritual Theory and Protestant Reform in Nineteenth-Century Zurich* (2004) and articles in *Numen, Method & Theory in the Study of Religion*, and the *Harvard Theological Review*. He serves on several steering committees, including the North American Association for the Study of Religion (NAASR) and the Institute for Cognition and Culture at Queen's University Belfast.

Mark I. Wallace is Associate Professor in the Department of Religion and member of the Interpretation Theory Committee and the Environmental Studies Committee at Swarthmore College. He is the author of *Finding God in the Singing River: Christianity, Spirit, Nature* (2005) and *Fragments of the Spirit: Nature, Violence, and the Renewal of Creation* (1996; 2002). He recently received an Andrew W. Mellon New Directions Fellowship for a research sabbatical in Costa Rica.

Teaching Ritual

Introduction

You will be amazed by the voices you hear in this book—voices of professors being personal about what they do in the classroom, what they think went well, what they fear went wrong, how they tried again.

Going into this project, I knew it was an opportunity to present the diversity of perspectives on ritual and the contexts in which it is being taught. So there are essays based on teaching undergraduate and graduate students, teaching in a variety of contexts (e.g., types of schools and departments), teaching with very different pedagogical goals and styles, teaching experimental courses and including ritual in more traditional courses, even co-teaching with colleagues who bring the possibly creative or disruptive perspective of another field. There was no effort, however, to provide "regional" coverage or avoid duplication of area specialties; experience for teaching by scholars also publishing in this area were the only criteria. You will see the variety that resulted as you turn these pages. Ritual has, from the beginning, been a topic enabling disciplines, styles, and purposes to come together and communicate with one another. This book, another example of this special quality, may help ensure that the disciplinary boundaries that so often take root at the college level will continue to be transgressed in at least one corner of the curriculum.

Aside from the easy task of assembling diverse expertise, however, I encouraged each contributor to be as individual in approach as his or her personality and experience allowed. I urged the contributors to speak to the *real* difficulties facing anyone planning to teach ritual in a traditional course or to develop a new course—specifically, how to simplify while representing the complexities of views on the subject. A book like this should be a thoughtful guide to the teacher new to the topic as well as the experienced professor looking for fresh angles and materials. This means it is not a methodical "how-to" book, but an account, in real voices, of the experiences of professionals on an assortment of courses. In the middle of all their drafts, several contributors wrote that their chapters had been among the most difficult pieces they had ever written. The writing was difficult, I surmise, because they were trying to formulate, in clear prose, the classroom techniques and rationales guiding what we do that usually lies unspoken and is often a matter of embodied knowledge. Many were also using a tone that was different from their usual professional one. In these pieces, they are striving to be completely frank in describing how a course succeeded, or not, and how the experience affected their outlook on the course. Therefore, some of the essays are very personal in recounting class experiences that proved to be self-revelatory or just wrong-headed. Other voices may be more formal, but they depart from established protocols to describe their various attempts to explore substantive issues that attend ritual in a variety of settings—not just the polished result. Although the materials, expertise, and the orchestration of a course by one teacher are not easily borrowed by another, these essays demonstrate how one's own area of scholarly expertise and interests can be used for courses with widely shared pedagogical goals. In fact, you will find their ingenuity rather stunning; they raise the bar for professional pedagogy very high.

All of the contributors are research scholars who have pushed our understanding of ritual in published analyses of distinct types of ritual experience or theory. Here, however, they describe the artistry with which they enable inexperienced students to reassess something that at first seems obvious, marginal, or simply invisible. Artistry or alchemy, this process is often hidden or ignored. Yet how a scholar-teacher transforms his or her voice to set the goals for a particular class *is* a learned skill. This book reflects the learning experiences of those in front of a classroom, but you will also see how the authors also imagined pulling their classroom experiences back into their scholarly work of discovery and interpretation.

Seeking diversity, the book has fully delivered it. Hoping for individual voices, I come away humbled and emboldened. Yet the contributions surprised me in another way. They showed a degree of coherence, even unity, in our perceptions of ritual that I was not aware existed. Time and again, authors share bibliographic reference points and stress similar aspects of ritual for their students. In a more latent consensus, they echo each other as to *why* to teach ritual in so many different courses: it is one of the most representative ways of being religious, and it comes under the radar of our students to present the vaguely familiar in a fresh way. By recognizing the central role of ritual as the flexible backbone of traditions and the clearest illustration of how we orient ourselves within the cosmos, teaching religion is both theoretically central and pedagogically compelling.

The unexpected coherence of these essays also comes out in the thoughtful preparation of material used. As John Nelson points out, many rituals from less familiar religions can be overwhelming, posing too many symbols, actions, and roles even to explain. If unexamined, these experiences of ethnographic overload can reinforce the worst forms of modern Orientalist exoticism. Examining them risks another kind of overload, however; I have long bemoaned the tedium that results when even the wildest shamanic trance is described in close detail and analyzed step by step, usually by reference to beliefs pulled in as representative of the authentic tradition. Well, authentic tradition is a slippery idea, as we know. Ethnographies of ritual that explain trance by reference to an enacted mental journey to visit the world of the dead are not wrong, of course, but they do not do justice to the shared features of ritual and the performative purposes of ritual.

These essays by seasoned teachers mediate the ethnographic record and the relevant experience of commonality, the homely example to analyze and the exotic film to parse. They describe what *works* in the classroom. As Nelson puts it, one must exercise the Buddhist value of *upaya*, choosing the form of instruction most appropriate for the audience of the message that you truly wish to communicate. With experience in and commitment to effective instruction, the contributors to this volume agree that ritual should be taught through attention to various widely found structural features and the types of experiences these features enable. This sort of thematic emphasis is, by any account, a relatively new way to teach religion, especially in a religious studies or theology department. It may still be controversial in places. Yet these ritual scholars conclude that ritual is too important a part of religion to be rendered secondary in the curriculum. To make the most of their conclusions, you need to heed the underlying challenges to our categories for religion, to pedagogical assumptions about the classroom, and to our habits of gentle self-censorship to conform to what our institutions overtly sanction.

The most effective sets of differences by which to organize these essays are the emphases, often minor, which the reader will see reflected in the three divisions of the book. The essays in the first section emphasize the personal experiences, usually religious, that are special to involvement in rituals. It could once be taken for granted that students would be familiar with some set of religious rituals, but that is no longer the case. Many students have no religious experience, or their experiences are too minimal and confused for them to draw upon. Their familiarity with civic rites or the rituals sponsored by various social institutions—such as high school graduation or freshmen orientation—must be pointed out to them; then they are amazed at what analysis reveals. Nonetheless, high school graduations do not fully explain why ritual is deemed so basic to social and cultural life, that is, why it has been called (a bit dramatically, perhaps), "*the* basic social act."[1] Freshmen orientation rituals also do not explain the significance attached to rituals basic to the religious communities that surround our students on campus and in the larger national community. Students are fascinated, of course, with bits and pieces of exoticism, from their rarely correct information about Mormonism to their generalities about shamanism and tantrism. They need a larger context within which to understand both the mundane and the fascinatingly foreign. They need to learn the analytic reflex, with a basic sense of theorizing in order to assess experiences with Buddhist meditation or Christian evangelicalism with which they may become involved someday.

In Part I, Richard Schechner starts things off by describing how he takes his class, step by step, into the more mystical of experiences orchestrated by ritual performances. He takes us through the variety of situations in which the teacher of rituals can be involved, from whirling in the dark to participating like a believer in the religious rites of a Brooklyn community. We and his students could have no better guide than this international expert in theater, ritual, and the performances of social communities in everyday life. The anthropologist Ann Grodzins Gold takes us on some of her peregrinations in the liminality of teaching, notably, "the rocks and stones" she lays out in large courses of undergraduates all looking for transcendence. How to teach "the continuity between external actions and internal states of being" when the "gulf" the class sees between lofty texts and meditative ideals is analogous to the gulf confronting her in her own fieldwork between the illiterate rites of the thousands of Indian villages and the textual ideals depicted by the tradition? She finds a key, and evidence of the distance in cultural understanding that she has traveled, when she ventures into a new course. In "Dancing Ritual," Sam Gill ruminates on the formal lack of interest in both ritual and dancing. From the perspective of religious practices, ritual and dancing are one and the same thing in many cultures, primarily oral cultures, but these equations of religion, ritual, and dancing remains relatively foreign for Americans students, despite their dancing events and at least one famous example of a dancing American religion. Experimenting with our reluctance to see any natural association, Gill takes his ruminations about the university as "a Christian theological project" into a class on ritual that refuses to ignore the body—and in which he had his students dance. In the end, the university may have looked pretty much the same, but his students—and Sam himself—felt significantly changed.

The field trip is a natural tool for teaching religion in communities of marked religious pluralism, which means almost every urban community in America and Europe. But escorting students to a Buddhist *puja* rite or a weekly Islamic service can actually distort their views of these religions; it would be like teaching Judaism through a field trip to a schul of the Lubavitcher followers of the late Rabbi Schneerson. There is so much more to the religion and the culture, beginning with a variety of sectarian views on how to be Jewish, Buddhist, or Muslim. How do you give students a picture of the whole in which to situate their field trip experience, the common human concerns as well as the unique historical experiences of these peoples? With "lots of work," the experienced teacher knows to answer! David Pinault is an experienced teacher, but one with the confident idiosyncrasies born of wide and repeated travel off the beaten track. His essay describes his efforts to navigate naïve students through the rich diversity of religion in Silicon Valley, while enabling them to encounter the real people behind the exotic facades. Along the way he recites for us some of the poetry that resulted from nineteenth-century encounters of the strange and the human.

Mark Wallace tells a different story, that of the teacher who must confront fresh reactions to 9/11. In a class on religion and ecology, he uses a variety of contemplative practices and social fieldwork projects, but unexpected rituals were born when he took the class into the woods. There the natural world created a liminal space in which his students were able to stop, sense, feel, speak, and reflect in healing forms of shared communication. Wallace's essay describes the experience of taking risks with a religion class, those that are planned, of course, but also the challenge of those that are unplanned. It this vein, it is only fitting that Ronald Grimes has the last word in a section devoted to ritual and experience, allowing *Teaching Ritual* to include the perfect piece for that purpose, although it was originally written for another venue.[2] Amid various reflections on the constraints and challenges of teaching, this essay describes what one learns when ritual is the curriculum. Grimes discovers the pedagogy of yielding the teacher's control to the very rites with which he has empowered his students.

Part II focuses on those teaching experiences, materials, and goals that emphasize the theoretical, ethical, and generally multi-analytical issues raised when one gives primacy to ritual and ritual action in the study of religion. Each essay contributes a very distinctive set of "rules of engagement." The substantive materials range from Shinto politics through revival meetings to the latest in cognitive theory. Yet each also explicitly addresses "why" ritual is the focus of a course on religion. In an essay that could fit into any of the divisions of this book, John Nelson describes teaching valuable lessons about the historical uses of ritual that often do not appear in our courses—for example, how Shinto symbolism could turn the emperor into a deity, evoking obedience and reverence from all his subjects. Nelson's course on Buddhism also undermines the assumptions with which students enter by stressing the role of ritual in propping up political power, which he demonstrates through an analysis of the ritual recitation of the Heart Sutra.

The current editors of the *Journal of Ritual Studies*, the anthropologists Pamela Stewart and Andrew Strathern, suggest a simple but novel approach to using the journal to provide discussions of key issues about ritual while introducing a wide range of ritual practices. In brief, they explore the conflict of local style and global norms, ritual invention, performance and performativity, embodied communication, as well as what ritual appears to suggest about human consciousness. They outline five assignments, each surely followed by several classes of discussions, creating a sophisticated introduction to anthropology's empirical and theoretical contributions to ritual. Mary McGann approaches our subject from the singular position of the engaged minister, the ritual leader, who is teaching the basics of ritual and liturgy to future ceremonial leaders. How is ritual taught from within a tradition, such as Christianity? McGann comes to her task with an unexpected, but very modern, set of credentials above and beyond her degrees in theology and liturgical studies: more than a decade of participation in an African American Catholic community for an ethnographic study of the role of music in ritual life, an experience that required her to master all the relevant anthropological and history of religions literature. The liturgical tradition is explained and passed on to another generation by engaging its diversity and current performative incarnations, not as a mere history of practice and theological meanings. McGann's concerns, in this complex example of the classic -emic and -etic distinctions, echo many specific arguments taken up in the other essays in this section, yet in the end she weaves a unique pedagogical resolution.

Ann Taves raises the problem of teaching ritual in relation to historically anti-ritualistic traditions that nonetheless developed ritual forms of their own, specifically, Protestantism in America. She begins by describing how she would revise a course that she has frequently taught to include more discussion of the issues at stake in the ritualism critique and reformulation. In developing the interplay between these modes of religiosity, Taves focuses on the revivalist camp meetings as described in the memoirs of a nineteenth-century Methodist. In lieu of any classroom performance of their own, her graduate students experience the first-person descriptions of a remarkable eyewitness by reading the rich observations and interpretations of a participant who is cognizant of the subtle reformulations taking place at every stage. Raising various questions—what was ritual to the participants, where did they make distinctions challenging their Methodist teachers?—Taves uses the work of recent theoreticians to analyze the styles and intentionalities of ritual action. Theodore Vial provides further discussion of the cognitive theories mentioned by Taves, after drawing a familiar ethnographic picture of the constraints placed on most courses in a small undergraduate institution. His course must satisfy the requirements of the department as well as other humanities programs, sometimes awkwardly conceived, and he cannot presume that anyone entering has the slightest familiarity with any major thinkers of the Western intellectual tradition. The goal of an omnibus course in the humanities that satisfies the "theory" requirement for religion majors and, at the same time, admits students who must be presumed ignorant of all the thinkers to be discussed could do worse, he finds, than start with criteria laid out by Jonathan Z. Smith. Vial explores the particular issue of how religious experiences become historical-cultural traditions. Along the way, he equips his students with a stimulating theoretical immersion, while offering readers a frank discussion of what worked and what did not. I do not know of a more efficient introduction to the main contenders in the debates of cognitive theory than what Vial lays out here.

My essay concludes this section with the admission that I have never taught a course that focused on ritual alone. After two books and too many articles, I was partly afraid that I would overwhelm my undergraduates with arguments that refute other arguments in a tightening circle of references that only I would be able to untangle. But the main reason is my interest in teaching them, in the short time I have them, about religion as a whole in terms relevant to their current probable experiences. My essay addresses the ramifications of, as well as strategies for, teaching ritual as a central feature of *religion*. As noted above, this marks an important change in the history of religions approach to both religion and ritual, and one of the functions of this book is to address specific issues that this change poses to teachers and scholars. It is a continual challenge to imagine how to teach religion, using ritual, in introductory courses, in courses on specific traditions, and in advanced classes that include more of the theory of the field and extended individual projects; these are some of the contexts in which I work through the particular place of ritual and the understanding of religion that I am presenting to my students. Teaching religion with a significant focus on ritual does not merely challenge our tradition of thinking about religion; it challenges every maturing religion major to try to make sense of the discrepancy in views about religion that they learn from other faculty.

The third and final section of the volume may be the most fun because it addresses the challenge of teaching ritual in courses that engage specific topics. These last chapters offer something for readers who searched through the first two parts of the book for ideas to use in courses that are already set or substantively constrained, but they also reward readers who want to reach beyond their own expertise. In particular, these chapters provide condensed backgrounds in various topics, to be included alongside more familiar materials in religion courses, for a new comparative focus. Simultaneously, these discussions broaden our understanding of ritual practices as healing rites *and* as tools in the teaching of undergraduate writing. In other words, you will hear the voices of scholars who gradually realized that a focus on ritual aided their teaching of other topics in religion to which they were committed. More than a mere organizing principle, ritual becomes a means of explicating the experience and structure of religiosity inherent in some unexpected (nonritual) forms of cultural practice. If Part I opens the book with the dynamics of teaching ritual experience, and Part II explores the theoretical reasons for foregrounding ritual in the study of religion, the contributions in Part III provide evidence that a wide variety of religious and cultural practices find fresh significance when analyzed as and through ritual.

Susan Sered and Linda Barnes deal with one of the earliest and still most ubiquitous forms of ritual activity in the human record: seeking the aid of a greater power in a quest for healing. Because of the enormity of the topic and the importance of keeping their students' experiences in mind, Sered and Barnes developed a cross-cultural typology as an expedient, not definitive, tool for organizing the key analytic features of ritual healing for individual and collective illness. Using the pedagogical exercises this typology affords, students discover nearly universal ritual strategies and motivations. Sao Paolo, Jerusalem, Shanghai, or Kiev—a class can readily suggest current American examples that match practices that at first seem so foreign and irrational. What is the common logic behind these rites and all the other curative practices of the American scene—from a doctor's visit to Twelve Step Programs, petitioner prayers, and the use of crystals? Sered and Barnes explore these ritual strategies and the religious experiences, cosmologies, and communities they can generate. In a more explicit version of the same starting point, Richard Gardner stresses the theme that religion, overly confined to concepts of belief and inner experience, is mostly a matter of what people do. Yet teaching religion as what people do is far from simple, and challenges every assumption about religion along the way. His materials are the Japanese arts of Noh and Kyôgen, traditional forms of performance still cherished in Japan today. He introduces a simple typology of ritual based on the particular needs of his materials and teaching, namely, rites that harmonize and rites that interpret the incongruities of life, which he applies to the subtle role of religious sensibilities in these traditions of dramatic action. With an intriguing compounding of questions, Gardner finds cultural definitions of ritual and artistic performance by examining the dramatic stories themselves because they typically center on the ritual actions of the lead actors, an approach some of Schechner's Indian material also suggests. Even those readers unfamiliar with the materials Gardner engages so deftly will find his conclusions surprisingly humorous.

The many facets of ritual performance are also the focus for Linda Ekstrom and Richard Hecht, who come together from different disciplines to teach a course investigating the relations of religion and contemporary art. To do so, they must explicate "religion" and "art" to students with little experience in either, and they have found that ritual provides the most effective opening for them to develop a variety of theoretical frameworks. They begin with an understanding of ritual's unique ability to hold together opposing orders of reality or, as Gardner might say, social incongruities. The modern "tradition" of processing the Virgin of Guadalupe around a Latino parish involves colorful

Aztec dancers in the street, in stark contrast with the Catholic mass performed within the church—"countervalent" performances roughly united
within the overall celebration of Las Mañanitas. Student ritual performances
become an opportunity to analyze more closely the expressive effect of choreographed symbolism, especially "whole-making" power. In a further development of performance and place, Lindsay Jones uses architecture as the
medium with which to explore ritual. He demonstrates the ability of defined
spaces to be performative events in themselves. Working through the theoretical complexities of comparative analysis, Jones explains his experiments
with two different course structures and projects. Real-world constraints on his
students dictated the more successful one for investigating the phenomenon of
the ritual eventfulness, apprehensive effect, and even abundant autonomy of
buildings, all ways in which our own creations come to flexibly structure our
reality.

Christopher Lehrich concludes this collection of writings on ritual by describing how ritual studies inform his teaching of undergraduate writing. If
the reader has stayed with the volume in the presented order of essays, Lehrich's essay will not seem implausible. Indeed, I was reminded of works on
ritual overlooked for years. I also presented Lehrich's method to my department in order to counter complaints that a single course (and its overworked
professor) could not be expected to encompass writing and a substantive topic
at the same time. Since they were used to a writing emphasis in small semi-
nars, my department colleagues were patient with a presentation on writing
in the introductory course on religion; but they grew visibly impatient with the
idea of teaching writing in large advanced courses responsible for so much
other content. Yet they were so impressed with a presentation on Lehrich's
formula that each faculty member wanted a copy of the drafted chapter. Lehrich's inventiveness simply underlines the evidence presented in this section
that in addition to unfolding so much of the world to our students, teaching
ritual also provides understandings that empower them to take less passive and
more performative actions to shape that world.

Whether through performative or cognitive analyses, ritual action holds an
important place in the study of religion. Long dominated by topics that theology holds central (scriptural texts, history of interpretation, and comparative
beliefs), history of religions finds in ritual practice a space within which to
develop theories of religion that are more uniquely its own contribution. To go
back and study scripture and belief from the perspectives forged by ritual
studies would certainly be the next step. The essays in this volume develop the
richness of ritual for religious studies, never more clearly than when forced to
explain itself again and again in the classroom. Some essays contain suggestions for how the next step might begin to be taken. To be in the classroom
teaching moderately interested undergraduates or more self-selected graduate
students has conventionally meant that one is not doing one's own research

and writing. Yet the classroom is a precious arena (and stage?) for thought—both performative thinking that forces ideas to make sense and have imme-diately useful ramifications, and the performative orchestration of thinking, that is, putting one's own airy castles aside to build with more diverse and conventional categories. As teachers, our contributions to this volume have been an opportunity to share those teaching and thinking performances, their connections, insights and recognitions of mistakes. We hope our readers will see in this record of teaching performances opportunities that they can seize and play out in their own inherently theoretical pedagogical practice.

NOTES

1. Roy A. Rappaport, *Ritual and Religion in the Making of Humanity* (Cambridge: Cambridge University Press, 1999), 138.

2. Grimes's essay originally appeared as "Zen and the Art of Not Teaching Zen and the Arts: An Autopsy," in Victor Sogen Hori et al., eds., *Teaching Buddhism in the West: from the Wheel to the Web* (London: RoutledgeCurzon, 2002), 155–69. Reprinted with the permission of the publisher.

PART I

Teaching the Experience through Encounter and Reflection

I

Living a Double Consciousness

Richard Schechner

Teaching ritual is incredibly difficult because the subject is so vast, with no general agreement on the basics, including what ritual is, how it works, what it feels like to perform a ritual or participate in one, and what its functions are. On the one hand, ritual is allied with the "sacred," another difficult concept to define. On the other, evolutionary biologists find human ritual rooted in animal behavior. Which came first, the activity or the meanings attached to the activity? There is agreement that rituals are repetitive, rhythmic actions. But so are factory work and obsessive behavior—which have also been called ritual or "ritual-like" (whatever that means). There are the public rituals of the state and church; the social rituals of families, clubs, professions, and identity groups; and the more or less private rituals of small groups, couples, and individuals. It is not easy to specify what these have in common or to distinguish among them. Many acts are upgraded to ritual status because "ritual" is a positive value word, linking an activity to the "sacred," another positive value word. But rituals can also be negative or bad if they are associated with groups such as the Nazis, devil worshipers, and other pariahs.

Given this tumble of possibilities and contradictions, by necessity I narrow my course to "aspects" of ritual or "problems" in ritual, or I offer a survey of some "ritual performances." I call my course "Ritual, Play, and Performance" because many qualities of ritual are also qualities of play both practically and theoretically; and because performance is my approach not only to ritual but to every subject I teach. That being said, "Ritual, Play, and Performance" is different each time I teach it, though there are some abiding themes and readings. The syllabus for "Ritual, Play, and Performance" as I taught it in the summer of 2004 at the School for Criticism and Theory, Cornell University, is the appendix to this article. I am sharing this redaction of the course because it was at Cornell that I first invited students to whirl in order for them to experience "light trance." That class's whirling is one key example in my exploration of six related themes: ritual experience; ritual formality; animal ritual; performing rituals; belief; ritual and theater.

Ritual Experience

The night of 20 July 2004, I guided fourteen PhD students and assistant professors into light trances by instructing them on how to whirl Mevlevi (dervish) style. In a semi-darkened rehearsal room at Cornell University's Schwartz Center for the Performing Arts, we spun to the flute and drum music beloved by the thirteenth-century Sufi sage Jalal al-Din Rumi, who was himself a professor until 1244, when at the age of thirty-seven he encountered the itinerant mystic Shemseddin Mehmet of Tabriz, who spun Rumi's life into another orbit.

Only one person in the class had spun before. For about an hour, the students let centrifugal force lift their arms while they kept their right palms up, their left palms down. According to Sufi teaching, this is a conduit for guiding energy from above through the body to the earth, like lightning. After whirling, we sat in a circle on the floor and talked.

The next morning I got an email from a participant:

> I felt distilled by the experiential dimensions of tonight's whirling dance and trance discussions. There is an invigorating spark and then a connection of stillness that I will always cherish. I am intrigued by the combination of velocity, vortex and centeredness that encapsulates the dance. How mystical and yet totally demystifying all at once! Many many thanks.

This man kept spinning after everyone else stopped, even after the music ended. In the darkened silence of the room, the rest of us listened to his bare feet lightly drumming on the floor. I extinguished the candles that were the only illumination and in darkness found him, slowly drew his arms to his side, embraced him, stood quietly with him, and then led him to the side. Without warning, I switched on the room lights. The sudden brightness was cruel. Most people guarded their eyes.

The next class we not only discussed the whirling but watched the Mead and Bateson film *Trance and Dance in Bali* (1939) and clips from Maya Deren's *Divine Horsemen* (1947–1951). Earlier, we had seen Peter Adair's *Holy Ghost People* (1967). More people shared their experiences of the whirling—and connected these to the experiences of those depicted in the films. We saw that certain bodily behaviors that characterized trance—bodily stiffness, trembling, "divinely inspired" utterances, loss of memory concerning exactly "what happened"—occurred across a wide range of cultures, so wide that diffusion of cultural traits did not seem to answer the question of why the similarities existed. We also talked about our interior experiences. Some people felt "swept away" by the music and movement; others felt "good" or "warm." I spoke about "brain tuning," when the activity of the two frontal lobes are in synchrony, and about the "oceanic" feeling such synchrony evokes.

At the same time, I went out of my way to demystify the experience. I pointed out that the Sufi mystics' whirling was preceded and accompanied by years of study and practice. We were starting with the sheer physical activity—a behaviorist approach—and registering the effects of the action. The mystics went much further than we could go. At the same time, there appeared, at least to some in the class, a ladder of possibilities. Even if we were only on the first rung, that was an accomplishment. "What's special," I said, "is that starting the climb up this ladder is nothing special. Anyone who can walk can do it." I also pointed out that there are many varieties of trance-inducing rituals. That's why I showed the films of trances in Bali, Haiti, and West Virginia. I find that experiencing and demystifying trance is an excellent way for students to experience ritual without needing to accept or even know the cultural or ideological context of the actions they are performing. The actions are autonomous. They work with or without cultural knowledge. It is possible to adapt and invent rituals. I realize that many are aghast at this. But I am getting ahead of myself.

Ritual Formality

Of course, rituals come in all sizes and kinds, from those linking humans to superhuman powers (possession trance, prayer, exorcism, and the like) to the everyday rituals (greeting, socializing, cleansing, and eating) to the rituals of the state, professions, clubs, and affinity groups. There are birth, puberty, courtship, marriage, death, and afterlife rituals. All of life—from the most mundane to the most special—is saturated with and marked by ritual. But what is ritual? It can be defined, as Roy Rappaport defines it, in a strictly formal way:

> I take ritual to be a form or structure, defining it as the performance
> of more or less invariant sequences of formal acts and utterances
> not encoded by the performers. (1979: 175)

Rappaport is not (here) concerned with meaning, function, metaphor, symbol, or anything other than a fixed progression of "acts and utterances." Frits Staal famously put it even more radically when he declared that rituals were "meaningless":

> A widespread but erroneous assumption about ritual is that it con-
> sists in symbolic activities which refer to something else. It is char-
> acteristic of a ritual performance, however, that it is self-contained
> and self-absorbed. The performers are totally immersed in the proper
> execution of their complex tasks... There are no symbolic meanings
> going through their minds when they are engaged in performing
> ritual... Ritual, then, is primarily activity. It is an activity governed by
> explicit rules. The important thing is what you do, not what you
> think, believe or say. (1979: 2–3)

Staal was discussing the performance of Agnicayana, a Vedic ritual of Kerala, India. But he generalizes from this instance. I do not want to (presently) argue with Rappaport or Staal. I want only to point out that their formalist position can easily be translated into the whirling experience I offered my School for Criticism and Theory (SCT) students.

At the SCT, I was interested in how the sheer action of whirling affected the students. This was based on an assumption that "ritual experience" is grounded in certain biological constants. For example, specific actions such as whirling according to known rules, generate predictable changes in electro-encephalogram rates and in brain chemistry, the release of endorphins, par-ticularly. The electroencephalogram indicates that a certain kind of experience is felt; the endorphins make people feel "oceanic" or "good"—lightly, natu-rally opiated. This kind of feeling of well-being can be associated with any number of ideological/religious/political (or whatever) cultural constructs.[1] These findings fit neatly with the ethological view that ritual is a specific genre of behavior that evolved over time rather than an ideology or set of beliefs, sacred or otherwise.

Animal Ritual

From the ethological perspective, rituals are actions designed to improve com-munication during encounters that could be trouble: hierarchy, mating, feed-ing, and turf. Where is each animal in the ranking? Who mates with whom? How is food found, hunted, and distributed? Who controls the territory and determines its boundaries? These are the basic questions of (at least) primate life. The answers—which are gendered—are much too complex to be discussed in any detail here. Suffice it to say that a complex language of ritual actions enhances communications and allows for both individuals to get what they need and for the group to function as a group. There are ritual displays of power, sexual prowess, and availability; rituals integral to gathering food, hunting, and sharing; rituals associated with defining/marking a band's boundaries and patrolling its territory. Sometimes pariah animals are driven from the group and its territory or murdered. Many of these rituals are strikingly similar to what happens among humans.

Among animals, according to ethologists,[2] ritualization involves transforming and transposing behavior common in non-ritual contexts into unambiguous behavior with high communication value that reduces the risk of deadly encounters. For example, a nibbling dog is very clearly signaling affection, the very opposite of what biting denotes. It's as if the dog is saying, "I am nibbling to show you that I could bite you but the fact that I am not biting you means that I like you." As Gregory Bateson put it, "These actions in which we now engage do not denote what those actions for which they stand would denote" (Bateson 2004: 122). Whether these kinds of action are ritual or play, as Bateson contends, is really a matter of interpretation. The realms of play and ritual more than complement each other; they overlap (see Handelman 1977). I make this point strongly in my Ritual, Play, and Performance course.

Eibl-Eibesfeldt specifies nine changes in behavior that occur during ritualization:

1. The behavior changes function.
2. The ritualized movement becomes independent of its original motivation and develops its own motivating mechanisms.
3. Movements are exaggerated and rhythmic.
4. Movements frequently freeze into postures.
5. Thresholds for expressing the behavior are lowered.
6. Several movements are compressed into stereotyped, simpler movements.
7. Behavior as signal becomes unambiguous.
8. The spatial orientation of the behavior changes from its ordinary occurrence.
9. Conspicuous body parts—horns, plumes, enlarged claws, fins, and so on—and bright colors develop over evolutionary time. (Adapted from 1970: 100–101)

These qualities are also found in human rituals Of course, humans have not developed conspicuous body parts, but our species is adept at costume, adornment, and makeup.

In my teaching, I try to open rather than close discussion regarding the relationship between human and nonhuman animal rituals and play. Sometimes we go to the zoo, notebooks and camcorders in hand, and try to note animal rituals. We then show the video and compare notes—connecting zoo ritual behavior with human ritual behavior. But we also discuss rituals from a Van Gennep–Turner point of view: rites of passage, social dramas, liminality, and so on. In all these instances—animal and human—I emphasize how rituals are designed to communicate between individuals, among groups, and across ontological lines: life/death, human/nonhuman (gods, demons, etc.). I also stress that clear communication is especially important when dealing with trouble, whether that trouble is actual or potential, coming from conspecifics or other beings, within or across realms of (actual or believed-in) existence.

But there is another dimension, too, very different from the notion that rituals are serious business that deal with trouble (hierarchy and power, mating, territory) or negotiate the passage from one life stage to another. This other dimension is the aesthetic-pleasurable. One culturally universal quality of rituals is that they bring out the best in people, aesthetically speaking. Think of music, masks, visual arts, dancing, singing, dramas. Ritual making is also often the occasion for pleasure taking: festivals, carnivals, feasting, lovemaking, drinking, and the like. If seriousness, even blood sacrifice (real or symbolically depicted), is one face of ritual, beauty and pleasure are another face. In my classes, we discuss how these two apparently contradictory tendencies interact. These are not incidental or epiphenomenal but are, rather, at the very core of what rituals are. The ritual performances of medieval and early Renaissance Europe provide one set of rich examples, while today's Trinidad Carnival and its offshoots offer another (see Enders 1999 and Riggio 2005).

But what about the rituals of everyday life? These are highly ritualized (see Goffman 1967). Most are not bridges over troubled waters, nor are they especially artistic—though some, like the Japanese tea ceremony, ritualize and aestheticize everyday activities. In fact, making art often involves the nine processes Eibl-Eibesfeldt identified as characteristic of the ritual process. But here I am referring to actions such as greetings (waves, handshakes), applauding after a performance, singing the national anthem at a public event, setting a table for dinner, following a "morning ritual" of toilet and ablution, and taking part in myriads of other routines. These do not transport individuals from one social or ontological status to another (though they do often mark a transition from one mode of public or private being to another); they do not release endorphins or change one's brain waves. So why are they called rituals? First, although the modes of existence they link are not momentous life stages, they are instances of disjunction in need of bridging. A greeting or a farewell temporarily binds or breaks a relationship; applause marks the end of the performance and signals a return to another kind of social life; the set table promises a sharing of food, an event almost always more significant than mere nutrition. The singing of the national anthem places the singers within a defined polity, whereas the singing of "Take Me Out to the Ballgame" puts one within a smaller, but very important time-out-of-time polity. Morning rituals transport a person from the interior and intimate life of sleep and dreaming to the more exteriorized daily social life. And so on. Probably every so-called "ordinary" ritual is a playing in the minor key of some more momentous act. Second, these kinds of expected acts are codes signaling the participants' agreement to partake of normative social solidarity, enacting/communicating shared values (whether or not these values are felt by all participating individuals).

These daily rituals occur along a continuum from the voluntary to the coerced. Completely voluntary activities are not likely to be rituals, though micro rituals—fleeting gestures and utterances, eyebrow flashing and unconscious smiles—are considered by some behavioral scientists as being both ritualized and involuntary: an intriguing paradox that what is "set" and "automated" at the micro level is voluntary when embedded in larger sequences of behavior. Then there are the cases of a person volunteering to perform a ritual in the interest of group solidarity. This was the case of my Cornell class. Each of them agreed to whirl—but once they made this agreement, they were obligated to whirl, not to hop, skip, or jump; even more, they were obligated to whirl in a prescribed way. Only if the students whirled in this manner, with each aware that the others were doing the same, would the full effect of whirling occur. There is encoded in ritual acts at least a hint of coercion, a script that "must" be followed. This coercion expressed as ritual behavior is integral to military, juridical, medical, and sacerdotal power. The rituals of ordinary social convention are less manifestly coercive but still compelling. On a strictly personal level, obsessive actions, repetitive and often exaggerated, displaced from their ordinary occurrences (Lady Macbeth washing her hands) appear to be rituals: they "must" be done, though quite frequently the performer does not know why. And then there is the pathological—the rocking of the autistic, the tics of the Tourette's sufferer. These are rituals in appearance only, rituals by association. It may not be quite so easy because there is a sliding scale from "healthy" to "pathological," with the polar categories open to ongoing redefinition.

Performing Ritual

In teaching ritual, I am particularly interested in the performing arts and ritual. This relationship is a two-way street. Art can "originate" in ritual, but ritual can also originate in art (see "From Ritual to Theatre and Back" in Schechner 2003). Also, I point out that the workshop-to-rehearsal-to-public-performance sequence is in itself a ritual process. Often I ask the class to read about the invented rituals of Anna Halprin (1979, 1995). Or I invite students to invent and perform a new ritual. If a new ritual is performed or is encountered in Halprin's work, we discuss how much of it consists of known actions and whether the "newness" is more a rearrangement than a true invention. Again questions arise concerning whether this kind of acting gets people closer to the experience of another or further alienates them.

Then, sometimes, I ask the class to use Victor and Edith Turner's "Performing Ethnography" (1982) as a guide to staging one or two rituals from "other" cultures. At the University of Virginia in Charlottesville, the Turners staged the Hamatsa ritual dance of the Kwakiutl and the Barok ritual of Papua–New Guinea. But the Turners did not always look to distant places for the rituals they had their students perform:

> One of our Virginia graduate students, Pamela Frese, who has been studying marriage (culturally, structurally, and in terms of social dynamics) in the Charlottesville area . . . elected to cast the entire anthropology department as participants in a simulated or fabricated contemporary Central Virginian wedding. . . . A Department of Religious Studies graduate student was cast as the minister. Both faculty and students were involved. . . . The "wedding" took place in the large basement of our house at Charlottesville—the "kiva" some called it. Afterwards, there was a "reception": upstairs with a receiving line, real champagne, and festive foods. At subsequent sessions students were asked to describe . . . their impressions. (1982: 34–35)

I have on occasion done similar things. Once, I invited McKim Marriott to perform a complex Hindu ritual in a dance studio at New York University's Tisch School of the Arts. This took several hours of preparation followed by several more hours of performance. The discussion began after the performance and continued into the next class, which I led after Marriott returned to Chicago. There is no substitute for experience; and if people can't go to the field, bring the field home insofar as you can.

The Turners offer in their article on performing ethnography some wise, if perhaps impossibly utopian, advice:

> Rituals, like law cases, should not be abstracted from the frameworks of the ongoing social process in which they were originally embedded. They have their source and raison d'etre in the ceaseless flow of social life, and in the social dramas within which communities seek to contain that life. . . If we attempt to perform ethnography, let us not begin with such apparently "exotic" and "bizarre" cultural phenomena as rituals and myths. Such an emphasis may only encourage prejudice, since it stresses the "otherness of the other." Let us focus first on what all people share, the social drama form, from which emerge all types of cultural performance, which, in their turn, subtly stylize the contours of social interaction in everyday life. In practice, this means setting apart a substantial block of time to familiarize students with the culture and social system of the group whose dramas they will enact. Such instruction should be interwoven with what Richard Schechner might call "the rehearsal process."

The resultant instructional form could be a kind of synthesis between an anthropological seminar and a postmodern theatrical workshop. . . . At least one session should be allocated to a close review of all aspects of the performance seen in retrospect. This should include subjective statements by the actors, the director, the dramaturg, and members of the audience if an audience was thought necessary. Much of the emphasis will be found to be on cultural differences, and the difficulties and delights of playing roles generated by cultures often far different from our own. In these occasions of intercultural reflexivity, we can begin to grasp something of the contribution each and every human culture can make to the general pool of manifested knowledge of our common human condition. It is in dramatics and dynamics most of all that we learn to coexperience the lives of our conspecifics. (47–48)

Belief

I am an atheist. I am also a Jew and an initiated Hindu. What is my position in relation to religious rituals and the belief systems they encode? Frequently, I ask students to attend religious services and celebrations as participant observers. We have made field trips to Pentecostal churches in Brooklyn and Harlem, a Ganesh temple in Queens, Purim in Brooklyn. One year, my ritual, play, and performance class prepared and celebrated a seder in my home— folding into the service, which itself takes the form of a lesson, even more levels of explanation and instruction. During one field trip to the Institutional Church of God in Brooklyn, a student—Jewish by birth and upbringing—was possessed by the Holy Spirit and declared herself reborn in Christ. She was anointed and carried into the bishop's chambers behind the pulpit. After thirty minutes or so, I met with the bishop and the young woman. I urged them to wait a few days to see if she still felt the same way before following up on her revelatory experience. I explained that although I did not want to interfere in her spiritual life or the church's call, I was also in parentis locus for this undergraduate student. Ultimately, after several trips back and forth to Brooklyn, she decided not to join the church. But her life was touched by the experience, and I do not know the long-term outcome of that Sunday morning.

At the somatic and aesthetic level, I enjoy enacting rituals—of faiths and groups I grew up knowing and of ones I experienced first as an adult. I do not feel like a hypocrite while participating in a synagogue service, a puja, a Holy Communion, or a Buddhist meditation. When I finish writing this on Yom Kippur 2005, I will drive from Manhattan to New Jersey and attend the neelah, or final service of the day, at the synagogue my great-grandfather founded and was the first rabbi of. But I know that when I recite prayers that I learned before

I knew how to read, my relation to those prayers and other "sacred" performances will not be the same as that of many others co-present with me.

I identify with these religious rituals culturally and historically. That is, when I celebrate the Passover seder, I am claiming my portion and place in Jewish tradition. When I sing *bhajans* or accept *prasad* in a Hindu temple, I am putting myself into another tradition and accepting, for the time being, its practices. When I take the Communion wafer on my tongue, I am "practicing" Roman Catholicism. Insofar as the actions are autonomous, I am what I do. Insofar as belief is necessary to make the actions efficacious, I am "playing." But I do not "believe" in the gods of Judaism, Hinduism, or Christianity. Well, actually, that's not quite it. While participating, I am overtaken by my own actions. Often, I am overcome with deep feelings, sometimes to tears. I interpret this emotion as a kind of regretful longing for the faith of my early childhood. Or it may be that rituals "work," whether they take the form of religious observances or rhythmic cheering at a Mets game. As Frits Staal noted: "It is characteristic of a ritual performance . . . that it is self-contained and self-absorbed. The performers are totally immersed in the proper execution of their complex tasks" (1979: 3).

My ritual tasks at synagogue, church, or temple are not complex, but at certain moments I am entirely absorbed in the doing of them. The feelings I experience at these times are more than a theatrical "as if" yet different from something entirely believed in. I am in a liminal emotional state and also performing a Brechtian "alienation effect." I am doing and watching myself doing. I encourage my students to find a similar "place" from which to experience and observe simultaneously. And I remind them of the instructions given to *bharatanatyam* dancers: Make the mudras with your hands and watch your hands as they form the mudras. You are dancing with yourself and for yourself, for the audience and for the deity. The actions I perform "in ritual" are subscribed to for the time being of the ritual performance: I did not invent these actions, but in doing them, I am reinventing them. The doing of the actions draws me deeply into the actions without asking that I comprehend (at the moment of doing) what those actions signify. Or maybe I am simply the messenger: the rituals communicate in their own code, whether or not I understand the code. Staal is right when he says that, sometimes at least, while performing a ritual, we are in flow, merged with the action entirely. Flow is not unique to ritual.[3] But the repetition and deep familiarity of a ritual, combined with the full sensory engagement—song, movement or dance, incense or other odor, tasting, utterance, participating in a group activity—help one surrender the I-self and merge with the Us-self, what Martin Buber called the Ich-Du.[4] I do not hide from my students my contradictory "stance" in relation to the rituals I practice and we study together. Quite the contrary, it is this double consciousness that I try to teach them.

Ritual and Theater

I am a "theater person" who has worked for more than 45 years as a director—
the one who oversees the workshop and rehearsal process, guides the actors
and designers, interacts with the playwright, and interprets or even modifies
the text. Sometimes I write plays or adapt older texts. My experience has taught
me that theater and ritual are very close to each other, involving processes of
displacement, transformation, exaggeration, repetition, and rhythmicity (see
Schechner 1985, 2003). The idea of the affinity of ritual and theater is nothing
new, dating back at least to Durkheim.

The Russian actor and director Konstantin Stanislavsky taught that the
words spoken and gestures enacted in a performance convey only some of
what's going on. Equally if not more important is what Stanislavsky called the
"subtext," the train of thought, motivation, and desire running beneath the
surface. The subtext is what the characters are "really thinking and feeling" no
matter what they say or do. Sometimes the subtext is in harmony with the
words and gestures, but often it is not. A character may say, "I love you," as she
kisses her husband, but actually mean "I am angry at you." Even more commonly, the subtext departs entirely from what is written and done. For example, a character says, "Pass the butter, please," and the other character does so.
A few words and a simple action. But these can embody a myriad of subtexts,
conveyed by tone and gesture, enacted with great subtlety but no less certainly.
An exercise for actors is to give them a text and assign a completely different
subtext. For example, one actor says, "Pass the butter" while conveying "I
desire you." The other actor passes the butter showing in that gesture, "Yes, I
know you desire me, and I want you, too." The actor's job is to speak the lines
and perform the actions in an ordinary way, but also communicate the subtext
to the other character and to the audience.

And here is a crucial difference between theater and ritual. In theater, the
subtext rules, whereas in ritual, the text rules. Even empty or hollow rituals, if
properly performed, "work," that is, accomplish what they are intended to do.
The bride's wish that she weren't marrying does not undo what the ceremony
and the signing of papers accomplish. Smiling and buoyant, blushing and shy,
or angry and morose make no difference with regard to efficacy. Ritual performers may wish they were in the theater, where, when the play is over, they
can step out of their roles and show that everything that happened onstage was
make-believe. But no such luck, or danger. Ritual is very close to theater, but
also exquisitely different. Ritual's actions are not make-believe; they are "make
belief": "invariant sequences of acts and utterances not encoded by the performers" enacted by "performers totally immersed in the proper execution of
their complex tasks." The outcome is binding.

NOTES

1. Norie Kawai and others (2001: 3419, 3423) found that some participants in rituals experience significant physiological changes that were evident when their blood was analyzed:

> For the first time, we have measured the plasma concentrations of several neuroactive substances: catecholamines, their metabolites, and neuropeptides, from subjects involved in ritual dramas under natural conditions. The results of the present study indicate that possession trances are associated with a significant increase in plasma concentrations of catecholamines and opioid peptides.... The results of the present study suggest that catecholamines and opioid peptides in the CNS [central nervous system] are involved in possession trances including markedly altered states of consciousness, memory, pain sensation, and behaviors. The present study represents a strong foundation for further characterization of the neuronal mechanisms underlying possession trances.

Oohashia and others (2002: 437, 444) isolated specific processes occurring in the brain of a person in a trance:

> The entire observation period of Subject 1, who became possessed, was categorized into two states: normal state (NS) and trance state (TS)....A positive correlation has been shown between the occipital alpha-EEG and the regional cerebral blood flow in the deep brain structure, including the thalamus. Therefore, we need to consider the possibility that a possession trance may be associated with a change of activity in deep-lying structures, including the thalamus.

2. There is a large body of literature on nonhuman rituals and on the relationship between nonhuman and human behavior—see especially Eibl-Eibesfeldt 1970; Cranach et al 1979; Konner 1982; Lorenz 1965, 1970–71, 1980; and Wilson 1975, 1996, 1998. Expectedly, the ethological approach has been controversial. It categorically rejects the notion that rituals "began" with or deal with the "sacred." The ethological approach assumes that rituals arise around encounters that are risky and dangerous. Humans are the only animals who try to deal with death conceptually and symbolically and who, in this regard, have imagined an afterlife and non-natural worlds or realms populated by gods, demons, and other beings.

3. Mihaly Csikszentmihalyi has authored a library on flow from theoretical as well as experiential perspectives. See Csikszentmihalyi 1975, 1988 (with Isabella Selega Csikszentmihalyi), 1990, 1996, 1999 (with Susan A. Jackson), and 2003.

4. I have kept Buber's German original—"Ich-Du"—because "du" in German is the intimate or personal form of the second person singular. Buber was suggesting a personal, even intimate, relation with God. "Thou" in English suggests the opposite, a formality and distance.

USEFUL MATERIALS

For an overview of my approach, see chapter 3 ("Ritual") in my books *Performance Studies—An Introduction*, 2nd ed. (London: Routledge, 2006) and *The Future of Ritual*

(London: Routledge, 1993). My views are informed by the theories of Victor Turner. Aside from his *The Ritual Process* and *Dramas, Fields, and Metaphors,* see *From Ritual to Theatre* (New York: Performing Arts Journal Publications, 1982) and *The Anthropology of Performance* (New York, PAJ Publications, 1986).

REFERENCES

Bateson, Gregory. 2004. "A Theory of Play and Fantasy." In *The Performance Studies Reader,* ed. Henry Bial, 121–31. London: Routledge. First published in: Bateson, Gregory, 1972. *Steps to an Ecology of the Mind,* 177–93. New York: Ballantine Books.
Bial, Henry, ed. 2004. *The Performance Studies Reader.* London: Routledge.
Cranach, M. von, K. Foppa, W. Lepenies, and D. Ploog, eds. 1979. *Human Ethology.* Cambridge: Cambridge University Press.
Csikszentmihalyi, Mihaly. 1975. *Beyond Boredom and Anxiety.* San Francisco: Jossey-Bass.
———. 1990. *Flow: The Psychology of Optimal Experience.* New York: Harper Collins.
———. 1996. *Creativity, Flow, and the Psychology of Discovery and Invention.* New York: Harper Collins.
———. 2003. *Good Business Leadership, Flow, and the Making of Meaning.* New York: Viking.
Csikszentmihalyi, Mihaly, and Susan A. Jackson. 1999. *Flow in Sports.* Champagne, Ill.: Human Kinetics.
Csikszentmihalyi, Mihaly, and Isabella Selega Csikszentmihalyi 1988. *Optimal Experience: Psychological Studies of Flow in Consciousness.* Cambridge: Cambridge University Press.
d'Aquili, Eugene G., Charles D. Laughlin, and John McManus. 1979. *The Spectrum of Ritual.* New York: Columbia University Press.
Durkheim, Emile. 2001 (1912) *The Elementary Forms of Religious Life.* Oxford: Oxford University Press.
Eibl-Eibesfeldt, Iraneus. 1970. *Ethology: The Biology of Behavior.* New York: Holt, Rinehart, and Winston.
———. 1979. "Ritual and Ritualization from a Biological Perspective." In *Human Ethology,* ed. M. von Cranach, K. Foppa, W. Lepenies, and D. Ploog, 3–55. Cambridge: Cambridge University Press.
Enders, Jody. 1999. *The Medieval Theater of Cruelty.* Ithaca: Cornell University Press.
Goffman, Erving 1967 *Interaction Ritual.* Chicago: Aldine.
Grimes, Ronald L., ed. 1996. *Readings in Ritual Studies.* Upper Saddle River, NJ: Prentice Hall.
Halprin, Anna 1975. *Movement Ritual.* San Francisco: San Francisco Dancers' Workshop.
———. 1995. *Moving Toward Life.* Hanover, Conn.: Wesleyan University Press.
Handelman, Don. 1977. "Play and Ritual: Complementary Frames of Metacommunication." In *International Conference on Humour and Laughter: It's a Funny Thing, Humour,* ed. Anthony J. Chapman and Hugh C. Foot, 185–192. Oxford: Pergamon.

Kawai, Norie, Manabu Honda, Satoshi Nakamura, Purwa Samatra, Ketut Sukardika, Yoji Nakatani, Nobuhiro Shimojo, and Tsutomu Oohashi. 2001. "Catecholamines and Opioid Peptides Increase in Plasma in Humans during Possession Trances." *Cognitive Neuroscience and Neuropsychology* 12, 16 (November): 3419–3423.

Konner, Melvin. 1982. *The Tangled Wing*. New York: Holt, Rinehart, and Winston.

Lorenz, Konrad. 1965. *Evolution and the Modification of Behavior*. Chicago: University of Chicago Press.

———. 1970–71. *Studies in Animal and Human Behaviour*. London: Methuen.

———. 1980. *The Foundations of Ethology*. New York: Springer-Verlag.

Moore, Sally, and Barbara Myerhoff, eds. 1977. *Secular Ritual*. Amsterdam: Van Gorcum, Assen.

Oohashi, Tsutomo, Norie Kawai, Manabu Honda, Satoshi Nakamura, Masako Morimoto, Emi Nishina, and Tadao Maekawa. 2002. "Electroencephalographic Measurement of Possession Trance in the Field." *Clinical Neurophysiology* 113: 435–445.

Rappaport, Roy A. 1979. "The Obvious Aspects of Ritual" In *Ecology, Meaning, and Religion*, 173–222. Richmond, Calif.: North Atlantic Books.

———. 1999. *Ritual and Religion in the Making of Humanity*. Cambridge: Cambridge University Press.

Read, Kenneth E. 1966 *The High Valley*. London: Allen and Unwin.

Riggio, Milla Cozart, ed. 2004. *Carnival in Action: The Trinidad Experience*. New York: Routledge.

Schechner, Richard. 1985. *Between Theater and Anthropology*. Philadelphia: University of Pennsylvania Press.

———. 2003 (1976). *Performance Theory*. London: Routledge.

Staal, Frits. 1979. "The Meaninglessness of Ritual" *Numen* 26, 1: 2–22.

Turner, Victor. 1969 *The Ritual Process*. Chicago: Aldine.

———. 1974. *Dramas, Fields, and Metaphors* Ithaca, N.Y.: Cornell University Press.

———. 1985 *At the Edge of the Bush*. Tucson: University of Arizona Press.

Turner, Victor, and Edith Turner. 1982. "Performing Ethnography" *TDR* 26, 2: 33–50.

Van Gennep, Arnold. 1960 *The Rites of Passage*. Chicago: University of Chicago Press.

Wilson, Edward O. 1975. *Sociobiology*. Cambridge: Harvard University Press.

———. 1996. *In Search of Nature*. Washington: Island Press.

———. 1998 *Conscilience*. New York: Alfred A. Knopf.

2

Still Liminal after All These Years: Teaching Ordeals and Peregrinations

Ann Grodzins Gold

Fall 1995 Prelude

On the first day of "Hinduism," an introductory course in which I spend more than half a semester on classical texts, I like to show students where I am coming from by giving them a slide show on "religion in the village"—that is, on my own ethnographic fieldwork. I have studied aspects of religion, culture and history in the same region of rural North India since 1979. The photogenic part of rural religion is, of course, ritual action. My slides display serious men and women making elaborate offerings and performing services before roughly carved but gaudily and elaborately adorned images of various deities.

In 1995, my third fall as a still insecure assistant professor of religion, my new TA was a young man with a nearly shaved head, a studded leather collar, and a Macintosh laptop as his constant companion. He would prove to be among the most effective assistants with whom I have worked. His interests, like those of so many graduate students attracted to study religion at Syracuse, lay more in philosophy and theory than in ritual practice.

As this earnest young scholar and I silently disassembled the slide projector following my opening lecture, he suddenly blurted out in a voice replete with muted astonishment but perceptibly tinged with dismay, "Oh Professor Gold, I thought you were going to tell them about the Brahman [absolute reality] and the atman [the self or human soul], but all you showed them were rocks and stones." As will soon unfold, this was far from my first jarring experience as an anthropologist in a religion department. Nonetheless, it remains in my memory as an epitomizing moment.

The mystical and difficult-to-discern identity of absolute reality with the self is, of course, one primary revelation in Hinduism's earliest philosophical understandings, derived from the *Upanishads* and often referred to as Vedanta. Euro-American scholars, both Orientalist and postcolonial, have admired Vedantic thought for centuries. Moreover, since at least the nineteenth century, movements to "reform" Hinduism from within—sometimes referred to as "neo-Vedanta"—have advocated a return to these foundations and simultaneously a rejection of later mythological narrative texts as well as popular ritual practices, including image worship and pilgrimage. However, only a small minority of those who understand themselves to be Hindu—generally persons belonging to particular enclaves of the urban educated elite—have consistently elected to shun the beloved narratives and practices of worship that pervade India's religious culture. Although authors of introductory religion textbooks never ignore Hindu ritual, they tend to draw upon Vedantic precepts to characterize the highest or deepest reaches of Hindu religious thought.

As an anthropologist dedicated to appreciating the worldviews of largely non-literate farmers and herders in rural North India, in my own writings I have tried hard to deconstruct the kind of gulf my TA presumed to exist between meditative self-realization and smearing roughly hewn stones with red paste while offering them soaked raw chickpeas. I chose to study pilgrimage for my doctoral research because I felt that it offered locations, practices, compelling sets of meanings, and a dramatic ritual complex that encompassed and integrated gross-external and subtle-internal. I was never disappointed. Every Hindu pilgrim I interviewed was quick to avow that God cannot be found in any sacred site, that boons cannot be purchased, that sins cannot be cleansed in any earthly waters. Yet the same persons boarded uncomfortable buses, made countless offerings, and bathed in every holy river. For me, this complex and untroubled adherence simultaneously to valuing and devaluing outer rites was the fascinating core of Hindu understandings, which rendered all dogma suspect but was nonetheless sustained by faith (Gold 1988).

In the classroom, I strive to teach a Hinduism premised on continuity between external actions and internal states of being, a Hinduism whose rituals are not meaningless and whose meanings are not disembodied. I think I eventually convinced my dubious TA of these continuities, and I trust that over the years I have convinced at least some of my students as well. Each semester I arrange an optional, extra-credit field trip to Syracuse's local Hindu temple, and, luckily for me, the priest there eloquently delivers a similar message with persuasive insider charm. Before and after making fairly elaborate offerings before gorgeously adorned marble images, he speaks to my students of ineffable divinities and inner realities.

The rest of this chapter is not about teaching Hindu rituals. However, the endeavor to link practice and context with precept and meaning carries forward to the comparative enterprises that are my central focus. Each key term in my title has more than one implication, and operates simultaneously at academic and autobiographical levels. The primary, academic sense of liminal evoked here is Victor Turner's—with due credit to Van Gennep (1960), from whom Turner adapted the tripartite scheme for "rites de passage" upon which he built and elaborated his own ritual theory. Turner expands on liminality as a ritual stage characterized by detachment, anti-structure, egalitarian bonding, and creativity—inevitably followed by a replenished return to social structure (Turner 1969). A secondary, personal sense of liminality relates to my own professional location as an out-of-discipline professor, anthropologist among the religionists—an edgy condition my opening anecdote sought to evoke. Of course, after more than ten years, my status no longer wears the guise of transition. It has perhaps become a variant that Turner might have called inferiority, marginality, or outsiderhood (Barnhill 1990; Turner 1974).

Just as the terms in my title have double meanings, so my contribution to *Teaching Ritual* will be similarly twofold. In explaining how I have remained rooted in ethnography while adjusting to the particular expectations students have for Religion courses, I hope at the same time to highlight key contributions—simple but powerful—that anthropology can make to teaching ritual practices.

When I commenced my doctoral course work in anthropology at the University of Chicago in 1975, the influence of Victor Turner, legendary master of ritual theory, was on the wane. I grasped this when he was introduced by one of his colleagues at an opening student-faculty reception as "Mr. Symbol himself." The sardonic bite, a Chicago specialty, was palpable. Impressionable by nature and susceptible to fashion at the time (though I'm surely ashamed of it now), I never took a course from Turner. The decision to study Hindu pilgrimage practices for my doctoral research came, ironically enough, after he had departed for the greener pastures of Virginia. Then I steeped myself in his and Edith Turner's writings, but never positioned my own project within a Turnerian frame—whether to argue for or against it.[1] In my thesis, later published as *Fruitful Journeys: The Ways of Rajasthani Pilgrims*, Turner's key concepts and their relevance to my findings appear occasionally, but only in the footnotes. Victor Turner will ultimately emerge as the outright hero of this chapter, paired of course with his coauthor, Edith Turner.

The following two sections describe two classes which involved "teaching ritual"—one that was bad and one that was good. The bad experience had to do with firewalking —the religiously orchestrated practice of walking over red-hot coals with bare feet. The good experience had to do with pilgrimage. In discussing the pedagogy of pilgrimage, I hope to demonstrate how and why

Turner's concepts remain valid and fruitful for understanding both students' own contemporary experiences and those of participants in other more obviously ritualized cultural worlds. Although anthropologists have roundly critiqued Turner's work on pilgrimage for several decades, his and Edith Turner's ideas remain valuable teaching tools offering modes of cross-cultural understanding accessible and relevant to students today.

Fall 1993 Ordeal by Fire

In the fall of 1993 I found myself appointed as Assistant Professor of religion at Syracuse University. Because I had been hired in the late spring, I was assigned to teach courses already in the catalog. One of them was titled "Comparative Themes and Issues in the Study of Religion" (REL 291) and had been deliberately designed to enable various faculty with highly diverse interests to fashion any kind of syllabus. I decided to focus my own section in the following fashion: "Three interconnected topics treated in depth provide a central focus for our study: healing rituals, religious narratives, and the roles played by charismatic figures such as saints, prophets, gurus, and ascetics." I selected these themes not only because they intersected with my own research interests, but also because they would allow me to borrow a few weeks of material from a course I had offered three years earlier while visiting in the department of sociology and anthropology at nearby Colgate University. The course I taught there was also a 200-level course and was also one for which the content varied by professor. It was titled "Religion, Culture, and Social Change" (SOAN 216). Both courses were intended to introduce the study of religion in their respective fields.

Unanticipated by me was the distance I had traveled between these two different if equally blandly formulated topics, and a correspondingly profound difference in student expectations. Certainly, had I paused to consider them, the two titles might have clued me into some contrasts between a social science approach to introducing the study of religion and a humanistic one. With hindsight, I can perceive that the religion title stresses a synchronic, panoramic view of religious thought, whereas the anthropology title implies a diachronic focus on culturally situated behaviors. More importantly, having nothing to do with catalog titles or descriptions, departmental auras create notions about course content. To put it crudely, students come to anthropology courses expecting to encounter exotic people's peculiar practices. This is why we can get them every time with Horace Miner's still acute '50s classic on the peculiar cleansing rites of the Nacirema (1956). By contrast, most first- and second-year undergraduate students come to religion classes anticipating the familiar. Euro-American thought, even in scholarly mode, was slow to grant the category of religion to those who did not cleave to Abrahamic monotheisms (Chidester 1996).

Undergraduate students are definitely perplexed about whether to grant this rubric to alien practices and theologies.

At Syracuse, REL 291 fulfilled a liberal arts core requirement in the humanities and thus attracted all kinds of students with no particular interest in religion. Nonetheless, those who choose to take religion courses rather than the alternatives in literature, philosophy, or art history—as I have learned in many subsequent seasons of freshman advising—often do so because they expect and need to find something comfortably predictable.

I opened REL 291 at Syracuse with an ethnography that had met with considerable success in SOAN 216 at Colgate: Loring Danforth's *Firewalking and Religious Healing: The Anastenaria of Greece and the American Firewalking Movement.* As a broad introduction to comparative religion, I chose William Paden's *Religious Worlds.* The concept of respectful travel among religious worlds seemed compatible enough with my anthropological lens. I expected that the combo of Paden and Danforth in the first four weeks of the course would smoothly transport my students between Greek firewalking and New Age firewalking so that both would illuminate the roles ritual and ritual symbols played in self-transformation and healing.

Danforth vividly describes a Greek community where icons of Christian saints are understood to have feelings and preferences. I found this remarkably similar to Hindu attitudes. In both traditions, the icons are theologically nothing but inert matter. Yet they must be treated with all consideration and courtesy if one is to obtain their blessings, and they may express unfulfilled desires by afflicting any persons who treat them with negligence or disrespect. Danforth quite brilliantly compares and contrasts firewalking in Greece and Maine, and is able to show how the symbolic potency of fire, as it burns and releases, spans the two contexts, even as individual motivations and specific problems addressed in the rituals dramatically diverge.

I knew the Anastenaria's behaviors and beliefs would unsettle student assumptions about Christian cosmology and practices, and thus "make the familiar strange"—a declared good in anthropology. Moreover, I sought deliberately to enhance that effect by showing the powerful, classic ethnographic film *Holy Ghost People,* about snake-handling Pentecostals in the American South.

My lecture notes from more than a decade ago give me only half the tale. But I know with the acutely painful sensation only a bad teaching experience can engrave into one's repressed consciousness that *Firewalking and Religious Healing,* which had worked so sweetly in my Colgate anthropology class, struck my forty-odd students in REL 291 as absurd, weird, and, above all, not what they had bargained for in an introductory religion course. My rebellious and grumpy class did not want to hear about the insignificant population of some remote corner of Greece whose firewalking practices appeared to defy science. The only thing they really wanted to know, which of course I was not able to tell them, was why some people do not get burned and others do. This knowledge gap upset them. They yearned for positivism; they abhorred multiple realities.

Danforth's final chapters on New Age marketing of self-empowerment through firewalking in the United States—rituals with an admission price—did not bring firewalking truths back home as I had planned. No, these impressed my students as still more over-the-top, comical, bizarre topics that simply were not worthy of being studied as "religious phenomena." From their point of view, this was left field—an aging hippie professor's bad idea.

As the midterm approached, I overheard one student joking loudly before class was called to order that Professor Gold's exam would require the students to walk barefoot over burning coals or possibly pick up poisonous snakes. I was mortified. Maybe this disciplinary cross-over was not going to work. I took half a class off my syllabus schedule to ask the students to tell me what they had expected to study when they signed up for "themes and issues." It turned out—big surprise to me!—that they were hoping to think about the religious worlds and rituals they already knew: baptism, bar mitzvah, weddings and the like. In other words, they wanted no part of dubious healing that was not medically approved nor of potentially self-deceptive spiritual transformations. Rather, they wanted rituals having to do with identity affirmation.

I revised my syllabus midsemester to allow students to organize presentations on traditions familiar to them, presentations that everyone (I among them) enjoyed a lot. Letting students teach what they know is a strategy that I incorporate whenever possible. They went to great lengths to bring ritual paraphernalia into the classroom—everything from phylacteries and prayer shawls to incense and gospel music. To many of them, it was quite enough of an intellectual adventure to step back from their own traditions, or those of their roommates, and to be fledgling analysts of these nearby religious worlds. They liked to apply the term "life cycle rituals" or "rites of passage" to their own experiences (and I, more than once, to my bemusement, found these phrases rendered in writing as "life style rituals" and "rights of passage"). My evaluations were at least partially salvaged. But Danforth's book, and the snake-handling film, were singled out for ire. I cannot blame Danforth for my fire ordeal. He had, after all, served me well in "Religion, Culture, and Social Change."

In the first week of both classes, SOAN 216 and REL 291, I had presented the students with eighteen academic definitions of religion, laboriously compiled. A majority of Syracuse students, to my utter surprise, had voted for Durkheim:

[Religion] is a unified system of beliefs and practices relative to sacred things, that is to say, things set apart and forbidden—beliefs and

practices which unite into one single moral community called a
Church, all those who adhere to them. (1965: 62)

Perhaps it was the word "church" that drew them to this; or perhaps it was the
clear separation of religion from the rest of life. Two years earlier, at Colgate,
the majority had favored Malinowski:

> Religion is not born out of speculation or reflection, still less out of
> illusion or misapprehension, but rather out of the real tragedies
> of human life, out of the conflict between human plans and
> realities. . . . Every important crisis of human life implies a strong
> emotional upheaval, mental conflict and possible disintegration. . . .
> Religious belief consists in the traditional standardization of the
> positive side in the mental conflict and therefore satisfies a definite
> individual need. . . . On the other hand, religious belief and ritual, by
> making the critical acts and the social contracts of human life public,
> traditionally standardized, and subject to supernatural sanctions,
> strengthen the bonds of human cohesion. (1931:641–642)

Looking back, it is easy to see that Malinowski's definition seems to apply
to healing miracles associated with firewalking far more aptly than does
Durkheim's definition, which reminds us rather of the sacraments neatly
packaged in sacred time and space. Malinowski's definition locates ritual in
mundane need; Durkheim's appears to locate it far from the everyday. I did
try hard to get the students in REL 291 to think about Durkheim's "collective
effervescence." I lectured with animation on the ways a shared and intense
experience among gathered humans might fizz, bubble, or foam in group consciousness. I pointed to this quality at firewalking events—but ultimately
failed to convince these students that such ritual shenanigans deserved their
attention as religious phenomena.

Fall 2003 Pleasant Journeys

Fast-forward ten years. I am full and fully secure, professorially and professionally. But in the classroom I feel my way, groping as ever. For the first time
in my many years of teaching, I have undertaken to offer a course titled
"Pilgrimage," coinciding with Syracuse University's College of Arts and Sciences semester-long Symposium—including art exhibits, musical performances and lectures—on the theme of "Journeys." I was nervous about the
syllabus—perhaps the most purely phenomenological, picaresque course plot
I have ever produced. My plan, such as it existed, was to look at religious
journeys and their meanings not only in ethnographic descriptions but in
other literary genres: memoirs, letters, poems.

Every element of religion unites in the pilgrimage process.[2] With this topic so close to my heart and my past, it seems that religious studies and anthropology; gross ritual actions and deep high truths; students' own worlds and the worlds of their cultural others all fluidly, magically converge and interpenetrate. Add to this the fact that folks in their late teens and early twenties love the ideas of journeys and quests: after all, they have been playing those video games all their lives. And then, there is Victor Turner.

I open REL 121 by assigning the students Turner and Turner's "Pilgrimage As a Liminoid Phenomenon," the introduction to *Image and Pilgrimage in Christian Culture* (1978). This represents one of the latest and most complete formulations of Turnerian pilgrimage theory, or so I recollected. When I reread the article, somewhat too late in the game, I realized with sheer panic that it was far too dense and too erudite for a 100-level batch of undergraduates to begin to comprehend. Nonetheless, their first writing assignment was to be based on Turner and Turner. Moreover, it had to offer them the chance, as I always try to do early in any semester, to talk about themselves. I did not want them to struggle and stumble now. My solution was to create a handout, a quick study, which I reproduce in full (see Response Paper 1).

I am proud of my handout, but I am equally ashamed of it, for I well knew it would make it far too convenient for them to do the writing task without reading the chapter at all. I guess I have to argue that the ends justify the means.

Although it indeed became clear in grading the papers that only a few students, mostly religion majors, troubled themselves to work through the article, everyone read the handout really carefully, even thoughtfully. They got the point. Not only that, they retained these ideas throughout our fifteen weeks. Assimilating this new vocabulary, they returned frequently of their own accord to the liminal nature of pilgrimage, to the experience of communitas, even to the distinction between liminal and liminoid. (They sometimes used "liminoid" oddly, as a noun; e.g.: "This pilgrimage is definitely a liminoid.")

Not a single Euro-American student in my smallish class had ever been on a religious pilgrimage; two Muslims from Near Eastern countries had been to Mecca, although not at the time of hajj. They had clearly signed up for the course because of this piece of their personal histories. Turner made fine sense to them. All the other students on our first discussion day presented passable and in several cases extraordinarily acute visions of liminoid experience and attendant communitas in "secular" contexts. We heard about Phish concerts, about sports teams in training, about several varieties of wilderness therapy programs, about a church trip involving community service in Mexico, about a retreat designed to enhance young African-American women's sense of identity and empowerment, and more. I start to imagine that the organizers of such events have read Victor Turner before ordering the T-shirts.

Bonded by collective storytelling, REL 121 spent the entire first half of the semester on two ethnographic case studies: Barbara Myerhoff's *Peyote Hunt:*

Response Paper 1: Shared Stories of Liminality and Communitas

Each response paper is usually more than one and less than two pages long. It should be typed in a 10-12 point font, or *neatly* written out in longhand.

Crucial Background on the Concepts

Liminality comes from Latin: *limen*, a threshold; in other writings the Turners have described it as "betwixt and between."

According to the Turners, liminality is a ritual stage during which participants are detached from their ordinary social routines and form new, status-free connections with one another—which the Turners call "communitas." The original model of a "liminal" period would be an initiation ritual, as in some tribal societies, that isolates adolescents for many days from their families and communities before returning them, transformed into adults.

According to the Turners, present-day pilgrimage, along with other similarly intense group experiences of modern society, has much in common with liminal periods. But it is "liminoid" or "quasi-liminal" because it is voluntary. By contrast, some small-scale societies require all persons to go through a single liminal experience.

Pilgrimage, like liminality, involves—the Turners say—release from everyday structure, removing and equalizing social differences, healing, renewal, reflection on the meaning of religious and cultural values. "A pilgrim is one who divests himself of the mundane concomitants of religion . . . to confront, in a special 'far' milieu, the basic elements and structures of his faith in their unshielded, virgin radiance" (p. 15).

Besides pilgrimage, other ritualized experiences in modern society that have been described as liminoid include spiritual retreats offered by churches, revival meetings, and Bible camps. Carrying the concept beyond realms we usually call religious, think about: family reunions, rock concerts, fraternity or sorority initiations, some forms of tourism, and organized wilderness camping such as Outward Bound programs.

Your Assignment

Read carefully Turner and Turner, "Pilgrimage as a Liminoid Phenomenon" and then describe an experience you have had, read about, or heard described that seems to you to fit the Turners' description of liminoid.

Be specific: if the experience involved a unified if temporary group identity; special clothes, practices, language, stories; a set of rules that are not customary or a collective breaking of rules that are customary; transmission of knowledge; or any other features associated with liminality—mention them.

The Sacred Journey of the Huichol Indians and Michalowski and Dubisch's *Run for the Wall: Remembering Vietnam on a Motorcycle Pilgrimage*. Pure serendipity caused these two books to be placed in such intimate proximity on my syllabus. Habitually, my syllabi slip into a conventional pattern: to begin with the "other" and return to the "self." That lazy scheme would have sent *Run for the Wall* to the end of the semester. But because one of its authors, Jill Dubisch, was visiting to give a public lecture in our Journeys symposium, I put her book about Vietnam veterans' annual, ceremonial symbol-laden journey from California to D.C. immediately after Myerhoff's book about the Huichol Indians' annual, ceremonial, symbol-laden journey to Wirikuta. Commonalities leapt out at us, and Turnerian insights provided a constant drone that promoted comparative analysis. Myerhoff was, of course, Victor Turner's disciple. Michalowski and Dubisch do not ride any big theoretical horse, only their Honda Gold Wing. But they do very convincingly argue and demonstrate that the Vietnam veterans' bike ride is a sacred journey:

> Like the pilgrimages associated with the major world religions, the Run combines a ritual journey with seriousness of purpose, ending in the arrival at a sacred goal. And like other pilgrimages, it can have a powerful, even transformative, effect on its participants. (2001: 15)

To conclude those weeks, I had my students generate lists of comparative points on the blackboard. Here are some of their observations, although not in the students' exact words:

The Run for the Wall is like the Huichol pilgrimage in that:

1. It is in tune with a sacred calendar.
2. It is a journey of self-transformatin and sometimes of healing.
3. It creates a sense of kinship among participants.
4. It marks novices, those who have never gone before. Novices are blindfolded by the Huichol at a certain stage of the journey; among the veterans, they wear bright stickers labeling them FNG for "fuckin' new guy."
5. It involves travel by stages through a landscape full of meaning and culminates in a place that is symbolically hyperpotent.[3] On both journeys, motivations include highly individualized quests for health and blessings, encompassed within a desire for participation in an intense collective experience.

My students also listed differences between the Run and the Huichol journey, although they argued over and qualified some of these. One clear contrast to which they pointed is the peyote hunt's culmination in hallucinogenic experience, whereas drugs and alcohol are forbidden on the Run. The Huichol deliberately assume the identities of their mythological predecessors;

some students thought the veterans lacked this altered or expanded sense of self; but others argued that the prisoners of war and the soldiers missing in action are in a sense spirit beings who accompany the riders and with whom they merge at times. Michalowski and Dubisch describe and photograph a "symbolic POW" portrayed captive in a "tiger cage" as a powerful emblem along the route (2001: 80).

One evident contrast on which all could all agree was that the Run, unlike the journey to Wirikuta, has no eternal heritage originating in mythic time, but rather belongs to history, and begins in a certain year. Related to this historical dimension is its public political message, whereas the Huichol journey seems to take place in a private religious world. Peter Furst's wonderful film of the Huichol pilgrimage, *To Find Our Life*, shows pilgrims in their brilliant embroidered clothing near a highway with trucks rushing past. It appears as if these pilgrims exist in a parallel, that is, a nonintersecting ritual dimension, a completely separate landscape. The veterans, by contrast, are intentionally visible and often draw media attention. This visibility is part of their raison d'être. (In discussions, needless to say, we got sidetracked to politics. We were, after all, living in the ominous shadow of a new war creating new wounds every day. But this is not my topic here.)

Pilgrimage teaches so brilliantly because religious journeys ring a set of recurrent themes that seem to resonate through highly diverse cultural contexts and religious worlds. Turner and Turner, even the boiled-down quick-and-dirty version thereof that the handout provided, help us to see these themes and to hear these chiming echoes. As a scholarly enterprise in anthropology, to argue for universals is suspect and often reductive. This is why the Turners' theories have met with so much opposition in the literature, where specific cases can always be mustered to refute them. However, as a pedagogic tool, under the right circumstances, to observe what is in common across traditions may help to open doors and windows. Or, to borrow a phrase from A. K. Ramanujan (1989), it may even turn mirrors (regarding one's own cultural practices—a Phish concert, let us say) into windows (seeing others as manipulating their ritual symbols and experiencing their sense of groupness in recognizable ways). This is the trick worked by a Turnerian approach in teaching comparative religion.

I shall not detail, but only highlight, the second half of the semester, during which we sampled smaller pieces of a wider range of pilgrimage phenomena, and considered the ways that different descriptive genres gave us access to different aspects of religious experiences. Poets, travel writers, insiders and outsiders enriched our views of ritual processes. Of course, we visited Graceland and argued mightily over Elvis's possible divinity. We also touched down in Guadalupe, Santiago, Kashi, Kailash, Shikoku, and Mecca.

A couple of excerpts from Wise and Thurman's *Circling the Sacred Mountain*, a Tibetan pilgrimage diary written in two distinctive voices, gave us, contrapuntally, Wise as down-to-earth, self-doubting, naïve pilgrim who frets over physical discomforts and his own spiritual malaise, and Thurman as tireless preacher of Buddhist truths who consistently incorporates each ritualized stage of the mountain's terrain into a narrative of pilgrims' progress. Together they work like stereoscopic lenses to bring a single journey and its cosmic psychology into focus.

For Islamic pilgrimage we read a number of hajj accounts in the wonderful anthology *One Thousand Roads to Mecca* (Wolfe 1997) containing travelers narratives that cover ten centuries. Ultimately, we turned inward to close the course with the Sufi allegory, *Conference of the Birds*—not a journey at all, but a compendium of teaching tales delivering, among other things, a message about why pilgrimage cannot bring you to your highest goals, but why aspirations to set forth in search of knowledge are nonetheless crucial.

Poetry offered some of the semester's most powerful glimpses of the paradoxical meaninglessness and power of religious journeys and accompanying ritual actions. The Journeys symposium brought both the Kabir Singers and the modern poet Karen Swenson to town. Students relished fifteenth-century Indian poet-saint Kabir's scathing critiques of ritual, including pilgrimage, both Hindu and Muslim. Kabir challenges, "Why bump that shaven head on the earth, why dunk those bones in the water?" (Hess and Singh 1983: 73), and his rhetorical question goes unanswered, implying that there is absolutely no good reason. Ritual is the antithesis of Kabir's devotion to the inner name of god.

Swenson, who also guides select tour groups in Tibet, was able to visit our classroom, and made a strong impression on the students. Her views are less trenchant than Kabir's. She read us some of her exquisitely crafted poetry, in which her positions seemed to us to shift. Sometimes Swenson gazes from a psychically alien space at other peoples' lives and rituals. But certain poems express partial participation. In poetic language, Swenson is able to transmit an understanding of ritual action and emergent meanings at which teaching strategies, and academic writings, can only clumsily hint. Her "Circumambulating Mount Kailash" captured for my class essential ways that pilgrimage may integrate outer movements and inner realizations. Yet Swenson was very frank about her position as a cultural outsider, making observations without access to local languages.

Even so, concise capsules of poetic epiphany yield teaching fruits of disproportionate size. I will conclude my contribution to this collective meditation on teaching ritual with a few lines of Swenson's verse. She evokes communitas with just the word "we"; she evokes liminal experience with the images of mountain, wind, and snow. With only the past tense "wheeled," she calls up not only a giddy mountainside whirl but images of Tibetan prayer wheels (which can, for outsiders, be emblems of meaningless "Oriental" ritual). The verb "to wheel" also summons the Indic notion of *samsara* or an endless round of redeath and rebirth to which desires and actions bind human beings but from which a pilgrim might be struggling to get free. Swenson's journey, like the Huichols' and the veterans', brings healing. In closing with some kind of return, she reminds us of reaggregation that completes the Turnerian model of ritual stages, although it always fails to fascinate in the way that liminality does. In speaking of new birth, the wheel's consequence, Swenson may allow into her poem a slight echo from Christianity, which unlike Buddhism puts a positive spin on this image. But birth also signifies the inevitable chains of samsara and the ways that returns never quite leave those who have undergone rites of passage in precisely the same form at the same place.

> The pass is well behind us now,
> wind singing in its snows.
> We've wheeled the mountain's hub along the brow
> of river bank, transgressions healed
> by the circumference of our strides
> which circle us to a new birth. (2004:221)

NOTES

1. Here my work differs from many significant studies of pilgrimage that followed Turner and attempted either to support or to refute his models. For one late and thorough example, see Eade and Sallnow 1991.

2. I am hardly the first to use pilgrimage to teach comparative religion, or world religions, at the introductory level. In fact, I knew that Diana Eck did so with famous success at Harvard, and I felt diffident about following in her footsteps. The AAR syllabus collection contains some other pilgrimage offerings.

3. See Turner 1979 on the accumulation of symbols in sacred centers; see Sturken 1997 on the accumulation of symbols at the Vietnam wall.

USEFUL MATERIALS

Aside from the books given in the reference list—especially Michalowski and Dubisch. 2001, Myerhoff 1974, Turner and Turner 1978, and Wise and Thurman 1999—the following may be useful to readers:

King, Christine. 1993. "His Truth Goes Marching On: Elvis Presley and the Pilgrimage to Graceland." In *Pilgrimage in Popular Culture,* ed. Ian Reader and Tony Walter, 92–104. London: Macmillan.

To Find Our Life: The Peyote Hunt of the Huichols of Mexico. 1969. Film. 16mm, 65 minutes, color. Film documents the ritual activities of a peyote pilgrimage by a group of Huichol Indians to the north-central desert of San Luis Potosi, Mexico. Creator: Peter T. Hurst, anthropologist; AV Service, Penn. State—Distributor, Spec Serv Bldg, 1127 Fox Hill Rd., University Park, Pa. 16803.

REFERENCES

Attar, Farid ud-Din. *Conference of the Birds*. New York: Penguin.

Barnhill, David L. 1990. "Basho as Bat: Wayfaring and Antistructure in the Journals of Matsuo Basho." *Journal of Asian Studies* 49: 274–290.

Chidester, David. 1996. *Savage Systems: Colonialism and Comparative Religion in Southern Africa*. Charlottesville: University Press of Virginia.

Danforth, Loring. 1989. *Firewalking and Religious Healing: The Anastenaria of Greece and the American Firewalking Movement*. Princeton, N.J.: Princeton University Press.

Doss, Erika. 1999. *Elvis Culture: Fans, Faith, and Image*. Lawrence: University Press of Kansas.

Durkheim, Emile. 1965 (1915). *The Elementary Forms of the Religious Life*. New York: Free Press.

Eade, J., and M. J. Sallnow, eds. 1991. *Contesting the Sacred: The Anthropology of Christian Pilgrimage*. London: Routledge.

Gold, Ann Grodzins. 1988. *Fruitful Journeys: The Ways of Rajasthani Pilgrims*. Berkeley: University of California Press.

Hess, Linda, and Shukdev Singh. 1983. *The Bijak of Kabir*. San Francisco: North Point Press.

Malinowski, Bronislaw. 1931. "Culture." *Encyclopedia of the Social Sciences* 4: 621–646.

Michalowski, Raymond, and Jill Dubisch. 2001. *Run for the Wall: Remembering Vietnam on a Motorcycle Pilgrimage*. New Brunswick, N.J.: Rutgers University Press.

Miner, Horace. 1956. "Body Ritual among the Nacirema." *American Anthropologist* 58: 503–507.

Myerhoff, Barbara G. 1974. *Peyote Hunt: The Sacred Journey of the Huichol Indians*. Ithaca, N.Y.: Cornell University Press.

Paden, William E. 1994. *Religious Worlds: The Comparative Study of Religion*. Boston: Beacon Press.

Ramanujan, A. K. 1989. "Where Mirrors Are Windows: Toward an Anthology of Reflections." *History of Religions* 28, 3: 187–216.

Reader, Ian. 1993. "Dead to the World: Pilgrims in Shikoku." In *Pilgrimage in Popular Culture*, ed. Ian Reader and Tony Walter, 107–136. London: Macmillan.

Sturken, Marita. 1997. *Tangled Memories: The Vietnam War, the AIDS Epidemic, and the Politics of Remembering*. Berkeley: University of California Press.

Swenson, Karen. 1994. *The Landlady in Bangkok*. Port Townsend, Wash.: Copper Canyon Press.

———. 2004. "Circumambulating Mount Kailash." *Poetry in Performance* 32:221.

Turner, Victor. 1969. *The Ritual Process: Structure and Anti-Structure*. Ithaca, N.Y.: Cornell University Press.

———. 1974. *Dramas, Fields, and Metaphors: Symbolic Action in Human Society*. Ithaca, N.Y.: Cornell University Press.

———. 1979. *Process, Performance, and Pilgrimage: A Study in Comparative Symbology*. New Delhi: Concept Publishing Co.

Turner, Victor, and Edith Turner. 1978. *Image and Pilgrimage in Christian Culture*. New York: Columbia University Press.

Van Gennep, Arnold. 1960. *The Rites of Passage*. London: Routledge and Paul.

Wise, Tad, and Robert Thurman. 1999. *Circling the Sacred Mountain*. New York: Bantam Books.

Wolfe, Michael, ed. 1997. *One Thousand Roads to Mecca: Ten Centuries of Travelers Writing about the Muslim Pilgrimage*. New York: Grove Press.

3

Dancing Ritual, Ritual Dancing: Experiential Teaching

Sam Gill

Prayer, Native American religions, ritual, and dancing are a few key words that label my abiding interests. They share an odd commonality, and that is that they all seem religiously ignored or, less dramatically, underappreciated by the academic study of religion. From a disinterested phenomenological point of view, this absence of attention seems striking. Prayer, ritual, and dancing are practically inseparable from religions across the globe and throughout time. For an academic study heavily centered in North America to all but ignore the indigenous traditions that are meshed with American identity seems likewise confounding. There are other factors that draw these disparate topics together. Stated as a lack, telling in itself, none of them is based in text. Put positively, all are centered on body.

Though texts of prayer and literature on how, why, where, when, and what to pray are common, prayer is as much as anything an action or attitude taken by the body—upraised arms and hands, folded hands and bowed heads, the spinning of wheels, the progression of beads, prostration—and the speech act of prayer is characterized by rote recitation, unending repetition and redundancy, or as an extemporaneous, internal performative. There is a marked absence of comparative academic studies of prayer.

Native American languages are exclusively oral; they have no texts. The very awkwardness of even labeling this characteristic is revealing. Even stated positively as "exclusively oral," we think of the negatives nonliterate, preliterate, illiterate, and the associated synonyms of stupid and primitive. Our inability even to label what characterizes them as anything but a lack is linked to why we ignore

Native Americans. In the late nineteenth century and well into the twentieth, processing the evolutionist agenda, it was common method to look to such peoples to establish the definitional benchmarks and the developmental patterns for religion and culture. Such peoples represented the primitive and archaic stages and states of being human. They revealed either the pre-religious state or the purest form of religion. Yet, once this stage and style of academic study passed, the religions of cultures without alphabetic writing were pretty much ignored by the academic study of religion, cast into that cesspool of "ethnic studies" (again, the term is worth thinking about) and left to anthropologists.

As I traveled among cultures in various parts of the world, I often asked someone on the road, "Where can I go to find some religious doin's?" And so often I've been directed to a dance event. I've found this in all Native American cultures, in Bali, in Java, in Ghana and Mali. And I know it would also pertain in many other cultures. Dancing and religious doin's are often nearly synonymous. And many dances that I would never have considered religious— tango, flamenco, and hip-hop are examples—are spoken of by at least some of their dancers as being religious. Other dances, particularly those of the West, are often described as being somehow "spiritual," the modern substitute for "religious." Such identification of dancing, which is unquestionably a bodily activity, reveals much about our perspective and how it shapes our appreciation of dancing and ritual and religion. To label dancing as "spiritual" is invariably done in the service of elevating its value. We seem unable to appreciate such body-based activities as ritual and dancing. We value spirit and mind so highly that anything of body must be denied its bodily character in order to have value. Of course, the academic study of religion pays little attention to the religions of Indonesia and West Africa and Native North America, but dancing is strongly identified with religion in Hinduism and, though rarely even mentioned so far as I know, it is also strongly valued in Christianity once we remember that the bulk of Christians, throughout Christian history, have lived outside the West, in Africa, Asia, South America, and Native North America, where dancing has not been separated from the church as it has been in Europe and North America. Yet the academic study of religion ignores dancing.

The paucity of attention given to ritual really needs no argument.

Though I think the most significant things I may have to say relate to teaching dancing, I want first to reflect on some efforts I made years ago to teach ritual. Among my University of Colorado colleagues, the question of whether to incorporate an experiential dimension in teaching ritual has been perhaps the most hotly debated issue of all my more than twenty years tenure. Doing rituals in an academic environment—apart from the unacknowledged and unquestioned rituals of the academy—are highly suspect. I fully agree. Though a quick aside to this aside is irresistible. Perhaps the largest public ritual in America today is that of academic graduation. It is, I think, no coincidence that academic garb and Christian liturgical garb are almost indistinguishable. Both render the body inarticulate. Both present human beings as floating heads. Analyzing the history of bodies in Western academic thought—that is, bodies disabled in deference to the all-important mind—correlates strongly and shares the same history as the European and American Christian body, which is distrusted and devalued when compared with the spirit. Holding that Western educational architecture and furniture, which are designed to place the body at rest, do more to shape and certainly limit education than the theories and ideas, and that these body attitudes strongly correlate with and are rooted in European Christianity, I argue that modern Western education is a Christian theological project.[1] One of the current sound bites for the University of Colorado is "minds to match our mountains" (I suppose we are to think of lofty rather than high or stoned), whereas the mascot most closely associated with CU athletics is a herd animal. Though I was fully disposed to attempt to teach ritual experientially, I nonetheless had some deep concerns about some aspects of the ritual lab work that was developing beginning several decades ago. Bringing together students of ritual and sometimes drama, these lab works often set the task as reenacting specific rituals of particular cultures. My concern was not only that such actions seemed disrespectful in some very fundamental way, but also that they could easily lead to misunderstanding. Other lab works have tended to draw students into intensely personal experiences accompanied by deep emotions. Though this kind of work clearly demonstrates some aspects of the power of ritual, my concern is that it fails to maintain boundaries appropriate to the modern academy and to the usual training of the faculty. In my view, these kinds of experiential teaching seem potentially dangerous and tend to manipulate students beyond standards of academic acceptability.

Still, to teach ritual sitting down, to restrict the study of ritual to reading and writing, seemed inadequate to me. I am fully convinced by the studies that demonstrate the inseparability of body and mind in such fields as gestalt psychology and cognitive science. George Lakoff's and Mark Johnson's many works are also quite convincing. If we take this mind-body interdependence seriously, we must carefully rethink most of our academic and pedagogical assumptions and practices. I found inspiration in the hard sciences where, notably, laboratory classes are standard requirements for undergraduate education. As I recall my own experience in science labs as an undergraduate, it wasn't getting the correct results that seemed to be the point of these labs. If it was, I failed miserably. Proving the theories, confirming the laws, seems not to be the most important part of science labs. It is the experiential side of it, having one's hands on something. Experiential learning is simply pedagogically powerful. So, I wondered, given that the study of ritual doesn't have the scientific counterpart of laws, theorems, instruments for observation and measurement, how can one even imagine teaching ritual without some experiential component? Wouldn't this be, I thought, like studying music without ever even hearing it? Wouldn't this be like studying painting without ever seeing it?

Well, it is rather more complicated to experience ritual while teaching it than it is to listen to music or see slides or reproductions of painting. Site visits are possible, audiovisual aids are useful, but bodily active experience of ritual seems also important. In state-supported schools, it might accurately be considered illegal to conduct religious rituals. In any general liberal educational environment, it should be considered disrespectful and inappropriate to imitate the rituals of others. This was part of my concern with the experiential approaches with which I was familiar. Further, it is naive to think one understands another's experience by briefly imitating his actions. I believe that this kind of appropriation of the surfaces of the rituals of others is inappropriate to higher education. I also think it usually unacceptable even for a faculty person adept at a particular ritual tradition to engage students in her or his practice. So what to do?

My experiment was a course I taught a couple times called "Ritual Drama" (a little Turner inspiration here). It was premised on my belief that any group of people can and often do constitute themselves—their identity, their interactions, their hierarchy, their resolution of conflict, their relation to "others," their methods of problem solving, their discipline of the aberrant, and so on—through the rites they establish and practice as much as by their definition and application of rules and laws. One could suggest that the definition and application of rules and laws are, in large measure, a codification of rites. My approach, then, was to charge class members with developing themselves as a group through the construction and practice of ritual.

I played two roles, which I did my best to keep entirely distinct and separate. As the instructor, I worked outside the actual classroom to assign readings and tasks for each class. These readings and assignments, which the students were given at the end of each session, focused on a particular aspect of ritual (say, how to incorporate a new member of the group). I assigned readings that dealt with the theories of such situations (e.g., rites-of-passage theories), and I provided relevant cultural and religious examples. I also provided the outline of a situation to be the focus for the next class meeting—for example, designating students to be the outsiders seeking incorporation in the group represented by the rest of the students. My second role was to be a member of the group. Once I entered the space of the classroom, I did my best to be simply a member of the group, with no distinction from the others. I refused students who, particularly in the beginning, looked to me for guidance or information or critique.

The principal rule for the group—set forth at the beginning of the semester and outside of the classroom space—was that action had precedence over analytical academic speech. Notably, as these groups formed themselves, their identity could not be separated from their academic interests, so they set aside time and space and methods for academic, analytical discourse as part of their ritual constitution. The group worked with all sorts of ritual issues, such as how to designate space, how to enter and leave space, how to treat guests, how to appear (clothing, etc), how to observe special days or occasions, how to discipline, how to exclude, how to reflect, how to determine hierarchy, and so on. While often taking insight from ritual theory or the practices of specific cultures, they had to create and practice their own rites. The rites created were practiced in the ongoing existence of the group.

My experience as both ritualist and teacher was valuable. My experience strongly confirmed that an experiential approach to teaching ritual is powerful. I believe that through these experiences we all learned some important things about ritual. Ritual is constructive and creative. It is affective and effective. It is negotiative and adaptive. If measured by fulfillment of intentions, it fails as often as it succeeds. It is artful. It is difficult to analyze, though not difficult to experience. It is full of meaning, yet it is difficult to articulate such meaning in other than tritely obvious terms. Details are important. Repetition and redundancy are essential and powerful. Ritual is of the minded-body.

Still, for me, the ongoing suspicion of such a course in a "class one research university," the enormous care required to keep such a course academically clear, the weirdness of maintaining a divided presence, the constant vigilance to restrict and limit the emerging ritual community to the service of only academic goals (itself an amazing testimony to the power of ritual) were more than I cared to regularly take on. I taught this course only two times. Both successful, both exhausting.

The teaching of these ritual drama courses corresponded with shifts in my life and my interests. Though I believe that there are clear limitations to the extent a teacher should disclose the personal, nonetheless, who a teacher is, what experiences (including personal) a teacher has had greatly shapes the learning situation. I rediscovered myself as a body through dancing—jazz, aerobic, hip-hop, African, and Latin American. As dancing became fundamental to my own personal reawakening, it began to bleed into everything I did. I began to recall that dancing had been central to so many religions I was familiar with. I had attended dozens of Native American dances that were religious rites. I had even written about some of these. The importance of dancing in my own midlife awakened me to the importance of dancing in religions. On the basis of a cursory review of dance literature, ethnographic and theoretical, I was taken aback by several factors. The academic study of religion gives little to no attention to dancing despite its being among the most common forms of religious action. Theories of dancing are almost entirely shaped by those trained in modern Western art forms of dancing, that is, by those who belong to the so-called "dance world." Though hundreds of ethnographic accounts exist documenting dances and dance cultures, dance ethnography is a tiny field, and its theories are poorly developed and little informed by the advances of social scientific and humanities theory. I found myself sucked into the study and teaching of dancing with many incentives: the pursuit of fuller appreciation of a form of action that is central and fundamental to my own life, but as understood through the inclusion of, and comparative consideration of, the actions of peoples in cultures around the world.

In the early 1990s, I collected dozens of ethnographic accounts of dance traditions. I invited students to read them with me, to think about them, and to try to contextualize them historically and religiously, and to investigate correlations and relationship between dancing and architecture and art and music and fashion and law and doctrine and belief and history. I began earnestly trying to come to terms with the academic challenges of understanding and appreciating dancing without dependence on the standard metaphors of text and language and propositional meaning. My students and I sat in chairs and read and talked and wrote, and, oddly, we didn't even watch videos. All the while, I kept feeling that something was missing. One day a student in the class spoke up. I think we were reading about dancing in Greek Orthodoxy. She informed the class that she actually knew the dance that we were discussing and that she could teach us a little of it if we wanted. Quickly we pushed back the chairs (and in the modern university, to actually be able to push back chairs is unexpectedly unusual) and followed her lead. We were dancing! Though our dancing was crude and unaccomplished, we nevertheless were experiencing the dance we had, minutes before, had no image or notion of at all, because the writings about the dance didn't, as is typical, include even the most rudimentary description of what the dance is like. In that moment, everything shifted for me. I suddenly knew what had been missing: the dancing.

That was more than a decade ago, and now I teach a two-semester sequence titled "Religion and Dance" to ninety students covering more than twenty-five dance cultures. I will describe that course in some detail, but first I must address the relationship between dancing and ritual lest I lose sight of my topic.

Dancing, of all human art and cultural forms, is arguably the most bodied, the most mind-body integrative. Dancing is the body. Dancing is done with the body as both the means and the outcome, both process and product. Though it is not possible to adequately present my views here, it is important to at least adumbrate them. I find that although dancing does many things—such as create and enact identity, negotiate differences, enact protest, ensue change—its role as being in some sense constitutive of being human is of greater interest. That is, as I understand dancing, it is inseparable from that which distinguishes us as human beings. Dancing is that which is the very source of the powers and behaviors and abilities that make us human. In terms of human development, dancing is prelinguistic. In terms of cultural

views, more than one religion—consider the Hindu form of Shiva, Nataraj—
sees the creation and destruction of the universe arising from dancing. Dancing is a kind of relationality—or to use Derrida's term, structurality, or to use
Baudrillard's term, seductivity, or to use Merleau-Ponty's term, reversibility—
that founds the very possibility of symbol and language and art and ritual. I
believe that dancing is more fundamental even than ritual and religion, and
that understanding dancing in these terms can be foundational to understanding ritual.

Dancing does what ought not to be possible, that is, dancing creates an
artifice, an other, something made up, something that is not the dancer, yet,
because this made-up thing, this artifice, is created of the body, it is experienced as self. I call this aspect of dancing "self-othering." It is the experiential
bridge between self and other. Arguably there must be some initial experiential foundation that underlies all the connectivities that constitute our humanity, those "this-is-not-that, but this-is-that" kinds of connections that
distinguish language, art, metaphor, ritual, and religion. Dancing is one of
these fundamental bodily experiences that make our humanness possible.

To begin to comprehend this not only helps us appreciate why dancing
and ritual are so often connected, even inseparable, but it also helps us understand why the academic study of religion—so focused on thought, language, text, and propositional meaning, indeed, focused on the meaning and
the truth—tends to ignore both dancing and ritual despite their near synonymy
with religion.

"Religion and Dance" is fairly evenly divided between traditional classroom activities—lecture, discussion, audiovisual presentations supported by
assigned readings and written essays—and experiential learning in a studio. I
arrange for teachers and artists, usually of the relevant culture, to teach and
demonstrate most of the dance/musical forms studied. Boulder's resources are
so rich that often these artists are of considerable renown. To prepare these
guest teachers, I tell them to present a 75-minute experience for the students as
if, in their whole lives, this studio is their only experience of this dance form.
Most include demonstrations. Thus studios are not simply beginning classes.
It is strange, ironically, that in a course that so extensively uses experiential
body-based learning, the very structure of the course enacts a rather rigid
mind-body split. The advantage of the experiential learning in the study of
dancing over that of non-dance ritual is that teaching dancing to those outside
of a dance culture is rather broadly accepted and practiced.[2] Indeed, partially as
a result of this course, I founded and continue to operate a school of world
music and dancing outside of the university.[3] I now teach dance there and find
it the most rewarding teaching I do. Certainly many cultures make distinctions
between what dance/musical forms are appropriate to teach to outsiders.
Dances acceptable to be taught are often similar to unacceptable ones. I think it
often has more to do with the context of the dances than the actual elements of

the dancing. Some people in some cultures strongly oppose anyone outside the culture doing the ritual dances. Some priestesses from the Brazilian religion Candomblé told me that without proper preparation, knowledge, guidance, and initiation, people who invoke the *orixas* through dancing could actually do harm. They were completely open, however, to the influence of the *orixa* dances on samba and other popular dance forms. It is also my experience that many Native Americans firmly oppose the learning or performing of their dances by anyone who is not Native American. I fully respect and abide by the wishes of anyone that the dances of their culture not be done by others. This attitude clearly says something important about how people understand dancing to be powerful and meaningful, to be inseparable from their identity, and we do discuss this attitude in class.

A brief overview of the two semesters of "Religion and Dance" will provide a clearer background for discussing issues of teaching. The first semester begins with an examination of the attitudes we have toward Africa and African dancing. We explore the implied primitivism of our inherited views of Africa as the "dark continent." We ask where these views came from and why they exist. Then we study the West African culture areas of Mali, Senegal, and Ghana. Each is presented as a culturally highly complex and diverse country that recently, as a product of colonization, has developed a sense of national identity. Students not only experience representative dance forms from each of these countries, they have a lecture demonstration on *djembe* drumming and on the griot tradition, with a kora-accompanied storytelling performance. Sometimes I am able to also invite an mbira performer/singer and a dancer from Zimbabwe.

From this grounding in Africa, we follow some of the African diaspora that accompanied forced slave trade. We begin in South America and work our way north. Argentine tango is traced from African roots through development in periods of European immigration, including the influence of tango danced in Paris and spreading throughout the world. In Brazil, we consider samba in the context of the development of carnival, capoeira with African and slave roots, and the *orixa* dances of Candomblé and the similar religions of Santeria in Cuba and Voudun in Haiti, all rooted in Nigerian Yoruban religions. The popular dances of Latin America are studied including bolero, salsa, and *rueda de casino*. For many of these dance forms, we consider how they have such strong cultural identities, yet have come to circulate the globe. We consider dancing in the context of commercialization and globalization. Entering North America, we study the history of black vernacular dancing from the early roots in cake walks and ring shouts through African influences on jazz and tap and almost every musical and dance form of North America. We study Lindy Hop and the way dance integrated races in New York City and other places decades before the civil rights movement. We study rock 'n' roll, break dancing, and hip-hop. We appreciate how dancing often arises among the poor and powerless to give them strength and identity. Certainly it is important in this approach to show that Africa provides roots for other dances. Yet, if left at that, it reinforces a kind of primitivism about Africa. Therefore, at the end of this course we return to Africa to study popular musical and dance forms. We find that recorded Cuban music, with its own West African roots, has highly influenced much African music since the middle of the twentieth century. We learn how the American blues circulates round and round from Africa to America and back. Highlife music, centered in Ghana, has exchanged influences with American jazz and other musical forms since the late nineteenth century. There are studios in most of these forms.

The second semester begins with *bharata natyam* in South India, where the deep historical and religious importance of this dance are explored. Javanese classical dance forms are considered next, along with the enormous Indian (both Hindu and Buddhist) influence on them that continues despite centuries of Muslim influence and rule. Balinese dance and music are examined in terms of their digestion of Hindu theology and mythology into a distinctly Balinese character. Then we go to North India to study Kathak dancing and Tabla drumming (showing the similarities and differences of Kathak compared with the dancing of South India) and to consider the influence of Islam on North India. Following the Gypsies or Rom from Rajasthan across the Middle East, we look at their dancing and remind ourselves that what we know as Middle Eastern dancing is often a conglomeration of the dances of peoples in Middle Eastern cultures and those of North Africa from Egypt to Morocco. Continuing on to Spain, we consider the complicated debates over the origins of flamenco and we take some time to consider the flamenco films of Tony Gatlif and Carlos Saura to appreciate how, in the contemporary period, filmic presentations of dancing certainly influence, more so than actual observations of the dances, the images held throughout the world of almost every dance form. Flamenco includes rhythm and guitar studio demonstrations as well as dancing. Finding ourselves in Europe, we consider dancing in the history of Judaism, Islam, and Christianity. In Islam, the attention is on the dervish turning dance of the Mevlevi Sufis.

Students' encounter with Christianity is often the most surprising for them. Certainly with many students being Christian and all students heavily influenced by Christianity, they often feel stunned and even angry that their experience of religion has been one in which dancing has been ignored or even forbidden. After studying so many cultures in which religion and dancing are so closely related, the absence of it in European and American Christianity is cause for concern for many. We look at Christian history to try to understand this attitude. Here we take a quick look at Christianity outside of Europe and America and find dancing to be common, though often transformed in ways that seem to limit and confine it when compared with dancing in these same cultures outside the church. We end the course with a consideration of ballet and modern and postmodern dancing followed by aerobic dancing, exotic dancing, and rave dancing.

Perhaps because students are so conditioned to see ballet as nonreligious, most are surprised to see a strong correlation of ballet ideals—simple values of good versus evil, emphasis on elevation and transcendence, gender roles, and so on—and Christian values. Ballet emerges from the same cultural crucible as did modern European and American Christianity. Though many students have had years of ballet training, surprisingly few have any knowledge of the history of ballet. To consider ballet as ethnic and as having a history seems to many of them, as also to those in "the dance world," to contradict their sense of ballet as "the dance."

At this point in the course, we begin to see that modern Western art forms of dancing—ballet in particular—have functioned as a prototype for our understanding of all dancing. This parallels European Christianity's serving as the prototype for our understanding of religion. Certainly, the continued cultural practice of having girls take ballet classes is one side of this. With ballet functioning as the prototype, we critically consider our dance typology and begin to discover the hidden pejorative connotations of such seemingly innocuous classifications as "ethnic," "folk," and "primitive." And we begin to see why, coming into this course, we would never think to connect dancing with religion or ritual.

Most students who take this course acknowledge that when they enter it, they don't think there is a relationship between dancing and religion. The strategy of each semester is to take the students on a journey far from what is familiar to them. This includes the study of cultures and dances they know little if anything about, but also it includes the presentation and consideration of dancing and music in terms they have never considered. The journey winds its way across enormous landscapes and mindscapes to arrive finally at some cultural and dance forms about which the students have considerable personal knowledge and experience—hip-hop and break dancing one semester and ballet, modern, and rave one semester. However, having taken the journey, they can now see and understand the familiar anew.

With every dance form and culture we consider, I introduce ideas and perspectives on dancing and how we understand dancing. Many of these ideas are of the rather pragmatic or functional sort: dancing creates and enacts identity (cultural, age, gender, and so on), dancing negotiates cultural differences (that is, dancing is a bodied form of cultural exchange), dancing creates and reflects history, and so on. But we move on to the much more complex ideas that dancing is self-othering, that dancing reveals something fundamental about what it means to be human. We critique the common theories of dancing as self-expression, as being language-like. We critique the whole base on which we try to attribute meaning to dancing. We critique contemporary Western ideas of dancing that tend to legitimize it by turning it into work and production. I find students remarkably open to explorations of dancing in these terms even though it is a large class at the sophomore level. Student essays are always focused on these broad issues and understandings of dancing and on how these views might be used to understand specific dance cultures.

Having explored this teaching of dancing, I don't want to lose sight of the core issue of teaching ritual. Dancing and ritual are not the same. But I believe their similarities are strong enough and important enough that my teaching of dancing provides some insights into the teaching of ritual. I certainly think that to include or even focus on dancing in the teaching of ritual has potential. From a theoretical point of view, the study of dancing and the study of ritual are very closely related. Many rituals are dance-dramas; many dances are done as ritual. Students' bodied experience of dancing as a component to teaching ritual is easily accomplished and broadly accepted. A comparative worldwide study of ritual and ritual dancing provides a magnificent theater for the construction and examination of ritual theory.

NOTES

1. See my "Embodied Theology."

2. Some may be concerned that the common image and expectations of modern Western cultures regarding men and dance—namely, that men don't dance; that white men, especially, don't dance; and that men who *do* dance are gay or effeminate—may discourage male participation in an experiential study of dancing and ritual. Yet these views are clearly a part of the subject. Break dancing, hip-hop, capoeira, tango, salsa, and many African dances are but a few of the dances that serve to define gender, and gender is defined differently through dancing from culture to culture. That male dancing is identified as gay or effeminate is readily identified in the context of this course as a particular historical and cultural view. Though I have always had more women than men in "Religion and Dance," the proportion of men in the class has been steadily growing.

3. Bantaba World Dance and Music (see www.DancingCircle.com) began operating in 1999.

USEFUL MATERIALS

Dancing. 8 video cassettes, 464 min. Chicago: Home Vision, 1993.

REFERENCE

Gill, Sam. 2002. "Embodied Theology." In *Religious Studies, Theology, and the University: Conflicting Maps, Changing Terrain,* ed. Linell E. Cady and Delwin Brown, 81–92. Albany: State University of New York Press.

4

The Field Trip and Its Role in Teaching Ritual

David Pinault

Field trips present an easy way to make a point that I try to impress on my students at the beginning of each academic quarter: the religions we study are not inert artifacts but rather are living traditions that are very much part of today's world. In the 1980s, when I first offered courses in religion at the university level, I experimented with various ways to teach students about the ritual aspect of religion. Watching videotapes of worshipers at prayer was not satisfying. Videos inspire complacency. In the classroom, my students felt safe. They could pay attention if they liked or simply nod off in the dark.

Somewhat better was the technique of in-class demonstrations of ritual. When I taught courses on Islam at Colgate University, a Muslim student in one of my classes was kind enough to offer to demonstrate the motions associated with *salat* (the five-times-daily prayer required of the faithful). The following semester, I invited to campus the imam of a mosque in nearby Syracuse, New York. He gave examples of both *tajweed* (Qur'an recitation) and a full-throated *adhan* (the call to prayer). This woke students up.

But I found that the most reliable way of engaging students in the study of ritual is to get them out of the classroom. Field trips to local places of worship, where students witness, document, and sometimes actively participate in religious services, have made my undergraduates aware of ritual's importance in the life of religious communities. The awareness comes at a price, one that not all students are ready to pay. "This class cuts way into my comfort zone," wrote one student in a summing-up at quarter's end.

Since 1997, I have taught courses in the Department of Religious Studies at Santa Clara University. The university is located some fifty miles south of San Francisco. With its immigrant populations drawn from throughout the world, the San Francisco Bay Area is home to just about every faith community imaginable. Partly to take advantage of this denominational cornucopia, I devised two courses that require all students to participate in field trips to local shrines and temples. One, titled "South Asian Traditions," is an introductory course that examines five religions of the Indian subcontinent—the Hindu, Buddhist, Jain, Islamic, and Sikh traditions. I draw attention to points of commonality and distinctiveness in these faiths by introducing the students to foundational concepts such as salvation, the sacred, myth, scripture, and ethics. During the academic quarter, we attend religious services associated with each of these five traditions, beginning with Hinduism and concluding with Sikhism (historically the newest of these faiths). The second course focuses on Islam. Field trips in this course are meant to bring out the diverse understandings within the Islamic tradition of what it means to be Muslim. Therefore we visit at least three different Islamic congregations, associated with the Sunni, Shia, and Sufi traditions, respectively.

Pedagogy and Teaching Plans

While working at Colgate and Loyola University in Chicago, I experimented with teaching ritual by sending students out in twos and threes to attend religious services on their own. But I quickly came to favor group visits, in which the entire class (or at least as many of the undergraduates as are available on a given day) and I travel together to the given site. On average, I arrange five such visits for each course per quarter. Each student is required to participate in at least two visits. Extra credit is offered for those who attend more. I take part in all the visits.

The system has its drawbacks. First is the workload. Before the quarter begins, I have to contact the custodians and priests of each shrine and schedule the visits. Then there is the business of carpooling. For each trip, I circulate a signup sheet to match drivers with individuals who need rides. All of us rendezvous on campus and travel together to the site of the day. The logistics can be complicated (for example, making sure that each driver has a copy of written directions to the site). Another challenge is that all the field trips take place outside classroom hours—Saturday night, Sunday morning, and so forth. Consequently, the course demands extra work of the students.

The latter point was the one that worried me the most when I first developed the field trips as a major part of the curriculum for my South Asia and Islam courses. I was afraid that no one would be willing to take these classes. And, in fact, every year I encounter undergraduates who tell me that they avoid my courses because of the claim that the trips would make on their free time. But there are compensations. The students that enroll and stick it out enjoy the comradeship generated by the shared experience of the field trips.

To maximize the benefit derived from the trips, I require that the students keep a fieldwork journal that they submit to me (in typewritten form) for a grade at the end of the quarter. In their journals they are required to include the following: (1) a description of the rituals they witness—the setting, the participants, the sequence of actions, and so on; (2) interviews with at least two members of each congregation (this requirement ensures that students actually interact with individuals from the host congregation instead of hiding among other Santa Clara students at the back of the shrine); (3) a discussion of links between field experiences and texts assigned for the course; (4) an analysis of media coverage (newspaper, radio, etc.) of pertinent local religious communities (Hindu, Muslim, etc.) in the Bay Area; and (5) personal reflections, in which students compare the experiences they had at the various sites and analyze the field trips in light of their own personal histories and prior experience with ritual. Throughout the quarter, I try to impress upon my students that even those with no nominal adherence to a particular religion are likely to have had considerable experience with ritual in the course of their lives.

Risks in Removing One's Shoes: The Challenge of Physicality

It is probably clear from the above that students sometimes find field trips involving religious ritual to be challenging and even threatening. Like most people, my students generally feel least threatened by the least unfamiliar. One of the less intimidating field trips I arranged while at Santa Clara University was to the San Jose branch of the Betsuin BCA (Buddhist Church of America). We sat in pews rather than on the floor, we sang from hymnals, and we heard a sermon from a priest dressed in robes that resembled a graduation gown. "A lot like church back home," wrote one Roman Catholic student in her journal (most of my students are from Christian backgrounds). "But," she added, "I wanted it to be stranger." (I will return to this topic of strangeness below.) Another student noted of the BCA visit, "I liked it that they let us keep our shoes on when we went inside." This comment formed the starting point for discussion in our first class meeting after the trip. I used the topic of footwear, as well as the pew arrangement and hymnals, to discuss the process of "Protestantization" and the assimilation of immigrant religions in America.

Things get riskier once the shoes come off. Such was the case with a visit I arranged recently to the Shiva-Vishnu Hindu temple in Livermore, California. No mere storefront, this. The outdoor statues of gods and goddesses, the carved Nandi bull by the entrance, the South Indian *gopuram* tower-façade: at first glance, little is familiar for most of my students. The kiosk where visitors must store their shoes is some twenty or thirty yards from the temple door. Early one cold winter morning I arrived with my students just after a night of rain. Dutifully, if reluctantly, we took off our shoes and made our way barefoot around the puddles to the temple entrance. I heard grumbling about wet socks and cold feet. "These trips are hard work," one student complained. Another, perhaps more willing to enter into the spirit of the venture, consoled him with the comment, "Hey, we're pilgrims."

Wet socks furnished a feet-first introduction for my students to the physicality of Hindu ritual. I timed our arrival for the early-morning ritual of clothing and awakening the god Vishnu. Together with Hindu congregants, we waited in line before the Vishnu shrine while priests concealed by a velvet hanging dressed and adorned the god. Like the other visitors, my students heard the priests' chanting, received the consecrated food offerings, and had the opportunity for *darshan*, the "auspicious sight" of the deity as it presented itself to the congregation for the reciprocal action of seeing and being seen. Prior to this visit, I had assigned to all my students in the "South Asian Traditions" course Diana Eck's textbook on the topic of "seeing the divine image in India." The Shiva-Vishnu temple visit, I hoped, would give them some taste of the *darshan* experience for themselves. They knew that they were required to observe visitors' interactions with the various shrines within the temple, and in their journals the students noted Hindu participants' prostrations, the donations of cash and fruit, and—especially—the concentrated intensity with which worshipers gazed at the flower-covered image of the god Vishnu. In reflecting on the acts of *darshan* they witnessed in Livermore, several students in our subsequent classroom after-action discussion made reference to Eck's description of "the ritual uses of the image": "Because the image is a form of the Supreme Lord, it is precisely the image that facilitates and enhances the close relationship of the worshiper and God and makes possible the deepest outpourings of emotions in worship" (1998: 46).

In classroom lectures prior to our field trip, I had spoken of the simultaneity and the decentralized quality of Hindu ritual at a site such as the Livermore temple, which has numerous shrines under one all-encompassing roof. I explained in my lectures that Livermore's Hindu community leaders had told me that they designed the temple to encompass these various forms of worship so as to offer a focal point for the Bay Area's diaspora Hindu population. This diverse population includes families that have brought from India a variety of devotional practices in honor of gods ranging from Mahadevi to Ganesha and Krishna.

But the field trip allowed my students to experience for themselves this unity-in-ritual-diversity. On our winter's morning visit, once we had taken part in the Vishnu wakeup ritual, some of my students wandered over to the Shiva shrine to watch as the Shiva-lingam was lustrated with gallons of milk and other liquid offerings. Meanwhile, bells rang as a family gathered around an *agni*-pit for a fire ritual presided over by a Brahmin priest. Nearby, other visitors circumambulated a table on which reposed statues of planetary gods. Still other visitors paid their respects before shrines to Lakshmi and Durga.

"Awesome, but exhausting," is the way one student reported on the Livermore trip. As for the Roman Catholic student who said that she wanted the BCA Buddhist Church visit to be "stranger": she reported with evident satisfaction that the Shiva-Vishnu expedition was "confusing and overwhelming and just what I wanted."

Cold, fatigue, stimulus-overload: more than one student noted in their journals what I would call a Rimbaudesque *dérangement* of the senses as an initial response to the Livermore field trip. In our classroom discussion after the trip, I mentioned the correspondence of T. E. Lawrence and quoted one of the early prewar letters he sent from Syria in 1911, in which the young Lawrence of Arabia tried to convey to his family the attractiveness of travel in exotic lands. In his Syrian correspondence, Lawrence describes himself as "an artist of sorts and a wanderer after sensations" (1954: 147). I went on to quote the poet James Elroy Flecker:

> Sweet to ride forth at evening from the wells,
> When shadows pass gigantic on the sands,
> And softly through the silence beat the bells
> Along the Golden Road to Samarkand. (1941: 168)

This led me to an excursus on Lawrence and Flecker as Edwardian-era aesthetes. For adventurers such as them, the point of travel abroad was to stimulate one's artistic imagination by experiencing the East in all its exotic splendor.

Such thinking of course is out of favor today. But in the context of teaching ritual, it might be just possible to rehabilitate Orientalist exoticism to suggest its pedagogic usefulness.

Orientalism, despite Edward Said's reductionist attempts to define it simply in terms of knowledge-as-domination, has also been concerned with other things, with the experience of the exotic as a way of testing and redefining oneself. Orientalism presupposes an interest in the world outside one's immediate range of the familiar and everyday. That can be a good pedagogic starting point, something a teacher can work with, infinitely preferable to a bored lack of engagement with the world at large.

Through informal surveys and office-hour conversations, I have learned from my students some of the reasons why they enroll in courses such as "South Asian Traditions" and "Introduction to Islam." Santa Clara University requires that all its students take three religious studies courses as part of their humanities distribution requirements. In fulfilling this requirement, many students decide that they want to study at least one religious tradition that is appreciably different from what they have known from childhood. And for students who happen to be Muslim or Hindu or Sikh, the field trips linked to my courses almost always expose them to at least some rituals that are markedly different from anything they have known in their family life. With regard to all my students, my hope is that the field trips take them out of their personal comfort zones. The way I sometimes put it to my students is that the field trips constitute invitations to imitate Lawrence in becoming, for one academic quarter at least, artists of sorts and wanderers after sensations. Such sensation-experiences may give them critical perspectives from which to reflect on both their own personal backgrounds and the faith-traditions being studied in the classroom.

Gathering these experiences, I warn them, will require of them considerable energy and initiative. At this point, I sometimes quote Flecker once more:

> We are the Pilgrims, master; we shall go
> Always a little further: it may be
> Beyond that last blue mountain barred with snow
> Across that angry or that glimmering sea
> ...but surely we are brave,
> Who take the Golden Road to Samarkand. (1941: 167)

Brave pilgrims, of course, have to expect to encounter discomforts. I don't always succeed in anticipating what will trouble my students. In our first field trip to the Sikh *gurdwara* (temple) in Fremont, we joined the line of worshipers who stepped before the Granth Sahib (a copy of the Sikh scripture) and bowed as a mark of respect. This didn't bother any of the Santa Clara undergraduates, with whom I had discussed the ritual in advance. But I'd forgotten to mention the *prashad*, the food offering given to worshipers after the bowing ritual. The *prashad* is a sweet gooey lump akin to cookie dough in taste and feel. "Too greasy to eat," was the whispered objection I heard from several students as we sat and listened to chanters reciting from Sikh scripture. These students weren't about to consume the *prashad*; but they were also afraid to be seen throwing it away for fear of showing disrespect. They lost all interest in what they were watching. Instead they focused on locating a restroom where they could surreptitiously dispose of the food and wash their hands. In class the next day, I heard numerous complaints of sticky fingers.

To put the stickiness in perspective, I had the students read anthropologist Valentine Daniel's description of his "first holy bath" during his fieldwork with Hindu pilgrims in southern India. It was only with the utmost reluctance, Daniel confesses, that he had joined the thousands upon thousands of devotees washing themselves in a sacred tank: "I crept through the praying, spitting, dipping, dripping, nose-blowing pilgrims, trying to find an area that had the least number of human beings per square foot." He describes the "strands of lumpy phlegm of pilgrims who had cleansed their lungs and throats by expectorating into the water." Daniel's response: "I scrambled out of the water as fast as I could, lest I retch into a public bathing pool and pollute it" (1984: 261–262).

A Golden Road, flecked with phlegm. In other words, I told my students, one has to recognize that in field trips, pilgrims are bound to encounter along the way the tangible realities of the physical.

More challenging than gooey fingers has been my students' experience with the rituals of the Naqshbandi Sufi order as practiced in Palo Alto. These rituals are challenging because they are so involving. Unlike the other Bay Area mosques we visit, the Palo Alto Naqshbandis actively encourage all visitors, Muslim and non-Muslim alike, to participate.

The Palo Alto *tariqa* (Sufi association) holds two evening gatherings weekly, on Thursday and Saturday nights. The evening begins with *salat*, followed by a communal potluck dinner. Thereafter, participants gather in a circle under the leadership of the shaykh to perform *dhikr*. Literally "recollection" or "remembrance" (of God), the term refers to the repetitive chanting of *al-asma' al-husna* (the "beautiful names" of Allah), together with the collective praying aloud of selected chapters of the Qur'an. The *dhikr* lasts some ninety minutes. Following this comes tea, dessert, and conversation. The whole event takes up four hours or more. I let my students know in advance that they are in for a long evening.

Before every field trip, regardless of the destination, I spend time in class preparing students for the experience. I encourage them to talk about what they expect to encounter. Among other things this is a way to help them address their fears. Certainly the Sufi field trip generates more anxieties than any of the other expeditions, and for a very simple reason. They know they are encouraged to participate.

I emphasize that they are by no means required to join in Muslim prayer. If they prefer, I tell them, they can simply sit and observe and take notes and receive no less academic credit. This is an important point to make, and not only because some students have understandable reservations about participating in alien rituals. The occasional student wonders whether I'm engaging in Sufi proselytizing—this, despite the fact that I remind my students that I'm Roman Catholic, not Muslim. (Some two years ago a student anonymously e-mailed my department chair a complaint to the effect that "Dr. Pinault is trying to make us worship Allah.")

But in fact, most students, even if apprehensive, are quite willing to have the experience of participating in Sufi ritual. Through films and classroom discussion before the field trip, they acquire some sense of what they will be doing.

Nevertheless, as the students invariably report in their journals, the actual experience is very different from simply watching a movie about Islamic prayer. This applies especially to the *salat*. The sequence of standing, bending, sitting, and prostrating oneself can be confusing, especially when one is trying to time one's actions so as not to disrupt a line of worshipers.

The week following our Sufi *tariqa* visit one quarter, I asked my students to write a brief reflection paper in response to an assertion by the scholar Michael Winter in his essay "Islamic Attitudes toward the Human Body": "One participates in the meanings of being a Muslim through ritual action, not merely through a profession of faith" (1995: 33). In their response essays, the students drew on their field trip experience in various ways. In describing the experience of *salat*, one undergraduate wrote that he had felt uncomfortable "being herded into line and being made to stand so close to the people on either side of me." (During group prayer, tradition dictates that there be no gaps and that participants come together to form a compact mass.) But he also acknowledged that the experience of being pressed into a formation of shoulder-to-shoulder worshipers gave him a vivid taste of something we had read about and talked about in the classroom. "These rituals," he wrote, "really make people feel their group solidarity."

Several female students focused on the fact that the women were required to worship at the rear of the mosque, behind the men. "I've never been made to feel second-class before," one young woman wrote. "Now I know what it's like."

The Palo Alto field trip and the sensation of being "made to feel second-class" led to one of the liveliest after-action discussions of the quarter: the question of women's status in Islam. One student compared the Sufi *tariqa* favorably with another mosque field trip we had made earlier that quarter, to the South Bay Islamic Association (SBIA) in San Jose. She pointed out that at the SBIA, women were required to sit behind a partition that completely blocked their view of the preacher and of the men's section. "In Palo Alto," she said, "at least we could see the imam. We were in the same room. We weren't completely segregated."

Several students then put in a good word for the SBIA field trip. The visit, they said, gave them a glimpse of what it's like to be in a community of Muslim women. They were impressed by the relaxed feeling in the partitioned-off women's section and by the sense of camaraderie they encountered. It felt good, one female student said, not to be worrying about whether any men were looking at them or judging them.

The ritual experience that dominates classroom discussions every quarter is the *dhikr* practiced by the Palo Alto Naqshbandi Sufis. As noted above, *dhikr* begins after *salat* and dinner. The *tariqa*'s prayer area is quite small. Participants gather in a circle. The lights in the room are dimmed, adding to the mood of intimacy. The group chanting that comprises the *dhikr* is quiet and slow-paced at the beginning. But in the course of the ninety-minute ritual, volume and tempo increase. All participants stay seated throughout the ritual (in contrast to other groups such as the Mevlevis, with their celebrated practice of "whirling"). Nevertheless, as the *dhikr* continues, many of the seated Sufis quiver and rock themselves from side to side in time to the beat.

The very evident emotion that becomes so manifest in the confined space of the mosque makes at least some students uncomfortable. I have taken undergraduates to this *tariqa* for more than five years and can predict the moment of acutest discomfort for my students. This is the point in the ritual when the Naqshbandis chant certain of the monosyllabic names of Allah such as *hayy* ("the Living") and *haqq* ("the Truth"). Each of these names is chanted thirty-three times, slowly at first, then with an accelerating intensity and force in which the combined voices rise almost to a shout. "It's like they were a team getting pumped up for a game," was one student's comment. Whenever the Sufis reach this point in the *dhikr*, at least a few students begin to look confused or embarrassed. They sometimes vent their embarrassment by giggling or whispering to each other. This happens despite the fact that we have discussed field trip protocol in advance and that I've reminded my students not to do things to disrupt the ritual. (Luckily, the *tariqa* members never seem thrown off by occasionally inappropriate student behavior.)

But these moments, too, have their pedagogic potential. In classroom discussions after the *dhikr*, I ask the students whether any aspect of the ritual made them uncomfortable. Sometimes they confess to a worry that the quivering and rocking and louder and louder chanting would get out of control. "I just wasn't sure what might happen" was how one student put it.

This remark led to a conversation on the ongoing dynamic tension in Muslim societies between Shari'a (Islamic law) and popular religious practices such as the Sufi *dhikr*. We examined the emphasis in the normative legal tradition on decorum and self-control in behavior (Reinhart 1990: 7–19; Pinault 2001: 29–55). Sufi *tariqas*, I pointed out, have often been accused by Muslim religious authorities of casting aside all notions of ethical restraint. Dervish whirling, music, and dance are considered to be symptomatic of moral abandon (Nelson 1985: 32–51; Pinault 1992: 147–151). Nevertheless, in Islam as in many other religious traditions, worshipers often crave a form of worship that creates an outlet for human emotion and that harnesses this emotion to trigger feelings of intimacy with the divine.

What we witnessed at the Palo Alto *dhikr*, I pointed out to my students, is the Naqshbandi solution to the tension between Shari'a and popular piety. Worshipers stay seated. No one rises to whirl or dance. Yet within this limitation, participants use the names of God and verses from the Qur'an (the recitation of which even the most orthodox cannot reject) to create rhythmic chants that lift worshipers to heightened states of spiritual experience. The Palo Alto Naqshbandi field trip gives students the opportunity to document for themselves the dialectic between decorum and emotionalism in ritual.

Problems, Polemics, and Politics

In the fall 2001 quarter, some two months after the September 11 terrorist attacks, I took a group of students from my "South Asian Traditions" course to visit the Sikh *gurdwara* in Fremont. As soon as we arrived, I noticed something I hadn't in my visit the year before: the presence of numerous American flags decorating both the exterior and interior of the temple. Our hosts were as hospitable and warm as ever in welcoming us. This time, however, the welcome was supplemented by leaflets that were distributed to all of us. The leaflets provided an introduction to the Sikh faith but also emphasized the patriotism and the American identity of California's Sikh population.

The anxieties besieging local Sikh communities became even clearer to my students on this field trip when one of the *gurdwara*'s custodians approached me and said that in addition to my own students, other non-Sikh visitors from the Fremont area were also there that day. He asked if I would be willing to give a short presentation to the mixed Sikh/non-Sikh congregation that was assembled inside the temple.

"Me? This morning?" I was caught by surprise. "Now?"

"Just a brief talk. Ten minutes."

I asked the man whether he had a specific topic in mind.

He did. "Please explain that our religion is altogether different from Islam."

The custodian's request highlighted one of the problems faced by Sikhs in our post–September 11 world: the tendency of many Americans to confuse Sikhs with Muslims. In the interviews conducted by my students that morning at the *gurdwara*, they learned about the human costs of ignorance and stereotyping. Religiously observant Sikh men, obligated by tradition to wear turbans and grow beards, conform more than do most Muslims to the prevalent American image of the face of Islam. Consequently, they have been subjected to misunderstanding and fear and at times have even been the targets of violence. My students collected stories in their interviews that day about what it means to negotiate the multiple identities associated with immigrant status, American nationality, and the Sikh faith. In their journals, my students wrote about the ways in which they saw the *gurdwara* serve as a community center and resource for helping local Sikhs deal with the challenges of the post–September 11 landscape.

A somewhat different kind of post–September 11 encounter arose the following year, during the fall 2002 quarter, when I taught an upper-level course for juniors and seniors titled "Islam and Modernity." Among the field trips I organized that quarter was one to a nearby Sunni mosque in the Bay Area (which I will leave nameless). I had phoned the mosque's "leadership committee" six weeks in advance to ask if we could attend *jum'ah* (congregational) prayers some Friday. Our hosts were kind enough to indicate that we were welcome to attend any Friday we liked.

The guest preacher on the day we attended happened to be a young Arab-American who (so we were informed) had studied Islam in Yemen. The sermon he gave was meant to be a response to the recent attacks by Christian evangelists on the moral character of the Prophet Muhammad. The specific charge to which he was responding, he said, was that of pedophilia with regard to the Prophet's marriage to Ayesha, the youngest of Muhammad's wives (Cooperman 2002: 3).

The preacher conceded that the Prophet married Ayesha when she was less than ten years old. Our speaker attempted to defend Muhammad by saying that the Prophet waited three years before consummating the marriage. The preacher tried to make the point that the choice of Ayesha as bride was an instance of divine providence. Her youth ensured that she would live long after Muhammad and be available for generations thereafter as a resource for believers concerning the *sunnah* (sayings and exemplary lifestyle) of her husband.

That, at least, was the point I think he was trying to make. Marring the presentation was his tone—strident, angry, and distressingly loud. On the one hand, the preacher reassured the congregation that these Christian evangelists could harm neither the Prophet nor the *ummah* (the community of believers). "When you spit at the sky," he announced, "the spit falls back on your face." On the other hand, he kept warning the congregation that Muslims in this country are surrounded by *kuffar* ("unbelievers," plural of *kafir*). To guard the purity of their faith, he admonished them, Muslims must avoid contaminating contact with *kuffar*.

For most of the students in my course, this was their first visit to a mosque. To judge from their journals and subsequent classroom discussions, they came away with vivid impressions from the field trip. Pedophilia. Spit on your face. Contaminating contact. Purity of faith. Avoid the *kuffar*. The effect, in short, was not felicitous.

In subsequent classroom discussions, I tried to contextualize this mosque sermon by putting into historical perspective the phenomenon of child-marriage. I noted that a variety of cultures have tolerated this practice. I also referred the students to a recent public-relations statement defending Muhammad's marriage to Ayesha. The statement was issued by a spokesman for the Council on American-Islamic Relations: "The prophet Muhammad didn't do anything not in accord with the norms of the time" (White 2002: 1). Nevertheless, the overall effect of this field trip—in which we encountered an angry, strident preacher and listened to a sermon that was so obviously defensive in tone—was to leave many of my students with a lingering negative impression.

Two Muslim students in my course were so upset with this sermon that they complained to the mosque's directors. Preachers like this, they said, ruin Islam's reputation in the eyes of Americans.

The complaint produced results. The next time I phoned to arrange a *jum'ah*-prayer field trip, the mosque's liaison person rejected the date I requested and insisted that we come on another date, to be specified by the leadership committee.

When I obediently showed up with my students on the date specified, we underwent a carefully structured experience. The preacher scheduled for the Friday of our visit proved to be significantly different in style from the last one I'd heard at this mosque. A white American convert, he sermonized reassuringly on themes of mutual respect, interfaith reconciliation, and the "root meanings" of Islam as a religion of peace. On previous visits, my students and I had been free after the sermon to mingle with the congregation and chat with whom we pleased. This time our liaison person kept us sequestered at the back and had someone bring the preacher directly to us as soon as the service ended. The preacher sat with us and talked to the students for some fifteen minutes. He made many references to hip-hop performers and rap singers and American pop culture in general, in what I took to be an attempt to let the students know that he understood them. "Islam respects Jesus," he went on to announce. But he catalogued Christianity's inadequacies and gave us what amounted to a supplemental mini-sermon on why he'd converted and how very satisfied he was with Islam. My students never did get to interview any other Muslims that day. We were supervised and maneuvered and shepherded every minute we were there. "Too much spin control," as one student noted in her journal. "And way too much proselytizing."

Classroom discussion of the field trip brought out an important point: sometimes the ethnographer inadvertently comes to influence how a faith community sees itself or at least how it chooses to present itself to the world at large. This insight was borne out during the same academic quarter by a field trip we took to an altogether different site, the JCNC (Jain Center of Northern California).

Located in Milpitas not far from the Santa Clara University campus, the Jain *bhawan* (temple) is quite new (it opened in August 2000). Our Santa Clara class was among the very first groups hosted by the Milpitas Jains. I had very high expectations for the Milpitas field trip. Knowing Jainism's teachings of respect for all living creatures and its emphasis on vegetarianism and nonviolence (together with its influence on the thought of Mahatma Gandhi), I hoped that my students would come away from this field trip impressed with Jainism and eager to learn more about this religion.

In fact, the results were very mixed. My students liked what they heard of the religion's teachings from Jain speakers during the field trip. But they were puzzled by the very conspicuous life-sized photographs on display in the temple showing emaciated gurus, and several students evinced distress at the ideal of self-starvation. Some undergraduates were put off by the general air of solemnity, silence, and austerity that prevailed as Jains went about their rituals of veneration before the statues of the *tirthankaras* (spiritual leaders who function as moral exemplars for the devout). The somber mood wasn't helped by the fact that so few worshipers were there (we arrived early on a Saturday morning) and that students had trouble finding individual worshipers to interview after we witnessed the rituals in the sanctuary.

But the Jains were eager to learn from this initial experience. Members of the JCNC leadership contacted me to gauge the students' response to the field trip. The Milpitas Jains reminded me that their temple is a very recent addition to the Bay Area's religious landscape. Many California Jains are immigrants who were drawn here by Silicon Valley's high-tech industries. Jain community leaders told me that they were eager to learn how best to present themselves in offering open-house sessions and educational programs to the public in Milpitas and the larger northern California region. I passed on these remarks to my students, who in classroom discussions made suggestions for how to improve the quality of the field trip. In turn, I conveyed these suggestions to the JCNC.

The result of these conversations was that the following year, when I brought another group of "South Asian Traditions" students to the Milpitas temple, the JCNC offered us a significantly different experience. As the students watched individual Jains perform rituals before the *tirthankara* statues, our guides pointed out how the iconography in this temple incorporates and harmonizes the distinct teachings of the Digambara and Svetambara traditions—the two major Jain denominations. They told us that the Milpitas *bhawan* was the first Jain temple in the world to achieve such integration. This led to a broader conversation about ways to address sectarianism and problems of communal divisiveness in South Asian traditions in general (a topic that had been introduced earlier in the classroom).

When we encountered the wall photos of emaciated Jain gurus, our guides took the opportunity to emphasize that Jainism does not advocate an adversarial attitude to the human body. Rather, they said, we should see such pictures as a reminder of the need to show respect for the earth and our environment. Tempering our appetites and our consumption of the world's goods helps us become less of a burden on the earth's resources.

This environmentalist lesson was reinforced when we left the sanctuary for the dining area. There volunteers served us a vegetarian meal and explained how Jain dietary ideals inculcate the values of living in balance with those around us and minimizing harm to other living things. The fact that the food was delicious helped the lesson go down.

On this visit, my students found that many congregation members were present to answer questions. Among them were two female monks from Rajasthan, who gave us a presentation on the faith's cosmology and doctrines and talked about the status of women in Jainism.

Students gave this field trip very high marks—a "report card" that I was glad to pass on to the JCNC leadership. More important, perhaps, was the collaborative and interactive quality of the experience. The local Jain community, my students, and I all learned from one another. In field trips such as this, my students and I certainly added to our knowledge concerning particulars of ritual. But we also glimpsed something of the ways in which immigrant faith communities undergo a process of reflection and continuously evolving self-presentation as they take their place in the changing religious landscape of the United States.

Acknowledgments

I thank my students at Santa Clara University, who have shared with me their reflections concerning the field trips we have ventured on together. The experiences recorded in this essay were possible only because of the patience and generosity of the various faith communities in the San Francisco Bay Area that welcomed my students and me. In particular I acknowledge the kindness of the following congregations: the Jain Center of Northern California, the Betsuin Buddhist Church of San Jose, the Naqshbandi Tariqa of Palo Alto, the South Bay Islamic Association, the Livermore Shiva-Vishnu Temple, and the Sikh Gurdwara of Fremont. For her encouragement and support, I thank Professor Catherine Bell, Bernard J. Hanley Professor of Religious Studies at Santa Clara University. I also thank Professor Becky Edwards of Loyola University, Chicago, for her generous assistance in helping me locate the source of the quotation from the correspondence of T. E. Lawrence that appears in this essay.

USEFUL MATERIALS

Those interested in the pedagogy of field trips and interfaith encounters in California's Bay Area will want to learn about Santa Clara University's Local Religion Project, which is directed by Professor Philip Boo Riley of the Religious Studies Department. See "Developing Local Religion Project" Web site (www.scu.edu/cas/religiousstudies/lrp/index.cfm). See also the discussion of the Local Religion Project in Paul Crowley, "Religious Studies at Santa Clara University," in the winter 2005 issue of *Santa Clara Magazine* (www.scu.edu/scm/winter2005/religious.cfm).

The topic of interfaith encounters in the context of university pedagogy is also treated extensively in Harvard University's "Pluralism Project," under the direction of Professor Diana L. Eck (www.pluralism.org). The electronic newsletter "Religious Diversity News," available via this Web site, contains numerous essays that are relevant to the subjects mentioned above. See also Diana Eck's book *A New Religious America* (Harper San Francisco, 2002).

REFERENCES

Cooperman, Alan. 2002. "Anti-Muslim Remarks Stir Tempest." *Washington Post*, June 20: A3.

Daniel, E. Valentine. 1984. *Fluid Signs: Being a Person the Tamil Way*. Berkeley: University of California Press.

Eck, Diana. 1998. *Darsan: Seeing the Divine Image in India*. 3rd ed. New York: Columbia University Press.

Flecker, James Elroy. 1941 (1922). *Hassan: The Story of Hassan of Bagdad, and How He Came to Make the Golden Journey to Samarkand: A Play in Five Acts*. New York: Alfred A. Knopf.

Lawrence, M. R., ed. 1954. *The Home Letters of T. E. Lawrence and His Brothers*. New York: Macmillan.

Nelson, Kristina. 1985. *The Art of Reciting the Qur'an*. Austin: University of Texas Press.

Pinault, David. 1992. *The Shiites: Ritual and Popular Piety in a Muslim Community*. New York: St. Martin's Press.

———. 2001. *Horse of Karbala: Muslim Devotional Life in India*. New York: Palgrave.

Reinhart, A. Kevin. 1990. "Impurity/No Danger." *History of Religions* 30, 1: 1–24.

White, Gayle. 2002. "Muhammad a 'Pedophile,' Baptists Told." *Beliefnet/Cox News Service*, June 12. Available at http://www.beliefnet.com/story/107/story_10762_1 .html.

Winter, Michael. 1995. "Islamic Attitudes toward the Human Body." In *Religious Reflections on the Human Body*, ed. Jane Marie Law, 36–45. Bloomington: Indiana University Press.

5

Experience, Purpose, Pedagogy, and Theory: Ritual Activities in the Classroom

Mark I. Wallace

The day after what we now call 9/11, I was scheduled to teach the second session of my class "Religion, the Environment, and Contemplative Practice." I had scheduled a three-hour class meeting in the Crum Woods, a forest preserve adjacent to the Swarthmore campus, where, in addition to discussing the assigned readings, the class would begin a series of group meditation and ritual practices that I had envisioned for this particular day in the semester. Under any circumstances, asking students to practice various meditation disciplines in an open classroom environment, in full view of their peers, is a risky proposition. But to ask them to take this risk immediately following such a traumatic event as 9/11 felt especially ill-timed. So I e-mailed class members before our meeting to see what they wanted to do; I assumed they would prefer to cancel class and make it up later. To my surprise, the students wanted to go ahead with the class as planned.

Experience

We first met in our regular classroom and then, without speaking, proceeded into the Crum Woods as a group, practicing a kind of silent walking meditation. Along the way, I asked each member of the group to experience being "summoned" by a particular life form found in the Crum Woods—red fox, clod of dirt, water strider, flatworm, gray squirrel, red oak, skunk cabbage, and so on—and then to reimagine themselves as becoming that life. After the walk through the woods, we gathered in a circle, thirty or so students and me, within a grove of sycamore trees in a meadow next to a creek.

At this juncture, I asked the students to use the first person in conveying a message to our group from the perspective of the individual life form they had assumed. Naturally, I explained that this was a voluntary exercise; no one should feel compelled to speak if he or she did not want to. If you imagine yourself, for example, as a brook trout or morning dove or dragonfly living in and around the Crum Creek, with the creek threatened by suburban storm water runoff and other problems, what would you like to say to this circle of human beings? This group activity is a variation on a deep-ecology, Neopagan ritual called "A Council of All Beings," in which participants enact a mystical oneness with the flora and fauna in an area by speaking out in the first person on behalf of the being or place with which they have chosen to identify (Seed et al. 1988; Hill 2000). A Council of All Beings ritual enables members of the group to speak "as" and "for" other natural beings, imaginatively feeling what it might be like to be bacterium, bottle-nosed dolphin, alligator, old growth forest, or gray wolf. Participants "become" this or that animal or plant or natural place and then share a message to the other human persons in the circle. The purpose of such a council is to foster compassion for other life forms by ritually bridging the differences that separate human beings from the natural world.

In principle, this sort of group activity seemed a good idea for inaugurating a new class format that I had learned about from colleagues, one that grafted earthen meditation practices onto an academic religious studies foundation (Gottlieb 1999: 33–58). As we sat quietly, waiting for someone in the circle to speak "as" his or her adopted life form, it became awkwardly clear to me that no one was ready to take on this sort of task. Shocked and traumatized by the previous day's events in New York, I silently wondered how I could expect my students to perform a strange ritual openly, especially since it appeared that some were, understandably, uncomfortable with "becoming" other life forms in the first place. Some of the students were shy, of course, and others did not want to do or say anything that might embarrass them in a group setting. As the minutes went by, I was certain I had been asking too much of them. After a half hour, no one had spoken, and I could feel the perspiration running down the inside of my shirt. I had been preparing this class for months, yet now I felt I should have proposed a more conventional alternative to a Council of All Beings ritual, at least in light of the sad events at the World Trade Center the day before.

Then something happened. "I am blue heron," said one member of the class. "I glide quietly through the creek in the early morning looking for something to eat. I break the calm of the late afternoon with my great wings as I take flight over the water and travel to new destinations. Humans, keep this watershed clean so that I can grace this place for years to come."

Soon other life forms spoke. "I am red-backed salamander. I live under rocks and deep down in the moist, fertile ground. I need the protection of this forest to dig for food and raise my young. I am worried that contaminants in the soil will make us sick to the point of death. Please care for the earth so that I can live."

Another voice: "I am monarch butterfly. I migrate through the open meadows in your forest looking for the milkweed plant on which I lay my eggs and my caterpillars feed. I brighten your day with my beautiful orange and black wings; I help other plants grow and pollinate with my nectar here and there. Please do not pave over the meadows and cut down the milkweed that I need for my survival."

And another: "I am black walnut tree. I add to the protective canopy of this forest. My heartwood is favored for your furniture making. The large nuts I drop to the ground are food for squirrels and mice and other forest creatures. I purify the air by absorbing the carbon dioxide you produce, and I produce oxygen so that everyone can breathe. Protect this forest and all its inhabitants."

The litany continued: "I am lichen . . . ," "I am holly bush . . . ," "I am crayfish . . . ," "I am forest wildflower . . . ," "I am worm . . . ," "I am mourning dove . . . ," "I am furry caterpillar . . . ," "I am tulip tree . . . ," and so forth.

After that long silence, the members of the class shared their eco-stories in polyphony of proclamations, soft-spoken entreaties, tears, and laughter. I feared the initial silence had signaled too much unease with the group ritual. Now I realized that the time of silence at the beginning of class allowed participants to gather their thoughts in a new vein, and discern what they should say as they assumed the identity of the particular life form who had originally summoned them during our forest walk.

Like the pattern of puzzle-like pieces of bark flaking off the trunk of the sycamore tree next to me, I became encircled by a medley of voices that reminded me and the others of our obligations to care for the forest. Sitting cross-legged in the open meadow, amid the occasional yellow jackets buzzing low as they foraged for food, my skin felt warmed by the mid-afternoon sunlight; the low gurgle of the creek nearby provided background music for our ritual gathering. Soon the class would end, and we would be back on campus, far from the forest. Yet for a moment here, we enacted our identities as fellow and sister members of this forest preserve in communion with the other life forms found there. We felt ourselves embedded in a sacred hoop greater than ourselves. As human citizens of a wider biotic community, we found ourselves surrounded by a cloud of witnesses who were calling us to our responsibilities for preserving the woods.

Purpose

The use of ritual in my teaching at Swarthmore stemmed from a Contemplative Practices Fellowship that I received in 2000 from the American Council of Learned Societies. The aim of these ACLS fellowships was to encourage university faculty to use nontraditional modes of active, contemplative learning to stimulate greater cognitive and emotional growth among students (Zajonc 2002). My fellowship enabled me to study and then incorporate ritual practices into a redesigned version of the religion and ecology class described above. My goal was to use classic sacred texts along with a variety of nonsectarian rites to show students how the world's religions, myths, and rituals have shaped humanity's fundamental outlook on the environment since ancient times. Beyond formal academic inquiry into the relationship between religion and ecology, however, the course had an unconventional practical aim: to enable students to consider adopting new insights into how they can live in harmony with their natural environments by means of fundamentally *experiential* contact with the actual sources of the ancient earth wisdom within various spiritual traditions.

The existential goal of this course, therefore, was for students to cultivate inner self-awareness and outward compassion for other life forms in a dialogical, interdisciplinary, and multireligious context. Ritual practices were to help class members learn strategies for coordinating the inner landscape of the heart with the outer landscape of the earth. The thesis of the course held that the world's environmental crisis is, at its core, a spiritual crisis because it is human beings' deep "ecocidal" dispositions toward nature that are the cause of the earth's continued degradation (Wallace 2005: 26–33). Our lives run opposite the crucial insight in the American Indian proverb, "The frog does not drink up the pond in which it lives." Regarding the environmental crisis as a spiritual crisis, this course sought to recover the biocentric convictions within different religious traditions as valuable resources for countering the utilitarian attitudes toward earth community now dominating the mind-set of the global marketplace we inhabit (Loy 2002).

Course topics included ecological thought in Western philosophy, theology, and biblical studies; the role of Asian religious thought in forging an ecological worldview; the value of Amerindian and Euro-American nature writing for environmental awareness; public policy debates concerning vegetarianism along with the antitoxins movement; and the contemporary relevance of ecofeminism, deep ecology, neopaganism, and wilderness activism.

In addition to requiring traditional writing and exam assignments, I asked students to perform ritual practices in the classroom, maintain contemplative journals, and do weekly field work focused on environmental renewal in the wider community. The purpose of these alternative learning activities was to promote liberatory cognitive development through an experiential understanding of certain aspects of spiritual life, on the one hand, and community-based social and civic responsibility, on the other. The degree to which religious rites and social service, as exercises in "secular spirituality," can function as positive forces in personal and communal well-being is much debated in ritual theory and religious studies (Van Ness 1996, 2004). Scholars have noted the tendency of many rituals to routinize regimes of power that control individual expression and repress social dissent (McWhorter 2004). While the relation of ritual to power is inherently dialectical (Bell 1992: 171–223), the salutary potential of ritual to productively enable self-transformation and the reordering of social relations has also been consistently documented (Driver 1998: 166–191; Grimes 1990: 145–157). I used ritual learning and service learning to enhance students' personal and interpersonal development in my religion and ecology class.

First, I introduced a series of quasi-religious practices in order to challenge students' inherited meaning structures, their basic worldviews, and open new possibilities for being in the world. In an open and nonsectarian environment, I made use of classroom-appropriate contemplative disciplines to deepen, elucidate, and sometimes challenge the insights gleaned from class discussions and the readings. Influenced by Ronald Grimes's establishment of a ritual studies laboratory at Wilfred Laurier University (Grimes 1990: 109–144), a spiritually inflected *practicum* was led by me, a guest facilitator, a student, or small group of students. We explored a selective variety of contemplative practices in this class: neopagan animal bonding ritual, Christian lectio divina meditative reading, Jewish prayer book contemplation, Zen Buddhist mindless sitting meditation, and Lakota medicine wheel ritual. Mindful walking and sitting, breathing disciplines, strategies for nonviolent relationships with plants and animals, nature observation exercises, and adapted individual vision quests supplemented other spiritually oriented rituals and were designed to aid the course's practical aims—that is, to assist students in their own understanding of how ritual can mediate more benign relationships of compassion and experiences of self-discovery.

Second, I also asked each student to commit herself or himself to a community-based fieldwork project and maintain a contemplative journal as a reflective record of her or his field activities. The fieldwork project focuses on some activity devoted to earth healing—for example, community development work, volunteering in a local arboretum, maintaining an urban garden, or working for social change in environmentally degraded areas. The journals sought to integrate personal musings, reactions to class readings and ritual activities, and reflections on field experiences. Traditional writing, artistic media, and Web page hypertext documents have all been used for the contemplative journaling. Service learning studies show that reflection about community-based education that is integrated into classes through regular discussion and written analysis increases students' cognitive development and capacity for citizenship (Eyler and Giles 1999: 187–208). Adapting metaphorically the vocabulary of Western mystical traditions, I have encouraged students to view the journal as their own interior chronicles of their "soul's journey" into itself and then back out again into service in the world.

Pedagogy

I had long wanted to revitalize my teaching by combining intellectual inquiry and ritual practice, but it took the "imprimatur" of the American Council of Learned Societies' Contemplative Practice Fellowship to ease my anxieties about the legitimacy of introducing quasi-religious activities into the classroom. My primary reservation about performance work in my pedagogy has always been the fear that I would be perceived as breaching the gulf that divides intellectual inquiry from religious practice (see this debate in Miller, Patton, and Webb 1994).

Understandably, many scholars of religion argue against blurring the lines of distinction that separate the academic *study* of religion from religious *practice* in order to secure the credibility of religious studies as an intellectually rigorous and ideologically nonsectarian mode of disciplinary inquiry (McCutcheon 1997; Wiebe 1999). The mantra that underlies this way of thinking is familiar to many of us: we do not *teach* religion, rather we teach *about* religion in as objective an environment as we know how to create. In no way, according to this viewpoint, should the wall of partition that separates the study of religion and the practice of religion be undermined; otherwise our hard-won standing in the academy as religious studies scholars would be compromised. Again, we would be seen as faith-based proponents of sectarian worldviews—theologians in disguise, as it were.

In many respects, I am sympathetic to this concern as an important hedge against the misperception of religious studies as a catechetical exercise interested in the indoctrination of students into particular forms of belief. If academic religious studies were to shade over into confessional theological studies, with classroom ritual used to inculcate particular religious persuasions, considerable confusion would arise about the important, if relative, distinction between the academic (nonsectarian) institutions' study of religion, on the one hand, and denominational college or seminary education, on the other.

Nevertheless, with this boundary question in mind, I think that is it possible to teach academic religious studies and use classroom ritual practices without sacrificing the intellectual integrity of the learning environment. Moreover, I have come to the conclusion that performance-based activities are necessary and integral tools in teaching the student, as a whole person, to better understand the depth and power of religious life and thought. To accomplish this end, I have needed to be methodologically clear about the nature and the purpose of the ritual practices in which I ask students to participate. Over time I have settled on the following criteria for developing student-centered rites that are, I believe, academically appropriate and intellectually enriching in a public classroom setting.

While classroom rituals provide genuine experiential insight into the meaning of religion, they should be practiced in a manner that is both culturally sensitive yet theologically vague. Performance activities rooted in particular cultural traditions provide students with a mediated experience of time-honored practices that enhance and deepen text-based learning. Engaging in a ritual practice borrowed from different mythopoetic cultures offers students a lived understanding of the significance of religious experience. But these practices should be taught to students only after the instructor determines which rituals can or cannot be appropriately imported into a secular classroom environment. Simple Buddhist sitting or walking meditation can be usefully relocated from a monastic to a public setting, but rituals that are sacred to the identity of a religion's devotees—such as a sweat lodge ceremony in Native American traditions or celebration of the Eucharist in Christian communities—would not make good candidates for altered use in a classroom setting.

The use of ritual language needs to be carefully edited to guard against possible misunderstanding by the uninitiated. Generally speaking, I make a point to exclude the iteration of theological beliefs that are not essential for a thoughtful, if partial, understanding of religious life through active, body-centered practices. It is not necessary to repeat the many names and attributes of the biblical God or chant the appellations of various Indian avatars to practice particular exercises in mindfulness drawn from the Jewish, Christian, and Hindu traditions, respectively. When avoiding the use of confessional theology in classroom rituals, however, the temptation for some scholars is to rely on seemingly "neutral" ritual practices, often borrowed from self-avowedly non-theological New Age traditions that do not entail the theistic beliefs that are integral to the monotheistic religions of the West, for example. But even quasi-religious practices are rooted in a theological (or a-theological) heritage of one sort or another, even if that heritage is antireligious, antitheological, or antitheistic. The best way to handle the question of theological language in ritual practice is to shape the cognitive dimensions of the classroom ritual so that the activity gestures toward, but does not invoke, the belief system that animates any ritual practice.

Classroom rituals should be practiced as analogous to a laboratory or studio learning experience, not as a liturgical exercise in inculcating confessional beliefs. This point may seem obvious to scholars of religion, but for students it can be unnerving to perform a modified Native American sacred hoop ritual and not feel correspondingly obligated to accept the religious worldview that has historically grounded this practice. I make the point with my classes that just as in laboratory sessions in biology or chemistry, on the one hand, or studio classes in art and music, on the other, a student learns more by actually *practicing* the discipline in question; so also in religious studies it can be intellectually enriching to engage in ritual practices, while still putting aside any personal subscription to the religious beliefs that underlie such practices. A studio art major learns about ceramics both by studying history and technique and by actually throwing a pot on a wheel and creating art herself. By the same token, by participating in classroom-appropriate ritual practices, students develop a more complex and nuanced understanding of the experiential dimensions of religion than what is available to them through textual studies alone.

Classroom rituals should be regarded as integral to the learning experience, but they should not be practiced by students who have personal objections to them. Academic ritual practices are an important exercise in active learning and should not be viewed as an occasional supplement to the essential activities of a class which, traditionally understood, entail classroom discussion, the reading of texts, and written work for exams and essay assignments. Rather, the use of ritual exercises underscores for students the importance of an experiential understanding of the performative dimensions of religious life. Through ritual, students can grasp something of the lived spirituality that characterizes particular symbolic communities. Nevertheless, at the outset of each term, I explain to students that this class is optional and that although religious and quasi-religious practices will be featured in this class as an exercise in learning-by-doing, students are not required to participate in particular activities if they find such activities objectionable. I do not require observant Jewish students to attend class during the high Jewish holidays. Likewise, I have colleagues in biology who do not require all laboratory students to perform dissections when particular students voice moral or religious objections to such procedures. Active learning rounds out academic religious studies by providing guided access to different aspects of the affective dimensions of religious belief and practice. Yet such access for students is best offered in the spirit of an invitation, not as a requirement that might be uncomfortable.

Theory

I have experimented with a variety of theoretical resources to better introduce and ground classroom performance practice in contemporary ritual theory. For example, I have used the work of René Girard, a literary critic and social theorist who analyzes ritual performance as the mainspring of cultural formation. Born in 1923, he is currently emeritus professor of French language and literature at Stanford University. In brief, Girard posits an innate capacity and drive to imitate the desires of others—what he calls *mimesis*—as a fundamental clue to understanding human nature, religion, and culture. Mimesis is the basic human impulse to copy what another person finds valuable and worthwhile; it is the instinct to acquire as one's own what is deemed desirable by another. Though mimesis is a natural feature of human subjectivity, more often than not it leads to tragic consequences. As the primitive desire to form one's identity in relation to another person, it is alternately the mainspring of social conflict as well as the origin of humankind's potential to form positive, lasting relationships with others. In this vein, I consider Girard's study of the human being via a series of stages and then analyze the relevance of Girard's project to understanding the value of ritual in the religious studies classroom.

Mediated Desire

A human being enters consciousness already overdetermined by the desires and expectations of its immediate caregivers and wider social group. As self-consciousness increases, human beings develop an ever-widening sense of self-centered on their developing feeling of ownership for what they consider to be their innermost hopes and needs. The first stage, then, in Girard's theory of the human condition is an analysis of humans' *mis*understanding of themselves as beings with innate desires. An initial problem develops because the subject misinterprets its desires as "natural" and "self-evident," yet it inevitably finds itself bound to a system of values and preferences that it neither understands nor is able to extricate itself from. Since the subject considers the generated needs and desires actually communicated to the subject by another to be self-generated, it suffers an existence in which, at least on one level, it is fundamentally self-deceived. At the wellspring of its existence, the self is opaque to the sources and motives of its own actions. Thus, for Girard, everything that generates the culture of a particular social group, from tastes in food to codes of behavior and divisions of labor, operates within the space of subconscious mimetic desire (Girard 1987: 3–47, 283–447).

Loss of Differences

The next stage concerns the power of mimesis, now referred to by Girard as *acquisitive* mimesis, to blur distinctions and merge identities whenever the subject becomes successful in obtaining the object of its desire. As long as attainment of the other's desires remains a distant and unreachable goal, there is no conflict between the subject and the mediator-of-desire, namely, that other person. But once the desired object is almost in the grasp of the subject, the potential for conflict arises. Now the mediator who had modeled attachment to the craved object becomes a rival who is seen to guard the subject from obtaining the object. Both parties see themselves in the other—imitating each other in a merging of their separate identities; the eventual result is a concomitant loss of distinctions between self and other, disciple and model (Girard 1977: 119–168).

The Scapegoat Mechanism

The merging of the separate identities into a single desire for a common object generates a loss of differences; this loss provokes an aggressive and, inevitably, a violent reassertion of the previous order in the interest of stable personal and communal identity formation. Therefore, in the third stage in Girard's analysis, acquisitive mimetic frenzy leads to a collapse of interpersonal and social distinctions, which in turn provokes reciprocal violence in order to shore up the threatened social structure. If everyone were allowed to carry out their mimetic desires unchecked, the system of differences, the hierarchy of values, the scaffold of distinctions that support and organize cultural identities would break down; the result would be social chaos. As Girard writes, "Order, peace, and fecundity depend on cultural distinctions; it is not these distinctions but the loss of them that gives birth to fierce rivalries and sets members of the same family or social group at one another's throats" (Girard 1977: 49).

In terms of group psychology, the gut-level response to the debilitating threat of unregulated desire is to turn a blind eye to the real cause of the problem, the raw compulsion to acquire the object desired by another, and impute to some unprotected "other" the cause of the community's dissolution into an undifferentiated and disordered state. This renders the chosen other a target for the community's rage over its loss of cultural order. The other has become the victim, the scapegoat, of the group's disintegration insofar as it functions to divert collective violence *to* itself and *away* from the real cause, the mimetic crisis. The solution to mimetic crises, Girard argues, is the prophylactic of scapegoating violence. In order to save itself from the inevitable corrosion of mimetic disorder, the community must periodically plunge itself into a paroxysm of violence toward a "guilty" scapegoat. Mimetic, imitative rivalry threatens to tear apart a society's order of differences and values unless it is regulated by a common agreement that some marginal member of the community has caused the problem, not everyone's unconscious and insatiable drive to imitate the other and possess what the other values. This subconscious agreement generates a temporary unity in the community of newly formed "persecutors" and temporarily resolves the mimetic crisis until the next rivalrous relationship gathers steam (Girard 1977: 250–318).

Religion Justifies Violence

The fourth stage of Girard's analysis of ritual and social life concerns the double valence of the victim: the scapegoat is now simultaneously regarded as both the *cause* of the community's disintegration and the *origin* of its newfound unity. "The return to peace and order is ascribed to the same cause as the earlier troubles—to the victim himself," Girard writes (1986: 55). This hard-won unity provides the basis and justification for the institutions, prohibitions, myths, and rituals that constitute the culture and religion of a particular group. Culture has its origins, therefore, in the mechanism that creates and destroys the scapegoat. All major cultural institutions function as inculcators of the myths, rituals, and prohibitions that undergird this way of social functioning. Political and legal institutions provide the routinized legitimation structures that reward and punish group members for obeying or disobeying the customs and laws that regulate the social order. And religious institutions operate to provide the curative sacrificial rites that recall the "good" violence that formed the community in the first place and prevented its descent into the "bad" violence of confusion and chaos. Girard argues that "*religion* in its broadest sense, then, must be another term for that obscurity that surrounds man's efforts to defend himself by curative or preventative means against his own violence" (1977: 23). In the Girardian framework, religious performance and religious ritual, along with most other cultural practices, operate both to render opaque and to legitimate the generative violence that founded the community. Religion functions to control further outbreaks of violence by deflecting the danger toward the "guilty other" who stands in place of the community's intractable mimetic problems.

Critically Appropriating Girard's Model of Mimesis and Religion

Girard argues that religion has its origins in sacrificial violence, which myths, rituals, and prohibitions serve to camouflage and justify. The founding unanimous outcry against the victim is the mainspring of cultural formation, and even modern society and current religious practice operate according to the code of the victim mechanism, a mechanism rooted in past events of mimetic conflict that engenders new rationalizations for further violence. Nevertheless, Girard's indictment of culturally mediated violence is not a generic indictment of all culture and religion as such. In fact, it is precisely at the point where his social theory appears to be most damning in its scope that he identifies an alternative range of mimetic and ritual practices that are relatively immune from the founding of religious rites based on scapegoats.

Girard maintains that there are actually two modes of mimetic expression that define the human condition: acquisitive mimesis, which leads to rivalrous imitation of others and eventual violence, and non-acquisitive mimesis, which imitates the healthy desires of others and does not descend into the whirlpool of violence and retribution. "On one side are the prisoners of violent imitation," he writes, "which always leads to a dead end, and on the other are the adherents of non-violent imitation, who will meet with no obstacle" (Girard 1996: 18). At another point he flatly declares, "Mimetic desire is intrinsically good" (64). Healthy mimesis opens up the self to the other without the drive to own or control the other; it is guided by the other's desires and actions with an eye toward the mutual welfare of both self and other, not the domination of the other by the self. Non-rivalrous cultural imitation is communion with, not possession of, the other. Non-conflictual mimesis is positive, transformative desire to be like the other, to find oneself in and through the other, all the while being vigilant to defuse the potential conflicts that come with imitative group behavior.

In my use of classroom ritual, I have found both aspects of Girardian mimetic theory useful in promoting constructive performance practices, and discussions, among my students. With reference to pacific mimetic activity, I regard the introduction of lectio divina meditative reading of the Hebrew Bible or Buddhist sitting meditation as complementary positive exercises in mimetic ritual. Students learn by reading and discussing, indeed, but they also learn by doing—and, in Girardian terms, by *imitative* doing. Learning to do spiritually grounded mindful activity is possible by sensitivity to the religious vocabulary and coded movements of the group in which one is ritually located. By practicing a sort of ritual teamwork, students look to their group peers as models for how to do nuanced performance work in the learning environment. In my mind, this is the central relevance of Girard's theory of peace-making mimesis: understanding the power of group process to nurture participants' capacities for empathy and respect for the lived reality of other persons.

I recently introduced my religion and ecology class to a modified practice of zazen sitting meditation, and I asked a former student of mine named Richard to lead the class in the practice. Students paid close attention to Richard's lucid explanation of the notions of mindlessness and emptiness in Zen practice and to his modeling of this practice through his own posture and breathing. After Richard finished his brief introduction to the philosophy and practice of this type of meditation, I volunteered that I myself sometimes practiced contemplative exercises to stem cravings for consumer items in a relatively affluent culture. And I noted that I am not always successful in this regard. As an aside, I then joked that I admired the cool British-club soccer jersey that Richard was wearing in class that day and that I hoped my occasional forays into meditation practice might help me move away from such acquisitive leanings. At this point, Richard, upon hearing about my desire for his shirt, smiled, took the shirt off, and gave it to me (he was wearing another shirt under the jersey), saying, "Here, I would like you to have this." Although I quickly thanked Richard, I was stunned and nonplussed. Yet all of us, in an atmosphere of almost reverent quiet, proceeded to leave the classroom and walk to our outdoor meditation space to begin the group zazen exercise.

I look back on this exchange with Richard about the jersey as illustrative of Girard's thesis that positive human formation occurs in places where peaceful mimetic activity is taking place. Richard's spontaneous extravagance modeled to me and my students his unspoken position that he would not be drawn into a sense of personal right to ownership; his practice of non-acquisitive mimesis was an example to the class of generosity in a group setting and concomitant avoidance of any adversarial tension. In other circumstances as well, I have seen group ritual generate other transformative surprises, underscoring

Girard's thesis that we learn by observation and that acts of mimetic generosity, such as Richard's, create positive environments in which individuals' formation as whole persons is productively carried out and is sometimes imitated by others as well.

As Girard emphasizes, however, mimesis is often not a positive force. Therefore, when a ritual is embarked upon in a classroom setting, it is very important to guard the activity from becoming a factious or divisive affair in which a student or students feel marginalized by the larger group. Girard is particularly useful as a hedge against naïve optimism that the introduction of group activities, particularly ritual, will somehow produce positive personal and social results. He reiterates that scapegoating others who do not "fit" into a particular group setting is more often than not the product of ritual activity. His caveat against most such group activities is a cautionary note to instructors to be sensitive to the emotional and interpersonal energy in the classroom whenever they are leading or participating in ritual-based learning. I try to be aware of the mimetic dynamics of the class so that if any student, through trying to imitate his peers in the class assembly becomes physically or spiritually ill at ease with the activity in question, we can gently renegotiate his level of participation in the group setting without provoking the attention of others.

Conclusion

In this essay I have tried to lay out the practical and theoretical prospects for ritual-based learning in the nonsectarian classroom in dialog with Girard's theory of mimesis and religion. In the course case study analyzed here, I am frank with my students that I have two objectives in teaching this course. On the one hand, the course is an exercise in critical thinking whereby I hope to familiarize students with a variety of worldviews toward nature and human beings' place in nature as can be gleaned through a comparative study of world religious texts and traditions. On the other hand, the course is animated by a moral concern to offer to students, through a study of the emerging discipline of religion and ecology, a potent resource for developing attitudes and behaviors that lead to sustainable lifestyles. Ritual plays a role in achieving both objectives, but it should be handled carefully—by attending to cultural sensitivities, the problem of theology in ritual, and the value of making ritual activity optional for some students. The class's exploration of ritual provides students with a limited experience of the potential of spiritual practice to ground the study of sacred texts experientially, and it may motivate students to cultivate mindful activities that lead to living in harmony with their neighbors and the wider systems that support life on our planet. Ritual is one of the means by which the ultimate goal of the course, transformational learning, is (I hope) achieved.

Finally, I have found Girard's theory of twofold mimesis to be an insightful theoretical voice in my attempt to understand better the nature and value of ritual practice. Mimesis, according to Girard, is a fact of life; the question it raises for ritual practice is whether we will practice enabling mimesis through nonrivalrous and nonaggressive imitation of others or become trapped in the whirlpool of conventional mimesis that leads to rivalry, envy, and ultimately personal and social disintegration. Healthy mimesis can be the source and product of classroom ritual, whereas acquisitive mimesis can lead to exclusionary and scapegoating behavior that warps the positive practice of classroom ritual. Many religious studies scholars are now willing to breach the wall that has long separated the study and practice of religion in modern institutions of higher learning. I suggest that this effort, if done with thought and foresight, can be effectively deployed so that students can learn about religion, in part, by existentially sampling aspects of the practices that have long carried meaning and value for devotees. To accomplish this end is to reinvent education in our time as intellectually robust "soul craft"—as critical inquiry through the study of texts and ritual practice that center on the needs of the whole person. Its critics notwithstanding, liberatory education for our time that is both head-intensive and heart-centered demands nothing less.

USEFUL MATERIALS

Readers may find René Gerard's *Things Hidden since the Foundation of the World* and *The Girard Reader* useful. Other works that may also prove especially helpful:

Barnhill, David Landis, and Roger S. Gottlieb, eds. 2001. *Deep Ecology and World Religions: New Essays on Sacred Ground.* Albany: State University of New York Press.

Gottlieb, Roger S., ed. 2004. *This Sacred Earth: Religion, Nature, Environment.* 2nd ed. New York: Routledge

Grizzly Man. 2005. Film. 104 minutes. Director: Werner Herzog. Lions Gate Films.

Smith, Jonathan Z. 2004. *Relating Religion: Essays in the Study of Religion.* Chicago: University of Chicago Press.

Zaleski, Philip, and Paul Kaufman. 1997. *Gifts of the Spirit: Living the Wisdom of the Great Religious Traditions.* San Francisco: HarperSanFrancisco.

REFERENCES

Bell, Catherine. 1992. *Ritual Theory, Ritual Practice.* New York: Oxford University Press.

Driver, Tom F. 1998. *Liberating Rites: Understanding the Transformative Power of Ritual.* Boulder, Colo.: Westview.

Eyler, Janet, and Dwight E. Giles, Jr. 1999. *Where's the Learning in Service-Learning?* San Francisco: Jossey-Bass.

Girard, René. 1977. *Violence and the Sacred.* Translated by Patrick Gregory. Baltimore: Johns Hopkins University Press.

———. 1986. *The Scapegoat*. Translated by Yvonne Freccero. Baltimore: Johns
Hopkins University Press.

———. 1987. *Things Hidden since the Foundation of the World*. Translated by Stephen
Bann and Michael Metteer. Stanford: Stanford University Press.

———. 1999. *The Girard Reader*. Edited by James G. Williams. New York: Crossroad.

Gottlieb, Roger S. 1996. *A Spirituality of Resistance: Finding a Peaceful Heart and
Protecting the Earth*. New York: Crossroad.

Grimes, Ronald L. 1990. *Ritual Criticism: Case Studies in Its Practice, Essays on Its
Theory*. Columbia: University of South Carolina Press.

Hill, Julia Butterfly. 2000. *The Legacy of Luna: The Story of a Tree, a Woman, and the
Struggle to Save the Redwoods*. San Francisco: HarperSanFrancisco.

Loy, David. 2002. "The Religion of the Market." In *Worldviews, Religion, and the
Environment*, ed. Richard C. Foltz, 66–75. New York: Wadsworth.

McCutcheon, Russell T. 1997. *Manufacturing Religion: The Discourse on Sui Generis
Religion and the Politics of Nostalgia*. New York: Oxford University Press.

McWhorter, Ladelle. 2004. "Rites of Passing: Foucault, Power, and Same-Sex
Commitment Ceremonies." In *Thinking Through Rituals: Philosophical Perspectives*, ed. Kevin Schilbrack, 71–96. New York: Routledge.

Miller, Richard B., Laurie L. Patton, and Stephen H. Webb. 1994. "Rhetoric,
Pedagogy, and the Study of Religions." *Journal of the American Academy of
Religion* 62: 819–850.

Seed, John et al. 1988. *Thinking Like a Mountain: Towards a Council of All Beings*.
Gabriola Island, British Columbia: New Society Publishers.

Van Ness, Peter H. 1996. "Introduction." In *Spirituality and the Secular Quest*, ed.
Peter H. Van Ness, 251–275. New York: Crossroad.

———. 2004. "Religious Rituals, Spiritually Disciplined Practices, and Health." In
Thinking through Rituals: Philosophical Perspectives, ed. Kevin Schilbrack. New
York: Routledge.

Wallace, Mark I. 2005. *Finding God in the Singing River: Christianity, Spirit, Nature*.
Minneapolis: Fortress.

Wiebe, Donald. 1999. *The Politics of Religious Studies*. New York: Palgrave.

Zajonc, Arthur. 2002. *Report on the Survey of Transformative and Spiritual Dimensions of
Higher Education*. Northampton, Mass.: Center for Contemplative Mind in
Society.

6

Ritualizing Zen and the Art of Writing

Ronald L. Grimes

I teach ritual studies courses. Sometimes I teach them ritually, sometimes not. However, even when I teach courses without "ritual" in the title, I occasionally teach them ritually. Ritual is not only a phenomenon that scholars turn into subject matter, it is also a way of engaging things. One can ritualize teaching as surely as one can ritualize sitting or eating.

One year, when I was on leave, Victor Hori, a part-time faculty member and Zen monk taught my course "Zen Meditation, Zen Art." Still robed as a monk, he created a stir among students. He spoke with authority that I could not muster, given my checkered history with Zen and my sparse writings about Buddhism in North America. Much later, after he began teaching at McGill University, Hori organized a conference on the teaching of Buddhism in North America. I was invited but did not attend, protesting that I was not a proper Buddhism scholar. Despite my obvious lack of qualifications, Hori persisted and eventually convinced me to write a piece on teaching Zen even though I was not at the conference. He pressed me, knowing that I sometimes brought ritual studies perspectives into my courses, including the Zen course. I finally yielded to his pressure after he agreed that I could tell the stories of two actual courses rather than reflect in a more theoretical or prescriptive way about teaching Buddhism.[1]

For twenty-odd years I have taught "Zen Meditation, Zen Art." When I first proposed it, darts arrived from several directions. A colleague at McMaster University assured me that I was less than qualified to teach it, my several years of Zen practice notwithstanding.

My Japanese was nonexistent; so was my Sanskrit. Chinese we didn't talk about. And I was no Buddhism scholar. What did I think I was doing?

I said I was not teaching classical Buddhism on the basis of classical or canonical Buddhist texts. I explained that the bulk of the course was on Zen and its acculturation in North America. I poked back by asking how qualified he was to teach the last leg of Buddhism's historical journey, the one that culminates in contemporary North America—my field, not his. I asked: Would we require that a course on Christianity in North America begin with Jesus and the New Testament? I doubt it. There are roots courses, I said, but there are also fruits courses. One is not better or worse than the other, just different. My colleague was unmoved by my quips, even though he knew I meant what I said.

Then there were members of my own university's Arts and Science Council, who, never having seen a course description involving Buddhism, read it with a mixture of bewilderment and bemusement. The first question was tossed out by a testy professor of English: "Why isn't this course being offered at the community college, where they teach bricklaying and underwater basket weaving and god knows what else? Surely, the so-called arts in this course description—can you believe it, flower arranging and martial 'arts'—have no place in an arts and science curriculum of a modern Western university."

Fortunately, a Japanese-sword-collecting colleague from the School of Business and Economics (quarters from which I did not expect support) sparred with my colleague from English and won straightaway. My only entry into that fray was to remind another inquirer that, no, I had not been hired to teach "theology and literature," rather "religion and the arts in North America," and that "the arts" were variously construed in different cultures and that, no, I did not think a course on Milton's *Paradise Lost* and Christianity would be a better alternative; the English department, thank you, was doing that.

Despite initial faculty skepticism, students liked the course. It was the mid-1970s, and Zen was in sync with the cultural mood. "Zen": the word rang mystical, if not true. Consequently, the first time I taught "Zen Meditation, Zen Art," it flew. The students said so, and I knew it. By the second and third times around, I realized that it was the most revision-free course I'd ever taught. Students arrived in droves eager for enlightenment and willing to practice zazen on the floor, chant sutras, or visit Zen centers in Toronto. Although students exited the course unenlightened, they developed a sense for the practice and its cultural ramifications. The only complaint was that the course was not *more* experiential. Why not practice zazen in the Ritual Studies Lab twice a week, they asked, and why not more tea ceremonies, a makeshift *sesshin,* and encounters with a few visiting Zen masters? Some years I relented and offered zazen outside class.

A few students from that era, especially those who sat, stay in contact some twenty-five years later. One is now a Buddhist priest; others have spent time in Zen centers and monasteries. Testimonies arrived, unbidden, extolling the course's life-changing, life-enhancing qualities. I did not set out to make converts, only to convey or evoke the sense of Zen. I believed—and still believe—that if students do not sense, as well as think, a topic, they will not understand it. Education is of the senses and emotions as well as the brain.

After those initial, successful years there was an interlude created by several converging forces: the requirement to teach other courses, sabbatical, my own struggles in a Zen teacher-training program, and the availability of part-time faculty with impressive credentials. For a decade or so I did not teach the course even though I sometimes wanted to.

Then came the academic year 1999–2000. Once again, I was scheduled to teach the Zen course. Fondly remembering the early days of the course, I anticipated it. But when students stopped by to sign up for the course—it had a waiting list—I found myself tipping backward rather than looking forward. The students talked about Zen in a tone that struck me as different, not what I remembered. They were mildly curious, hoping to be entertained. They were not looking for masters or expecting to be enlightened.

By midterm it was evident to both my teaching assistant, Barry Stephenson, and me that something was not taking, that we were failing to cultivate a sense for Zen among the students. So we resorted to more dramatic means. We arranged a debate. Students were to come to class in the persona of a Zen teacher; they could pick which one. They didn't have to dress up, but they were to maintain the demeanor, attitude, and speech of a Zen master they had read about. In an attempt to have them encounter Zen as embodied in named and located persons rather than as a set of generic ideas and practices, the course had introduced them to half a dozen practitioners whom they now got to "be."

In class, Barry and I provoked debate among the dramatized Zen masters. If we couldn't inspire them, then we would tease them into crawling into someone else's skin. Two Zen teachers, themselves the spiritual offspring of a common master, were pressed to take up their differences in public. An entrepreneurial teacher was confronted with students who thought he had lost touch with the point of the practice. Marginalized and exploited female Zen students confronted marginalizing, cavorting American male teachers.

Even though students playing the roles had absorbed few of the details of the lives they were representing, once they loosened up, they did enter into the spirit of dharma-horsing-around (however unlike dharma combat it may have been).

Later in the course, we tried another performance strategy. When it became all too obvious that the students did not understand koans, that, in fact, they were not even intrigued by them, we resorted to acting out. Barry became the Zen master and I, his student. He got to slap me, publicly, and, coached by our rubrics and texts, we stood on desk tops, acting the fool in search of the oxlike self. But the best we could do was titillate a lethargic, slightly bemused audience. They marveled that we would make such a desperate spectacle of ourselves.

A key component of the course was the final "Zen and the art of" project. The number of "Zen and the art of" books is large. Many of the books are junk, but they reflect North American ways of selectively adapting and distorting historic Zen. A major aim of the class is to attend to the values that determine patterns of adaptation and modes of distortion. And the populist artsiness of the American "Zen and the art of" industry is a good example for study. My aim in having students study this motif is partly to incubate their creativity and partly to inculcate a healthy iconoclasm. Doing so successfully requires a delicate balancing act.

I had remained foolishly hopeful right up to the very end, even though the course was one of the flattest I had taught in thirty years. But the "Zen and the art of" projects set me back. With each new paper, I was faced with my own failure to teach even the most basic ideas, attitudes, and practices that I had set out to inspire in the Zen course. The students wrote as if they had not taken it.

Students were allowed to write on an Asian art traditionally associated with Zen—haiku, tea, Noh, sumi, and so on—or on a Western art such as photography, sculpture, literature, poetry, or dance, provided they first conducted research on a traditional Asian form. If students chose to pursue a project on a Western art, they were to read about Zen's relation to the traditional arts of Asia, particularly Japan, as well as study some of the "Zen and the art of" literature that saturates the North American market. Then they were to ask, for instance, What would it mean to engage in photography as an extension of practice, as if it were a Zen art? Photographers were advised to look at the Zen Mountain Web site for examples.

In addition to discussing ways a specific art and a distinctive religious tradition interact, students were invited to submit their own art and to describe the process, for instance, of shooting and developing. In the "old days" of the Zen course students had begged to be allowed to experiment and practice with Zen and art. But this time the requirement was met with incredulity and indifference, with only an occasional flash of interest.

The papers written about Asian arts inevitably emphasized form, content, or technique, and they stuck closely to the scholarly texts they had read; largely they summarized sources. Those written on Euro-American arts emphasized spontaneity and personal expression. Despite repeated lectures and discussions on the Western acculturation of Zen, students inevitably settled on flow or spontaneity as *the* Zen quality and then wrote entire papers showing how their photographs, shot five years ago, surprisingly exhibited this very quality.

One student opened a project this way: "Chaung-Tzu once said, 'Flow with whatever may happen and let your mind be free. Stay centered by accepting whatever you are doing. This is the ultimate.' To me, this is the essence of Zen and the art of photography. When one can concentrate on the pictures they are taking and be free from all the surrounding distractions, not only will they be happy with the results, but they have captured the Zen way. Although there are multiple ways to do this, I think the three most important are being flexible and spontaneous, being 'in the moment' of where you are, and being personal with your work instead of detaching yourself from it."

This student not only assumes Zen art has an essence and cites a Taoist to illustrate a Zen Buddhist attitude but talks as if happiness with results is the obvious aim of Zen. In this view, the proper Zen way to achieve that goal is to tune out the surroundings (even though course readings and lectures repeatedly emphasized that Zen meditation was not about tuning out distractions or quelling thoughts). The writer, by no means a poor or even mediocre one, emphasizes flexibility and spontaneity despite the fact that zazen, the most basic of Zen Buddhist practices, is so heavily structured that expressions of spontaneity usually violate its decorum. The student's paper identifies "the Zen of" an art with its expression of the personal, despite the fact that Zen monks shave their heads, dress alike, obey their teachers, and otherwise comport themselves in ways designed to quell the ego rather than enhance the personality. In short, the writer of this paper sees only *similarities* between the style of her photography and the style of Zen. To me, the *differences* were blatant. When the Western way of photographing is laid alongside either Zen practice or Zen-influenced Asian arts, I have to work to find continuities. We had repeatedly talked about the ritual grounding of Zen, about learning by imitation, about formality, and about structure. Never mind, Zen is spontaneity, presence to the moment.

The student told about having been forced in a high school photography class to shoot a roll of film a week for twenty weeks. The subject matter was the schoolyard itself. She experienced the assignment as boring but nevertheless included some stunning old photographs along with this comment, "All of these pictures are pictures that I may not have taken had I not been forced to adapt to my surroundings; however I was pleased with the results." So even though she knew that there had been a rigid structure to the assignment, and that it, in part, was responsible for her photographic success, Zen was still about flexibility, spontaneity, and self-expression. What did the assignment teach her? She quotes Lao Tzu, not a Buddhist: "Softness triumphs over hardness."

I wrote in her margin: "Zen photography is not merely about spontaneity. If you hadn't had the rule that forced you to photograph, you wouldn't have discovered the scenes you shot. The story you tell here is *not only* about adaptability and flexibility, as you seem to believe, *but also* about a strict form: Shoot a roll a week on and off the school grounds. The story is not about the triumph of softness over hardness, but about the integration of softness (be flexible) and hardness (follow the rules). Right?"

This student was one of the better ones in the course. I cite her paper as an example not because it was among the worst but because it was among the most articulate. Like the others in class, she had heard me say that Zen is not identical with spontaneity, or even with presence, and certainly not with personality enhancement—that's what North Americans *want to find* in Zen.

But saying is not teaching.

I was struck by how doggedly and systematically students were able to tune out what they had learned—rather, what I *imagined* they had learned. Regardless of how I squeezed the balloon of their brains, they returned stubbornly to the shape they originally had. Some force greater than I, "the culture," was responsible. Even though many students equated "the Zen" or "the art" of something with spontaneity, they neither noticed nor articulated the contradiction involved in submitting paintings or photographs done several years ago. Old photos and high school artwork were pulled out of drawers. Many of the projects implied the title: "Zen and the art of *retrospective* interpretation of *old* works of art *as if* they were executed under the influence of Zen practice." It had not occurred to me that an "art of" project would elicit such desperate or lackadaisical methods, so I had not written into the course requirements, "You cannot hand in old artwork" any more than I had specified, "You may not hand in papers from last year's courses." I had assumed that a new course meant new work. I had assumed too that the heavy Zen emphasis on attending to the present would elicit present-oriented experimentation and research. I expected students to pay concentrated attention to the details, fluctuations, and foibles of the creative process. I was dead wrong.

I had hoped that students would raise and explore difficult questions and struggle out loud with some of the perpetual quotation marks that plague courses on contemporary North American Zen:

- Would a "Zen photographer" sensibility search out "natural" rather than industrial content?
- Is a black-and-white photograph "more Zen" than a color photo?
- Does "the Zen of" something consist of its content? Its style? The attitude with which it is done? The manner of its performance?
- Should a "Zen photo" look more "Japanese" than "American"?
- Does photography become a "Zen art" when preceded or followed by meditation?
- Is "the Zen" of an art dependent upon how it is interpreted (rather than how it is executed)?
- Is an edited or touched-up photo by definition a "non-Zen" photo? (After all, you can't erase or edit the tracks of an ink brush.)

Wrestling with such questions in lectures did not guarantee that they would be considered in projects. Why not? Why was I so unsuccessful at eliciting paradox, play, irony, iconoclasm, and the other processes that had made the course work so well in years past? I've considered obvious ways of accounting for the failure of the 1999–2000 version of RE 298, "Zen Meditation, Zen Art": I am getting old and stale; this was a remarkably stupid bunch; the failure was a mere fluke and things will improve next time around; Tibetan Buddhism is now in, and Zen is out. But in the end, I have concluded that the most decisive factor is the cultural milieu, the culture of learning at university and in the larger culture surrounding and permeating it. The problem was not merely that Zen no longer has the exotic appeal that, say, Tibetan Buddhism has; it was that students resist rather than long for creativity and experimentation in the classroom. They are desperate to be given explicit rules and directions, preferably coupled with marks that can be achieved by following them. They are disoriented, even threatened, by paradox, silence, simplicity, playfulness, and the other "virtues" that made Zen and student life seem so obviously connected in the 1970s and 1980s. In short, the milieu makes "audience reception" of this course content much more difficult than it was a quarter of a century ago.

The social stream in which we all swim is not the stream that once was. We professors talk about religious traditions and religious studies topics as if they are eternal verities, which a good teacher can teach anytime, anywhere. In actuality, certain traditions and practices make better, or at least easier, sense in one time or place than in another. Teaching about Zen now is different and, for me, more difficult, than it was two decades ago because the motivating predispositions have evaporated. Even though it may well be deluded to enter a Buddhism course looking for enlightenment or for a master, that is at least a motivation. It is easier by far to redirect a motivation than to create one.

But the story I tell is not entirely dreary. Near the end of the course, two students working jointly on Zen and the art of tea asked if they might supplement their paper on traditional tea ceremonies with one performed for, and with, the class. Of course, I said. In years past, I had been flooded with initiatives like this, so I was grateful for this single glimmer of hope.

On the evening of the class, the two young women came by my office at 6:15 to set up for a 7 o'clock class. I took the lateness of arrival, the harried looks on their faces, and the presence of a boom box as bad signs. Barry accompanied them to the room they were preparing as their tea hut. At a quarter to 7, when I arrived and figured out they were using beer cups, plastic flowers, and paper cut-out stepping-stones leading down the hall to their tea-hut classroom, I wanted to go home and pull weeds in the back yard. If I had sensed even the slightest tinge of irony in their demeanor, I'd have danced a jig.

Would I be the chief guest? they queried. Yes, of course, but what is my job? I asked, ever the educator. I should enter first, they said, and wash my hands so the other guests could see how it was supposed to be done. And I should leave last.

What music is on your CD player? I queried. It was some soupy, dreamy, astonishingly inappropriate piece. I suggested: Silence would be quite fine. No, they said, we want music. Well, okay, if you want music, I said, how about something a bit more in keeping with the spirit of the ceremony? Sure, they said. I hurried away and returned with Tony Scott's "Music for Zen Meditation," only slightly more appropriate. When improvising, improvise.

I didn't know whether to laugh or cry during the demonstration/ceremony. So I did neither. The ethos was that of a grade four Shakespeare play or a Christmas pageant. We were awkward and self-conscious, and none of the actions showed much sensitivity to the tea ceremony or suggested that educated choices had been made on the basis of serious reading. I was not expecting a replication, only something "in the spirit of" Zen. We sat uncomfortably on the hard tile floor, having tiptoed across the treacherous white cardboard stepping-stones, which, not having been taped down, slipped this way and that across the hall floor.

Not until the hot tea began to burn my hand through the plastic beer cup did I settle down into my belly and notice that several other participants were doing likewise. For ten minutes perhaps we sat sipping hot tea and watching our self-consciousness fade. For a few moments even the spilling of tea and the shifting of untrained, weary bones became part of the event. A few "guests" drifted off into boredom; a few were embarrassed; but most began to inhabit the cluttered, sterile place and actually taste the tea.

Ceremony over, we returned back across the bridge of cardboard stones to our regular classroom. Expecting criticism or indifference, I opened with a preface calculated to protect the two students, whom I addressed publicly: "I appreciate your courage in taking on such a difficult topic. I am also delighted to have had time in the midst of end-of-term madness to sit and sip tea that warms the hands and belly. So let me ask your classmates: 'If you were to perform a Canadianized tea ceremony, what would you do that is the same or different from what your two classmates have just done?'" I was hoping to elicit gentle critique and some comparison of Japanese tea and Canadian tea (or even Canadian beer).

The first response came quickly and energetically from a student who had regularly been critical of the class. "This is the highlight of the course," she exclaimed. "Now, for the first time, I get it," she said.

I believed her. The outpouring from other students echoed her sentiment. The enthusiasm and sense of recognition were so pervasive that I felt free to joke about the beer cups, the music that *almost* got played, the slipping cardboard stones, the plastic flowers, and the jammed-up desks that had surrounded us like a stack of ghostly bones in an elephants' graveyard.

The truth is that I would have been embarrassed had the ceremony been witnessed by any of my finely tuned, linguistically well-educated colleagues who teach university courses in Buddhism. It would not have measured up to their expectations or mine, and it would have been loud testimony that I had failed to teach Zen or the art of anything. The ceremony lacked simplicity. It lacked precision. It lacked silence. And it lacked attentiveness. Never mind the fine points of gesture and posture, its tone and tenor were off.

But something worked despite all that. The beer-cup tea ceremony became the high point of the course. I reminded myself that the rite was not of my doing and that it transpired despite my resistance and self-consciousness. It succeeded despite me, despite the course, despite the two students, even despite itself. Ritualizing, it seems, can work even when it fails.

Writing Religion

This story is not quite over. Running simultaneously with RE 298, the Zen course, was RE 400, "Writing Religion," a required course for religious studies honors students in their last year. As fate would have it, the course had only a dozen students, which meant it could be held in the Ritual Studies Lab, which, as karma would have it, is outfitted with just that many *zafus* and *zabutons*. "Ah," I said to someone, "writing close to the floor: good for the ass, the bones, and the soul."

The course is partly a reward and partly remedial. It is a reward for those who, in their last days at university, have finally learned enough to wish they could write well. It is remedial for those who not only don't, but also don't care that they don't. Half the class consists of creative or personal writing on religious themes; the other half is analytical. The first half is soft, nurturing, and vaguely Buddhist; it aims at producing a story or personal essay. The second half is hard-edged, secular, editorial, and critical; it aims to produce an article for a scholarly journal. Each student's writing goes through multiple drafts and multiple readers.

Aside from the choice of Natalie Goldberg's *Writing down the Bones* as one of the books for the first half, everything "Buddhist" about the course came about by accident or improvisation. One afternoon a student complained about writing trash (actually, she called it "shit"), so we did some deliberate trash writing and needed a god to whom we might offer such stuff. I remembered there was a sleepy-eyed, tilted-to-one-side Mexican Buddha in the closet; he would do. So out came a bowl, the Buddha, and a bell with which to mark the moment for feeding trash to the Hungry Buddha of Bad Writing. Had there been a Goddess of Bad Writing in the closet, we'd have used her too.

Then the obvious dawned: Why not offer Buddha some good writing too? Christian and other students were invited to bring Christian and other gods for our improvised writing altar. We would not play favorites here. The advantage of Lord Buddha, I teased, is that he is indifferent to judgments of good and bad.

Isn't he?

Almost by accident "Writing Religion" became as much about religion as it was about writing. Why learn only about the craft of *writing* religion? Why not play along the edges of a *religion* too? Write Christian. Write Hindu. What does it mean to write not only using this or that technique but to write in, or at the edge, of this or that religious practice?

Education by indirection.

Indirectly, the writing course became more of a Zen course than the Zen course was. We sat. We drank tea. We wrote. We shared what we wrote. We trashed what we wrote. We treasured what we wrote. We offered Buddha the fruits of our writing. When celebrating, we blew bubbles over his dozing head. When disappointed, we burned or shredded writing trash.

The writing course was not a proper Buddhism course, but it kept becoming one by indirection and happenstance. Since this was a workshop, not a lecture course, aphorisms and *teisho*-like utterances popped out on their own accord. In addition, the space of the Ritual Studies Lab had its own mind about such matters, since it has been the scene of several decades of ritual experiment and critique. It, we noticed, seemed to be asking for aphorisms to be posted on the door, painted on the wall, and written in green ink on writers' hands so they would not be forgotten: "Show. Don't tell." This is the standard advice of creative writing teachers. Uttered repeatedly atop round cushions and punctuated by bell ringing and incense burning, the attitude is absorbed from underneath the writerly consciousness. While we debated the placement of commas and jerked misplaced modifiers into line, we also cultivated writing attitudes. Excerpted rightly, writing about writing can easily be made to echo sentiments that we North Americans have learned to associate with Zen:

> Writing is not...an art but breathing. (Anais Nin)
> The ideal view for daily writing, hour on hour, is the blank brick wall
>   of a cold storage warehouse. Failing this, a stretch of sky will do,
>   cloudless if possible. (Edna Ferber)
> Only the hand that erases can write the true thing. (Meister Eckhart)
> Every time I sit at my desk, I look at my dictionary, a Webster's
>   Second Unabridged with nine million words in it, and think: All
>   the words I need are in there; they're just in the wrong order.
>   (Fran Lebowitz)
> We must write where we stand; wherever we do stand, there is life.
>   (John Updike)
> If you wish to be a writer, write. (Epictetus)

One reason religions are so poorly understood is that they are so flatly and unevocatively described. One reason they are woodenly described is that we were never taught how to attend carefully and fully to words. Both as students and as teachers we spew them, rushing from term paper to term paper, then article to article. We don't sit with them. Writing in the Lab, we sat with words, sometimes even a word.

When I inquired how many people revised papers submitted for courses, one student raised her hand. For everyone else, revision, editing, and searching for just the right word were foreign activities. So "Writing Religion" became a course about attending, dwelling, pausing, and taking time with words. Words are treasures, we said, yet eminently deletable. Every word is special, even sacred, you could say. Even so, every word is subject to deletion. What we learned about writing in RE 400 was not much different from what Zen teachers say about an inhalation or exhalation.

Natalie Goldberg's *Writing down the Bones* is not only a Zen book, it is a period piece and cultural artifact. The stench of popular psychology, Western aestheticism, and the American workshop circuit are all over it. It stinks not only of Zen but of American Zen. Americanized Zen writing is very different from Japanese calligraphy, not just in form or content but in fundamental sensibility. But Guatemalan Christianity differs radically from Roman Christianity, and African Caribbean religions differ remarkably from Ashanti religion. So how much does it matter whether the Buddhism taught is North American rather than Japanese or Korean, whether it arrives indirectly in a writing course or directly in a Zen course? They all reek, and they should; that is the nature of acculturation.

Is writing under Goldberg's tutelage "Zen" writing? Or merely American writing? Or turn-of-the-millennium writing? The answer to the question does not matter much. For the purposes of the course what mattered was that students learn to care about writing and then develop a writerly rhythm: attend, discard, treasure; attend, discard, treasure; attend fully, then discard. Have no attachment to a word, phrase, paragraph, or paper, yet write something you treasure passionately. Just remember: Treasuring has a life span. Today's treasure will become tomorrow's discard.

In the Ritual Studies Lab and with Goldberg's assistance, we ritualized the act of writing. In other versions of the course, the aim had been the production of a work of verbal art or scholarship. In this version, the aim was to perform the act of writing in a ritualized manner. It just so happened that the ritual idiom was indebted to Zen Buddhism.

At the beginning of the course, I hung a blank scroll on the wall. This is how Ritual Studies Lab courses always begin. I invited students to sign it using traditional Japanese ink and brush. I gave no mini-lecture on calligraphy. "In your own good time," I said, "please sign the scroll, thereby formally entering the course. Write: 'I am a writer,' then sign your name below that."

Most participants sat still. I had made the task of signing in too heavy. After a while, I made the task less onerous: "You may mean whatever you wish by those words: 'I aspire to be a writer. I am hot stuff because I am published. I am a student, therefore I write papers, therefore I am, by definition, a writer.'"

Whatever students meant, they had to discover or invent it in the act of putting brush to scroll. Their first act required them to attend to a signature and to do so with an uncharacteristic intensity. The advice, "Every word in a story or article is like your name signed at the bottom of a check," is not much different from the advice, "Let every breath be your last" or "To sit is to die."

When the writing course was over, I felt it a success. When the Zen course ended the same week, I felt it a failure. Where I had intended to teach Zen, I had not. Where I had not intended to teach Zen, I had. In authoring this autopsy it occurs to me that perhaps I taught neither Zen nor writing but only Pauline theology: That which I would do, I have not done, and that which I would not do, I have done.

I teach Buddhism and I teach writing in unorthodox ways, but not because I think either is special. The arguments for "experiencing" Zen are no stronger than those for experiencing, say, Anishnabe or Muslim religion. The line between teaching and practice is fine, never easy to walk, but it is always worth trying. If I were teaching Christianity, I'd likely have students singing hymns in class. Pressed to defend the practice, I say something like: "Such subjunctive experiences, however complex and dangerous, can be effective ways teaching."

I do not claim that everyone should teach every course on Buddhism or writing in this way, only that an embodied, "participatory" pedagogy is a valid form of teaching and learning and that it is not a propagandistic move aimed at making converts.

The quotation marks around "experiencing" and "participatory" are necessary. They signal the crucial subjunctive. An "as-if" marker does not render experience and participation unreal, but it does flag them, suggesting that the reality of the Zen and the writing that I teach is peculiar, even fictive. But fiction, like ritual, has real consequences.

Acknowledgment

This essay was originally published as "Zen and the Art of Not Teaching Zen and the Arts: An Autopsy," in *Teaching Buddhism in the West: From the Wheel to the Web*, ed. Victor Sogen Hori, R. P. Hayes, and J. M. Shields, 155–169 (London: RoutledgeCurzon, 2002). It is reprinted here and in *Rite Out of Place: Ritual, Media, and the Arts* (New York: Oxford University Press, 2006) with the permission of the publisher.

PART II

Teaching the Questions through Issues and Theories

7

Teaching Ritual Propriety and Authority through Japanese Religions

John Nelson

Few topics in the classroom have the potential to integrate mind and body the way studying ritual does. We can talk to our students about its theory, history, and symbolism until we're blue in the face, yet we know this is one of those topics—like the taste of strawberries or how a musical score actually sounds—that requires an experiential, performative encounter. Through a class's voluntary participation in a simulated ritual event, we can try to bridge those gaps between intellect and emotion, between understanding and experience, and between passivity and action. We may not always be successful in reaching our learning objectives through these admittedly artificial and structured activities, but there is no better way to impress upon students the viability of ritual (and ritualizing activities) as a social force that can and does actually move people. Ritual has helped to launch blitzkriegs, kamikaze attacks, jihads, and even genocide. It has also helped to focus civil rights and anti-war demonstrations, to commemorate critically important events in our lives, and to empower groups and individuals of all social classes to address and engage the vexations of their worlds.

Working to frame content and performance are the political dimensions of ritual—its authority, legitimacy, social impact, and intentionality. Among the many ways we approach the topic in our classrooms, surely one of the most ongoing and important should be how we demonstrate the power of an activity that is culturally constructed and oftentimes arbitrary, yet can still reach into both the psychology and emotions of large numbers of people and help move them to act in specified ways.

Students need to know that ritual is neither natural, wholly consensual, nor always willingly joined. Its activities, symbols, themes, and participants articulate a particular order that has a coercive authority. The political dimension of ritual events is tangled in a complex web of agency, resources, and power that has legitimated the rule of kings, popes, tribal leaders, prime ministers, presidents, and governments in visible and tangible ways. Likewise, this legitimation can work to elevate above the mundane world key rites of passage, domestic holidays, auspicious events, or even a nation's foreign policy. When secular, ritual oils the wheels of government from city councils to the floor of the Senate, providing decorum, "magical utterances" that frame space and time, and symbolic resonance with the founding values or myths of a particular sociocultural order. When religious, rituals reference and usually seek divine intervention to guide, coerce, cajole, and control (a hundred other verbs could apply here) the interactive relationship between human and transhuman realms.

The exercise and display of authority by designated specialists is at the heart of ritual. Whether it be in determining or maintaining the site of the event, the themes it will address, the language it will use, or the conditions for participation as well as the bodily conditions of participants, at each phase a choreography of order attempts to discipline and define how the cosmos *should* operate. If we elide or downplay in our teaching the politics of how rituals come into being or the strategies behind the ways they're performed, we render our students myopic to some of the principal dynamics of religious traditions as well as to some of the most dramatic political events of our day.

There's a saying in my home discipline of anthropology that to understand ourselves, we make a detour through the Other. I have never been entirely comfortable with the self-serving implications of this statement, but I have learned it is mostly true. Teaching ritual within a course on religion or anthropology provides the opportunity to use ethnographic material that is both radically different from what students know and yet is organized in a meaningful way. Ethnographic investigations of Nepalese mortuary practices, Inuit coming-of-age celebrations, or Chinese geomantic building placement all reflect back upon our own normative constructions of the world. We see with fresh eyes (accompanied by respect, tolerance, and appreciation, one hopes) that there is more than *our* sociocentric way to organize reality.

Japan's two dominant religious traditions, Buddhism and Shintō, provide examples I use in the classroom to make three key points about ritual. First, despite obvious differences, I want students to see there is nonetheless considerable thematic resonance among ritual practices worldwide. Prayers in an ornate Catholic church, in an ancient Buddhist temple, or at a makeshift shrine beside a busy highway are all cousins to one another. Second, ritual is a practice fundamental to societies worldwide and is thus part of an expressive human heritage in ways similar to graphic arts, dance, or theater. Finally, ritual activities are among the oldest techniques on the planet that consistently dislodge individuals from the clutches of their limited worldviews. Through a variety of strategies, ritualizing activities promote perspectives that can renew or redraw the cultural blueprints for one's existence. Although I'm most interested here in the politics of ritualization, I will attempt to provide a bit of context for activities that may usefully illustrate the points I've just mentioned.

The Context of Ritual in Japan

Teaching about Japan's many expressions of ritual practice can be surprisingly straightforward. This straightforwardness need not imply a reduction of the complexities and subtleties of a diverse religious heritage into conceptual boxes simply for convenience. Just as the historical Buddha was reported to employ *upaya* ("skillful means") and choose only those modes of communication appropriate for the audience at hand, so should instructors follow suit if they hope to convey some of the dynamism and excitement of ritual in Japan. Rituals specific to certain sects or denominations may be fascinating to present and discuss, but they tend to overwhelm most undergraduates in introductory or survey courses. Either the tradition is too unfamiliar, or the symbolism is too abstract, or students lack sympathetic resonance with the farmers, priests, businesspeople, or politicians for whom the ritual is designed. We will see in a moment a couple ways to minimize this cultural distance, a distance made all the more formidable by religious ways of acting and thinking that may strike students as odd.

There are thematic categories relevant to and consistent with all ritual practices in Japan—from Agonshû to Zen—that serve as open doors into this fascinating topic. Whatever the religious tradition, ritual occasion, or specialist in charge, one can always focus on four themes shared by ritual worldwide: (1) the condition and comportment of bodies, (2) symbolic gestures and objects, (3) the stylized performance of petitions, sutras, or prayers, and (4) strategies of empowerment framed by authority. As we will see in a moment, the fourth theme plays a dominant role in Japan, acting like a gravitational force upon the other three.

As the Japanese never tire of reminding those residing elsewhere, theirs is an island nation subject to a panoply of dramatic forces shaping social and cultural development. Four distinct seasons and a temperate climate create superb growing conditions for vast forests, rice agriculture, and other crops. Japan is also embraced by several powerful ocean currents that provide a steady supply of fish, seaweed, and crustaceans. But there are also monsoon rains, a typhoon season that lasts from July to November, unpredictable earthquakes, volcanic eruptions, and a long history of epidemics and pestilence. If that isn't enough to foster a desire for some means of control over these potentially destructive variables, we can also add political upheavals (usually violent at first) that have caused centuries of civil war, internecine conflict, and (more recently) imperialism, colonialism, and fascism.

In a volatile environment like this—where deities (called *kami*), buddhas, bodhisattvas, and demons were thought to intervene directly in the affairs of society and government—we can document the importance of and regard for rituals promoting stability, order, normalcy (especially related to health), and harmony. As subheadings embedded throughout the preceding categories, rituals in Japan, like those elsewhere, can also legitimate common origins and interests, empower select individuals (including people historically without much power, such as women), and negate or deny threats (including death) that challenge the legitimacy or survival of the individual or group. Most rituals in Japan are focused on gaining tangible benefits in *this* world (*genze riyaku*), with concern for one's own salvation or the afterlife of close kin coming in a close second.

To many foreign observers, the practitioners of ritual practices in Japan display a puzzling tendency to swing from Shintō to Buddhist to Christian-based rituals, with apparently little regard for the actual content of these religious traditions. Despite their dominance on the domestic religious land-scape, those are not the only traditions with which the Japanese interact. A young couple may start married life together by holding their wedding in a chapel built specifically for this purpose, with an ordained Christian minister conducting the ceremony. The prayers, references to a powerful yet loving deity, hymns, and setting enhances the exotic cultural ambiance and fulfills the couple's desire for a unique event. Should this couple later find them-selves unable to conceive a child, they may visit a Shintō shrine to petition a particular *kami* to enhance virility, fertility, or both. To cover all possible variables, they might also go to a traditional Buddhist temple or perhaps that of a new religion to pacify the unhappy spirit of a fetus aborted years earlier that could be blocking their plans. Each of these traditions certainly has specific ways of believing and acting, but what matters most are the spiritual and pragmatic benefits (*goriyaku*) accessed via their rituals. To put it another way, why should a person afflicted with a serious medical condition worry about the specific ingredients of a medicine, as long as it alleviates their pain or symptoms?

Ritual activities and practices associated with religious institutions in Japan can range from those performed by priests at Buddhist temples, Shintō shrines, or in a new religion based on some syncretic blend of the two. At the same time, idiosyncratic adaptations of a formal ritual are freely enacted by anyone in need of that ritual's efficacy: a farmer concerned about his rice crop, a new mother worried about her sick baby, or a businessman anxious about falling sales. By doing so, they gain a sense of relative empowerment, psychological balance, and control via the ritual's blueprint for an ideal reality. Rituals both ancient and contemporary have long been thought to enhance those divine forces which imbue conditions beneficial to individuals and society—productivity, fertility, safety, or stability to name a few—as well as to exorcise influences thought to be harmful or defiling.

With such a rich stew of possibilities, how can we find those that best nurture understanding about ritual propriety and authority? Returning to matters of pedagogy and "skillful means," it has been my experience that by emphasizing the practical nature of these rituals and how they are designed (via the four categories mentioned earlier) to promote health, healing, revitalization and so on, students can easily make an imaginary leap into another cultural perspective. They might very well have numerous issues in their own lives—anxiety about academic performance, troubles with significant others, money problems—that a ritual from Japan can address in a positive way. There may also be topics or problems too delicate or controversial to address openly where again, a detour through the Other may help illuminate the self.

Shintō's "Emptiness of Symbolic Forms," or How an Emperor Became a Deity

Since Japanese religions are often presented in chronological order, many instructors begin with "Shintō." Standing in dramatic contrast to conventional, Western notions of religion, Shintō has no centralized dogma, no charismatic founders, no weekly worship services attended by a congregation, and, perhaps most strikingly, no sacred texts. These characteristics have served to advance an autonomy and freedom at the local level leading to widely diverse practices and beliefs.

However, at Shintō institutions closer to the centers of political power, the tradition has been and remains a viable means for legitimating regimes, ensuring social and political stability, and making sacred via ritual everything from the coming harvest to the nation's wars. Like other religions pressed into service for political agendas (think of contemporary Islam or evangelical Christianity), a dramatic shift toward centralized power and control is most conveniently encouraged through ritualizing strategies—some of which will be demonstrated in a moment.

For most Japanese today, the Shintō tradition is represented not by a specialized, problematic term or the darker parts of its recent history as a tool for imperialism, but through specific occasions. These include visiting shrines at certain times of the year or at critical stages of the life cycle, participating in periodic festivals, or simply (as the saying goes) "turning to the deities in times of trouble." The deity or *kami* can be anything mysterious, marvelous, uncontrolled, strange, or beyond human comprehension. As in any interpersonal relationship characterized by moods, events, and situations, Shintō rituals addressed to *kami* likewise employ strategies aimed at controlling the temperament and degree of influence of these volatile deities. The rituals that one can perform privately, or those performed on one's behalf by priests, address a wide range of known contingencies as well as those that might be stalking or preventing one's good health or prosperity. Presented with the proper attitudes, bodily comportment, offerings, and "beautiful words," like an honored guest the *kami* are obliged to act appropriately in ways that assist petitioners.

A typical Shinto ritual unfolds in three movements. With an emphasis on the body to bring about both the ritual itself and enable its concerns to be conveyed to the deities, it is essential that whoever participates first be purified. As we will see in a moment, one can perform this ritual privately at a water basin, or be purified by a priest waving a paper wand (*haraigushi*) over one's head. Next, the purified body enacts specific gestures and postures that are thought to resonate with and tap into cosmic orders of power and benefits. Finally, participants are rewarded for this exacting attention to detail with a kind of communion, one that connects sacred time and place with the everyday (but not profane) world.

What may sound like a rather abstract template for purification and petition translates into a classroom (or outdoor) activity that students both enjoy and remember. The activity also serves as a foundation for the lessons of relative empowerment gained via authoritative control. To reiterate, the idea behind this activity is to structure an environment in which students can experience firsthand the tension, drama, focus, and symbolism of a typical ritual one might perform at a Shintō shrine. In this sense, the dynamics of this ritual (called *hairei*) have a generic quality, one that might be applicable to many religious traditions.

To perform a *hairei* ritual, three "stations" are set up beforehand where purification, petition, and finally communion can be experienced. While waiting their turn to participate, students begin a report (to be handed in at the conclusion of the activity) that describes the three stations and the activities occurring at each location.

At the purification site, students rinse their hands in a left-right-left hand sequence symbolizing the *yang-yin-yang* dynamic that purifies and revitalizes participants before they petition the deities. A basin with clean water and a ladle (preferably one with a long handle) is set on a table, while an empty trash receptacle (with pine needles, a few evergreen sprigs, leaves, or some other organic material at the bottom) is placed on the floor. A student will use the ladle to dip a small amount of water and then pour it into her left hand, with water trickling through her fingers and into the receptacle on the floor. She does this for her right hand and once more pours a small amount of water into her left hand, which is then raised to her mouth and used for a brief rinsing purpose only, with the defiled water spit into the receptacle. Symbolically, with the participant's bodily impurities drained away into the receptacle, defiling actions and words have also been cleansed.

The remaining water in the ladle is then trickled down the handle so as to prepare it for the next participant. Napkins or paper towels are at the ready for drying hands and mouth afterward (this paper also goes into the receptacle). After being purified, a student waits to serve with a clean paper towel the next participant who finishes the purification.

At the second station, students petition the deities about a private, personal concern. The notion of the divine (*kami*) in Shintō is very flexible, pluralistic, and fluid. To shift attention away from Western or Christian perspectives of the divine, it is best to represent some local natural landmark— a giant tree, mountain, or simply the direction of the rising or setting sun—as an expression of the *kami* to which the petition is being offered. Students kneel on the floor in pairs, facing an "altar" (a chair works fine, with the altar facing any direction but north) upon which is placed some image or object that might evoke a resonance with the *kami*. The instructor has prepared in advance two small branches or stems from an evergreen tree, bush, or plant (symbolizing vitality), each no shorter than ten inches in length. Students are given these stems and told to hold them using both hands so that the base of the stem points toward their heart. They then approach the altar on their knees, advancing first with their left leg, then right, then left again. Before they offer their branches, they reverse the stems so that they point toward the altar, symbolizing a connection between themselves and the *kami*.

What comes next is the highlight and raison d'être of the ritual, where space and time pivot to address the deity. Still in the kneeling position, students bow twice (bending forward from the waist), clap their hands twice (each clap symbolic of a *yang-yin* dynamic), and bow again (*yang*) in a final gesture of empowerment and new beginnings. They back away from the altar on their knees (left, right, left legs) and then stand and make a final, shallow bow.

Their purpose completed, participants then move to the communion site, where they pour a tiny sip of *omiki* (which is none other than saké, itself a gift from the *kami* via rice) and partake of some thin rice crackers. Students pour the *omiki* for each other, and then clap once before drinking. After they've finished their ritual meal, which functions as a transitional bridge between sacred and domestic domains of time and space, they find a seat and work on their report, detailing what they've just accomplished, how they felt while doing it, and the concern they hoped the *kami* would empower them to deal with effectively. The act of writing serves an additional purpose by keeping the students engaged while their classmates proceed through the ritual.

Although the preparation takes a little forethought (one water basin, one trash receptacle, one ladle, napkins, two evergreen sprigs, altar symbol, sake, rice crackers), I've used this reenactment of what goes on within most Shintō shrines as an effective and enjoyable means to convey the importance of a disciplined body in performing each stage (see Nelson 1996). The initial foray into the power and mystery of ritual is in itself a worthwhile learning goal suitable for half of one ninety-minute class period. As is the case with most hands-on, experiential activities, students find the simulated ritual both exacting and entertaining. Students report they felt anxious and "stressed" in trying to do each phase correctly, even though they had been coached, seen videos, and watched other students perform the same actions over and over. They also noted that the ritual focused their attention in significant ways, bringing them into a "here and now" in which each sound, smell, or action resonated with significance. They see and feel how gestures, bows, and symbolic orientations—expressed through their body—can serve to address their own concerns through the language of ritual.

In discussions about the activity, I emphasize how Western, Judeo-Christian–based societies have very few ritual resources that help connect us to our environment, or to sites where something significant has occurred. I encourage students to try out the yang-yin-yang hand-clapping and bowing ritual (called kashiwade, literally "oak/kashiwa" and "hand/te, de" based upon the oak tree's union of male and female) whenever they see a beautiful sunset, visit a lovely place, or want to otherwise apply brakes to the flow of time and space and ritually acknowledge something of significance. By doing so, they become ritual specialists who have the knowledge and skill to impose order and meaning on a fleeting world.

To stop at this point would be to shortchange both our students and the interdisciplinary field of ritual studies. What is lacking from the above exercise is a sense of history, sociocultural context, and, perhaps most important, an understanding of authority that can both shape and spin the ritual into more broadly encompassing spheres of reference.

In the class meeting following the simulated ritual, we retrace its various phases so that symbols, movements, and goals are once again clear and present. Then, standing beside the image or object that occupied the makeshift altar, I announce that an important political shift has occurred since the last time we met. Henceforth, in addition to the familiar representation of the kami associated with some natural presence, there will also be a photo of the Japanese emperor named Meiji (r.1867–1912) to be treated with even greater reverence than the local kami. Placing this photo (easily available online) side by side with the object representing the nature kami elicits quite a reaction from the class, as I'll discuss below.

History informs us that the Meiji emperor, Mutsuhito, was at the center of a kind of "civic" Shintō that Japan's social architects developed as the ideological heart of a late-nineteenth-century program of modernization. It was a powerfully coercive ideology—later enforced by the law and police—using mythology and ritual to blend ideas about ethnicity, race, patriotism, and duty into an emotionally charged nationalism. From the 1890s forward, this ideology became the legal obligation of every Japanese to study in school and to observe as civic duty. Many rituals at shrines nationwide were systemized so as to conform with newly instituted liturgical guidelines issued from Tokyo.

This dramatic and radical policy obscured centuries of religious complexity and tradition at the local level by instituting an emphasis upon serving the emperor as a manifestation of the state. This is not to say that all shrines, priests, and communities willingly and without dissent adopted these practices, or that the practices themselves were uniformly observed. There was resistance to and subversion of directives coming from the central government. But since there were financial rewards and patronage attached to compliance—and a manufactured atmosphere of crisis and threat (akin to post–9/11 in the United States)—local priests and their institutions more often than not acquiesced to the new standards as much for economic reasons as for civic, religious, or patriotic ones.

Once the photo of emperor Meiji occupies center stage on the classroom altar, a number of reactions take place among the students. The first is one of invasion and mild irritation—*Who is that guy? And what's he doing on our altar?*—similar to what the majority of Japanese people initially experienced. As noted earlier, one of the primary ways the new central government of 1868 devised to break with the past and usher in a new era was to fashion an invented tradition that reemphasized the importance of the emperor as both father of the nation and grandson of the gods. The emperor and other transcendent "national" deities (in particular, the *kami* of the sun was made synonymous with the imperial lineage) were installed among local shrines, and the whole system was then bolstered through a nationwide system of schools. For almost eighty years, Japanese students were taught that Japan had been created by the gods, that the emperor was a descendant of those gods and thus divine himself, and that Japan's sacred duty and destiny in Asia was to "expel the (foreign) barbarians" and liberate ethnic populations oppressed by Western colonialism.

A second wave of reaction from the students focuses on how to resist or somehow subvert the new ritual paradigm emphasizing the emperor. There is usually discussion about "reclaiming" or "retaking" the ritual (as if it were territory lost to some enemy force) in order to not anger the local nature *kami* with which "we" must live in harmony or else suffer consequences. Students suggest alternative altars, new ritual practices, or nonparticipation as modes of resistance, and they come up with innovative ways to treat the central image: to ignore, reposition, veil, or otherwise deconstruct it, none of which would have been permitted by state authorities at the time of course.

When students see (and, somewhat surprisingly, *feel*) the relative ease with which familiar ritual practices can be hijacked by those in power, it drives home Catherine Bell's assertion that ritual does not *appropriate* minds and bodies so much as *engage* them in a set of tensions that involve both domination and resistance (1992: 213). During eight decades, Japanese leaders cultivated through specific policies, the mass media, new institutions (such as state Shintō shrines), and the educational system a complex emotional cluster of sentiments (pride, crisis, loyalty, fear) centered upon the nation state. Convinced that their country was under a constant threat of invasion and colonization, the Japanese saw civil liberties abridged, religious freedom constricted, and ideologies of self-sacrifice and service to the emperor exalted in art, literature, theater, and the media. We now know it was a path to delusion and disaster for all involved, a path made smoother in part by the strategic use of ritualizing practices.

Empowerment and Submission within "Buddhist" Ritual

Many students come to a course on religion that discusses Buddhism having already been exposed to a number of provocative bits of information from popular culture. They know (but aren't sure why) Buddhism is culturally "cool." They know it has been featured in several recent Hollywood films, that its vocabulary and imagery are displayed in advertisements, song lyrics, and in the names of music groups, and (perhaps the most significant of all) that it rated an entire episode of the animated television series "The Simpsons." With this kind of cultural presence, an instructor's job is both easier *and* more challenging in converting these preexisting expectations into resources for learning.

For example, it usually comes as a shock to students to learn that the religion first came to Japan from Korea and China in the early sixth century *not* for its doctrines of compassion, emptiness, or the practice of meditation but for its stabilizing, regime-enhancing rituals. Throughout the long history of Buddhism in Japan, its temples (like those in Thailand, Tibet, Sri Lanka, China, and Korea) have always relied first on the patronage of powerful rulers and lords and only when necessary upon contributions from the lower classes. Though the value of patronage is emphasized in many sutras and teachings— and extends across all social classes—individuals with money, territory, and political influence have played tangibly important roles in the spread of various kinds of Buddhism. Elaborate rituals and prayers promoting the stability of earthly kings and rulers, in whom "kingly law" and "Buddhist law" mutually reinforce each other, have been central to the survival and propagation of Buddhism throughout Asia.

For many centuries in Japan, Buddhist rituals (centered in temples but also conducted *in situ*) and rituals for the benefit of the *kami* (centered in shrines or at sacred sites) were seen as mutually reinforcing and interdependent.

Because the *kami* were considered to be manifestations of Buddhas and bo-dhisattvas (*honji suijaku*), the Japanese were free to use whichever tradition provided the greatest resources for accessing worldly benefits. To return to the medicinal metaphor mentioned earlier, Buddhist and *kami*-oriented rituals were complementary interventions that could lead to a cure for one's troubled condition. After the Meiji revolution in 1868, however, shrines and temples were forcibly separated into two distinct traditions, with a revised Shintō (having the emperor as its head priest) now privileged as the spiritual engine propelling the state's agendas of modernization.

Given this history, it was business as usual that Buddhist priests and administrators during the period of Japan's rapid modernization (1853–1943) allowed their temples and rituals to accommodate the central government's nation-building agendas. Priests from all sects had been struggling to over-come a much-maligned, 250-year association with a repressive feudal regime that had used temples to register and monitor both rural and urban popula-tions. After the 1868 "imperial" revolution that ensconced the emperor as the figurehead of Japanese government, Buddhism in Japan endured a brief but destructive persecution (1870–1874) that saw many temples destroyed, price-less icons and artwork burned or vandalized, and legions of priests forced to return to lay life. Buddhist leaders were anxious to regain their status and properties, as well as participate in the heady triumphalism of Japan's military victories over China (1894), Russia (1906–1907), and Korea (1910).

This brief detour into history is necessary if students are to take the next step in understanding of how authority, and the power that sustains it, can shape ritual activity. As the Zen priest Morinaga Soko reminds us, "Until you have subjected yourself to some discipline, you should not put too much faith in your own willpower."[1]

The multifaceted relationship between authority and ritual activities is well illustrated in the fact there is probably no practice more fundamental and universal among Buddhist traditions than the recitation of texts. The primary means for enacting ritual I've stressed throughout this discussion—the condition and comportment of bodies, symbolic gestures and objects, stylized linguistic performance of petitions, sutras, or prayers, and strategies of empowerment—are all fully present in sutra recitation. Although the content of sutras is fairly consistent (depending on whether one uses original texts or translations), it is the *application* of the content toward a specific recipient that creates merit (for both parties) and activates the sutra's spiritual power. This, too, is among the most long-lasting characteristics of Buddhism in Asia.

We find examples of merit-generating chanting at temples in every country where Buddhism is still practiced. Chris Ives has shown how the early Indian notion of "divine kings," who embody the dharma through their rule, has been at the heart of numerous relationships between Buddhist institu-tions and political rulers throughout Asia (Ives 1999). At Myōshinji, a head temple for the Rinzai sect of Zen in Kyoto, Japan, bimonthly services for the health of the emperor and stability of his reign are conducted by the priests and monks in the main hall. At other temples as well—Tendai, Shingon, Sōtō Zen, Pure Land, and True Pure Land—similar services recognize the emperor's birthday or other occasions of national concern. It is one thing to chant a text such as the famous "Heart Sutra" for the spiritual benefit of oneself or one's immediate community, but quite another to direct the merit toward a recipient (such as the emperor) deemed worthy by institutional authorities. One might feel as if one is but a hired hand laboring for someone else's salvation!

To convey some of the hierarchies of power at work in Buddhist rituals, I use a class activity that begins with distribution of copies of an excerpt from a well-known sutra (either the Lotus, Diamond, or Heart). I project an overhead (or Web site) image at the front of the classroom that has a Buddha statue on an altar and ask students to imagine they are sitting in a gilded temple hall with high ceilings overhead and soft tatami grass mats under their legs. If no one objects, I burn a little incense as well. I then demonstrate how the sutra is to be chanted—emphasizing its rhythms and steady cadences—but do not offer explanations about the meaning of the text. A few lines from the "Heart Sutra" will serve as an example:

> With no hindrance of mind—no hindrance therefore no fear,
> Far beyond all such delusion, Nirvana is already here.
> All past, present, and future Buddhas live this Prajna Paramita
> And attain supreme, perfect enlightenment. (Smith 1999: 178)

Before attempting a more formal, group recitation, I ask students to think of their own situation and needs as well as those of someone dear to them, someone who could benefit from extra attention, care, or compassion. I remind them that even if the meaning of the sutra is obscure (or profound) to the person chanting, the transfer of merit does not depend on one's intellectual grasp of the subtleties of Buddhist doctrine. Just saying the words activates the spiritual power of the teaching.

I then have the class stand. At the front of the room, I first bow to the group—hands together in front of my chest in the traditional gesture of greeting and acknowledgment—and they return the bow. Standard ritual protocol then requires a bow to the main image, but I pause here to remind them of earlier discussions about the distinction between an image as object of devotion and as a symbol for a metaphysical construct. If students feel comfortable bowing to an image that represents the potential within human beings to transform themselves, I encourage them to do so.

Returning to the "script," I bow again to the projected image and then hold up the text with both hands, asking the class to follow suit. (Having a bell on hand to mark the beginning and ending of the recitation is a nice touch, but not essential. Most temples would also use a rhythmic instrument of some sort to set the pace for the chant, but because English translations don't convey easily into syllabic parts the way a character-based language such as Japanese or Chinese does, setting a rhythm can also be dispensed with. For a good example, hear the Heart Sutra chanted at http://www.spokanebuddhisttemple.org/Audio/englishheartsutra.mp3.) We then proceed slowly and carefully through the text. After the last syllables have faded (and the bell is struck again), I put down the text and ask the students to join me in a final bow to the idea-in-the-image. I then turn to face the class, and we bow facing each other a last time.

By the time the activity is finished, students will have encountered the three categories of ritual mentioned earlier (bodily comportment, symbolic objects, stylized performance) and several versions of authority. First, the sutra's content and meaning have a *gravitas* shaped by the tradition of communal practice. Just as the Twenty-Third Psalm is regarded as a definitive text from the Old Testament, most Buddhist sutras are likewise afforded an authenticity and authority conferred by the centuries. Like any text, sutras have been constructed, aligned with intellectual themes, and edited into final versions. Nonetheless, by chanting the text, students can enter briefly into an imagined community—the Buddhist *sangha*—that has grounded its faith traditionally in the magical efficacy of these teachings. The text's reputation and veneration brings together vast linguistic, cultural, social, and political differences into the fold of the Buddhist tradition.

Another kind of authority is encountered in the performative delivery of the sutra. Students try to synchronize with the chant, and in doing so submit to the flow and rhythm of stylized language and group dynamics lest their single voice stand out as separate (and embarrassing). By harmonizing with the group, participants give the text a greater momentum in its application which is, of course, the whole point of the ritual. Once they get the hang of it, students usually find the practice of chanting to be nonthreatening and even relaxing. They see parallels with Christian prayer or responsive reading and, though the content is different, find the ritual atmosphere for communal prayers and sutras fairly familiar.

The final form of authority is also the most obvious: deciding who receives the sutra's merit. Transferring merit to one's friends, family, or to those less fortunate than ourselves is no problem. However, should I ask them before the final recitation to direct merit to the U.S. president—who most would agree could certainly use more wisdom—they usually bristle before remembering that, as nominal Buddhists for one class period, they are supposed to be compassionate. Again, as we encountered earlier in the Shinto ritual, a tension develops between compliance and resistance. One of my goals for this activity is to hope that students attempt to identify sources of agency and power inherent in any activity shaped by objectification, hierarchy, and tradition, three of the characteristics of what Bell terms "ritualization" (1992: 212).

In the activity at hand, deciding who should benefit from the merit of the sutra leads to other related questions. What if one were asked to transfer merit to the so-called terrorists around the world who, for one self-righteous reason or another, have become the new enemies of Western civilization, religion, and progress? They are ignorant of the harmful consequences of their actions and so, it might be reasoned, need our spiritual assistance in gaining compassion and insight. What about sex offenders, corporate criminals, or other reviled individuals who have harmed countless people and been condemned by society? If the merit of a sutra is to reach and transform those who suffer or who are responsible for causing suffering, then why not reach out to individuals whose activities could be said to minimize suffering because they benefit, enable, and sustain our current way of life? Like the patrons of Buddhism in earlier times, that line of thinking would qualify as recipients of merit key executives from computer and software corporations, oil, automobile, and airline companies, bank presidents, media CEOs, and so on. Shouldn't Buddhists desire that all these systems continue to function smoothly, given that massive suffering would result were they to fail?

Students see very quickly that sutra chanting, like prayer, can be used to promote certain political causes as well as imbue these causes with an aura of legitimacy. Buddhist priests and monks the world over operate through institutional and organizational hierarchies, in which the relationship between junior and senior is formalized and traditional. Having faith and trust in one's superiors—who, one believes, are at an advanced stage of spiritual development—is fundamental to institutionalized Buddhist practice. If the senior monk within a temple or monastery is instructed by the abbot to henceforth include merit-generating sutras on behalf of a particular family or organization, he has little recourse but to do as he is told. In turn, the more junior monks will not question the senior monk's directive because they know it does not originate with him. It is also important to remember that unlike Christian, Judaic, or Islamic prayer—in which the agency of God makes things happen—in Buddhism, merit originates from individual effort. Since merit is generated by the *correct* articulation of the sutras, one can easily imagine subversive monks merely going through the motions, mumbling, or otherwise dulling the efficacy of the prayer. By now, it should be evident how one high-ranking priest can influence an entire institution on key political or social issues. Rituals such as sutra recitation help provide expressive venues and the authority sustaining them, through which this focusing can occur.[2]

Conclusion

We've seen how two examples from Japan's main religious traditions can provide lessons about the authority that structures ritual performance and determines who receives the ritual's intended blessings. Because ritual privileges action and builds consensus through expression instead of explanation, a flow of symbols, gestures, ceremonies, and drama create a seductive presence that crowds out analysis. Put another way, the characteristics of ritualizing activities combine to build a persuasive momentum that can be coercive, emotional, and empowering, but is always a moving target for any real-time assessment. Think for a moment of a presidential inauguration (or funeral), memorial services for victims of 9/11, state funerals, the pledge of allegiance, university graduations, or any other ceremony conducted on a public stage. As numerous authors have noted, ritual serves political power well by producing, as David Kertzer puts it, "bonds of solidarity without requiring uniformity of belief" (1988: 67). Issues that might provoke controversy, conflict, or anxiety can be wrapped within the guise of an activity whose themes highlight reassurance and unity.

After studying and experiencing ritual authority within Japanese religious contexts, students may have new tools for unraveling densely complex events, even those that occurred on September 11, 2001. I've received a number of papers on how the World Trade Center site quickly became a sacred space, with its own rituals and ceremonies for honoring and removing different categories of victims (firefighters, police, civilians). Some papers have shown how, as the nation mourned and tried to recover from the shock of this day, only certain articulations of order—similar in some ways to the orderings of ritual—were found to be culturally acceptable. The ritualizing strategies that depend on order (formality, traditionalism, invariance, and of course strategic empowerment and authority) help explain the symbolic surge of flags, patriotic slogans, normative values, national myths, and religious language asking God's blessing on America.

Studying the consensual and coercive dimensions of ritual has aided another part of 9/11 analysis evidenced in student papers. They argue that understanding why and how the attacks took place was delayed because of the political and religious emphasis on unity. Few people in the mainstream media or government were ready to look beyond the ideology of crisis and inquire about failures of domestic security, or question U.S. foreign policy in the Middle East as fostering conditions out of which extremism would emerge. Questions of a theological nature were equally unwelcome, especially regarding why God would bless one country and not another, or why an American, evangelical version of God privileged a selective morality of a good "us" against an evil "them."

At the risk of sounding naïve or overly idealistic, I believe that teaching ritual can help prepare students to better understand some of the most dynamic situations of our complex world. Examples taken from contemporary, historical, and ethnographic sources provide detailed insights on how politicians frequently appropriate and even hijack religious and ritual traditions (as was the case in Japan leading to World War II) to better carry out their agendas. Many students see an immediate relevance and application of this information for the post–9/11 world. Because they have experienced through structured classroom activities how ritual participation requires submission to various kinds of authority, they may also develop a critical awareness of situations in which consensus rather than individual expression is privileged. If we can foster through our teaching even a few of these perceptual breakthroughs, we will have made a small contribution to enhancing social justice and civic responsibility.

NOTES

1. Morinaga's account of becoming a Zen priest is one of the most instructive and poignant essays on the subject. He pulls no punches in educating readers about the ordeals he endured, made all the more trying by his stubbornness. Students are amused by his initial errors and lack of understanding, but the quote above, coupled with some kind of ritual activity (especially meditation), usually checks their feelings of superiority and problematizes their own sense of self-control. (See Morinaga 1988: 27.)

2. Although some scholars consider the complicity of Japanese Buddhist institutions and leaders with military agendas during World War II an exception rather than the rule, it is an instructive example that illustrates dramatically how religion can serve political ends. Priests from Zen, Pure Land, True Pure Land, Nichiren, Shingon, Tendai, and other sects actively aided and abetted the invasion and occupation of foreign countries under the aegis of a divinely instilled "Japanese spirit" that was to serve as the guiding light of a revitalized Asian civilization. Priests served near the front lines as counselors and missionaries, advised military leaders (as they have always done in Japan), and, along with Buddhist scholars at leading universities, compiled voluminous justifications about the important role of Buddhism in promoting the emperor's wars and advancing what they saw as the nation's divine destiny (see Ives 1999).

REFERENCES

Bell, Catherine. 1992. *Ritual Theory, Ritual Practice*. Oxford: Oxford University Press.
———. 1997. *Ritual: Perspectives and Dimensions*. New York: Oxford University Press.
Ives, Chris. 1999. "The Mobilization of Doctrine: Buddhist Contributions to Imperial Ideology in Modern Japan." *Japanese Journal of Religious Studies* 26 (spring): 83–106.
Kertzer, David. 1988. *Ritual, Politics and Power*. New Haven, Conn.: Yale University Press.
Morinaga, Sogo. 1988. "My Struggle to Become a Zen Monk." In *Zen: Tradition and Transition* ed. K. Kraft, 13–29. New York: Grove Press.
Nelson, John. 1996. *A Year in the Life of a Shinto Shrine*. Seattle: University of Washington Press.
Smith, Jean, ed. 1999. *Radiant Mind*. New York: Riverhead Books.

8

The Camp Meeting and the Paradoxes of Evangelical Protestant Ritual

Ann Taves

The discussion of ritual in Protestant contexts raises some peculiar questions for ritual studies because the value of ritual, understood in the traditional Christian sense, has been contested within Protestantism. Though ritual was explicitly rejected by many Protestant traditions as "dead formalism," Protestants nonetheless engaged in practices that scholars would typically describe as rituals. This raises the question of how we might best understand ritual-like practices in the context of "anti-ritualistic" traditions. Posing this question provides students with an opportunity to reflect on indigenous and scholarly definitions of ritual, critique the scholarly presuppositions that have informed traditional approaches to ritual studies, and test more recent approaches to ritual using Protestant sources.

To get at these issues, I would work with a ritualized Protestant practice, such as the camp meeting, assigning students historical documents related to the camp meeting and secondary readings from the scholarly literature on ritual. I would alert students from the outset that key terms such as "ritual" and "formalism" have different meanings in the indigenous and scholarly contexts, and I would set them to exploring the gap and its implications. I would begin by having students analyze a narrative account of a camp meeting and texts that illuminate the indigenous polemic that swirled around the camp meeting. Having surfaced the antiritual polemic embedded in the camp-meeting tradition, I would have them consider camp meetings as "ritual-like activities" using the criteria laid out by Catherine Bell (formalism, traditionalism, invariance, rule governance, sacral symbolism, and performance).

Finally, I would have the students revisit the dichotomy between ritual and experience upon which this type of antiritualism is premised and consider whether the hostilities between "formalists" and "enthusiasts" might not be more adequately conceived from a scholarly perspective as conflict between two "modes of religiosity" (Whitehouse 2004), both of which can be understood to involve ritual and experience, albeit of different sorts.

Though I have used the camp-meeting material in a variety of courses, I have not framed it in relation to ritual studies per se. In large part, this was because of the embedded antiritualist polemic, which I have not wanted to obscure by redescribing the camp meeting as ritual. I have, however, discussed camp meetings in the context of a course on religious practices. I find the recent shift to a practice-centered approach, which forgoes universalistic definitions of ritual, much more congenial to the analysis of ritualized practices in overtly antiritualistic traditions. This approach, however, is insufficient if it allows us to consider such "antirituals" in isolation from the rituals they are critiquing. A modified version of Whitehouse's modes of religiosity that allows us theorize the interplay between more and less formally ritualized practices in the internal life of a tradition provides a framework for situating antiritual polemic and overcoming the traditional dichotomy between ritual and experience.

Background

The Protestant polemic against ritual was premised on a sharp distinction between ritual (understood as liturgy or rite) and faith (understood in terms of belief and/or experience). While Lutherans and many Reformed Protestants stressed the importance of belief (faith) over ritual (works), other Protestants stressed the importance of an experience of faith, which they typically attributed to the action of the Holy Spirit. Such Protestants, labeled as "enthusiasts" by their critics, valorized religious experience at the expense of ritual, argued for the necessity of an experience of "the new birth" or conversion, and disparaged those who were initiated into the tradition by ritual means alone (e.g., the sacrament of baptism) as mere formalists. The experiential critique of ritual was embraced most fully by the radical seventeenth-century Puritans; by Pietists, Methodists, and other revival-oriented Protestants during the eighteenth and nineteenth centuries; and by twentieth-century Pentecostals, charismatics, and most born-again (modern-day evangelical) Christians.

The experiential critique stands in contrast to the liturgical and sacramental understanding of ritual promoted by the Eastern Orthodox, Roman Catholic, Anglican, and (some) Lutheran traditions. In these traditions, ritual and experience were not sharply dichotomized. Ritual was viewed as efficacious (rather than superstitious or magical); the sacred was believed to be really and paradigmatically present in the sacraments (the ritual was not viewed as "empty"); and spiritual development was a matter of growth in community rather than marked by a specific "event."

Despite their polemic against ritual, experientially oriented Protestants developed any number of practices that they hoped would increase the likelihood that conversions would occur. In the early seventeenth century, New England Congregationalists noted the recurrence of "seasons of grace" in which numerous persons experienced conversion, prayed for them to recur, and, when they did, took to calling them "revivals of religion" (Crawford 1991). In the eighteenth century, Presbyterians gathered for "sacramental occasions," Baptists for "big meetings," and Methodists for "quarterly conferences" (Schmidt 1990; Richey 1991). During the early years of the nineteenth century, these gatherings coalesced to form the "camp meeting," a temporary gathering in a designated location where many preachers preached and many listeners experienced conversion over a period of several days. In the early nineteenth century, Charles Finney devised methods for promoting revivals of religion in urban areas. Within a Protestant vernacular, these various types of meetings (whether seemingly spontaneous or carefully planned) were not understood as rituals, though they may have included a ritual such as Communion (McLoughlin 1959). Revival-oriented Protestants might well have acknowledged that these occasions did become highly ritualized over time, but such an acknowledgment would most likely have carried negative connotations and thus preserved the underlying dichotomy between ritual and (authentic or pure) experience.

The dichotomies between faith and works, belief and practice, and experience and ritual that informed the Protestant break with and polemics against Catholicism are mirrored in much of the scholarly literature on ritual (Smith 1987: 96–103; Bell 1997: 80–81). Because the oppositions embedded in the scholarly definitions parallel the dichotomies inherent in the Protestant attack on ritual, and in some instances are clearly derived from them, subsuming antiritualistic Protestant practices, such as camp meetings and revivals, under the rubric of rituals not only sounds oxymoronic to Protestants and scholars of Protestantism but, more important, obscures the indigenous antiritual polemic embedded in the practices themselves. The shift from a focus on ritual, universally defined, to a focus on ritualized practices and the process of ritualization, as proposed by Catherine Bell (1997: 80–83), provides a means of undercutting both the oppositions embedded in universalistic definitions of ritual and traditional Protestant polemic. Most important, this shift allows us to move away from a reified understanding of ritual as historically decontextualized "rite" to the analysis of features, which we as scholars associate with ritual, along a series of historically embedded continua. Finally, the historical recontextualization of ritual allows us to make a clear distinction between what we, in our context, and our sources, in theirs, mean or meant by ritual and allows us to move between the two points of view.

Introducing the Camp Meeting

Though references to "camp meetings" are rare before 1800, large outdoor gatherings of various sorts were common in a number of Protestant traditions during the late eighteenth century. The three most important were the Presbyterian sacramental meetings, the Methodist quarterly conferences, and the Baptist "big" or "great" meetings. The earliest camp meetings were cooperative ventures undertaken among Methodists, Presbyterians, Baptists, and others, but the cooperative arrangements soon broke down and they became largely Methodist affairs (Richey 1991: 21–32; Johnson 1985: 50–51).

Methodists of various sorts wrote of their experiences at early-nineteenth-century camp meetings. I regularly use the descriptions contained in the memoirs of Zilpha Elaw to introduce students to the camp meeting. Elaw was a free woman of color from the Philadelphia area, who eventually became an unofficial Methodist preacher. She had a conversion experience and joined a local Methodist Episcopal society in 1808, after which she began attending camp meetings. She describes in detail two camp meetings in her memoirs; both were held in New Jersey, one in 1817 and the other in 1821. At the first, she experienced what Methodists referred to as "sanctification" and at the second, she received "a call to preach."

Elaw provided extended descriptions of the way space and time were typically organized at such meetings. With respect to space, she said: "A large circular inclosure [sic] of brushwood is formed; immediately inside of which the tents are pitched, and the space in the centre is appropriated to the worship of God, the minister's stand being on one side, and generally on a somewhat rising ground." She describes the physical layout of the camp, the nature of the seating, and the way that fires, lamps, and candles were used to illuminate the camp at night. Camp meetings, both in the North and the South, were interracial events. How relations between the races were configured spatially seems to have varied. Although many camp meetings separated blacks and whites, Elaw does not give the impression that she as a free black woman was encamped or seated in a distinctive space. The only seating she mentioned (and she was seated) was located "in the space before the platform" (Elaw 1986: 65).

Elaw's description of the way time was structured at the meeting was more elaborate than most, though she and others agree on the basic format. At dawn, a person walked around the camp blowing a trumpet to awaken the people. Shortly thereafter, people began to sing and then prayed in or near their tents. As the sun rose, a sermon was preached, followed by breakfast. Preaching resumed again about 10 o'clock, followed by a midday meal. There was more preaching in the middle of the afternoon, supper at sunset, and more preaching after supper by candlelight. The meetings typically took place over a weekend and lasted several days. Elaw infused her account of these activities with biblical allusions. The persons who awakened the people with trumpets were described as "watchmen [who] proceed round the inclosure, blowing with trumpets to awaken every inhabitant of this City of the Lord." When preaching began at 10 A.M.:

> The trumpets sound again to summon the people to public worship; the seats are all speedily filled and as perfect a silence reigns throughout the place as in a Church or Chapel; presently the high praises of God sound melodiously from this consecrated spot, and nothing seems wanting but local elevation to render the place a heaven indeed. It is like God's ancient and holy hill of Zion on her brightest festival days, when the priests conducted the processions of the people to the glorious temple of Jehovah. (Elaw 1986: 65–66)

The richness of Elaw's description allows students to explore how camp meeting participants steeped in the Bible would have understood the event. Using a King James Bible and a concordance, students can use Elaw's text to analyze the layout and the practices associated with the camp meeting in relation to the biblical account of the Israelites encamped with the tabernacle in the wilderness, the temple in Jerusalem, and the land of Zion. After introducing the concept of typological exegesis, which illuminates how later (Christian) readers read themselves back into earlier (Jewish) texts, students are able to see how participants in the camp meetings were using traditional means (reading themselves back into the biblical texts) to literally and figuratively construct a new religious practice (the camp meeting). (On typology, see Bercovitch 1972: 3–46; Landow 1980: 1–64; Cherry 1980: 14–25.)

To illustrate the typological relationship between the camp and Zion, I have students examine the practices associated with circling the camp. When Zipha Elaw described the trumpet blower as a "watchman," who "proceed[s] round the inclosure, blowing with trumpets to awaken every inhabitant of this City of the Lord," she not only sacralized the wakeup call, but sacralized the camp as the "City of the Lord" (Elaw 1986: 65). As depicted in Ezek. 33: 1–3, it was the duty of Zion's watchman to watch for the coming of the sword of the Lord and notify the people so that they might repent. Elaw wrote that on the last morning of the camp meeting, ministers "form[ed] themselves in procession and march[ed] round the encampment; the people falling into rank and following them." After circling the camp a number of times, "the ministers turn aside from the rank, stand still, and commence singing a solemn farewell hymn; and as the different ranks of the people march by, they shake hands with their pastors, take an affectionate farewell of them, and pass on in procession, until the last or rear rank have taken their adieu" (Elaw 1986: 65–66). Collections of nineteenth-century "shape note" songs include such songs as "Zion's Walls" and "Heavenly King," which were likely sung by ministers and people as they marched around the encampment (Taves 1999: 116).

Ritual and Experience: The Polemics of Formalism and Enthusiasm

Though to a twenty-first century scholar, the camp meeting may seem an obvious example of a ritual or at least a ritualized event, I would pause before discussing the camp meeting as ritual to re-embed these meetings in the polemics of "formalism" and "enthusiasm" that surrounded them in the early nineteenth century. Two texts are particularly helpful in this regard: John Fanning Watson's *Methodist Error; or, Friendly Christian advice to those Methodists who indulge in extravagant emotions and bodily exercises* (1814); and the camp meeting song "The Methodist and the Formalist." Both claim the mantle of "true Methodism," while at the same time seeking to discredit the other. "Methodist Error" depicts the camp meetings as occasions for "enthusiasm"; "The Methodist and the Formalist" characterizes those who condemned the meetings as "formalists" (Taves 1999: 111–114).

In *Methodist Error*, Watson emphasized that he was not opposed to "extravagant emotions" or "bodily exercises," such as fainting, crying out, or shouting, when they took place in private. He objected to such expressions when they took place in the context of public worship, whether in church or at a camp meeting. George Roberts, a Methodist preacher, put the matter more plainly when he stressed that what reformers found most offensive about this new style of worship was not "the involuntary loud hosannas of ... pious souls, [but] ... forming jumping, dancing, shouting, & c. into a *system*, and pushing our social exercises into these extremes" (quoted in Taves 1999: 78). The problem, from Roberts's perspective, was not with isolated spontaneous expressions of feeling, but with the systemization or, in contemporary language, the *ritualization* of emotion and bodily action. Watson discussed this process in terms of the formation of habits and marked the habits he deplored in terms of class and race. Thus, he wrote, those who "learn a *habit* of vehemence [are] ... mostly persons of credulous, *uninformed* minds; who, before their change to grace had been of rude education, and careless of those prescribed forms of good manners and refinement, of which polite education is never divested—and which, indeed, religion ought to cherish. They fancy that all the restraints of conduct, viz. 'sobriety, gravity and blamelessness,' is a formality and resistance of the Spirit;—and so to avoid it, they seem rather to go to the other extreme, and actually run before it" (quoted in Taves 1999: 77).

I would have students note the sharp opposition between the "habits of vehemence" that Watson deplored, on the one hand, and the "restraints of conduct" that he advocated, on the other. Watson explicitly framed these "habits of vehemence" as "enthusiasm" and linked his condemnation of enthusiasm with the condemnations of enthusiasm made by Protestant luminaries from John Wesley to John Locke. Watson acknowledged, however, that his opponents viewed the situation very differently. They viewed sobriety and restraint as "formality and resistance of the Spirit." Rather than avoiding the behaviors to which he objected, they actually encouraged them as manifestations of the Spirit (Taves 1999: 76).

Singing was a primary point of contention in the controversy. Watson was particularly critical of the new spiritual songs sung at camp meetings because they fostered, indeed infused, the habits of vehemence he decried. Watson provides firsthand descriptions of the way that these new spiritual songs were improvised in the context of camp meetings. They were, he said, *"merry* airs, adapted from old *songs,* to hymns of our composing: often miserable as poetry, and senseless as matter, and most frequently composed and first sung by the illiterate *blacks* of our society." The songs aroused feelings that were often expressed in movement, sometimes with all the "precision of an avowed *dancer."* Those who attended the early camp meetings often stayed up all night, he said, "after the public devotions had closed... singing tune after tune... scarce one of which were in our hymn books" (quoted in Taves 1999: 109–110). Those Watson condemned referred to themselves as "shouting Methodists" or simply as "Methodists" and undoubtedly were among those responsible for the many camp meeting songs that were later set down in shape note songbooks and collections of white and black spirituals. Among the songs that have come down to us from the early nineteenth century, there is one titled simply "The Methodist." From it we learn not only that Wesley's followers in America were "despised... because they shout and preach so plain," but also that they proudly referred to themselves as "shouting Methodists" (Taves 1999: 76–77).

"The Methodist and a Formalist" was the shouting Methodists' answer to John Fanning Watson. Sung at camp meetings with verses alternating between the "Methodist" and the "Formalist," it reenacted an alleged formalist's visit to a Methodist camp meeting. The song contrasts the burning desire of the true Methodist longing for Zion with the curious formalist who, in contemporary terms, was just checking out the scene. The formalist reveals that he was offended by the "groaning and shouting," distracted by the cacophony of sound, and unable to pray. As the dialogue unfolds, the Methodist and the formalist debate the nature of true religion and its scriptural basis. The formalist is ultimately overcome by the Spirit and winds up "rolling prostrate on the ground," filled with the love of God. "The Methodist and the Formalist" provides our fullest surviving articulation of the theology of the shout tradition and, indeed, was a direct theological response (or provocation) to *Methodist Error.* In many ways a study in contrasts, both claimed the mantle of authentic

Methodism and both devoted much attention to Scripture. Though both readings of Scripture were infused with the presuppositions of their respective traditions—"enthusiastic" and "enlightened"—their respective depictions of the scriptural passages that informed the shout tradition were largely in agreement (Taves 1999: 109–116).

The Camp Meeting as a Ritual-Like Activity

Of the six characteristics of ritual-like activities identified by Catherine Bell— invariance, rule-governance, performance, sacred symbolism, traditionalism, and formalism—sacred symbolism is the one most obviously evident in the case of the camp meeting. Formalism, at least on the surface, is the least evident. The others are all present to some degree.

I begin with *sacred symbolism*. Bell indicates that symbols take on ritual-like attributes when they do two things: "differentiate some places from others by means of distinctive acts and responses" and "evoke experiences of a greater, higher, or more universalized reality" (1997: 259). As a biblical "type" or, more broadly, a symbol of Zion, the camp meeting did both these things. Understood as the holy land, as Zion, and as heaven here below, participants clearly viewed the camp meeting as set apart from ordinary places in both space and time. Ritualized actions, such as the watchman circling the camp and blowing the trumpet, the rising ground under the preachers' stand, and the parting ceremony in which preachers and people circled the camp in farewell, all signaled the special nature of the meeting. The biblical allusions to the holy city of Jerusalem and the temple as the site where God dwells, which infused these ritual actions, evoked experiences of a greater, higher, and more universalized reality.

The characteristics of *invariance* and *rule-governance* are somewhat more complex. Participants and supporters clearly viewed camp meetings as having a recognizable rule-governed organizational structure. Though the structure was not invariant—examination of accounts suggest that they differed in various ways from time to time and place to place—it was critics, such as John Fanning Watson, who were most likely to see the camp meeting as disordered and chaotic. Watson, who was largely oblivious to the spatial and temporal structures described by the meetings' proponents, focused instead on what he viewed as the chaotic welter of emotion that arose in the context of the camp meeting.

Bell characterizes *performances* as multifaceted sensory experiences that create a sense of condensed totality and cognitively order the world. Camp meetings were performances in that sense. Anthropologists, however, borrowed the language of performance from the theater, in which context, in the popular mind at any rate, performance still carries the connotation of agency and control. Events that occur on stage are the controlled result of intentional voluntary acts. Both critics and supporters of camp meetings viewed the emotional aspects of the meeting as largely uncontrolled. Supporters viewed the experiences of conversion, sanctification, and calling associated with the camp meetings as uncontrolled because they were, in their view, acts of the Holy Spirit. Although the Holy Spirit responded to prayer and petition, it was not, in the participants' view, subject to human control, and neither the Holy Spirit nor its devotees were thought of as performers. In the eyes of participants, the camp meeting and the theater were worlds apart. Nonetheless, critics watched like hawks for evidence that participants were merely performing. A friend of John Fanning Watson's observed with satisfaction how people ostensibly struck down by the power of the Spirit immediately rose from the ground and proceeded to their seats when the trumpet blew for preaching (Taves 1999: 99).

With respect to *tradition*, the evidence is also mixed. The camp meeting drew upon the tradition of field preaching for conversion inaugurated by John Wesley and George Whitefield in England and disseminated by Whitefield throughout the American colonies. As a large outdoor gathering, the camp meeting had precursors in the sacramental meetings, big meetings, and quarterly conferences of various Protestant traditions. It drew upon standard biblical tropes and methods of devotional reading. Nonetheless, the camp meeting qua camp meeting was viewed then and now as an early-nineteenth-century invention. The sense that the camp meeting (and the outdoor preaching services from which it derived) broke with the traditional church service marked it as *both* antitraditional *and* special. In a context in which church services were viewed as traditional and routine, the camp meeting was marked as special precisely because it broke with tradition.

Given the indigenous Methodist polemic against *formalism*, this aspect of ritualization should be considered most carefully. Bell illustrates this aspect of ritualization in terms of the differences between formal oratory and informal speech. Given the prominence of preaching at camp meetings, students could be asked to consider the camp meeting in relation to occasions ranging from (on one extreme) the read sermon in the context of a highly formalized liturgy to (on the other extreme) the impromptu street sermon addressed to passersby. On such a spectrum, the camp meeting falls somewhere in the middle. Sermons, which were delivered orally rather than read, struck a balance between convention and spontaneity. The preaching was enough like formal oratory that those who publicly challenged the proceedings were typically portrayed as disruptive hecklers. It was informal enough that, at least in the early years, the spontaneous, seemingly involuntary shouts and groans of the devout were encouraged by some and tolerated by others. Camp meetings can be understood as "semiformal" in other respects as well. The setting, for example, might be construed as semiformal because of its conventionalized layout and its impermanent, outdoor setting. Time, too, was a mix of the formal and informal. The day was carefully ordered, but not all blocks of time were devoted to structured activities, thus creating space for spontaneity, improvisation, and, as believers would have it, the action of the Holy Spirit.

Although these characteristics allow us to locate the camp meeting relative to certain characteristics commonly attributed to ritual, establishing that the camp meeting was indeed "ritual-like" according to certain criteria does not provide an adequate framework for understanding the camp meeting in the context of the polemic between formalism and enthusiasm. As a final task, I would have students wrestle with the problem of contextualization with particular attention to two issues. First, the analysis of a singular practice, such as the camp meeting, in light of a set of criteria leaves us with the impression that we can understand the camp meeting as a thing-in-itself. If the controversy between "formalists" and "enthusiasts" tells us anything, it signals that the camp meeting cannot be understood apart from the "formalism" against which it was a protest. To gain a clearer perspective on the camp meeting, we need an approach that does not view the camp meeting as a ritual-like activity unto itself, but as a ritual-like activity that stands in relation to other activities— most notably, the Sunday worship service. Second, the six attributes, with their emphasis on rules, invariance, tradition, performance, and formalism, tend to reproduce the traditional Protestant distinction between ritual and experience. To gain a clearer perspective on the camp meeting, we also need an approach that undercuts the opposition between ritual and experience.

Ritual and Experience Reconsidered: Formalism and Enthusiasm as Two Modes of Religiosity

As an alternative to traditional approaches to contextualization, I would have students read chapters 4 and 6 of Harvey Whitehouse's *Modes of Religiosity* (2004). I would ask them to consider the thesis that Whitehouse's theory of religious transmission effectively undercuts the opposition between ritual and experience by reframing formalism and enthusiasm as two competing modes of religiosity, doctrinal and imagistic, each with its own distinctive emphasis in terms of ritual and experience. The thesis can be broken down into two claims: (1) that Whitehouse's two modes each have their own distinctive emphases in terms of ritual and experience, and (2) that formalism and enthusiasm correlate with Whitehouse's two modes. The first claim is relatively easy to defend; the second leads students into current discussion of Whitehouse's theory among scholars.

In Whitehouse's framework, the doctrinal and imagistic modes are not correlated with ritual and experience. Rather, because rituals are frequent in the doctrinal mode and infrequent in the imagistic mode, experience takes a different form in each. In the doctrinal mode, in which rituals are regularly repeated, the level of emotional arousal is low, and much of the cognitive processing of the rituals takes place in implicit memory—that is, through processes independent of conscious thought or control. The chief experiential danger in the doctrinal mode is tedium and the resulting sense of simply going through the motions (Whitehouse 2004: 65–70). This seems to provide a fairly apt description of what "enthusiasts" referred to as "formalism." In the imagistic mode, in which rituals are infrequent, the level of emotional arousal associated with ritual is high, and episodic or "flashbulb" memory is engaged, such that participants remember the particulars of these infrequent rituals in vivid detail. These infrequently performed rituals trigger "spontaneous exegetical reflections" that are "often experienced as personal inspiration or revelation" (Whitehouse 2004: 70–74). On the surface, anyway, this is very suggestive. The Methodist movement within the early-eighteenth-century Church of England and camp meetings within early-nineteenth-century American Methodism can both be interpreted as providing highly arousing rituals at infrequent intervals. In both instances, high-stakes preaching for conversion by itinerant preachers at large outdoor events (infrequent rituals) led to episodic (and thus more vivid) memories and spontaneous exegetical reflection (on intensely felt experiences).

Whitehouse positions the two modes dichotomously and defines each mode in terms of a series of mutually reinforcing attributes. Students, like the scholars who debate Whitehouse's theory, might struggle with this feature of the theory and question whether the camp meeting fits neatly into Whitehouse's description of the imagistic mode. The underlying problem, Ilkka Pyysiäinen suggests, is that the Protestant conversion experience exhibits elements of both modes. Thus, Pyysiäinen (2005) argues:

> Although conversion is a phenomenon that typically happens in
> a doctrinal context, it is nevertheless a phenomenon that does not
> quite fit with Whitehouse's description of the doctrinal ideal type. It
> is a sort of imagism with doctrinality: the psychological variables have
> an imagistic content, while the social variables have a doctrinal
> content. (160)

Cognizant of the mixed character of most actual religious phenomena, Pyysiäinen refers to phenomena as more or less imagistic or doctrinal and suggests that phenomena of both types can be found within stable traditions. In such contexts, they tend to perform different functions: "Imagistic-like phenomena provide individual motivation while doctrinal-type phenomena offer systems-level tools for the preservation of stable traditions" (160).

Instead of dichotomizing the imagistic and doctrinal modes, Pyysiäinen argues that imagistically oriented revival movements play an important role *within* doctrinal traditions:

> Doctrinal religiosity develops slowly but has strong staying power: revivalism does not undermine doctrinal religiosity but supports it. Conversions are reactions to inherent problems in doctrinal religiosity; they derive their motivational power from imagistic-like phenomena but combine them with elements of doctrinality. The important thing is that one experiences an intimate connection with some counterintuitive agent. Episodic memories of conversion experiences are then always activated when a doctrinal summary is activated. (161–162)

Interpreted this way, we can view the camp meeting as existing in a dynamic and creative tension with an increasingly formalized Methodist Sunday service, just as the Methodist movement as a whole originally existed in a dynamic and creative tension with the Church of England. "Formalism" and "enthusiasm" were the epithets that Anglicans and Methodists used to characterize the doctrinal and imagistic poles within their tradition. Though these indigenous terms set ritual and experience in opposition, Whitehead's distinction between doctrinal and imagistic modes of religious transmission, as modified by Pyysiäinen, provides a more adequate framework for analyzing the relationship between ritual and experience in various contexts within a tradition.

USEFUL MATERIALS

"The Methodist and the Formalist" (originally published in the *Hesperian Harp*, comp. William Hauser [Philadelphia, 1848]) in Johnson 1985: 262–264 and available on the web at http://www.thunderstruck.org/revivalflames/SHOUT2.htm.

Ruth, Lester. 2005. *Early Methodist Life and Spirituality: A Reader*. Nashville, Tenn.: Kingswood Press.

Social Harp (Early American Shape Note Songs). Rounder Select, 1990. This collection contains "Zion's Walls" and "Heavenly King," mentioned in the text.

Watson, John Fanning. 1814. *Methodist Error*. Philadelphia. This text is difficult to acquire, but excerpts appear in Taves 1999, 76–117.

REFERENCES

Bell, Catherine. 1997. *Ritual: Perspectives and Dimensions*. New York: Oxford University Press.

Bercovitch, Sacvan, ed. 1972. *Typology and Early American Literature*. Amherst: University of Massachusetts Press.

Cherry, Conrad. 1980. *Nature and Religious Imagination from Edwards to Bushnell*. Philadelphia: Fortress Press.

Crawford, Michael. 1991. *Seasons of Grace: Colonial New England's Revival Tradition in Its British Context*. New York: Oxford University Press.

Elaw, Zilpha. 1986. "Memoirs of the Life, Religious Experience, Ministerial Labors of Mrs. Zilpha Elaw." In *Sisters of the Spirit*, ed. William L. Andrews, 49–160. Bloomington: Indiana University Press.

Johnson, Charles A. 1985. *The Frontier Camp Meeting: Religion's Harvest Time*. 2nd ed. Dallas, Tex.: Southern Methodist University Press.

Landow, George P. 1980. *Victorian Shadows, Victorian Types: Biblical Typology in Victorian Literature, Art, and Thought*. Boston: Routledge & Kegan Paul.

McLoughlin, William. 1959. *Modern Revivalism: Charles Grandison Finney to Billy Graham*. New York: Ronald Press.

Pyysiäinen, Ilkka. 2005. "Religious Conversion and Modes of Religiosity." In *Mind and Religion: Psychological and Cognitive Foundations of Religiosity*, ed. Harvey Whitehouse and Robert N. McCauley, 149–166. Walnut Creek, Calif.: AltaMira Press.

Richey, Russell. 1991. *Early American Methodism*. Bloomington: Indiana University Press.

Ruth, Lester. 2000. *A Little Heaven Below: Worship at Early Methodist Quarterly Meetings*. Nashville, Tenn.: Abingdon.

Schmidt, Leigh. 1990. *Holy Fairs: Scottish Communions and American Revivals in the Early Modern Period*. Princeton, N.J.: Princeton University Press.

Smith, Jonathan Z. 1987. *To Take Place: Toward Theory in Ritual*. Chicago: University of Chicago Press.

Taves, Ann. 1999. *Fits, Trances, and Visions: Experiencing Religion and Explaining Experience from Wesley to James*. Princeton, N.J.: Princeton University Press.

Whitehouse, Harvey. 2004. *Modes of Religiosity: A Cognitive Theory of Religious Transmission*. Walnut Creek, Calif.: AltaMira Press.

9

Ritual from Five Angles:
A Tool for Teaching

Andrew Strathern and Pamela J. Stewart

Ritual is a complex concept that provides both challenges and opportunities in teaching. It can be compared to the topic of kinship:
though general definitions of kinship have been sought in vain, the
term "kinship" immediately resonates in a meaningful way with
every student. This is true for ritual as well. Even if the definitional
debates are interminable, the topic is easily recognizable to students, and everyone can say something about it. In both cases,
therefore, one teaching strategy is to ask for "folk" definitions
from students themselves and then have them explore the interesting discrepancies that emerge.

Since its inception in 1987, *The Journal of Ritual Studies,* which
we co-edit, has published many seminal articles on the definition,
recognition, and interpretation of ritual practices. The *Journal*'s approach has been interdisciplinary from the start, enriching the scope
of contributions and broadening the base of conversations about
theory. Indeed, its corpus of contributions can be a useful resource
for teaching ritual, and this chapter would like to demonstrate how
this potential can be realized, using just five articles from recent
issues analyzed in the manner of a graduate or upper-level
undergraduate class.

The five articles we have chosen for this task all consider current
themes in religious studies, ritual studies, and anthropological
studies: the local and the global; ritual and invention; performance
and performativity; embodiment and communication; and ritual
and human consciousness. The last theme here is perhaps the
broadest and relates directly to the long traditions of analysis of

ritual in Durkheimian terms. The first four obviously connect with special aspects of contemporary theorizing at large. Questions of the relationship between local and global, of performance and how meanings are communicated by it, of invention and improvisation, and of the special role of embodiment in processes of communication are characteristic of ritual analyses but are also found widely outside them. So the first teaching task in relation to these topics might be to show exactly how the study of ritual can be especially effective in looking at the broader settings of, say, analysis of the local and the global components of action. Second, we might ask how these articles work to illuminate their topics. And third, we might ask how they can be turned into effective teaching tools. The last question is less crucial for advanced levels of teaching, but even at these levels, students often ask questions such as "How does this impinge on *my* interests or *my* proposed dissertation topic?" and the only answer that can be given is to show how the student's own topic and those tackled in an article or book under consideration meet in some general arena of interpretive debate of a theoretical kind.

We will look at these questions in turn. First, however, we will give an account of the main lines of analysis in the articles themselves. The articles we have chosen are:

1. Frank Korom's "Reconciling the Local and the Global: The Ritual Space of Shi'i Islam in Trinidad" (13, 1 [1999]: 21–36).
2. Jone Salomonsen's "The Ethno-Methodology of Ritual Invention in Contemporary Culture—Two Pagan and Christian Cases" (17, 2 [2003]: 15–24).
3. Gavin Brown's "Theorizing Ritual as Performance: Explorations of Ritual Indeterminacy" (17, 1 [2004]: 3–18).
4. Michael S. Merrill's "Masks, Metaphor, and Transformation: The Communication of Belief in Ritual Performance" (18, 1 [2004]: 16–33).
5. C. Jason Throop and Charles D. Laughlin's "Ritual, Collective Effervescence, and the Categories: Toward a Neo-Durkheimian Model of the Nature of Human Consciousness, Feeling, and Understanding" (16, 1 [2002]: 40–63).

Synopses of the Articles

1. Frank Korom's article takes up, through ritual studies, a theme that has been classic in contemporary anthropology since the 1980s: the relationship between the local and the global. Like many authors since the work of Marcus and Fischer (1986), Korom uses the occasion of writing his article to critique the underlying concepts involved. After tracing an emphasis on "the local" to Kenneth Pike's emic/etic contrast and Clifford Geertz's "local knowledge"

concept, Korom notes that the idea of the local has itself been problematized by writers such as Arjun Appadurai and Ulf Hannerz, on the grounds that "the local" is not to be seen as bounded or monolithic. Rather, it is in a dynamic relation with other contexts; and so, moving quickly to ritual, "ritual loci may thus become sites of contestation where global concerns are debated and negotiated for political, economic, and ideological reasons" (21). Korom takes Islamic practices as his context for illustrating this proposition. Since Korom wrote his article, the political significance of the variations within Islam has become more acutely obvious in world affairs at large. In particular, the pressures exerted by "Islamist" elites from national centers on local, predominantly rural populations for whom Islamic practices have long been mingled with practices from other contexts have become more evident than before, as the struggle to create a transnational form of doctrinal Islam develops in dialectical opposition to "the West." Korom's own purpose is rooted in his studies in Trinidad. He aims to show how "one small community of Muslims on the island-nation of the Republic of Trinidad and Tobago creates its own peculiar brand of local knowledge through discourses concerning the ritual construction of space" (22). But he also, at the same time, wishes "to suggest some of the ways in which Trinidadian Shi'i Muslims theologically connect with their global brethren" (22).

On one hand, then, the study is about how a local population "adapts Islam" to its own purposes. On the other, it is about how, in doing so, the people connect themselves globally to other Shi'i Muslims. The same kinds of processes, we may note in passing, are likely to apply in other religious contexts, such as Christian ones.

In the Trinidad contexts, the adherents of Shi'a Muslim practices connect themselves during the ritual time known as Hosay "to a common core of worldwide practice" (24). Hosay refers to Hosayn/Husayn, the prophet Muhammad's grandson who was killed in Karbala, Iraq, in 680 C.E. Mourning for Hosayn is the central ritual act involved, and Hosayn's sufferings come to stand for the sufferings of local people who feel themselves to be abused and humiliated. Militant Muslims in Trinidad connect themselves to the revolution in Iran, Korom notes (25), via this notion of suffering. The idea of linkage or connection is expressed in the miniature mausoleum made for Hosayn with a cross-section of locally grown reeds binding it together at its center. The reed represents local values, but it binds the local to the global image of the mausoleum itself. In another sense, the adherents assert their difference from worshipers elsewhere, saying, "This is Trinidad, not Iran!" There is, therefore, an ongoing dialectic between the local and the global at work here. Ritual has a privileged, but not unique, place in this dialectic because it is a vehicle for overt, conscious local statements about identity, which people themselves conceptualize in relation to broader contexts.

2. Jone Salomonsen examines particular, local expressions of another global-ized ritual phenomenon, neopagan witchcraft, and conducts an internal com-parison with mystery rites for teens in the First Church of Christ, Connecticut. Consciousness is again to the fore here, because the ritualists involved ex-plicitly appropriate themes from the work of anthropologists and religious studies scholars. The overall theoretical message is that ritual knowledge is not essentialized but "is contextual and always in the making" (15), and the article focuses on the ethnomethodology whereby people actually undertake ritual inventions.

Salomonsen's first ethnographic case is on the Reclaiming community in San Francisco, which has a ritual conducted for the menarche of teenage girls, to "celebrate the girl's embodied way of being female as something essentially good and normal" (16). The blood of menstruation is celebrated as marking the girl's body as sacred rather than as a sign of impurity (see Stewart and Strathern 2002b for a comparative essay on the powers of menstrual fluids). The ritual for each girl is customized, and in one instance that the author observed, the circle of women who conducted the ritual "were inspired by various menstruation narratives and initiation themes from tribal cultures, in particular the Pueblos" (17). One part of the ritual for this girl was designed to "cut the cord" between the girl and her mother; another was to make her aware of the goddess figure central to neopaganism; a further part to re-introduce her as an adult into the community of women; and the remaining part was an exchange of gifts at which she "received a magical necklace from the community" (18) and announced her new name as Aurora (dawn). The ritual's structure consciously accorded to classic theories of initiation as ex-pressed by Van Gennep, but its specifics were all newly invented.

A similar drive to innovation within a broad framework is seen in the First Church of Christ rituals from New England, in which a minister of the church revived "what he felt was the lost rite of Christianity, that is, an initiation rite for young people . . . in a form similar to tribal societies. His sources were biblical literature . . . and extensive studies of Turner, van Gen-nep, Eliade, and Jung" (19). The initiation program he devised centered on "four thematic pillars: Society, Self, Sexuality, and Spirituality" (20). Rituals were used to *teach* the young people involved, with the aid of a "trance in-ductor," usually played by the minister himself.

In her conclusion, Salomonsen alludes to Fredrik Barth's (1990) dis-tinction between the guru and the conjurer, in which the guru imparts "radically decontextualized" knowledge, whereas the world of initiation is like that of the conjurer in which everything is "radically contextualized" or em-bodied in the specifics of a particular performance (23). Korom also stresses the particular, embodied form of knowledge encapsulated in the Trinidad Shi'a rituals he studied. Embodiment, performance, and improvisation are all linked together.

3. Gavin Brown's interest lies in conceptualizing ritual as performance. He explores the meaning of the term "performance" itself in this context. Brown starts from an observation by Catherine Bell that theorizing in ritual continues to draw on a "diverse heritage" of approaches (3). Accepting this as broadly accurate, he nevertheless suggests that the trend has been to concentrate on "what ritual intrinsically represents or achieves" (3) and that the term "performance" signals this trend.

Brown sees performance as a mode of human action that constitutes an event. Performance is connected to a script that designates how the action is to unfold. A performance therefore has to engage with variability and indeterminacy because the script is not always followed, as a result of human vagaries. Though a performance can follow its script, it may also displace it (5). Therefore there is a dynamism at work, through the creative tension between a script and its enactment. Brown notes Victor Turner's work on performance, in which Turner argued that performance may be not simply an expression of culture but an active agent of change. Brown concludes: "Performance is, therefore, fundamentally about transformation; it is dynamic cultural activity" (6).

Brown sees himself here as rehabilitating the idea of ritual from the pejorative perceptions of it that emerged over time in Europe, in which "ritual" was contrasted with "true religion," as a mere set of external forms. If we see ritual instead as performance, with creative capacities built into it, these pejorative perceptions, he says, are dispelled (8). He draws further on Victor Turner's (as well as Richard Schechner's) work here, citing Turner's use of the concept of "social drama." Turner's social dramas—sequences of action in which conflict is expressed and, if possible, resolved—can be seen as kinds of ritual performances, with all their capacities to effect change through processual mediations of social relationships. Meanings of ritual also emerge through performance, not just in the script. Indeterminacy may be found in the space of liminality, in Turner's terms, in which performers enter into a state of communitas, "a momentary suspension of normative social relations" (14). From the structuralist viewpoint of Turner's earlier work, this suspension was seen as being in the service of reestablishing the social order; but in his later work, he saw it as a reflexive act, collapsing the subject and object of performance and making the liminal space of performance an arena of indeterminacy, culture in the "subjunctive mood" (15). Similarly, scholars of ritual studies today, says Brown (citing, for example, Bell 1998), are taking a reflexive approach to their own work, interrogating "their own performances as ethnographers and academics" (15).

In his conclusion, Brown notes that although ritual is thought of as ordered and invariant, "the scholar finds that the condition of indeterminacy lies at the heart of ritual form" (16). Brown's article is a theoretical exercise, and he does not proceed to exemplify his argument with any detailed cases.

The next article in our series is also theoretically ambitious, but takes the ethnography of masking as its empirical arena of inquiry.

In terms of reflexivity, it is interesting to note that Gavin Brown was, at the time of publication of his article in the *Journal of Ritual Studies,* a doctoral candidate in the Department of History, University of Melbourne. His Ph.D. work, however, is listed as ethnographic, on ritual in Australian Catholic culture from 1901 to 1962 (18).

4. Michael Merrill's article is also concerned with experience and with how ritual actually works to create transformations. In particular he considers "the influence of altered states of consciousness induced during masking on the belief states of performers and participants" (16). The question of altered states of consciousness, classic to the analysis of ritual behavior, is also implicit in the first two articles, by Korom and Salomonsen. Merrill's article is an ambitious exercise undertaken to further the theorizing of practices of ritual masking in terms of notions of trance and spirit possession, seen as cross-cultural constants. Though the ideas in Korom's and Salomonsen's articles are readily absorbed, Merrill's article presents more challenges as it moves into hermeneutic, philosophical, and psychological realms. It does depend, however, on a classic Van Gennepian and Turnerian theme, that of liminality, and it offers a special definition of metaphor in line with the author's purpose: "Metaphor is the means to produce expanded consciousness" (17). He accordingly sees masks as "metaphoric archetypes" integrating creative personal endeavors with "institutionalized behavior" (17). Seeking to transcend semiotic approaches (such as those used by Donald Pollock 1997), Merrill argues that we need to consider the realm of the unconscious to understand exactly how masks can create transformations in people: for example, how they may bridge the gap between the human and the divine.

Merrill then launches into a discussion of altered states of consciousness (ASC) that parallels much discussion generally undertaken in the last decade or so, for example by Michael Winkelman in his theory of shamanism (see, e.g., Winkelman et al. 2004) and by other writers such as Charles Laughlin and C. Jason Throop (e.g., Laughlin and Throop 1999) and Ian Prattis (e.g., 2002). Merrill argues that the wearers of masks may experience a form of ASC and that this entails an embodied experience "of the unity of spirit and matter" (26). Given this unity, the masked dancer may both feel under the control of spirits and nevertheless be able to execute the complex dance steps that the ritual requires. We may comment that the equivalent "Western" term for this kind of capacity is "inspiration." In the Papua New Guinea context, about which we have written extensively, it would be called "seen in a dream" (*pulere enanea*) in the Wiru language of Pangia in the Southern Highlands Province (see, e.g., Stewart and Strathern 2002a), as something given externally and therefore as an "objective" force. In Merrill's formulation, this becomes the power that enables ritual performers to discover their essential selves.

Merrill's article reaches outward in an effort to bring to us a theory of masking and embodiment that extends beyond the social and the semiotic. A comparable encompassing scheme is sought in Throop and Laughlin's article, to be considered below, but on very different baselines.

Merrill, like Brown, was a doctoral student at the time his article was published. He had earned an M.A. from the Religious Studies Department of the University of South Florida in 2001 and was studying for his Ph.D. in the Communication Department of the same university. Whereas Korom's and Salomonsen's articles represent grounded work by scholars further along in their careers, Brown's and Merrill's represent the efforts of early-career scholars to make a theoretical mark.

The final article represents a collaboration between an early-career and an established-career scholar, and is perhaps the most ambitious of all five articles in its intentions and scope.

5. Throop and Laughlin return in their article to the work of Emile Durkheim and his "theory of a ritually generated social epistemology" (40). They link their exposition to contemporary theorizing by considering some current work, especially in neuroscience, that they see as a logical extension of Durkheim's ideas. Their aim is to arrive at a "cultural neurophenomenology" that could underpin "a modern version of Durkheim's theory" (40). The emphasis on neuroscience bears comparison with Merrill's appeal to this realm of inquiry in his article on masking which we have just discussed. Throop and Laughlin's use of neuroscience is more comprehensive in its coverage.

The fundamental categories of experience are not, say Throop and Laughlin, following the work of Ann Rawls (1996), the same as collective representations, which "are little more than cultural conventions" (42). Rather, they are the conceptual frames that order the contents of experience. In Durkheim's argument, it is in ritual that these conceptual frames are forcefully presented to the individual, mediating between individual and collective understandings of reality. Throop and Laughlin see in this work of Durkheim an attempt to set up a "proto-social phenomenology" (43), especially in the context of his studies of "collective effervescence" on large-scale ritual occasions, which Durkheim saw as the source of religious feelings. In Throop and Laughlin's view, this position gives Durkheim's work a phenomenological cast. It also makes him, in a sense, an early exponent of embodiment theory. Further objectified, of course, Durkheim's theory does become one in which society is "the force that defines religious power" (44), and this is how Durkheim's theory is generally represented. Throop and Laughlin, however, insist on a return to Durkheim's own starting point in the subjective experience of individuals in collective events.

This starting point also enables them to link Durkheim's ideas to contemporary work on how human cognition is related to varieties of bodily experience. They cite the work of Antonio Damasio (e.g., 1994, 1999) in this regard, but also Lakoff and Johnson (1980), D'Andrade (1995), and Thomas Csordas (1997), before moving to "biogenetic structuralism," a term Laughlin deployed in his earlier work. This approach attempts to integrate anthropology, psychology, phenomenology, and neuroscience together, advocating a method of introspection as a means of ascertaining properties of the mind-brain complex (49). The method results in a notion of "somatically generated cartographies of inner space" that are said to be the foundation for ideas about space (50). Shared psychic experiences of effervescence result from people's shared capacities to construct imagined realms and to infuse these with emotional values, especially in contexts of trance. The authors cite !Kung San trances and Tibetan Tantric Buddhist notions of psychic energy (52). These examples enable Throop and Laughlin to link "effervescence" to ASC (53), which can occur both within and outside of ritual contexts. Here we can see how an idea of trance or ASC also links four of the five articles we have chosen for discussion: Korom discusses heightened emotional experience in the Hosay rituals; Salomonsen pinpoints trance as a factor in the initiations she discusses; Merrill invokes ASC as a way of exploring the experience of maskers; and here Throop and Laughlin cite ASC as related to "collective effervescence."

The authors conclude with the thought that if Durkheim had known about current theories in neuroscience, he would have dropped his opposition to psychological explanations and would have instead pioneered a cultural neurophenomenology (55).

Discussion

1. Ritual studies as a means of looking at broader analytical and topical questions: in this regard, all of the articles show neatly how the study of ritual can make a contribution to broader issues. Korom's article does this most clearly, through its intersections with the local/global debate. As it happens, his choice of the ritual of Hosayn's sufferings in Shi'ite observances resonates poignantly with subsequent events in Iraq. We recently edited a special issue of the *Journal of Ritual Studies* titled "Contesting Rituals: Islam and Practices of Identity-Making" (Stewart and Strathern 2004), which contains a number of studies of Islamic rituals. One by Liyakat Takim, also on Shi'a ritual in Iraq, might well be studied along with Korom's article.

Salomonsen's article addresses questions of change and ritual invention against the backdrop of wider changes in gender and social relations generally in American society. The recourse to ritual as a way of articulating ideas about change can be seen as a way of asserting personal agency and commitment in community contexts that may otherwise be dominated by secular values. Ritual invention is thus both a sign of change and an active response to it. From our work in Papua New Guinea we have written about similar processes in relation to dealing with various aspects of change such as new concerns about mining companies (see Stewart and Strathern 2002c).

This argument is thus easily extended to ethnographic contexts. It applies well to the theorizing on religious change in many parts of the world, for example the Pacific (see, e.g., Robbins, Stewart, and Strathern, 2001). Also, millenarian movements and processes around the year 2000 illustrate this point (e.g., Stewart and Strathern 1997, 2000). Much anthropological theorizing has focused on explaining why movements labeled as "cargo cults" tend to have a religious and ritual focus. One answer to this question is that ritual action is fundamental to human action in general (Rappaport 1999), because it represents a fusion of emotive, conative, and ratiocinative elements in collectively instigated form. Today, the emphasis might be on the improvised character of ritual action in these contexts of change. Brown's article on indeterminacy in ritual would fit well with such an emphasis.

Merrill's article and Throop and Laughlin's intersect with a growing arena of theorization both on ASC as a phenomenon and on "neurohermeneutics." Stephen Reyna's book "Connections" (2002) gives a useful and ambitious overview of these trends. In teaching terms, one might well wish to compare this trend with Csordas's concept of a cultural phenomenology based on embodiment. Students could then be introduced to other works that take embodiment as a central focus or a point of significant departure (e.g., Stewart and Strathern 2001; Strathern and Stewart 1998; Lambek and Strathern 1998; Strathern 1996). In a sense, the new hermeneutics based on the image of neurological connections can be seen as giving content to one aspect of embodiment, the processes by which meanings are made in and through people's bodies.

Throop and Laughlin also situate their approach within phenomenology, so other works on phenomenology, such as those by Michael Jackson (e.g., 1989), could be brought into play here. Ongoing work on cognition by Dan Sperber and Maurice Bloch (Bloch 1998, 2005) is also relevant. Ritual may be seen as a slowed-down and elaborated version of processes that occur in everyday actions at much faster rates or shorter intervals. In this way, ritual can be seen as "built out of" everyday experience, just as Durkheim saw religion as built out of the experience of effervescence.

2. How do these articles achieve their ends? Here, students should be asked to outline the strategic ways in which authors have mounted their arguments There is always, of course, the citation of parallel literature, and sometimes an invocation of a particularly relevant idea from another author, as in

Salomonsen's use of Fredrik Barth's contrast between the guru and the conjurer. This literature can be updated: Barth's contrast is similar, in some ways, to that later developed by Harvey Whitehouse between doctrinal and imagistic modes of religiosity (see Whitehouse et al. 2002).

Korom's article signals that little had been written on possible ways to reconcile the categories of the local and the global in Islamic studies; his article shows how to do this for one case study. His answer is that the narrative of the sufferings of Hosayn is both particularized in Trinidad and connects the Trinidad adherents to a global context. The *same symbol* thus comes to have both local and global aspects.

Salomonsen achieves her ends by means of a neat internal parallelism between the neopagan and Christian rituals of initiation she has studied. The ethnographic demonstration is clever, and the implication that ritual bricolage is at work in both cases also patently emerges from her study. The strategy is clearly, therefore, inductive and empirical.

Merrill's and Brown's ways of going about their business are different. Both want to say something about ritual *in general*. To do this, Merrill appeals in the end to depth psychology. Brown contents himself with closely examining meanings of terms and, via the work of Victor Turner, with demonstrating that indeterminacy of some sort is implied in ritual action. Students might be asked to critically evaluate the "leap" into psychology that Merrill makes and to find examples to work with in assessing Brown's arguments regarding ritual and indeterminacy. How indeterminate can ritual actions be? How can they lead to cultural transformations? Who proposes and who resists such transformations? Changes may also be proposed rather than actual and may then suddenly "come into being." An example would be the issue of same-sex marriage in the United States and some other places. Here the form of the ritual itself is not changed, in essence, but the permitted or suggested composition of the ritual players is.

Throop and Laughlin lay out the structure of their article explicitly. They tell us what the argument will be and how they will illustrate it. Their main focus is on concepts, and their agenda is to bring Durkheim into the fold of cultural psychology, by interpreting effervescence as akin to ASC. Theory, methods, definitions, examples, and generalizations are brought comprehensively together. One could ask, however, for more in-depth examples, and perhaps for more evidence regarding effervescence and ASC: an article by Melanie Takahashi and Tim Olaveson (2003) on "rave" behavior does address this issue, albeit in the context of psychotropic drug use.

3. Turning articles into effective teaching tools: we have already given examples in passing of how students can be asked to explore further the authors' topics. The articles do not cover all aspects of theorizing in ritual, although they refer to a good spectrum of current writing on the topic. Our summaries

of them were also selective, aimed at elucidating their interrelated content rather than accounting for everything in them. After reviewing them, it is clear that they are very well adapted for teaching, especially at the graduate level. We envisage them as forming a module in a broader course on ritual studies: a module called "Examples of Contemporary Theorizing." They could advantageously be read, we think, in the order in which we have presented them here. Other sets of articles from the *Journal of Ritual Studies* would also be suitable to cluster together as a teaching core for classroom use.

In the set of five articles that we have selected, Korom's and Salomonsen's articles present few difficulties of interpretation for students or instructors. Merrill's and Brown's articles present a challenge requiring greater in-depth exploration of the materials. Students are likely to enjoy reading and thinking about these materials. What holds this set of five articles together is an emphasis on choice, change, consciousness, and agency, and this is a thread on which many substantive points can be tied together.

Finally, Throop and Laughlin's article can be used as a model of how to lay out a whole argument and support it. Students should be encouraged to check their analytical steps by reading Durkheim's texts themselves; moving to work by commentators; looking at other writings by the authors and likeminded theorists of consciousness; and, finally, considering how this reframing of Durkheim affects or does not affect his famous propositions regarding treating aspects of society as sui generis phenomena. We are reminded here of a piece of professional folklore about the social anthropologist Alfred Reginald Radcliffe-Brown, in which it is claimed that in the first draft of his now classic book *The Andaman Islanders,* he used the word "psychological" repeatedly in his explanations; but after reading Durkheim, he altered the adjective to "sociological." Clearly, Throop and Laughlin would like to see that adjective altered back again, but with a different sense from its usage in Durkheim's time. In the discipline of ritual studies, the changes are rung in and rung out again, and although history may almost repeat itself, it also keeps on changing: perhaps this is a good illustration of Gavin Brown's concept of indeterminacy.

USEFUL MATERIALS

A good, thematically organized collection of studies in the anthropology of religion, which can be used to provide a general resource for students wishing to explore topics in ritual studies, is edited by Michael Lambek and titled *A Reader in the Anthropology of Religion* (Blackwell, 2002).

Apart from a continuous stream of both ethnographic and theoretically oriented contributions to the analysis of ritual which have appeared in the *Journal of Ritual Studies* since its inception in 1987, there have been a number of special issues of the *Journal* (listed below) that could prove especially useful for classroom study. Over the many years since beginning our joint work as coeditors of the *Journal,* we have sponsored six of these special issues, as a way of drawing attention to the *Journal*'s special role in highlighting the significance of rituals in social processes.

JRS 3, 2 (1989), "Korean Ritual Thematic Issue," with an introduction by Clark W. Sorensen.

JRS 6, 1 (1992), "Art in Ritual Context," with an introduction by Kathleen Ashley.

JRS 7, 1 (1993), "Ritual and Sport."

JRS 14, 1 (2000), "Ritual and Food."

JRS 14, 2 (2000) and JRS 15, 1 (2001), "Time and the Millennium."

JRS 15, 2 (2001), "Charismatic and Pentecostal Christianity in Oceania," guest editors Joel Robbins, P. J. Stewart, and A. Strathern, with a note by the coeditors of the *Journal* and an introduction by Joel Robbins.

JRS 18, 2 (2004), "Contesting Rituals: Islam and Practices of Identity Making," with an introduction by Andrew Strathern and Pamela J. Stewart.

JRS 19, 1 (2005), "Asian Ritual Systems: Syncretisms and Ruptures," with an introduction by Pamela J. Stewart and Andrew Strathern.

REFERENCES

Barth, Fredrik. 1990. "The Guru and the Conjurer." *Man* 25, 4: 640–653.

Bell, Catherine. 1998. "Performance." In *Critical Terms in Religious Studies*, ed. Mark C. Taylor, 205–224. Chicago: Chicago University Press.

Bloch, Maurice. 1998. *How We Think They Think: Anthropological Approaches to Cognition, Memory, and Literacy*. Boulder, Colo.: Westview Press.

———. 2005. *Essays on Cultural Transmission*. Oxford, England: Berg.

Brown, Gavin. 2004. "Theorizing Ritual as Performance: Explorations of Ritual Indeterminacy." *Journal of Ritual Studies* 17, 1: 3–18.

Csordas, Thomas. 1997. *The Sacred Self: A Cultural Phenomenology of Charismatic Healing*. Berkeley: University of California Press.

Damasio, Antonio R. 1994. *Descartes' Error: Emotion, Reason, and the Human Brain*. New York: Grosset/Putnam.

———. 1999. *The Feeling of What Happens: Body and Emotion in the Making of Consciousness*. New York: Harcourt Brace.

D'Andrade, Roy G. 1995. *The Development of Cognitive Anthropology*. Cambridge: Cambridge University Press.

Jackson, Michael. 1989. *Paths toward a Clearing: Radical Empiricism and Ethnographic Inquiry*. Bloomington: Indiana University Press.

Korom, Frank. 1999. "Reconciling the Local and the Global: The Ritual Space of Shi'i Islam in Trinidad." *Journal of Ritual Studies* 13, 1: 21–36.

Lakoff, G., and M. Johnson. 1980. *Metaphors We Live By*. Chicago: University of Chicago Press.

Lambek, Michael, and Andrew Strathern, eds. 1998. *Bodies and Persons: Comparative Perspectives from Africa and Melanesia*. Cambridge: Cambridge University Press.

Laughlin, Charles D., and C. Jason Throop. 1999. "Emotion: A View from Biogenetic Structuralism." In *Biocultural Approaches to the Emotions*, ed. A. L. Hinton, 329–361. Cambridge: Cambridge University Press.

Marcus, George, and Michael Fischer. 1986. *Anthropology as Cultural Critique: An Experimental Moment in the Human Sciences.* Chicago: University of Chicago Press.

Merrill, Michael S. 2004. "Masks, Metaphor, and Transformation: The Communication of Belief in Ritual Performance." *Journal of Ritual Studies* 18, 1: 16–33.

Pollock, Donald. 1997. "Masks and the Semiotics of Identity." *Journal of the Royal Anthropological Institute* 1: 581–598.

Prattis, Ian. 2002 "Mantra and Consciousness Expansion in India." *Journal of Ritual Studies* 16, 1: 78–96.

Rappaport, Roy. 1999. *Ritual and Religion in the Making of Humanity.* Cambridge: Cambridge University Press.

Rawls, A. W. 1996. "Durkheim's Epistemology: The Neglected Argument." *American Journal of Sociology* 102, 2: 430–482.

Reyna, Stephen. 2002. *Connections: Mind, Brain, and Culture in a Social Anthropology.* London: Routledge.

Robbins, Joel, Pamela J. Stewart, and Andrew Strathern, eds. 2001. "Pentecostal and Charismatic Christianity in Oceania." Special issue, *Journal of Ritual Studies* 15, 2.

Salomonsen, Jone. 2003. "The Ethno-Methodology of Ritual Invention in Contemporary Culture—Two Pagan and Christian Cases." *Journal of Ritual Studies* 17, 2: 15–24.

Stewart, Pamela J., and A. J. Strathern, eds. 1997. *Millennial Markers.* Townsville, Queensland, Australia: JCU, Centre for Pacific Studies.

———, eds. 2000. "Millennial Countdown in New Guinea." Special issue, *Ethnohistory* 47, 1. Duke University Press.

———. 2001. *Humors and Substances: Ideas of the Body in New Guinea.* Westport, Conn.: Bergin and Garvey.

———. 2002a. *Gender, Song, and Sensibility: Folktales and Folksongs in the Highlands of New Guinea.* Westport, Conn.: Praeger.

———. 2002b. "Power and Placement in Blood Practices." In "Blood Mysteries: Beyond Menstruation as Pollution," ed. Janet Hoskins. Special issue, *Ethnology* 41, 4: 349–363.

———. 2002c. *Remaking the World: Myth, Mining and Ritual Change among the Duna of Papua New Guinea.* Washington, D.C.: Smithsonian Institution Press.

———, eds. 2004. "Contesting Rituals: Islam and Practices of Identity-Making." Special issue, *Journal of Ritual Studies* 18, 2. Also in book form in the "Ritual Studies Monograph Series," Durham, N.C.: Carolina Academic Press, 2005.

Strathern, Andrew. 1996. *Body Thoughts.* Ann Arbor: University of Michigan Press.

Strathern, Andrew, and Pamela J. Stewart. 1998. "Embodiment and Communication: Two Frames for the Analysis of Ritual." *Social Anthropology* 6, 2: 237–251.

Takahashi, Melanie, and Tim Olaveson. 2003. "Music, Dance, and Raving Bodies: Raving as Spirituality in the Central Canadian Rave Scene." *Journal of Ritual Studies* 17, 2: 72–96.

Takim, Liyakat. 2004. "Charismatic Appeal or Communitas? Visitation to the Shrines of the Imams." In "Contesting Rituals: Islam and Practices of Identity-Making," ed. Pamela J. Stewart and Andrew Strathern. Special issue, *Journal of Ritual*

Studies 18, 2. Also in book form in the "Ritual Studies Monograph Series,"
Durham, N.C.: Carolina Academic Press, 2005.

Throop, C. Jason, and Charles D. Laughlin. 2002. "Ritual, Collective Effervescence,
and the Categories: Toward a Neo-Durkheimian Model of the Nature of Human
Consciousness, Feeling, and Understanding." *Journal of Ritual Studies* 16, 1:
40–63.

Whitehouse, Harvey, et al. 2002. Book Review Forum of *Arguments and Icons:
Divergent Modes of Religiosity*. Reviews of Whitehouse's book by: Brian Malley,
Pascal Boyer, Fredrik Barth, Michael Houseman, Robert N. McCauley, Luther
H. Martin, Tom Sjoblom, and Garry W. Trompf. Reply to reviews by Harvey
Whitehouse. *Journal of Ritual Studies* 16, 2: 4–59.

Winkelman, Michael, et al. 2004. Book Review Forum of *Shamanism. The Neural
Ecology of Consciousness and Healing*. Reviews of Winkelman's book by: Stewart
E. Guthrie, Richard J. Castillo, C. Jason Throop, Pablo Wright, and Mary Douglas.
Reply to reviews by Michael Winkelman. *Journal of Ritual Studies* 18, 1: 96–128.

10

Teaching Rites Ritually

Mary E. McGann

Like ritual, teaching and learning are always contextualized. I teach
Christian liturgy in a Catholic graduate school of theology, situated
in an ecumenical and interfaith consortium. Hence my perspective on
teaching ritual may differ from that of teachers in other settings.
In contrast to those who introduce students to the unfamiliar ritual
contours of whirling dervishes or a Sufi dhikr, I guide students into
a deeper understanding of their own tradition, while inviting them
to appreciate the ritual traditions of others.[1] Moreover, courses in
Christian ritual in this setting are integral to the professional formation of our students, who are master's candidates preparing to be
lay or ordained liturgical leaders, chaplains, teachers, catechetical
instructors, and leaders of faith communities, and doctoral candidates preparing for advanced teaching and scholarship in the field
of liturgical studies. Beyond enrichment, what is at stake in their
study of ritual is no less than a shaping of their professional identity.

  In addition to the uniqueness of my academic setting, twelve
years of participating in the ritual life of an African American
Catholic community and the writing of a major ethnography of
that community's musical and ritual performance (McGann 2004)
have uniquely affected my pedagogical assumptions and teaching
strategies. I first encountered the vibrant community of Our Lady
of Lourdes in San Francisco in 1993—a time when I was seeking
to expand my horizon of Catholic ritual practice and to hone skills
for interpreting its diversity. From the outset, the dynamism, at
times communal passion, of this community's worship created a
dramatic counterpoint to the more reserved ritual experience that

had shaped my liturgical imagination. Caught up week after week in the exuberant pulsing of drums, the vibrance of impassioned gospel singing, the candor of freely offered testimony, the dynamism of interactive preaching, the hush of communal prayer, I felt strangely at home in this Catholic ritual, although still a stranger to most of its cultural realization. Slowly, my "going through the motions"—a unique point of entry into the rituals of others— enabled me to cultivate the feelings, intentionality, and sense of meaningfulness experienced by members of the community.

Immersion in this experience convinced me that encountering lived practice is critical to understanding a liturgical tradition, even one's own. Since liturgy is, by its very nature, performative, teaching liturgy must put students in touch with the living tradition, in all its diversity, and teach them to pay attention to what takes place. Despite the seeming universality of ritual practices within a tradition, rites are always locally enacted. The sheer performativity of rhythmic movement, voiced praise, hushed prayer, and personalized gestures of engagement that drew me into the flow of ritual enactment in a small church house in San Francisco *is* the living tradition—the manner in which one community shapes and hands on the tradition to future generations. Inviting students to encounter this living practice, to attend to the manner in which local customs and cultural resourcefulness are at work, is to invite them into a process of "traditioning" that has been at work since the origins of Christian liturgy.[2]

Moreover, my participation in the rich textures of this African American community's worship underscored the centrality of the human body to what transpires ritually, relationally, and spiritually. Paying attention to the range, style, and energy of bodily communication within the ritualizing community— evocative gestures, expressive sounds and words, and rhythmic movements— as well as to the resonance I discovered within my own body, I began to grasp the significance of what was taking place. As community members interact bodily in space and time, people assume their places, socially and ecclesially— the relational body, described by theologians as the Body of Christ, is actively negotiated. Likewise, it became clear that spiritual power and authority do not simply reside in one or a few ritual leaders, but flow through the fluid exchange of communication and interaction within the whole ritualizing community. This was especially evident in processes of music-making, where the bodily and vocal expressiveness of singers, especially the women, becomes an icon of divine presence and activity. Other community members interpret the expressiveness of these women singers as an impulse of the Holy Spirit, and, through their own bodily and verbal responses, affirm their spiritual power and ratify their authority to "preach the word" musically.

In sum, I learned that what transpires in the ritual/ization of this vibrant community in San Francisco is less an encapsulation of meaning, as previously formulated theologically or doctrinally, and more a richly textured confluence of processes—spiritual, social, personal, religious, familial, ecclesial—that are the stuff of both tradition-making and theology. Moreover, the community's engagement in the ritualizing process yields its own discourse—a shared, image-laden and cultivated way by which participants describe and interpret what takes place—offering students of ritual a rich counterpoint to other ways of understanding and interpreting liturgical practice.

Teaching Rites Ritually

The pedagogical outcome of this gestation can be summed up quite simply: I teach rites ritually. I approach them as lived practices, always contextualized, embodied, and culture-laden. I invite students to come to know their tradition as a performing tradition—an amalgam of rites and ritual practices that have unfolded historically through diverse local enactments—and to access this tradition through learning strategies of empathetic participation, ethnographic attentiveness, and serious inquiry into historical, cultural, and theological sources that offer interpretations of what takes place.[3]

I have honed this general approach into three ways of teaching rites ritually, each of which enables a particular kind of "ritual knowing" that is pertinent to students at specific stages of their studies. The first, which fosters what I call *foundational ritual knowledge,* is effective ecumenically, inviting students who are insiders to their own tradition to widen their perspectives on their own experience and to appreciate liturgical rites that are not their own. The second, which cultivates *performative ritual knowledge,* has taken shape in the specific need to teach students of my own denomination how to conduct their own rites. This pedagogy enables students to develop ritual competencies needed in their professional ministries. The third iteration focuses on *scholarly ritual knowledge,* which prepares doctoral students to become scholars and teachers in the field of liturgical studies. In addition to an exploration of ritual theory, "teaching ritually" in this instance includes challenging students to observe how ritual theories are constructed so as to shape their own interpretive frameworks and to prepare for ethnographic study of particular ritualizing communities.

As I show how these varying modes of ritual knowledge play out in three types of courses, it is my hope that one or all of these examples may find resonance with others who guide students into a deeper embrace of their own traditions and an appreciation of the ritual traditions of others.

Foundational Ritual Knowledge

Foundational courses have three aims: to expose students to the complexities of contemporary liturgical practice; to introduce them to the historical evolution of rites and their theological interpretation; and to enable them to assess how rites become effective/efficacious for particular ritualizing communities. Although these goals are accomplished across a cluster of courses, my focus here will be on my introductory "Liturgy and Spirituality" class, highlighting some of its pertinent teaching strategies. The course usually attracts some thirty-five students, who come from a wide variety of cultural backgrounds and who represent several Christian denominations.

I begin the course by inviting students to write their own "liturgical history": to create a kind of ritual memoir in which they give conscious attention to those taken-for-granted, yet highly formative experiences—cultural, familial, catechetical, spiritual, and ritual—that have shaped their understandings and practice of liturgy. Some have been empowered by their experience, others alienated, at least for a period in their lives. Students are surprised to discover the variety of factors, both positive and negative, that have shaped their attitudes: the influence of parents or teachers; the impact of a childhood experience of night vigils in a darkened cathedral or the intimacy of a teen retreat; the significance of cultural rituals cultivated within their family or community.

Besides heightening students' self-awareness of their own ritual formation and establishing personal starting points for their learning, this exercise has two other outcomes. First, it becomes a springboard for intercultural and interdenominational conversation. As students share their personal liturgical histories in small discussion groups, difference immediately comes into play. Diversity within and across denominations becomes evident. A sense of self and other is evoked, and a personal doorway into the ritual experience of others is opened. Second, students' discovery that their experience of liturgy has been shaped by a host of historical factors opens a window on how the larger tradition has been shaped by myriad social, religious, political, and geographic influences.

My second starting point for the course is to offer students a framework for exploring liturgical rites performatively. This takes the form of a set of "action coordinates"—dimensions of the performative event—that can help students "map" what is taking place as a rite unfolds. These coordinates are eightfold: an assembly of people who enact the rite; ritual leaders and ministers; the Word of God (Christian and Hebrew Scriptures); the "word of the church" (ritual words from the tradition or arising from participants); ritual action of various kinds; song and other musical expression; time; and space. While this set of ritual coordinates bear resemblance to those delineated by Ronald Grimes (1995: 26–38), I draw them directly from theologian Jean Corbon (1988: 32–34). These eight components, Corbon claims, have been fundamental to Christian worship since the beginning, thus making them amenable to the analysis of historical as well as contemporary ritual/ization.

Immediately after this framework is introduced, the lights in the room are darkened and we are engaged (via large-screen video projection) in the enactment of adult immersion baptisms on Easter night in a suburban Texas Catholic church. A multigenerational community stands clustered around a huge open pool, the church darkened, faces lit by candlelight. The presider of the rite, vested in white, stands knee-deep in the flowing water of the pool. Those to be initiated, invited one after another to enter the water, are asked to affirm their intent to be baptized, then submerged in the pool's warm waters. Women wait with huge terry towels to wrap the wet bodies as they emerge from the pool, while chanted music suffuses the room and weaves sonic connections among the many participants.

Having engaged vicariously in this rite, students explore how it has unfolded through an interplay of the eight action coordinates: how the circular arrangement of the persons around the pool mediates a particular awareness of the identity of the community; how varied roles, from holding towels to submerging bodies in flowing water, shape a sense of relatedness; how gestures take on greater significance than words in communicating meaning; how music inhabits space; how time and its perception are affected by environmental darkness; and how concentrated attention to the physically strenuous action of initiating new members, and of witnessing the action, makes time stand still. It becomes clear to students that accessing rites in this way is significantly different from reading a ritual text, script, or written description of the same rite.

The course as a whole is divided, more or less equally, into two segments—one focusing on the historical formation of rites, the other on contemporary practice. Keeping concerns of performativity, diversity, embodiment, and contextualization in the foreground, my approach to both historical processes and contemporary practice has certain common strains. First, we view rites from the perspective of the actual experience of worshipers. Historically, this is aided by texts that explore the architecture, music, books, and vessels that were used in various periods and diverse contexts—what worshipers actually saw, heard, touched, tasted (Foley 1991). I supplement this reading with videos that examine, archeologically, the visual and spatial dimensions of past ritual performance. Second, we trace how diverse ethnocultural perspectives and performances have shaped the tradition from the first century onward. Students are surprised to discover that issues of multicultural performance, geographically variant practices, and tensions over heterodox and orthodox practice were as present in the earliest centuries as they are today.

Third, we explore how nonliturgical sociopolitical forces have influenced traditional ritual strategies. A brief look at Christian ritual life in fourth-century Jerusalem, for example, reveals the imprint of the Roman Empire on liturgical practice: large basilicas replaced earlier "house churches" as the preferred place of assembly, with the bishop's chair substituted for the emperor's throne in the apse of the building; processions, a popular civic practice within the Empire, became a characteristic element of Christian liturgical performance; and *Kyrie eleison!* (a shout of praise to the emperor) was adopted as an acclamation of the divine. Inviting students into an imaginative reconstruction of this process of assimilation and change enables them to better grasp how their liturgical tradition has been shaped historically.

Fourth, we examine forms of "explanatory discourse"—theological and mystagogical texts, as well as normative ecclesiastical statements—in relation to contemporaneous ritual practice. For example, ecclesiastical prohibitions regarding certain ways of ritualizing may tell us more about what *is* going on in liturgical practice than what is *not*. Fourth-century legislation "forbidding women to baptize and teach, to enter the sanctuary in ministerial functions, to exorcize, to bless, to anoint, and to heal has to be read as pointing to liturgical functions" that women were actually doing (Berger 1999: 17). Indeed, throughout the course, I invite students to adopt a "hermeneutic of suspicion" regarding what might be missing or misrepresented in how rites have been remembered and recorded—for example, in their portrayal of women's involvement and leadership. Selective memory continues today, affecting our perception of the tradition as a whole. Finally, we examine how rites are always embedded in the power-laden fabric of ecclesial/social life and thus are deeply related to issues construed as nonritual—ethics, social justice, and issues of inclusion. This is especially important in our exploration of contemporary ritual/ization because students are often negotiating their own attitudes toward the interface of liturgical practice, ethical choices, and social responsibility.

Critical to students' learning is their encounter with lived practice. Hence, in addition to the expected elements of the course—assigned reading, lecture, and discussion—I engage them in a number of experiential forays into liturgical diversity, both cultural and denominational. First, each student is required to participate in the Sunday worship of three communities that are denominationally and/or culturally other than their own. This is often done is small groups, students inviting each other to experience their traditions. I encourage them to talk with a few participants after the service, inquiring about their experience of liturgy in this setting. As a simple follow-up assignment, students are asked to record one key insight they have gained about the particular tradition and one realization about themselves. Second, to supplement my Catholic perspective, I invite several colleagues to address the class, exploring the unique ethos and customs of their particular traditions: Greek Orthodox, Lutheran, Anglican, African American Catholic, Latino Catholic, Vietnamese Catholic. We conclude each of these classes with a brief ritualization that immerses students in the sights and sounds of the tradition just portrayed—the smell of rose-scented incense wafting before a set of icons as we engage in the flow of prayers of Greek Orthodox "Compline"; an exuberant, guitar-accompanied singing of *Las Mañanitas* as we gather around candle-lit image of Our Lady of Guadalupe; the richly harmonized sonority of four-part hymn-singing as we explore the sonic dimensions of Lutheran and Anglican practice; and the rhythmic swaying of bodies to the repetitive lyrics and highly improvised accompaniments of African American gospel songs and spirituals.

Third, each class session throughout the semester is preceded by an optional full-length video presentation that is cued to the topic of the evening. Some offer archeological/pictorial entry into the worship settings of former eras; others explore contemporary liturgical performance in a specific part of the world—places as diverse as Papua New Guinea. Malawi, Vietnam, Guatemala, Alaska, San Antonio, and Chicago. Entering these experiences vicariously, students' ritual imaginations are stretched and informed. They discover, for example, the central role of communal dancing in rites of many African and Melanesian cultures; the range of ritual roles undertaken by women and men in Latino and African American settings; the manifold architectural and natural settings in which rites take place in parts of Asia, Oceania, and Africa; and the broad range of music-making strategies that mark the ritual performance in Latin American and Polynesian communities. About half of the students attend screenings of these videos, with the proportion growing as the semester progresses. For this reason, I incorporate short clips in class presentations.

Finally, I conclude the course with a brief "ethnographic" project which I invite students to pursue in small groups: participating in the liturgical practice of one local community over a three- to five-week period so as to explore the questions, What makes rites work for people? What makes them efficacious? I send them out equipped with what Ronald Grimes calls a "map of the ritual field"—a set of questions that cluster around the eight "action coordinates" that I introduced earlier in the semester: an assembly of people, ministers, time, space, the Word of God, the word of the church, music, and performative action. This map becomes a framework for their paying attention to what takes place ritually and spiritually, and for describing it in some detail. Moreover, I ask them to explore how these central components intersect and shape each other in the course of the ritual/ization, and how they affect the manner in which the community makes meaning within the liturgical action. Their conclusions, which they present to me in an hourlong report, often accompanied by audiovisual materials, becomes a last arena for synthesizing many of the threads of the entire course.

Performative Ritual Knowledge

A second cluster of courses focus on the development of ritual competencies that students will need to enact rites in their professional ministries: skills for leading, orchestrating, inventing, participating in, or musically accompanying the liturgical performance of particular communities. These competencies require two kinds of learning. First, students need cognitive knowledge *about* particular rites—a familiarity with the texts, options, and sequence of actions involved in such rites as baptism, Eucharist, funerals, and rites of healing, as well as an awareness of what is claimed theologically about each in official discourse. Second, perhaps more important, they need knowledge *of the rites*— a holistic knowledge of the ritual action itself, an embodied awareness of the performative power of each liturgical rite. This performative knowledge begins, I believe, when "the body minds itself"—when a student's intuition, emotional intelligence, affective sensibilities, and aesthetic awareness become engaged in a discovery of how rites are effectively performed by particular communities.

I team-teach a course for students preparing to preside at liturgical rites as lay or ordained leaders. Like other modes of ritual leadership—proclaiming sacred texts, leading communal movement or song, animating an assembly— skills for presiding are rooted in the body. We begin our first class with exercises in breathing, then move to short sung aspirations, then to small units of speech. Students are invited to form two groups which, facing each other, engage in call-response patterns of short spoken or sung phrases from group to group. This group interchange gives a felt sense of the communal context within which individual leadership comes into play. Once established, individual students experiment with taking the lead by setting similar ritualized exchanges in motion between themselves and the group as a whole—first with sung/spoken words, then with bodily gestures. Next we explore how traditional liturgical gestures of blessing, of anointing, and of laying on of hands might be enacted—an experimentation that continues throughout the semester. Our goal is to enable each student to discover a personal sense of her or his "body-in-action" and "in-relationship," not through a fastidious application of rubrics but by discerning what style of gesture and tone of voice will elicit the ritual engagement of others—a discovery-in-action of the "for whom" and "on whose behalf" students will assume leadership.

The classroom becomes one of several ritual laboratories, along with a small chapel, a large church, and other ritual spaces for domestic rites. Students are asked to prepare ritual events in small groups and to assume different roles in their performance. Before each ritual/ization, we experiment with aspects of the rite to be performed: blocking how persons will be arranged in the ritual space and how movement within the space will unfold; exploring dynamics of pacing and timing, of face-to-face and person-to-group interaction; and experimenting with how the "scale" of each ritual space demands differing styles of ritual leadership. Once ready, students invite friends, family members, and other students to participate in the events, thus simulating an actual ritual context—a live baby for baptism, a mourning family for a funeral rite.

Supportive and critical feedback is essential to students' growth into effective ritual leaders. A feedback session immediately follows each experimental rite, followed by written feedback from students and professors. This juxtaposition of experimentation and feedback helps students move beyond self-consciousness to a fuller discovery of their own competence and inner authority to lead. It also sensitizes them to the entire spatiotemporal event, enabling them to better prepare and orchestrate future rites. For example, in feedback sessions, we focus on the whole flow of the event we have just experienced, reflecting on how patterns of alternation within the action—such as sound/silence, rest/concerted effort, word/song, emotional peaks/contemplative resting places—affected people's participation. We assess the evocative quality of actions with particular ritual objects such as water, oil, bread, wine, and the appropriateness and effectiveness of each gesture. We discuss the affect of various environmental factors on those of us who have participated—light/darkness, spaciousness/clutter, color/texture, closeness/distance. We explore, as well, how the particular arrangement of persons in the space influenced how they perceived themselves to be agents of the rite, and how ready they were to take their respective roles.

Throughout the course, we put special emphasis on developing cultural awareness and intercultural communication skills. Since context is critical to how rites become effective—to how, for example, a grieving mother is comforted or a newborn initiated into the community—learning to adapt the flow, texts, and gestures of a rite to match a community's particular cultural sensitivities is vital to students' growth as ritual leaders. The cultural mix of the class becomes a basis for intercultural learning activities that help develop greater ritual sensitivities. Take, for example, hospitality. Inviting German, Euro-American, Latino, and Korean students to each "show," without words, how welcome and hospitality are expressed in their respective cultural settings brings a range of responses: a handshake, a pat on the back, a warm *abrazo*, a respectful bow. How, we ask, can these simple but evocative gestures be translated into the whole tone of a ritual event—its musical, spatial, interpersonal, devotional qualities—especially those rites which specifically focus on welcoming new members? Finally, we explore how particular cultural customs can be woven into the ritual enactment: highlighting, for example, the ritual and social importance of *padrinos* in the baptismal rites of Latino children, or the honoring of parents in a Vietnamese wedding rite. These cultural sensitivities—become bodily and interpersonal awareness—enable future ritual leaders to connect their own ritual competence with the sensibilities of diverse communities.

Scholarly Ritual Knowledge

A third arena for teaching rites ritually is our doctoral curriculum and the preparation of students to become scholars and teachers in the field of liturgical studies. It is important to note here that the study of ritual performance per se has not always been part of liturgical scholarship. Conceived primarily as a normative discipline, historical and theological studies of Christian liturgy have traditionally focused more on ritual texts and structures than on the performative dimensions of the tradition. Spurred on by the enormous cultural flux and denominational liturgical reforms that began in the 1960s—which called attention to issues of ritual change, diversity of practice, processes of inculturation, and local meaning-making—liturgical scholars have turned to the insights and methods of cultural anthropology and ritual studies to enable them to deal with the emerging pluriformity.

In my own academic setting, liturgical studies is understood to be a tripartite interdiscipline: liturgical history, liturgical theology, and ritual studies. Doctoral students are required to develop competency in all three areas and to be able to integrate their varying methodological perspectives. Because performance, diversity, embodiment, and contextualization are increasingly vital concerns to both theological and historical studies of liturgy, ritual studies will be foundational for students' future scholarship.

Within this interdisciplinary framework, I team-teach a doctoral seminar called "Ritual Studies as Liturgical Studies." The goal of this course is twofold: to expand the hermeneutical, analytical, and theoretical frameworks that students bring to their scholarly pursuits of rites and ritual practice, and to introduce them to ethnographic methods for the study of ritual performance. Implicit is the need for students to stretch beyond denominational perspectives and to situate Christian liturgy within the larger framework of ritual as a human cultural practice. Students lead seminar discussions, providing information about the particular scholars whose writings are to be discussed and presenting their own research.

We begin the course by asking students to identify *what ritual is* and *what ritual does*—that is, to name their current assumptions about ritual/izaton. This exercise helps situate their initial interpretive frameworks. It also provides students with a way of tracking their growth over the semester. Returning to this exercise at the end of the course, a change in their perspective is always evident. Early in the semester, students are inclined to define ritual as symbolic, formal, and repetitive action, by which participants act out texts that connect them with their past and future and with one another. At the conclusion of the semester, students' interpretive frameworks are far more nuanced and open-ended; they now might describe ritual/ization as culturally oriented/contextually localized ways of acting; as intersecting processes, social and bodily; as negotiated fields of energy dynamics; as strategic markers of identity.

The heart of the course is a critical reading of four ritual theorists whose work has significantly influenced liturgical scholars—Clifford Geertz, Victor Turner, Ronald Grimes, and Catherine Bell. We set the work of each in conversation with a cluster of other scholars who either critique or build on their respective theoretical frameworks. Students are given the task of unearthing each author's intellectual history—tracing the academic institutions in which they have taught, the schools of thought that have influenced them, other theorists with whom they have interacted, and the anthropological/ethnographic research they have pursued. The purpose of this exercise is integral to the goals of the course: that students will not simply imbibe theories, wholesale and uncritically, but rather will observe the theory-construction process itself, insofar as this is possible. Tracing influences and academic commitments reveals this process and invites students to become self-aware and self-critical about the persons, contexts, biases, and ideological commitments that influence how they construct their own hermeneutical practices.

As we pursue these various theoretical approaches to ritual/ization, through seminar discussion and accompanying written assignments, several questions recur: How do the analytic categories of each theorist construe ritual practice? Is ritual assumed to be a universal category of human action? If so, what are its defining characteristics? How is it situated vis-à-vis other human practices? How is agency construed—does "ritual" act, or do ritual agents act? How does ritual/ization relate to social change? To religious meaning-making? To cultural resourcefulness? To power and politics? How do the theories explored situate the role of the theorist in relation to ritual performance? And how have the respective theories of each scholar informed that scholar's empirical research?

Complementing this probing of ritual theory, students engage in individual research, developing their own hermeneutical approach to a particular aspect of ritual performance—for example, ritual change; power and authority; the body in ritual/ization; ritual texts and language; the realm of the "sacred"; orality and literacy; the invention of tradition. As they construct new interpretive frameworks, based on a scrutiny of the work of several scholars, students begin to identify how the field of ritual studies will shape their liturgical scholarship and serve as one "community of accountability" within their interdisciplinary pursuits. Moreover, they begin to apply the hermeneutical approaches they develop to specific forms of ritual practice that hold interest for them: the veneration of ancestors or shamanistic performance in a Korean cultural setting; the emergence of queer liturgy in a large metropolitan Christian church; the practice of Ash Wednesday in a rural Episcopalian parish.

Finally, the seminar links these theoretical/hermeneutical explorations with the ethnographic research process itself. As liturgical scholars, students will need skills for documenting emerging practices, for exploring cross-cultural differences in the enactment of common rites, and for in-depth research into the embodied ritual practice of particular communities. We introduce these skills in this course through an in-depth reading of two ethnographic accounts—*A Precious Fountain* (McGann 2004) and *Every Time I Feel The Spirit* (Nelson 2005)—each of which focuses on the liturgical practice of an African American community, one Roman Catholic, one AME. We ask, How was the research carried out? What interpretive strategies were engaged? What modes of narrative and ritual analysis have the authors used to access the religious experience of each community? What do these evocative accounts offer liturgical scholars?

A subsequent course, which I am currently designing, will offer students hands-on practice in ethnographic field research methods—such as intentional participation, writing field notes and descriptive accounts, conducting interviews—and will explore issues of intercultural communication and reflexivity, as well as ethical concerns that arise in doing field study. Here I draw on my own research, described at the outset of this chapter, and on the constructive approach I have developed for integrating empirical research into the work of liturgical scholarship (McGann 2002, 2004). Over a period of several semesters, each student will engage in a long-term study of one community's liturgical practice, creating an initial ethnographic presentation of her own work.

Hence, we come full circle. Teaching rites ritually, in the various pedagogical incarnations I have described in this chapter, begins and ends with empathetic participation, ethnographic attentiveness, and serious inquiry into historical, cultural, theological, and local sources that offer interpretive perspectives on what takes place ritually. In an academic setting in which the study of Christian ritual is formative of students' professional identity, I feel an imperative to teach performatively. Rites, after all, belong to people, to communities that, in their ongoing encounter with divine mystery, shape and hand on the tradition in unique and culture-laden ways. Teaching rites ritually honors the ritual integrity and embodied theology implicit in the plurality of performances that make up a tradition.

Acknowledgments

I am grateful to the leaders of Our Lady of Lourdes Parish, San Francisco, for permission to use material from my research there; to my co-teachers, William Cieslak and Andrea Bieler who helped construct aspects of two of the courses described; to colleagues who have stretched the ecumenicity of my courses with their presentations; and to students in my various courses for insights and research topics mentioned.

NOTES

1. In speaking of "their own tradition," I imply the complex, denominationally diverse "Christian tradition" as a whole. When referring to specific denominational practice, I indicate this clearly. In claiming to invite students to "appreciate the ritual traditions of others," I do this explicitly with reference to Christian denominational diversity. Implicitly, I believe that inviting students to enter the ritual performance of other Christian communities prepares them for a much broader ritual encounter across religious traditions.

2. Tradition, as Catherine Bell notes, is not created once; it is "constantly produced and reproduced, pruned for a clear profile, and softened to absorb revitalizing elements" (1992: 123). This process, which I refer to as "traditioning," has marked the history of Christian practice. Indeed, the incorporation of local custom has been a primary way in which the liturgical tradition has evolved.

3. My purpose in this essay is to focus on the ritual/performative dimensions of my pedagogy, which I consider foundational. I give less attention here to the theological dimensions of liturgical practice which is integrally related (See McGann 2002: 58–81).

USEFUL MATERIALS

Books

Aside from the books in the reference list—especially Grimes 1995 and McGann 2002 and 2004—the following may be helpful to readers:

Collins, Mary. 1987. *Worship: Renewal to Practice.* Washington, D.C.: Pastoral Press. (See especially pp. 59–132).
Kelleher, Margaret Mary. 1997. "Ritual Studies and the Eucharist: Paying Attention to Performance." In *Eucharist: Toward the Third Millennium,* ed. Gerard Austin. Chicago: Liturgy Training Publications. (See especially pp. 51–64).

Videos/DVDs

Fiesta: Celebrations at San Fernando, San Antonio (Thomas A. Kane, producer). New York: Paulist Press. 1999.
Fire in the Pews. Oblate Media and Communication Corporation (African American Catholic Liturgy). 1987.
Holy Image, Holy Space; Icons and Frescos from Greece. Part I: Windows to Heaven. Astoria, NY: GOTelecom. 1988.
Inori: Japanese Prayer (Fr. Mario Bianchin, producer). Pontifical Institute for Foreign Missions, IWANAMI Productions. N.d.
Re-Examining Baptismal Fonts. Collegeville, Minn.: Liturgical Press. 1991.
The Dancing Church: Video Impressions of the Church in Africa (Thomas A. Kane, producer). New York: Paulist Press. 1995.
The Dancing Church of the South Pacific (Thomas A. Kane, producer). New York: Paulist Press. 1998.
The Drums of Winter (Uksuum Cauyai). University of Alaska Museum (Yup'ik Eskimo dance in social and spiritual life). N.d.

The History of the Mass. Chicago: Liturgy Training Publications. 2001.
This is the Night. Chicago: Liturgy Training Publications. 1992.
The Reason Why We Sing. Chicago: Liturgy Training Publications. 1995.

REFERENCES

Bell, Catherine. 1992. *Ritual Theory, Ritual Practice.* New York: Oxford University Press.
Berger, Teresa. 1999. *Women's Ways of Worship: Gender Analysis and Liturgical History.* Collegeville, Minn.: Liturgical Press.
Corbon, Jean. 1988. *The Wellspring of Worship.* New York: Paulist Press.
Foley, Edward B. 1991. *From Age to Age: How Christians Celebrated the Eucharist.* Chicago: Liturgy Training Publications.
Grimes, Ronald L. 1995. *Beginnings in Ritual Studies,* rev. ed. Columbia: University of South Carolina Press.
McGann, Mary E. 2002. *Exploring Music as Worship and Theology: Research in Liturgical Practice.* Collegeville, Minn.: Liturgical Press.
———. 2004. *A Precious Fountain: Music in the Worship of an African American Catholic Community.* Collegeville, Minn.: Liturgical Press.
Nelson, Timothy Jon. 2005. *Every time I Feel the Spirit: Religious Experiences and Ritual in an African-American Church.* New York: New York University Press.

II

Teaching the Cognitive Approach

Theodore Vial

Teaching a cognitive approach to ritual presents the same opportunities and challenges as teaching other approaches. Some traditions or theorists seem to be obvious inclusions on the syllabus. They are self-evidently great, as we learned in graduate school. The cognitive science of religion is, however, relatively new, exciting to some and irritating to others in equal measure, controversial, and only now moving into the canon of scholarship on religion. It does not come with an oral tradition of what texts are the key ones, what groundwork must be laid to make them comprehensible, what strategies allow a teacher to make them accessible to students. All the reflective questions demanded of teachers as they prepare a syllabus are unavoidable as they consider adding a cognitive approach. Why should it be there? How does it relate to other material on the syllabus? What should they have the students read?

The Teaching Context

Until recently, I taught in a department of religious studies at a small, church-related liberal arts college. Religious Studies 340, "Ritual Studies," was an upper-level undergraduate class, for which the only prerequisite was prior completion of one class in the humanities. This is a standard prerequisite for upper-level religious studies classes, which is designed to give ready access to non-majors, while at the same time keeping students from getting in over their heads in classes that demand heavy reading and analysis of difficult texts. "Ritual Studies" was one of two classes that fulfilled the "theory" requirement for religious studies majors, so it was designed to help them understand that phenomena can be approached with different methods with different results, to give them some exposure to major figures from whom the field traditionally has taken its bearings, and to give them a taste of some current issues in religious studies. (I plan to offer a similar course, including the cognitive approach, to graduate students at my current institution.)

The class also fulfilled two requirements in the college's General Studies program: it was a writing course (students averaged one of these per semester) and it was a "values" course. Students took two classes from each of several "frames of reference," including, for example, classes that introduced them to the empirical approach, historical method, questions of aesthetics, and so on. The values category was a hodgepodge intended to get them to understand the role that different "faith perspectives" play in human society, to attend to "normative issues," and to understand and criticize "faith-experiences and value-experiences . . . in a rational way." I am citing the language of the General Studies committee from the Virginia Wesleyan College Web site. For my purposes in this class, I interpreted all this to mean that the class should look at rituals from different kinds of societies, both familiar and "exotic," and analyze these rituals using various theoretical approaches. With only one general prerequisite, I could not presume that anyone came into the class having read Freud, or Durkheim, or any specific theorist.

What, then, is a course like this for, one that is both a service course for the college's general studies and a required class for majors? The general goals of undergraduate education, the specific goals of my college's values category, and the education of religious studies majors, meet in Jonathan Z. Smith's discussion of the reasons for the academic study of religion in *Imagining Religion*.[1] A successful class, especially in the humanities, will "provide exempli gratia, an arsenal of classic instances which are held to be exemplary, to provide paradigmatic events and expressions as resources from which to reason, from which to extend the possibility of intelligibility to that which first appears novel" (113). We need examples, and examples of attempts at intelligibility. Smith describes the tension between "religion imagined as an *exotic* category of human experience and expression, and religion imagined as an *ordinary* category of human expression and activity" (xii, italics in original). A compelling strategy, especially with undergraduates, is what Smith calls "defamiliarization": "making the familiar seem strange *in order to enhance our perception of the familiar*" (xiii, italics in original). When the students have seen that religious activities of the Pomio Kivung in Papua New Guinea are at one level quite similar to the activities of American Protestants with which they are familiar, they have learned both to move beyond gawking to attempts at intelligibility; and they have learned that the everyday phenomena around them are in fact just as extraordinary. Everyday phenomena will become interesting, require reflection, and require explanation. Though far beyond the scope of this essay, this means that this class in ritual studies was designed with what I take to be the most basic goals of a liberal arts education in mind: to initiate students into the examined life, and to do so in such a way that they develop the analytical tools required for full participation as citizens in a democratic society.

In addition, majors should have some familiarity with "touchstone" thinkers, especially if they plan to attend a graduate program in religious studies or seminary. But I assume that a fair number of the people, places, and theories will be forgotten by the time they cross the graduation stage, so such familiarity cannot be the primary goal of the major. More important, the process of making ritual intelligible through various means teaches unforgettable things about religion and religious studies. Students will grasp some of the ways that religious traditions interpret and reinterpret—that is, the way they become traditions. And they will see the same thing happening with scholarly traditions. If they are really insightful, they will see that these two processes share many parallels (another nice Smith point; see 100–101).

The Cognitive Science of Religions

Although sessions related to the cognitive science of religion are drawing increasingly large crowds at professional meetings, it is likely that teachers of religious studies will have less familiarity with this approach than some of the others discussed in this volume, and so I will say a few introductory words about the approach in general.

The cognitive science of religion begins with the plausible assertion that the basic unit of cultural and therefore religious transmission is the individual human mind. Though people are clearly shaped by the culture in which they reside, cognitive science dissolves many of the frustrating questions about what culture is by assuming that culture is the shared patterns of ideas and behaviors of individuals. Ideas and behaviors are not somehow stored "out there" but are located "in here." To the extent that an idea or behavior is widely disseminated across a population of individuals, we call that idea or behavior cultural.

If that is the case, then the structure of the human mind will play a significant role in which behaviors or ideas are widely shared. An idea that is easy to remember is more likely to be "in" the minds of more individuals, and is therefore more likely to be widely disseminated and ultimately part of a culture than is an idea that is difficult to remember. There are, of course, cognitively costly ideas that are in fact widely shared (algebra and Trinitarian theology, for example). But in these cases there are special societal institutions that are devoted to their active promulgation (middle schools and churches).

An early strand of the cognitive science of religions took its cue from Richard Dawkins's concept of memes. A meme is an idea that can be replicated and therefore shared by many individuals. For Dawkins, it is precisely analogous to a gene. Dawkins applies the tools of evolutionary biology to these memes. Ideas easy to remember are fitter, and more likely to survive and reproduce, than are ideas difficult to remember.

This is an intriguing analogy, but it seems to rely on a rather Humean concept of the mind as a blank slate, rather than a Kantian concept of mind as an active shaper. Most current cognitive scientists, who work in the tradition of Chomsky and the role of the mind in generating grammar, find the "epidemiological" approach of Dan Sperber a more plausible account of the spread of ideas and behaviors. When we talk about ideas that are easy to remember or hard to remember, we are talking less about the ideas themselves than about what the human mind is like, such that it allows us to process some things easily and others only with great difficulty. Ideas are rarely copied directly from one mind to another. The patterns of shared ideas and behaviors will have a great deal to do with human mental processes, and these mental processes are the focus of the cognitive sciences. The human brain has evolved to handle certain tasks relevant to our survival and reproductive success. Humans share these tasks and processes. We therefore tend to shape ideas and actions in similar ways; they tend to group around certain "attractor positions," and this accounts for widespread similarities across a culture and among cultures.

From the beginning, there have been two tracks in the cognitive science of religion, one focused on religious ideas (gods), the other on religious actions (rituals). I will of course be most interested in religious actions in this chapter, but I will mention one application of cognitive science to religious ideas because it provides such an accessible example of the general approach.

There is evidence that, in much the same way that children seem to develop a language capacity at a certain age and can learn complex lexicons and syntaxes quite "naturally," so too they develop other mental capacities at specifiable points in early cognitive development. For example, very young infants begin to expect that solid objects will not pass through each other. Children at a later stage learn to attribute minds to other "agents" and account for their movements by attributing to them perception, desires, and intention. In other words, children and adults have what psychologists call a naive physics and a naive psychology, among other capacities.

Justin Barrett describes the mind as a set of specialized tools, each handling different tasks, mostly unconsciously. These tools include "describers." For example, when your mind has identified something as an object, it automatically ascribes to it all the properties of a bounded object. If something seems to initiate its own actions, your mind ascribes to it agency, which includes properties such as desire, intention, and thought (cognitive scientists call this the theory of mind).[2] This is a cognitively efficient system because it does not require your mind to observe and remember a set of characteristics for each object it encounters—describers (tools) merely identify something and attribute to it all the characteristics of the appropriate category.

Barrett and Boyer have found in experiments that over time people are more likely to remember stories that include agents or objects that violate one of the assumptions of these describers. In other words, if your mind has identified something as an object, and yet the story attributes to it some aspects of mind (a listening statue), this story will be remembered better than stories in which no violations of assumptions occur, and it will be remembered better than stories with merely odd components (a table made of cheese, for example, which is odd but violates none of your mind's descriptor assumptions). Such stories, in other words, have selective fitness, and will be widely remembered. The hypothesis is that violating one assumption makes such stories worth remembering because they are interesting, but not too cognitively demanding to be remembered and transmitted easily. Barrett has termed these concepts "minimally counter intuitive."[3]

The other track of the cognitive science of religions began with the work of E. Thomas Lawson and Robert N. McCauley on ritual first published in *Rethinking Religion*.[4] They argued that ritual participants represent ritual action to themselves in cognitively structured ways. Ritual participants have intuitions about correctly formed rituals, much the same way that speakers who cannot articulate rules of grammar nevertheless can produce and recognize correct sentences in their native dialects. For Lawson and McCauley, the proper place to begin the study of ritual is with these intuitions, this ritual competence, rather than with ritual performance. This competence can account for many of the features of ritual behavior quite apart from the semantic or theological meanings of the agents, actions, and objects in any given ritual. Lawson and McCauley are interested in the deep, generative grammar of ritual. It is precisely this focus on structure rather than meaning that makes their admittedly demanding publications seem to so many to be much ado about nothing. At the end of the intellectual workout, they are not interested in interpreting the rituals or saying what they mean, which leaves many feeling unsatisfied.[5]

Lawson and McCauley argue that humans represent all actions to themselves in categories or slots of agent, action, and object (though not every action has an object). Religious ritual relies on this cognitive apparatus that handles all actions in the world. On their definition, though, what makes an action a religious action is that in one of these slots we will find a representation of what Lawson and McCauley call a culturally postulated superhuman agent (or CPS agent). This CPS agent may appear directly in a slot or may be embedded in a previous ritual. For example, when a priest baptizes an infant, we find a superhuman agent embedded in the agent slot, because the priest can legitimately perform this ritual by virtue of his or her previous ordination, which is legitimate by virtue of the previous ordination of the bishop, which eventually leads back to the founding of the church by Jesus.

Lawson and McCauley argue that we can make certain predictions about rituals based on where in the representation we find the CPS agent most proximately implicated (agent, action, or object). The more proximate the CPS agent (i.e., the fewer embedded rituals it takes to get to a superhuman action), the more central this ritual will be to a religious tradition. And, rituals in which the CPS agent is found in the agent slot will not be repeated (baptism), whereas rituals in which the CPS agent is found in the action or object slot will be repeated. Lawson and McCauley do not say much about why this is except to repeat that "when the gods do something . . . they do it once and for all."[6] There are of course rituals in which CPS agents appear in more than one place (communion, for example). But the criterion is one of proximity. If your tradition teaches the real presence, then the CPS agent is directly present in the object slot (bread), and less directly present in the agent slot (priest). Communion will therefore be central and repeated.

Soon after Lawson and McCauley's work began to appear, Harvey Whitehouse's "modes of religiosity" theory also started to attract attention. Whitehouse and Lawson and McCauley have collaborated on several projects, but there are significant differences between their theories. Whitehouse's is, first of all, a theory of religion, not ritual. He argues that one finds in historical accounts and in ethnographies two basic modes of religiosity, the doctrinal and the imagistic. He does not isolate a single variable that distinguishes these modes; rather, each mode is a "basin of attraction" around which sets of characteristics tend to cluster. The doctrinal mode codifies revelations into a logically coherent linguistically transmitted body of doctrines. Remembering such bodies of doctrines requires frequent repetition, leaders who can cast the doctrines persuasively, orthodoxy checks to curtail mutation of beliefs, and so on. The imagistic mode, in contrast, tends to transmit revelation through sporadic collective action, using "multivocal iconic imagery."[7] Weekly Protestant church services are a good example of the first; initiation rites of the Baktaman (often called "rites of terror") are a good example of the second.

This is a cognitive theory because, Whitehouse argues, what allows a religious tradition to succeed, its "fitness," is the ability of the members of that tradition to remember its concepts and rituals, and their motivation to pass them along to others. Each mode relies on a different mnemonic strategy to accomplish this. The doctrinal mode relies on semantic or scripted memory, which requires a great deal of rehearsing of doctrines and rituals—in other words, repetition. The imagistic mode, in contrast, relies on what some psychologists refer to as "flashbulb memory"—single traumatic and meaningful events stored in episodic memory.

In an outstanding ethnography, *Inside the Cult*,[8] Whitehouse describes his fieldwork among the Pomio Kivung of Papua New Guinea. The Pomio Kivung have a largely doctrinal religious tradition. The grueling schedule of ritual repetition and carefully enforced orthodoxy lead to what Whitehouse calls the tedium effect. While he was there, a splinter group resembling a cargo cult broke off from the mainstream movement in an effort to cause the immediate return of the ancestors. This splinter group was largely imagistic, creating new and ever more striking rituals. In the end, the members of this group were reabsorbed into the mainstream movement, but, Whitehouse argues, they brought with them a renewed vitality and motivation. It seems that the advantage of the imagistic mode is that it sustains both memory and motivation; its disadvantage is that it forms only small, closely knit groups. Though the doctrinal mode is easily transported and can form large anonymous communities, it seems not to be sustainable by itself over the long term. Large, successful traditions, then, will have some pattern of interaction of the two modes.

There is a fair amount of overlap between the theories of Whitehouse and Lawson and McCauley. Each focuses on cognitive processes underlying ritual practice, and each is concerned to highlight the factors that aid memory and motivation and so give religions a selective advantage. McCauley and Lawson's most recent book, *Bringing Ritual to Mind*, argues that what they call the "ritual form hypothesis," that is, paying attention to which slot in the representation of action holds the superhuman agent, can account for all the data more efficiently than Whitehouse's modes theory can, including even Whitehouse's ethnographic account of the Pomio Kivung. Whitehouse has recently responded to this claim, both at conferences and in a chapter in his most recent book, *The Modes of Religiosity*.[9] One could, then, structure a very nice course on the process of theorizing (defining, classifying, arguing, explaining) taking these exchanges as an example.

One of the odd features of the cognitive science of religions, particularly pertinent for a course in ritual studies, is that it is no simple matter to relate the two tracks (the religious ideas track and the ritual track) to each other. I will have more to say about this later, because it has a significant effect on what readings make for good assignments when studying ritual. Although the leading figures in the religious ideas track (Justin Barrett, Pascal Boyer, and Scott Atran among them) pay their respects to Lawson and McCauley, they tend to have very brief, unsatisfying discussions of ritual. Their accounts of why minimally counterintuitive agents make appearances in rituals, or where rituals originate, or the kinds of work they do, have a very ad hoc feeling to them. In their turn, Lawson and McCauley pay their respects to these other theorists, but their theory does not require them to say what the origin of CPS agents is or why they survive. In fact, there seems to be some tension between the concept of a minimally counterintuitive agent and a CPS agent whose acts are effective "once and for all."

Religious Studies 340

If the general aim of a college course is defamiliarization—that is, the dual process of practicing strategies of intelligibility for that which seems foreign and, at the same time, looking at the extraordinary character of that which is familiar—then there is no one set of data or one ritual theorist that must necessarily be included on the syllabus. A cognitive approach does have the advantage of exposing majors to issues and debates currently occupying the field of religious studies, but there are plenty other of theories that could also claim space in the semester. Why, then, use a cognitive approach in an undergraduate class? One reason is its claim that although cultures vary, the underlying cognitive structures that organize cultures do not. This claim makes very clear to students who have had little exposure to religious traditions other than their own just how familiar these other religions can be. Many of the classical approaches to ritual leave a strong dose of otherness intact at the end of the day, as do some more contemporary theories to a lesser extent. It does not matter to the cognitive sciences if data come from hunting, agricultural, or technological societies. Students do not have to make the imaginative leap that, were they to live in a society like such-and-such, they too would find this a rational way of operating. The root assumption is that minds are minds and that the patterns thrown up for examination by cognitive theories look the same across kinds of cultures. This is not necessarily a strength of the theory; rather, it is a pedagogical advantage at a small church-related liberal arts college.

The model of intelligibility it asks students to accept is one with which they are familiar. Many of them are not yet skilled at hermeneutics, and it does not ask them to be. It claims to use the empirical method. (This is also not without its interesting controversies, which can be pursued depending on how the course is set up. I know biologists and psychologists who are skeptical of the level of empiricism at work here, and I know sophisticated theorists in religious studies who will argue that the empirical method is precisely the wrong model to pursue.) Again, I am not claiming a strength for the theory here so much as that it ties in with a kind of knowledge that students assume unproblematically is real knowledge. They may need to enter the debate about the extent to which that is true, but in the meantime there are fewer hurdles for them to go over to see something like a cargo cult as intelligible and familiar.

Though few students come into the class well read in Kant, Freud, or Chomsky, they do come in with the culturally influenced assumption that there are things going on in their minds to which they do not have direct access. Just as Chomsky shows that what is so fascinating about language is precisely those things we assume to be so common and ordinary, a cognitive approach exposes them to one way of looking at very familiar ideas and behavior in a new light.

There are challenges to teaching a cognitive approach. Perhaps the greatest is simply the logistical question of picking appropriate readings. But for the pedagogical reasons mentioned above, I have found it worthwhile to accept these challenges. That is not to say that I have not suffered through some pedagogical failures and made the students suffer through them with me. I now present a brief outline of the course as a whole, a discussion of some of the strategies for teaching a cognitive approach that I have tried and will not try again, and some of the solutions that, for now, seem to work well.

"Ritual Studies" usually enrolled between fifteen and twenty-five students (courses at my college were capped at twenty-five), mostly juniors and seniors. One of the features that consistently worked well over the years was the requirement that students attend in person at least four extracurricular events: an athletic event, a religious ritual that is not part of their own tradition, an academic lecture,[10] and a play or concert. I required this because the goal was to get them to master different strategies of intelligibility, which means understanding a theory well enough to apply it in a context that the theorist him- or herself did not. This is particularly critical in ritual studies because so many of the theories are presented as critiques of other theories and come with very little thick description of historical rituals as a way of testing their adequacy. Thus it would be easy for a good idea never to be tested even by its proponent.

All the assignments in the course were geared toward using the theories. In papers and in in-class presentations, students were always asked to explain some ritual or aspect of a ritual. What would Durkheim say about the homecoming game? Where would Eliade and Smith agree and disagree on last Sunday's communion service? What strategies of ritualization are being wielded to negotiate power structures in an academic lecture? Without these applications, students never really master the ideas. They also became very astute at picking out shortcoming of theories when they take them from the theorists' own data and put them into play with data of their own choosing.

When I began teaching "Ritual Studies," I made individual students responsible for presenting a theory to the class. This had very mixed results. If the presentation did not go well, the whole class's understanding of an important theorist suffered. I was then left with the dilemma of guiding the presentation from the back row too much for the good of the student practicing presentation skills, or too little for the benefit of the students trying to come to terms with the theorist. I kept in-class presentations on the syllabus because that practice is part of a liberal arts education and because it ratchets up the level of student participation and ownership of the educational process.

But I began to teach all the classes on theorists, and the students took that material and presented applications of theory to the ritualized events they have attended. In a graduate-level seminar, I will revert to student presentations of theorists.

The semester was divided into three sections, with the headings (1) What Is Ritual? (2) Classic Views, and (3) Some Contemporary Criticisms. It is useful to have some grand narrative to help students place individual theorists in context, both the context of the thinker's own time and work and in the trajectory of thought about ritual. Though there are several good anthologies and overviews of the field (works of Catherine Bell and Ronald Grimes, for example), I have never had much success as a teacher with anthologies and textbooks (though they provide invaluable orientation to scholars). My own solution, also not perfect, was to have students work through Roy Rappaport's *Ritual and Religion in the Making of Humanity* over the course of the semester.[11] That solution was not perfect because Rappaport's book is not easy going for undergraduates and it is, frankly, quirky, especially at the end. But it unfolds as a real argument in the course of which he takes up and discusses almost all the theorists we covered. So the students saw how these thinkers fit into at least one pretty good account of what has come before in ritual studies, and get one example of a thinker using and criticizing these approaches. Rappaport is also eye opening in his adamant claim that in the beginning was the deed. Ritual is "the social act basic to humanity" (31). When I asked students at the beginning of any class to define religion, they almost universally came back to some version of belief in god(s). Rappaport very forcefully claims that ritual behavior lies at the core, and in fact generates eternity as well as society (222). That is an argument that I would like students to take seriously in this class.

Readings changed somewhat each semester in response to how things had gone. In the course's most recent iteration, the "What Is Ritual?" portion included Jack Goody's "Against Ritual"; Arnold Van Gennep's *The Rites of Passage,* chapters 1 through 3 ("The Classification of Rites," "The Territorial Passage," "Individuals and Groups"); and Rappaport, chapter 2 ("The Ritual Form").[12]

The "Classic Approaches" portion included the chapter "Liminality and Communitas," from Victor Turner's *The Ritual Process;* Clifford Geertz's "Deep Play: Notes on a Balinese Cock Fight"; "The Positive Cult," from Emile Durkheim's *The Elementary Forms of Religious Life*; Sigmund Freud's essay "Obsessive Actions and Religious Practices"; selections from Mircea Eliade's *The Sacred and the Profane* and *The Myth of the Eternal Return*; and J. Huizinga's chapter "The Nature and Significance of Play as a Cultural Phenomenon," in *Homo Ludens.*[13] I did not see any point in shying away from the best readings. After all, the most important goals of the class were less to disseminate information about specific theories than to exercise the student's analytical abilities with important arguments. Textbooks generally do not provide such exercise. But students at most colleges usually have a wide range of abilities, and so I found it wise to assign the best but to excerpt ruthlessly and then to provide time in class and in office hours to assure that students could understand the readings.

Once they were familiar with some of the important touchstones in ritual theory, students were in a good position to understand more recent work and to see how a scholarly tradition of criticism, application, and innovation unfolds. The cognitive approach fell under a third heading, Some Contemporary Criticisms. This section also included Warner's "An American Sacred Ceremony," David Parkin's "Ritual as Spatial Direction and Bodily Division," Steven Lukes's "Political Ritual and Social Integration" (this is a nice set of people working out of a Durkheimian model and yet using it in different ways), Bell's articles "Ritual, Change, and Changing Rituals" and "Discourse and Dichotomies: The Structure of Ritual Theory" (these articles get to the heart of Bell's arguments very efficiently, and I have found them to be more accessible to students than is *Ritual Theory, Ritual Practice*), most of the rest of Rappaport's *Ritual and Religion in the Making of Humanity*, and Jonathan Z. Smith's "The Bare Facts of Ritual."[14]

Since I first taught this course in 1997, I have included the cognitive approach. In my experience the greatest challenge has been to pick appropriate readings. The first year, I screened Frits Staal's movie *Altar of Fire* (1976) and lectured on the analogies between deep grammar and ritual structure. Though the students enjoyed the movie, they lacked enough background to make much sense of it, and the lecture on deep grammar was less than a success. Much of the leading work on the cognitive science of religions, as stated above, focuses on religious ideas rather than actions. For theoretical reasons I find these works' treatment of ritual inadequate. In addition, as a practical matter it is difficult to excerpt the chapter on ritual from them because they make little sense without the other chapters, which would occupy too much space on the syllabus. Texts from the ritual cognitive track tend to fall into two groups: gruelingly difficult, and easy but unhelpful. I have tried both. In the grueling category is Lawson and McCauley's first book, *Rethinking Religion*. It is not impossible for undergraduates, but one has to move slowly. The best success I have had with this book requires reading it in tandem with Chomsky's *Syntactic Structures*.[15] But in a general course on ritual theory, this took us too far afield and occupied too much of the syllabus. I have not yet tried McCauley and Lawson's second book, *Bringing Ritual to Mind*. Two features caused me to shy away from the book for a course like this one. First, it includes a detailed review of current scholarship on flashbulb memory. This is thick going for those with no background in this branch of psychology (which would include most of my students), and it is a bit far afield for this class. Yet it would be difficult to excerpt from the book without it. Second, McCauley and Lawson's argument is framed largely in terms of their ability to explain Whitehouse's data in *Inside the Cult* better than he himself can. Although this is exciting for those in the field of ritual studies, my sense is that students would have a hard time following the text without a prior reading of Whitehouse. And one of the most interesting questions raised by McCauley and Lawson's book is whether they have presented Whitehouse's theory in a way that he would accept. One could structure a fascinating course around this, but in a course designed to cover a number of approaches, this would take up an inordinate part of the semester.

As for readings on the easier overview side, I have assigned Lawson's "Cognitive Categories, Cultural Form and Ritual Structures."[16] To make this useful, giving the theory in enough detail that students could actually apply it, I found I had to present the "harder" version of Lawson and McCauley in class anyway, so this ended up being a time loser rather than a time saver.

The solution that worked fairly well the last couple of times I taught the course was to assign Whitehouse's *Inside the Cult* as an example of the cognitive approach. There are several advantages to using this book. It is an engaging ethnography that reads almost like a novel. The students loved it. Its portrayal of the Pomio Kivung exposed them to a religious tradition that is unfamiliar to them, but it gives enough detail and enough background so that it makes sense. It portrays participants in this "foreign" tradition as historical agents affected by and making their own way in the modern world. In other words, they are not presented as archaic, which forms a nice contrast to much of the data in the section on classics. It presents enough data to support the theoretical claims that arise at the end of the book. (Many of the other readings on the syllabus present interesting theories, but not much data to test them.)

There are also serious disadvantages to using this book. It does a nice job of making the point that ritual behavior is based on cognitive structures, in this case different mnemonic and motivational strategies. But in doing so it takes no notice of Lawson and McCauley's work on the ways ritual actions are represented cognitively by participants. I find this an insignificant disadvantage for liberal arts undergraduates, who are not being trained to become scholars of religious studies. Those heading off to graduate school will have the tools to read Lawson and McCauley when they get there.

One of the strengths of the book, its wonderful thick description, is also a practical drawback. Students need to get through a large number of pages before getting to the theoretical payoff. I tried to make this drawback worthwhile by using the ethnographic data as grist for the theory mills of others. One very successful final project asked students to create a flow chart representing Rappaport's "cybernetics of the holy." Rappaport sees ritual as part of a system that provides corrective feedback to support or alter or overthrow social systems. This system can easily be displayed graphically. Students went through Whitehouse's ethnography to see if the pattern of ritual change he describes could be placed into this flow chart in a way that does justice to the data of the Pomio Kivung. The students who chose this project enjoyed it, and they really nailed down both Rappaport and Whitehouse.

Because Whitehouse claims there are two basic modes of religiosity, the doctrinal and the imagistic, with many different features, including different ritual patterns, students began to see these patterns everywhere. Two projects stand out in my mind. One was by a woman beginning college after working for many years. She had participated in a De Colores weekend (a weekend designed to regenerate Christian commitment), and came away from her class presentation both excited and temporarily shaken by the similarities between her experiences and the experiences of the mainstream and splinter groups described by Whitehouse. (She has continued on to seminary, and I expect she will one day be a very adept ritual specialist.) Another student was similarly excited to have a new way of looking at the religious summer camp most of the youth from her rather strict and doctrinal church (Associate Reformed Presbyterian Church) attended each summer.

These, then, are the choices I have found that work best to this point. Each semester brought some adjustment to the syllabus. For those interested in incorporating a cognitive approach to ritual in their teaching, I encourage them to keep track of the Web site of the Institute for Cognition and Culture at Queen's University in Belfast (http://www.qub.ac.uk/icc/). This is an institute founded by Harvey Whitehouse (and currently directed by Tom Lawson) that is becoming the institutional clearinghouse and driving force behind much of the work in the cognitive science of religion. There is a great deal of literature appearing, and this is a good place to track the development of the field, and perhaps to find new readings that avoid some of the difficulties I mention above. There are many important and unresolved debates surrounding what is, after all, a very new body of research. It is not clear to me that the cognitive science of religions will fulfill some of the grander promises of its pioneers. But it may. In any case, I have found it to be an extremely engaging and successful way to introduce and practice the central goals of a liberal arts education in a class on ritual theory.

NOTES

1. Jonathan Z. Smith, *Imagining Religion: From Babylon to Jonestown* (Chicago: University of Chicago Press, 1982).

2. See Justin L. Barrett, *Why Would Anyone Believe in God?* (Walnut Creek, Calif.: AltaMira Press, 2004), chap. 1. Pascal Boyer presents similar views in *The Naturalness of Religious Ideas: A Cognitive Theory of Religion* (Berkeley: University of California Press, 1994); and in a more popular form, in chap. 3 of *Religion Explained: The Evolutionary Origins of Religious Thought* (New York: Basic Books, 2001). *Why Would*

Anyone Believe in God? and *Religion Explained* are probably the most accessible point of entry for those looking for orientation in the field of the cognitive science of religions.

3. There are a couple of obvious issues under debate among cognitivists: first, some important religious concepts seem to be maximally counterintuitive (the Christ of Chalcedon comes to mind); further, this theory has not yet explained why some minimally counterintuitive concepts are widespread and believed, whereas others are just widespread. This is referred to as the Santa Claus problem, or the Mickey Mouse problem.

4. *Rethinking Religion: Connecting Cognition and Culture* (New York: Cambridge University Press, 1990).

5. See, for example, Michael P. Levine's claim that their theory "does not tell us about . . . the nature of ritual, its function, or what it means. Simply put, it does not tell us anything about ritual that is of interest." "A Cognitive Approach to Ritual: New Method or No Method at All?" *Method & Theory in the Study of Religion* 1 (1998): 42.

6. Robert N. McCauley and E. Thomas Lawson, *Bringing Ritual to Mind: Psychological Foundations of Cultural Forms* (Cambridge: Cambridge University Press, 2002), 122.

7. These modes are fully described in *Modes of Religiosity: A Cognitive Theory of Religious Transmission* (Walnut Creek: AltaMira Press, 2004). A good introduction is Harvey Whitehouse, "Modes of Religiosity: Towards a Cognitive Explanation of the Sociopolitical Dynamics of Religion," *Method & Theory in the Study of Religion* 14 (2002): 293–315.

8. *Inside the Cult: Religious Innovation and Transmission in Papua New Guinea* (Oxford: Oxford University Press, 1995).

9. Whitehouse, "Theoretical Challenges," chap. 8 of *Modes of Religiosity.*

10. Before attending this lecture, students read the foreword and pages 1–9 and 69–75 of Kevin Sheard, *Academic Heraldry in America* (Marquette: Northern Michigan College Press); and Jean La Fontaine, "Invisible Custom: Public Lectures as Ceremonials," *Anthropology Today* 2 (1986): 3–9.

11. See my review in *Religion* 34 (2004): 261–263.

12. Jack Goody, "Against 'Ritual': Loosely Structured Thoughts on a Loosely Defined Topic," in *Secular Ritual,* ed. Sally F. Moore and Barbara G. Myerhoff (Amsterdam: Van Gorcum, 1977), 25–35; Arnold Van Gennep, *The Rites of Passage* (Chicago: University of Chicago Press, 1960).

13. Victor Turner, *The Ritual Process: Structure and Anti-Structure* (Ithaca, N.Y.: Cornell University Press, 1969), 94–130; Clifford Geertz, "Deep Play: Notes on a Balinese Cock Fight," *The Interpretation of Cultures* (New York: Basic Books, 1973), 412–453; Emile Durkheim, *The Elementary Forms of Religious Life,* trans. Karen E. Fields (New York: Free Press, 1995), 330–391; Sigmund Freud, *Collected Papers,* vol. 9 (The Institute of Psycho-Analysis and Angela Richards, 1959), 115–127; Mircea Eliade, *The Sacred and the Profane: The Nature of Religion,* trans. Willard R. Trask (New York: Harvest, 1959), 11–12, 20–36; Mircea Eliade, *The Myth of the Eternal Return or, Cosmos and History,* trans. Willard R. Trask (Princeton, N.J.: Princeton University Press, 1959), 3–34; J. Huizinga, *Homo Ludens: A Study of the Play Element in Culture* (Boston: Beacon Press, 1950), foreword and 1–27.

14. W. Lloyd Warner, "An American Sacred Ceremony," in *American Civil Religion*, ed. Russell E. Richey and Donald G. Jones (New York: Harper & Row, 1974), 89–111; David Parkin, "Ritual as Spatial Direction and Bodily Division," in *Understanding Rituals*, ed. Daniel de Coppet (London: Routledge, 1992), 11–25; Steven Lukes, "Political Ritual and Social Integration," *Sociology: Journal of the British Sociological Association* 9 (1975): 289–308; Catherine Bell, "Ritual, Change, and Changing Rituals," *Worship* 63 (January 1989): 31–41; Catherine Bell, "Discourse and Dichotomies: The Structure of Ritual Theory," *Religion* 17 (April 1987): 98–118; Jonathan Z. Smith, "The Bare Facts of Ritual," *Imagining Religion*, 53–65.

15. Noam Chomsky, *Syntactic Structures* (The Hague: Moulton, 1957).

16. E. Thomas Lawson, "Cognitive Categories, Cultural Form, and Ritual Structures," in *Cognitive Aspects of Religious Symbolism*, ed. Pascal Boyer (Cambridge: Cambridge University Press, 1993), 188–206.

USEFUL MATERIALS

Altar of Fire. 1976. Color. English text and narration. 58 min. Produced by Robert Gardner and Frits Staal. Berkeley: University of California, Extension Media Center.

Barrett, Justin. *Why Would Anyone Believe in God?* Walnut Creek, Calif.: AltaMira Press, 2004.

McCauley, Robert N., and E. Thomas Lawson. *Bringing Ritual to Mind: Psychological Foundations of Cultural Forms*. Cambridge: Cambridge University Press, 2002.

Whitehouse, Harvey. *Inside the Cult: Religious Innovation and Transmission in Papua New Guinea*. Oxford: Oxford University Press, 1995.

———. *Modes of Religiosity: A Cognitive Theory of Religious Transmission*. Walnut Creek, Calif.: AltaMira Press, 2004.

12

Religion through Ritual

Catherine Bell

That I have never taken a course on ritual is probably not at all surprising since my formal education ended many years ago, just as Victor Turner's early books were becoming ubiquitous on college and university campuses. However, it seems a bit odd even to me that I have never *taught* a course on ritual or, more precisely, a course *just* on ritual. Yet there are two good reasons for this, both emerging from the particular context in which I teach religion. Located within a liberal arts college housed within a larger university with distinct graduate schools, my department has no graduate program in religious studies. So whenever I give some thought to this lacuna in my teaching repertoire, I always conclude that any plan for an *undergraduate* course on ritual would inevitably raise two problems. The first, and more trivial, is whether to use my own books in class: they contain nearly all the content I would want to teach. My second book on ritual, *Ritual: Perspectives and Dimensions*, was not written to be an undergraduate text, but it certainly swallowed up all I had learned while teaching ritual in various contexts. Naturally, a course would engage other texts to explore many approaches, and I might even be able to ignore my own authorship, but my lectures would inevitably rely heavily on the material I had personally processed. I would teach the history that I have written or the theories I believe I have effectively critiqued and "improved." Even if I held back my own books, I fear I would inevitably overwhelm the students with details and defensive diatribes in arguments with unseen colleagues about points coming freshly to *my* mind but totally meaningless to a captive class of undergraduates.

Underlying this little dilemma is the fact that teaching students how to critically engage books, lectures, movies, and cereal boxes has been central to me as a teacher. How could I put them in the difficult (and rather unfair) position of having to be bold enough to critique the teacher's book or question the teacher's overly enthusiastic opinions?

I have asked colleagues who do assign their own work how they deal with this issue. Some reply that they don't; rather, they use their own work as a type of neutral textbook (is this possible?) and then employ a critical approach with regard to the other readings, usually primary sources. Other colleagues admit that they have tried it and soon abandoned the effort because it ultimately made everyone uncomfortable. One colleague, however, acknowledging all of these problems, remains determined to teach students that polite critical assessments are okay in the classroom (and beyond!), even if *he* has to demonstrate it by critiquing one of his own articles ("Now, what *was* I thinking when...") to get responses in kind. Recently I experimented using my 1992 book, *Ritual Theory, Ritual Practice,* in an advanced seminar. After working through appreciative critiques of seven or eight other readings in the historical study of religion, I assigned the first third of the book as an exercise in (a) analyzing a complex argument, (b) identifying the point(s) of one's confusion, and (c) expressing that confusion intelligently in writing using the literary mannerisms available for just this purpose. Although my mind is not made up about the value of the assignment, the format avoided the worst problems I have feared and led to some critical assessments.

Aside from this substantively minor reason, the second reason for never having taught a course on ritual is more grounded in my sense of the discipline of religious studies. Working with the expectation of having most of my students for only one course in the whole of their undergraduate careers, I am not convinced that a course dedicated to ritual is the most useful one I can provide, no matter how it might incorporate other pedagogical goals. My concern probably dates back to the late 1980s when I had the opportunity to design my own introductory course rather than continue to teach what my predecessor had made so popular. This was about the time that E. D. Hirsch's *Cultural Literacy: What Every American Needs to Know* (1988) was the object of much critical debate in what would prove to be the emerging culture wars. Somewhat playfully and with no allegiance to the Hirschean principle behind the project, two colleagues and I decided to try to draw up our own lists of what we thought every student taking the religion requirement should learn (and know?) by the time they graduated. Our different subdisciplines (theology, church history, and history of religions) made us suspect the results would differ, but the differences proved to be so great that it was comical to see our defensive ignorance of so many terms one or the other thought to be, or thought should be, common knowledge; inevitably, we disagreed over the importance of anything one of us did not know. Perhaps there would be greater congruence, we concluded, if we employed some real discipline and narrowed our lists significantly (Hirsch had five thousand "essential" names, phrases, dates, and concepts). Could we manage to be sufficiently austere, and confident in our sense of selection, to pare the lists to a mere ten items?

As I remember it, the other two reasonably decided a few weeks later that they had better uses for their time. But I doggedly worked on a ten-item inventory of minimal competency in religious studies, withstood their condescension when they reviewed it, and continued to tweak the last item or two on the list for several more years. However unrealistic it may have been, this project primed me to design an introductory course less around my own disciplinary strengths than around those issues that were arguably most useful for students, that is, what would make them at least "literate" (per Hirsch) in the study of religion and religion's main cultural extensions. With the idealism of a relatively new teacher, I fashioned a flexible ten-week course (for the quarter system) that was designed to make the students address why religion has taken the shapes that they were seeing around them, why it offered them the particular personal choices placed before them, and how it might be otherwise. In this context, ritual was clearly a central topic—and not the most difficult to make relevant and appealing.

A graduate course on ritual would be more straightforward, although not without some critical choices about presentation, most notably whether to start with data (a series of classic and current rites), the history of inquiry into ritual, or simply the most influential modern theories. Context, that is, the type of graduate program, would make a difference, but the foregoing options would still remain. And, to be honest, I suspect I would decide the course's approach either according to whatever issues or questions were uppermost in my thinking at the time, or how much time I had to prepare. Reality always trumps one's paper-based idealism, so it is usually better to take it into consideration from the beginning. With an undergraduate course, however, both realism and idealism dictated a different set of options.

What Is Ritual?

The introductory course that I have taught now for at least a dozen years, like so many others taught in comparable institutions, presents a number of key topics as avenues for depicting and understanding the social life of religion (social does not simply mean "to an outsider").[1] The fact that ritual is one of just four topics in this ten-week course reflects my view of its centrality; but it is joined, and contextualized, by three other topics, namely, symbol and myth, scripture and interpretation, and types of religious communities dealing with change. Only in discussing scripture do the students feel that they are on somewhat familiar ground, which fits with their starting notions of what

makes up religion; these tend to range from inchoate images of popular culture to rigid orthodoxy of some stripe. Yet these notions are also the starting
point of the course. I have learned to make clear from the outset that the course
is about religion as a social phenomenon; in other words, whatever else religion might be in regard to relationships with God or other formulations of
the divine, much of religion as we meet it from within and without is inevitably (and often sadly) a matter of human institutions trying to express and
live out these relationships with God. We need to try to understand the variety
of religious communities and institutions since they are so much a part of our
world, not just as they may appear in the news, but more surely in terms of
their diverse and rarely acknowledged cultural assumptions—how they are
linked to internalized and projected cosmologies capable of influencing very
personal engagements as well as committed political activism. Students readily
discuss many examples of the way religion is an active part of the current
global village—and often a confusing part at that.

The question then becomes, Can we understand religion as a social phenomenon in terms more general and analytical than those used when religions
present themselves? At this point, I give the class what has come to feel a bit
like a "canned" performance, dramatically describing how nearly every social
scientist since the very rise of the field has predicted that religion would gradually decline and fade away, with a few notable theologians suggesting their
own versions of its "death." These experts argued that science now provides
better explanations for the nature of the cosmos; modern technology promises
to do away with the poverty that has made people supplicate higher powers and
hope for more in the hereafter; and psychology could provide a better guide to
inner growth than could a minister or the functional equivalent, people who
are rarely schooled in psychological problems of basic development. These
idealistic expectations were explicit before World War II, even lingering on as
unexamined assumptions up through the 1960s. The class always has a good
laugh at how this vision of progress has gone awry, as seen in the continuing
history of challenges to scientific explanations such as evolution by religious
fundamentalists, or the failure of technology to dispel poverty and the suspicion that for all its benefits, it may have created new forms of scarcity. Certainly
there are real difficulties accessing truly useful psychological resources unless
one is wealthy, living in a large city, or a clear danger to oneself or the public. I
use Mary Douglas's 1982 article, "The Effects of Modernization on Religious
Change," which boldly challenges her colleagues to admit the obvious: that in
the wake of the Islamic revolution in Iran and the more general climate in the
Middle East, as well as the politically powerful rise of the Christian evangelical
Moral Majority, it was clear that the social sciences failed miserably to understand basic aspects of religion.

Since the experts have not had the right answers, I tell the class, the larger
question—what is religion?—will rightly be the focus of the course. They

write out their own answers in a few sentences, some of which we read. They usually give four types of answers: religion as divine revelation and humans living in accord with it; religion as a psychological crutch for those who cannot deal with reality; religion as a moral system dressed up as a cosmology; or "I don't know." We put these away until the last class, when we can see if and how their views have changed—although I am lucky if the class has any time for it. Since the social scientists so obviously failed to understand religion, as Douglas puts it, basic questions about it remain wide open for the students to engage. Moreover, I assure them that the course will not give them any answers, nor have I any up my sleeve. It is a *real* question. We will, however, explore some major social theories to appreciate and critique their contributions; the course will also add to the students' store of knowledge about various religions so that they have a better basis for engaging theoretical considerations. By the end of the mere ten weeks available to the course, they can expect to come to their own conclusions, certainly tentative, but at least articulate and defensible.

The question of why religion has continued to thrive when most of the social scientists of the nineteenth and twentieth centuries expected it to fade away makes clear to students the limits and failures of experts, the openness of basic questions, and the active role that the course expects them to take. The four sections outlined in the syllabus attempt to provide them with resources—theories and data—for forging their own answers in a series of projects. The first section, symbols and myths, introduces the psychology and phenomenology of religion; the second section, on ritual, presents basic anthropological theory; scripture and interpretation looks at the history reconstructed by biblical studies and then the interpretive role of theology; the last section, how religious communities change, provides rudimentary schooling in the sociology of religion. Along the way, the main readings use Hinduism, Ndembu religion, Christianity, and Islam as their data, while shorter readings for paper projects applying theory to data add examples from many other areas. In each case, the idea is to identify where a theory has proven insightful and arguably useful, and where it is weak by virtue of significant counterevidence or because it avoided addressing key issues. The strategy of introducing a topic that the experts had failed (so far!) to analyze and predict correctly serves to situate each student in the driver's seat as an analyst of theories and methods, encapsulated within the admittedly limited if flexible rubric of the four main topics I selected.

The first section explores psychological theories of symbols and phenomenological treatments of sacred space, time, and myth, ending up with the "hero myth" theory and papers applying these ideas to the sacred cow in India, the Lady of Guadalupe in Mexico, or Aztec human sacrifice (Harris 1977; Wolf 1958; Sahlins 1978). Then we are ready to turn to ritual. Lectures start with Van Gennep's insight into how rites of passage create the effect of a change of nature or status, a transformation of social status, by the simple use of move-ments in space, from passing through arches and bowers to more elaborate journeys of initiation. At the same time, the students are reading two chapters from Victor Turner's *The Ritual Process* (1969). In these pages, Turner also presents Van Gennep's model of the three-stage rite of passage (separation, liminality, assimilation) in order to generate his own theory of ritual as a dialectical interplay of structure and anti-structure (*communitas*). Just as Ann Gold describes in chapter 2 of this volume, the highly visual ideas of Van Gennep and Turner are immediately appealing to the students because they can apply them to their own experiences (with endless references to weddings and fraternity initiations!). When Turner spins his ritual model, and theory of its social purposes, into an extended explanation of the historical "stages" in America from the 1950s to the 1970s, the students follow right along with continued enthusiasm. But I call them up short, accusing Turner of letting a good theory get terribly inflated, starting with ritual structure and going on to forces of historical causation. Although Turner's theory is interesting specu-latively, its sweeping breadth raises questions of evidence. We discuss the sort of proof needed for a theory and the attraction of theories that start small and specific but grow to try to explain a great deal more—an idea that will be picked up again later. Students are a little dismayed to realize that one-theory answers to the nature of ritual (and religion, or culture itself) may be mis-leading.

The paper projects for the ritual section give them accounts of two different ritual scenarios to analyze using three models they have learned: Mircea Eliade's idea of ritual as a return to *illo tempore*, the time before history, by reenacting the deeds of the gods (ancestors, etc.) who created a cosmos out of the original chaos; Van Gennep's three-stage rites of passage; and Turner's dialectic of structure and anti-structure (Eliade 1954; Van Gennep 1960; Turner 1969). I might give the students accounts of girls' initiations among some American Indian tribes, the twentieth-century American bar or bas mitz-vah, or the "temporary monkhood" of a young boy in Thailand (Lincoln 1991; Robinson 2001; Swearer 1995). When required to apply as many models to each ritual as possible, students demonstrate to themselves the viability of multiple perspectives and theoretical formulations.

During the first course section on symbols and myths, the students tend to be rather uneasy, especially in regard to Freud's theory of the Oedipal roots of religion. This is *not* what they expected in a religion course; nor is it any-thing like what they have thought of as religion. The examples they analyze in the writing assignment, which ask them to use the psychological and phe-nomenological theories studied in class to explain real data, do little to ease their discomfort. However, after a few classes on ritual in the second section, the students seem to "get" it a bit. They begin to appreciate what a theory is, how wild it might seem, how wildly it might be applied, what agendas it can serve, and how it can be examined, modified, shot down, or developed further. They have had comparable experiences—at least, the rites of passage underlying their high school graduation, their college "orientation" process, and their growing New Year's Eve party expectations—and the theories explicate them in a way that makes sense and adds to their grasp of the depth of the cultural routines they take for granted. However, I point out to them, many of the rites discussed so far are not "religion" in the usual sense of the word; we still have to try to figure out what religion means. Freshman orientation cannot be considered religion, so why does it have a ritual structure? Is it religion really watered down, or are rites not confined to religion in the first place?

At this point, I will introduce a grossly simplified version of Durkheim's theory of religion as cultic activity and social formation; if the students' eyes are not too glazed over, I will also introduce the basics of Mary Douglas's ideas on the parallelism of the personal body and the social body, my own theory of the goal of ritual mastery to be used beyond the rite itself, and maybe even J. L. Austin on performative utterances (Douglas 1973; Bell 1992; Austin 1975). The last examples of ritual theory, tossed out to them without any supporting readings, are undoubtedly beyond most of the younger students in the class. Yet they enjoy the lecture as one rabbit after another can be pulled from the hat of theory. It pushes their sense of the "play" of theories, while tackling the larger issue of the relation between religion and ritual. However, I have had times when students became sullen or rebellious about theories that appeared to be trying to explain them, making their deeply prized bits of personal independence suddenly drown in a sea of cultural determinism. If I catch a sizable manifestation of this attitude early, a good discussion can be had. If I do not see it happening, the students drift away intellectually and emotionally, and a great deal of effort is required to pull them back to an active stance.

What Is Religion?

Religion was not always introduced in this manner. I certainly never had any such overview of topics or methods of inquiry, not even anything that could be considered an introduction at all. The closest thing was the philosophy of religion or the world religions course, the latter still popular among students and some faculty, but its cookie-cutter reconstruction of a handful of religions has become almost impossible to teach (Masuzawa 2005). General introductory courses per se do not seem to have appeared in significant numbers until the 1980s, when they were apt to be half theological and metaphysical materials (concerning God and theodicy), perhaps a novel or movie about an Eastern religion, and then a journal for some sort of self-reflection. In the 1990s, college introductory courses were more apt to analytically tie course materials to what some spectrum of scholars in the field were currently reading, thereby admitting psychology and anthropology, in particular. Currently, introductory religious studies course may well lean heavily on anthropology to supplement phenomenological resources, and more often than not they disregard theology completely. Of course, the social study of religion has been trying to distinguish itself from theology for many decades now. It is also undeniable that theology is not interested in religion per se; it offers few modern discussions of how to understand other religions or address the challenges posed to exclusive claims to truth by the religious plurality of an age uncomfortable with further evangelization. Yet as a dimension of religion, the theological writings of a religious tradition (or any other means by which a tradition interprets its unchanging sacred revelations) are unquestionably an aspect of religion that students know about and should learn how to contextualize. To add theology as a topic, alongside ritual, is not very easy, but the student response is quite rewarding. They enjoy making (provisional) sense of things in the world they know, being able to place what they have met (to some degree) within a larger picture.

Multiple caveats accompany the introductory course's exercises in method and perspective, stressing that these theories not only remain open to debate, they necessitate it—having failed to predict the future of religion very accurately. Eventually, the exercises seem to reassure the students that there are larger pictures within which their cacophony of experiences can be analyzed and even stuffed into pigeonholes if they are so inclined and—this I am less confident about—that there are transferable techniques of analysis with which to pursue such investigations. Most of all, the presence of theology as a topic keeps in the air the question that forms the theme of the introductory course: What is religion—and who is to say? By the time we get to the theology section, they have learned to ask whose perspectives are admissible. Do not all perspectives come with cultural limitations as well as insights? And why, in an academic setting, is it appropriate to want more than private answers for these questions?

Most of the course introduces religion in terms of psychology, comparative mythology, ritual, and sociological change, all of which foreground the explicitly non-theological approaches that have become so dominant in the twentieth century. For students, like most people who think of religion as a matter of ideas about divine beings that one either believes or does not, these methods of social analysis are a surprise, almost unwelcome to some and too welcome to others. Yet they bring important experience. Though quickly appreciating the importance of family and communal rites, students also know that participation in such rites can be expected even when personal conviction regarding the values or beliefs espoused in the rites are lacking. They can imagine the performative act as religiously expressive, or simply socially effective. When they come to appreciate the extent of their own involvement in

civic rites, club rites, and college ceremonies, some students are a bit dis-
tressed: the knowledge undermines their own carefully measured sense of
distance between themselves and organized religion of any sort, or they undermine the distinct religious identity they may have cultivated, since all these
other innocuous rites engage them in communities that take their other,
secondary identities as uppermost. For students with strong religious convictions, the distress is worse when religion is presented, at least in part, as a
matter of social categories and ceremonial action, rather than religious convictions about primal revelations. Yet few reject the course material; they
choose instead to work their way through it. And it is the ritual section that
seems to convince them of the value and applicability, however limited, of the
theories presented.

In one simple classroom exercise, the students must research and bring
in a "posture" typical of the ritual life of a particular religious tradition—
kneeling in prayerful supplication, receiving baptism in a river, standing to
chant a specific invocation to each of the gods of the four corners, lighting
incense to the ancestors, singing gospel hymns, praying on a prayer rug
facing Mecca, or lighting the candle at sundown with a blessing that marks
the beginning of the Sabbath. The students are usually very imaginative in
seeking out the familiar and unfamiliar, researching it and coming to appreciate the beauty of the act. Moreover, the physicality of acting ritually in
unusual ways seems to provide avenues for externalizing their questions and
unease. The discussions have been very stimulating. And although the
adoption of such postures can smack of high school or late-nineteenth-century
forms of parlor entertainment, we also have the opportunity to discuss the
artificiality of our actions in the classroom and the importance of context in
understanding such activities. They are aware that conflicts over "whose tradition is it?" have arisen when the religious practices of one people are taken
and used by others in very different contexts; this is most likely to be experienced as more than mere sacrilege when the people already feel victimized
by other forms of cultural exploitation. Yet the pedagogical result, delivered
very gradually and often incompletely, is the ability to understand and articulate the importance of activity itself, the often secondary nature of doctrinal
formulations, and the mystery of personal religious experience in a context of
cultural expectations and social models.

Religion in Full Context

The introductory course I designed focuses on some of the main topics and
analytic categories used by historians of religion, all geared to emphasize how
to employ and evaluate theories of religion (or anything else, of course). If the
spectrum of ways to analyze religion dominates at the introductory level,

secondary courses focusing on specific traditions are opportunities to explore ritual acts in the very thick of another cultural and historical context. Though I have had to teach all of the Asian traditions at one time or another—and frequently in comparative courses using Christian, Jewish, or Muslim material—changes in the curriculum have gradually allowed more focus on my main areas of formal competence. In teaching Chinese religions or Buddhism in all its Asian (and some American) forms, there have been many opportunities to use ritual practices to explore religion as more than a pantheon of deities and a set of beliefs formulated to look like the other "world religions."

In fact, it is impossible to teach Chinese religions as primarily a matter of beliefs with some rites attached. Though I do not draw students into the debates that have engaged me professionally, I do introduce them to the question "What is religion?" in the context of Chinese culture, and to the question of how much we should focus on ritual practices or the formulations, usually textual, of beliefs (and who might have held which ones). These issues throw into relief the problems that come with all the assumptions of even a vaguely Judeo-Christian background. Breaking out of the Christianity model of religion is necessary even to understand its siblings, Judaism and Islam. It is no less necessary on the other side of the globe. Ancestors and ancestor rites, a divinatory cosmos, the many meanings of "the way," and centuries of interaction with very different ways of being Buddhist—in all these cases, rituals make the outlines of religious diversity become clearer, even when they are glossed by the perfect bit of textual imagery from Zhuangzi or Zhu Xi. Yet the many formulations of religiosity found in China challenge the imagination of anyone raised within the Judeo-Christian-Islamic paradigm, suggesting to them that either China is *really* different, or maybe we have a very simplified understanding of what has been going on behind the neat outline of our dominant paradigm.

In a modest variety of courses, I suggest that the cultural importance of ceremony in tribal as well as official court rituals around the globe arguably makes ritual a starting point for the project, however open-ended, of understanding religion. But the process is complicated by the realization that we cannot assume that ritual or religion are essentially the same sort of thing everywhere. So a course on the religions of China or Japan or a course covering Buddhism from India to California will often fall into the easier stance of surveying religious-like cultural history; it is a different sort of course when taught as an opportunity to question the nature of ritual and religion, challenging the basic ideas with which we engage that cultural history. Such courses, therefore, destabilize assumptions and neat definitions about what religion is. I certainly am thoroughly destabilized by now and know that a few students felt more than a bit challenged! One religion major declined to take a required course with me for a couple of years, willingly telling me it worried him, until his senior year when he finally signed up for my course on Buddhism. He was a thoughtful Christian and had not wanted anything to disturb his beliefs. I recommended he talk it out with his Jesuit advisor, who was responsible for finally convincing him to enter the Buddhism course. He did not love the course, but by senior year he was mature enough to be interested and drawn into the comparisons with what he knew. Finally, unsure what to do a paper on, he picked up on a reference I made to the problem of involuntary losses of semen by Buddhist monks when sleeping, a topic that was much discussed for its problematic implications of a loss of physical control and lingering forms of sexual desire. The student did a fine paper, one that I quoted in class for years after. By coming to understand in greater depth Buddhist views of the body, and the ritual controls expected of it, he found some common ground on which to understand the differences and similarities of Buddhism and Christianity.

Over the years, a teacher works up a few extended examples, such as the Japanese imperial enthronement ceremony, stretching from what it known of its origins to the curious arrangements in the most recent one, that of Akihito. Chinese ancestor rites allow for multiple examples that contrast the formal Confucian canon with the irrepressible forms of folk religion. In developing small examples, different types of religiosity are encountered—village religion, the regional religions of market-linked towns, the religion of the cultured elite, and the ceremonial life of the court itself. In addition, there were the religious movements of charismatic leaders, which led to political campaigns, much suffering, and cultural changes. The more subtle logic of various Chinese rites of "self-cultivation" can be shown to play out in the history of Daoism, alongside stages in the sinification of Buddhism, the modernization of Confucianism, and even the "reeducation rites" of the Cultural Revolution at the hands of the Red Guards.

Students, of course, have a hard time figuring out how such materials will fit into the examination structure, although they do figure it out. Students know they may be at a disadvantage when they step into one of my classes if their only previous coursework addressed Christianity, but I think the disadvantage is quite different from what they imagine. It is not one of knowledge, but perspective. Christianity is the religious tradition least likely to be taught with reference to its key rituals. In most religious studies departments, undergraduate courses on Judaism and Islam naturally discuss some of the main ritual components of these traditions, often presented as more orthopraxic in orientation than Christianity. They also deal with the significance for a Jew or Muslim of the ideal of living a life defined by observing all of the ritual responsibilities laid out for a man and a woman. There are always classes celebrating a seder at Rosh Hashanah, or making visits to mosque services, as David Pinault describes. Yet courses on Christian history or theology that refer to the liturgical expressions of key doctrinal ideas will do so without ever examining what these liturgical expressions mean to anyone but theologians.

We have all been *trained* to present religion as systems of ideas, which are primarily attested to by texts. Should we happen to study Confucianism or Islam, we would take for granted a bond between religion and culture that is broken only occasionally by various modern pressures to accommodate religious plurality and secular democracy. In other words, we learn about Confucian and Islamic cultures, noting the continuities and discontinuities between the textual bases and traditional ritual practices. Religion defines culture. Yet Christianity is presented as noncultural, undetermined by any cultural forces, even though it has resided on the same continent for most of its existence. If there are winds of change in the air, they come as departments of religion begin to see the need to pay greater attention to global Christianity. That involves the study of Christianity in a multitude of cultural translations, appropriations, or even defensive accommodations. Yet in view of the unarticulated relationship of Christianity to culture, teaching the globalization of Christianity could still defeat the issue: it might underscore the peculiarity that *our* religions are relatively distinct from culture; in other words, religion and culture are distinct at home, but joined when foreign. The inclusion of ritual would make it impossible to ignore this issue. Indeed the Christian churches of Sierra Leone include their culture primarily in their rituals and thereby present the Vatican or the Anglican communion with the need to express concern about such sources of disunity.

The study of ritual practices has had a second-class standing among religious studies faculty and has elicited zero interest among students who are looking for exotic knowledge and strange experiences. Although I have a rationale for not offering a course just on ritual to undergraduates, it is true that I fear no one would show. Introductory texts increasingly include a chapter on ritual, which is an improvement conceptually. But to my mind, such chapters tend to reinforce student perceptions that rites are boringly familiar when they are not incomprehensibly strange; for them, it's the ideas or the art or the history that interests. To amuse myself as much as anything, I have approached the ritual component of my introductory course as a personal challenge. Each time I teach it, there is the opportunity to understand better how rites relate to symbols, doctrinal revelations, textual interpretation, and the inevitable processes of social change—and how to teach these relations more effectively. It is a challenge to figure out how to present ritual not as a grand "theory of everything," as Turner does, nor as just a chapter in a text on religion. My goal is to show the fundamental role it plays in integrating thought, action, and tradition, that is, in making a functional holism of the most routine experiences of religion—a holism that is one of religion's most powerful attractions.

NOTE

1. This course is under development as an introductory textbook (tentative title, *What IS Religion?*) due out in 2009.

USEFUL MATERIALS

Books

Bell 1997 and 1998 and Turner 1969 may be particularly useful for readers who want to adopt recommendations made in this chapter. Also of special interest are the following:

Cooke, Bernard, and Gary Macy. 2005. *Christian Symbol and Ritual: An Introduction.* New York: Oxford University Press.

Grimes, Ronald, L., ed. 1996. *Readings in Ritual Studies.* Upper Saddle River, N.J.: Prentice-Hall.

Turner, Victor. 1969. *The Ritual Process: Structure and Anti-Structure.* Ithaca, N.Y.: Cornell University Press.

Videos

Altar of Fire. 1976. Color. English text and narration. 58 min. Produced by Robert Gardner and Frits Staal. Berkeley: University of California, Extension Media Center. The only detailed film recording of one of the world's oldest rituals, the Agnicayana, a Vedic sacrifice to the fire god Agni. Like the other documentary films listed here, this video demonstrates the sheer complexity, tedious work, and variety of opinions that go into any performance of the tradition.

The Funeral. 1988. Produced and directed by Juzo Itami (Itami Productions). 123 min. Los Angeles, Calif.: Republic Pictures Home Video. A black comedy about an actress and her actor husband who, when her father dies, must be the chief mourners and observe the three-day traditional wake. They learn their "roles" from a video called "The ABCs of Funerals." Excellent satire on the cheap consumerism of modern Japan and the power of ritual to break through it now and then.

The Japanese Tea Ceremony. 1993. Color. English narration. 30 min. Produced by NHK, Japanese National Television. Princeton, N.J.: Films for the Humanities and Sciences. A particularly detailed account of all the preparations behind this supposedly simple ritual, accompanied by a discussion of the "way of tea" (*cha-no-yu*) that focuses rather exclusively on one significant seasonal tea ceremony as performed by the heir of the Omoto Sen-ke family, one of the leading schools of tea in Japan.

Kuan Yin Pilgrimage. 1988. 56 min. Produced by Prof. Chin-fang Yu. A documentary filmed in China that records the 1987 celebrations of the birthday of Kuan

Yin, a Buddhist ("goddess") bodhisattva, in the T'ien-chu monastery in Hangchow and on P'u-t'o Island, with discussion of pilgrimage practices to Buddhist monasteries there.

Puja: Expressions of Devotion. 1996. 20 min. Produced and distributed by the Arthur M. Sackler Gallery of the Smithsonian Institution. A basic introduction to this ubiquitous form of Indian worship with a general overview that compares puja in the home and at the temple. A final, unnarrated section presents good footage of household Durga puja in western India and a Chandi puja in an outdoor shrine in Orissa state in eastern India.

REFERENCES

Austin, J. L. 1975. *How To Do Things with Words.* 2nd ed. Cambridge, Mass.: Harvard University Press.

Bell, Catherine. 1992. *Ritual Theory, Ritual Practice.* New York: Oxford University Press.

———. 1997. *Ritual: Perspective and Dimensions.* New York: Oxford University Press.

———. 1998. "Performance." In *Critical Terms for Religious Studies,* ed. Mark C. Taylor, 205–224. Chicago: Chicago University Press.

Douglas, Mary. 1973. *Natural Symbols: Explorations in Cosmology.* New York: Vintage Books.

———. 1982. "The Effects of Modernization on Religious Change." *Daedalus* 111, 1 (winter): 1–19.

Eliade, Mircea. 1954. *The Myth of the Eternal Return or, Cosmos and History.* Translated by Willard R. Trask. Princeton, N.J.: Princeton University Press.

Harris, Marvin. 1977. "The Origin of the Sacred Cow." In *Cannibals and Kings: The Origins of Cultures,* 211–229. New York: Random House.

Hirsch, E. D., Jr. 1988. *Cultural Literacy: What Every American Needs to Know.* New York: Vintage Books.

Lincoln, Bruce. 1991. *Emerging from the Chrysalis: Rituals of Women's Initiations.* Rev. ed. New York: Oxford University Press.

Livingston, James C. 2001. *Anatomy of the Sacred: An Introduction to Religion.* 4th ed. Upper Saddle River, N.J.: Prentice Hall.

Masuzawa, Tomoko. 2005. *The Invention of World Religions.* Chicago: University of Chicago Press.

Robinson, George. 2001. *Essential Judaism: A Complete Guide to Beliefs, Customs, and Rituals.* New York: Simon and Schuster.

Sahlins, Marshall. 1978. "Culture as Protein and Profit." *New York Review of Books,* November 23: 45–53.

Smart, Ninian. 1995. *Worldviews: Crosscultural Explorations of Human Beliefs.* 2nd ed. Englewood Cliffs, N.J.: Prentice Hall.

Smith, Huston. 1991. *The World's Religions: Our Great Wisdom Traditions.* Rev. ed. San Francisco: HarperSanFrancisco.

Swearer, Donald, K. 1995. *The Buddhist World of Southeast Asia.* Rev. ed. Albany: State University of New York.

Turner, Victor. 1969. *The Ritual Process: Structure and Anti-Structure*. Ithaca, N.Y.: Cornell University Press.

Van Gennep, Arnold. 1960. *The Rites of Passage*. Translated by M. B. Vizedom and G. L. Caffee. Chicago: Chicago University Press.

Wolf, Eric. 1958. "The Virgin of Guadalupe: A Mexican National Symbol." *Journal of American Folklore* 71: 34–39.

PART III

Teaching the Medium through Contrast and Engagement

13

Teaching Healing Rituals/Ritual Healing

Susan S. Sered and Linda L. Barnes

Rituals preserve and change people, things, and situations. The study of ritual allows us to think about what is being preserved; the change that is being sought; and how that change is expected to be effected, by whom, and through what means. Healing, too, involves bringing about a change, whether understood as restoration to an earlier state or as transformation to a new one, in relation to the experience of affliction or suffering, matters that lie at the heart of many religious traditions. Insofar as suffering and affliction are understood differently within different traditions—whether as an existential state or a condition susceptible to alleviation—the scope and meaning of healing will vary.

Though they may not use the word "heal," scholars generally represent rituals as healing social relationships (with people, spirits, and gods; from oppression, violence, feuds, mistaken alliances); as healing personal and social identities; and as healing misfortunes of various sorts. If rituals are understood to be transformative, then the phrase "healing rituals" may be a redundancy. Indeed, is healing rituals a heuristically useful category, or so broad a concept as to lose any sort of analytical efficiency? Is it more useful to designate a subset of rituals as healing rituals, or to identify the healing aspects of latencies or potentials intrinsic in diverse rituals?

The virtue of acknowledging the wide set of phenomena experienced as healing rituals (even if ultimately we find it more useful to work with a smaller subset of phenomena) is that it points to how ubiquitous and diverse healing rituals are, and how they span a gamut that includes behaviors which students may view as exotic, superstitious, and ridiculous, and behaviors that they themselves engage in without thinking of them as rituals. In our work with students in the United States and in Israel, we have found that students are better able to see and interpret these connections if they (1) develop a typology of afflicting forces, (2) formulate a typology of ritual healing techniques and procedures;[1] (3) examine the process of healing; and (4) determine what is meant by efficacy—the outcome of healing.[2] Such typologies and interpretive frameworks, though in no way exhaustive, provide a way of getting at the extraordinary complexity and diversity with which people engage healing. They enable comparison, as opposed to allowing the facile conclusion, "Oh, well, then everything is healing!"

Afflicting Forces

Underlying all ritual healing practices are beliefs regarding what it means to be ill and beliefs regarding the causes of illness: the forces (natural, semi-natural, or supernatural; external or internal; cosmic or personal) that cause affliction. The etiology, or explanation given for an illness, may take multiple forms. One broad category traces illness to personal failings, whether in this life or an earlier one. The failings include:

- unhealthy living;
- succumbing to imbalance, whether physical, humoral, emotional, energetic, or some other construct;
- suppressed anger, jealousy, or fear, coming under the heading of sickening emotions;
- anti-social feelings;
- an inability to manage stress;
- sin or moral failing;
- insufficient faith;
- ritual impurity;
- inattention to ancestors and/or ghosts.

In such cases, illness may be interpreted as the manifestation of a punishment (including karmic outcomes carried over from other lives), a test, or the natural outcome of imbalance. Collective failings may be read as the corruption of an age or recognized in social disharmony, potentially resulting in collective affliction.

Illness may also be blamed on others. It can be attributed to other individuals, as in

- the "sins of the fathers" visited upon their children;
- trauma, whether physical or emotion, inflicted by another person;

- curses and other expressions of anger or envy, as in "evil eye";
- sorcery or witchcraft directed in ways intended to afflict.

The living agent can also be collective, particularly in cases involving environmental ills, structural violence, social inequities, and related social trauma.

The dead can be sources of illness, whether through a genetic legacy (one way of representing ancestral influence) or through ghost affliction (whether one's own angry ancestors, or somebody else's). Evil forces such as Satan or demons can also be causative forces, as can God or gods. In the latter case, it is common to construe the illness not only as punishment, but also as a test—a spiritual wake-up call—or in relation to some lesson the person is expected to learn. In some cases, no personalized force is identified. Illness is viewed as simply an aspect of the way of the world—whether through biologically based agents like germs and infection, an impermanent reality, or bad luck. Etiological explanations may also combine factors from different categories.

When presenting different healing rituals to students, asking them to identify the etiological variables named by the different ritual participants provides an important framework for understanding the ritual response to the particular illness or affliction. It is also useful to ask them to identify the target of the affliction. Ask not only, "Is it individual or collective?" but "What aspects of the person or collective have become sick?"

A Typology of Ritual Healing Procedures—Techniques and Methods

This typology lets us see relationships and connections among rituals that would normally not be treated together, because some seem so distant and some so mundane. We see these typologies as food for thought rather than as definitive models. The fun of teaching with them is that people with different knowledge backgrounds can contribute to fleshing out and refining them. These techniques, or procedures—"who does what to whom with respect to medicines administered, prayers recited, objects manipulated, altered states of consciousness induced or evoked" (Csordas 1988)—are closely intertwined with what healing is understood to mean.

In his 1960 book, *The African Religions of Brazil,* Roger Bastide noted that religious healing lends itself to the "law of accumulation." Since healing rituals aim to be as effective as possible, healing practitioners tend to accumulate many and diverse rituals in order to maximize the possibility of efficacy (1978: 278). Altars of healers in contemporary Latin American societies and altars of healers in contemporary Asian societies often bear a striking resemblance to one another in that both include ritual objects from almost every corner of the world: crystals, holy water, six-pointed stars, Buddha statues, crosses.

Recipients of healing often take that law even further, availing themselves of multiple healing modalities and the services of multiple healers in the quest for health (however that is construed in a particular situation). The pursuit of healing sometimes leads to modalities that typically are understood to stand in contradiction to one another, and to healers whose religious identity would, in other circumstances, preclude social contact. Thus, for example, the Kurdish Jewish women studied by Sered recall non-Jewish Kurds coming to Jewish healers and Jewish women patronizing non-Jewish healers in Kurdistan early in the twentieth century. Although general social contact between Jewish and non-Jewish communities was limited, it was understood that in the pursuit of healing one would try all possible solutions. In the Chinese community studied by Barnes, people might resort both to Christian churches on the one hand, and to ancestor-related practices on the other, along with herbal remedies, to make sure that all the bases had been covered.

The size of healing repertoires varies, as does the degree of openness to healers and healing techniques from outside one's own tradition. Christian Science represents one extreme in which non–Christian Science healing is frowned upon, and the techniques of healing are limited to prayer and reflection. At the other end of the spectrum, we can identify some affluent Americans (stereotypically assumed to live on the West Coast) who try out every new holistic healing fad and New Age hero who comes along.

Given the avidity with which human beings seek healing, and the pace at which new techniques and combinations of techniques emerge, a comprehensive list of ritual healing techniques and procedures would be an impossibility. There are, however, several categories that can, in one form or another, be identified in many cultural settings. Though this is far from a hard-and-fast rule, it often is the case that the pursuit of healing begins with simpler or more straightforward (less expensive, less elaborate, less specialized) rituals and progressively moves on to more complex ones.

One of the simpler clusters of healing techniques centers on the manipulation of sacred or symbolic objects. This cluster was addressed prominently in the writings of early anthropologists who identified subcategories of "contagious magic" (contact with objects understood to carry particular power) and "sympathetic magic" (the use of objects understood to resemble the desired effect). Though the pejorative meanings often associated with magic are not particularly useful, the recognition that objects are ritually manipulated in particular ways is quite useful. Along the lines of contagious magic, ritual healing techniques include wearing an amulet written, blessed, or manufactured by a saint or other holy person. Along the lines of sympathetic magic, ritual healing techniques include the *milagros*—the tiny legs, arms, hearts, and so on that represent the body parts or organs in need of healing that are placed into receptacles at Catholic shrines and churches in Mexico and Texas.

Another cluster of healing techniques centers on prayer and meditation. The variations within this cluster are many: Who prays—the individual in need of healing or someone else on that individual's behalf? Is the prayer spontaneous and idiosyncratic or does it follow a set liturgical formula? Is the prayer understood to be effective because it elicits divine response or because it calms the emotions or centers the mind of the person who prays or meditates? Is the ritual silent and private or recited aloud? In contemporary American society, healing prayers occur privately, as when they are recited under the breath by millions of people going into surgery, and as part of public extravaganzas, such as revival meetings of various sorts.

A third cluster of healing rituals have to do with removing the object, experience, emotion, force, spirit, or person that is understood to cause illness. Roughly speaking, this cluster includes confession, exorcism, and purification of various sorts. A well-known example here would be the shamanic healings described by Boaz in which the shaman sucks the "sickness" out of the body of the patient. In many settings, the removal is verbal, narrative, metaphorical, or symbolic. Public and private, and voluntary and forced confessions of sins and misdeeds are other manifestations of extraction techniques: the sickness-causing information, guilty feeling, or wicked or aberrant thought is removed from inside the individual and, in one sense or another, is dissipated or neutralized. Purification techniques include physical cleansing practices such as washing and spiritual practices such as a meditation that eliminates impure thoughts. Often, the physical and spiritual aspects of purification rituals are inseparable. We think here of biblical laws of ritual immersion after menstruation or contact with the dead. Clearly, immersion in water washes away blood and other bodily effluvia. Yet the immersion also is understood to transform the individual into a spiritual state in which s/he can participate in the religious life of the community. When outsiders are targeted as the source of sickness in the body social, as has happened historically in response to some immigrant groups (Kraut 1995), the larger collective may erupt into violence and adopt ritualized forms of quarantine and/or expulsion—often unjustly—with the idea of purifying and healing itself.

In contrast to the previous cluster, which has to do with removing something, our next cluster has to do with inserting something into the person in need of healing. The most obvious examples in this cluster involve the ingestion of medicine of one sort or another. The ritual aspects of this cluster take a variety of forms: techniques of ingestion, techniques of collecting or preparing the medicine, and so on. In some instances, the something that is ingested or inserted is material in nature and understood to work on fairly straightforward biological principles: an herbal tea, for example. In other instances, the something has both material and spiritual aspects: for example, drinking water in which a paper with a verse from the Koran, a Buddhist sutra, or the Bible has soaked. Even substances that may seem to be material can be understood to work in a nonmaterial way: An example here would be homeopathy, in which the pills that are ingested are understood to work on an "energetic" level. The insertion of devices such as acupuncture needles adds an additional tangibility to the concept of insertion, coupled with energy manipulation, and it occurs in the context of a set process: for example, the acupuncturist reads the patient's pulse, looks at his or her tongue, and listens to the narrative of symptoms.

A fifth cluster of techniques involves touch. We include here techniques ranging from massage to laying on of hands of different kinds. At the most basic level, we think of the common human act of rubbing a body part that hurts. At the other end of the spectrum we think of the practice of Reiki healing, in which the touching is done on the astral or energetic level rather than through direct contact with the patient's skin. As a healing technique, touch is particularly multivalent. Its effectiveness can be understood in physical terms such as relaxing muscles or increasing blood flow, in emotional or social terms such as creating warm and healing interpersonal connections, and in spiritual terms such as channeling the power of divine entities.

One of the largest cluster of healing techniques has to do with the induction of trance and other altered states of consciousness. In many cultures, either the sick individual or the healer carries out some sort of practice that results in the elicitation of healing dreams (in which the dream itself heals or reveals healing knowledge). Healing trance and spirit possession, as in, for example, the zar rituals in parts of Africa, are elicited through drumming and dancing. In other contexts, altered states of consciousness in the healer, the patient, or both are elicited through substances such as mushrooms or tobacco, through sleep or sensory deprivation, through repetitive or hypnotic types of motions, through singing or chanting, or through meditation. The neurophysiological mechanisms by which altered states of consciousness heal have been explored thoroughly by Michael Winkelman (e.g., 2000).

A related cluster of ritual techniques falls under the general rubric of performance. In several works Tom Csordas develops the notion that healing performances create moods and special enchantment of experience that serve to engage the patient in the therapeutic process. Robert Desjarlais emphasizes ways in which healing rituals use music, visual stimuli, taste, and kinesthesia to "wake up" the patient and thus effect the healing. Desjarlais identifies healing techniques that invoke "wild images" that excite the senses, stir the imagination, and lead to healing via inducing sensory attentiveness and engagement (1996).

Healing settings often include some sort of ritualized social interaction. These interactions may be understood as an essential component of the healing process in that they represent reconciliation with gods, the community, particular social networks, spirits, or ancestors. The specific ritual practices often involve gathering the relevant people and spirits together in one place where some sort of public confession or ceremonial forgiving script is played out. Sometimes the spirits or ancestors who are part of the ritual interaction are made present or embodied through individuals who are understood to be possessed by the spirits. Other times, the ritualized gathering may be more symbolic, with people or spirits represented by drawings or other objects.

A final ritual cluster of ritual techniques has to do with some form of cognitive restructuring, that is, practices that encourage the patient or other participants to see or construe their affliction in a new or "healthier" way. Storytelling often is the means by which the cognitive restructuring is effected. Through the recitation of myths and tales that have cultural or spiritual resonance, the patient comes to see his or her own suffering as a part of a larger cosmic unfolding. Christian Science offers a clear example of cognitive restructuring: the work of the Christian Science healer is to help the patient understand that his or her suffering is not real.

In order to enable discussions of these typologies, a pedagogical exercise might include presenting students with a range of healing rituals—an Episcopal service of healing for those living with HIV/AIDS; devotion to saints and pilgrimage to holy tombs and relics; wearing amulets; spirit possession in traditions such as Santería or Candomblé; a Wiccan healing circle; prayer chains; a Korean shaman at work; a charismatic service of the Pentecostal Assembly of God; and a biomedical appointment with a physician—and asking them to apply the typology to each one, looking for all the aspects that apply. Discussion of how students have categorized each example can then include their rationales for doing so.

Procedures as Settings and Roles

Part of the procedure of ritual healing involves the settings in which rituals take place, as well as the roles played by healers, communities, and other forces. Healing rituals take place in a variety of settings and structures. At one end of the spectrum, we think of an individual who engages in a healing practice alone in his or her own familiar, domestic setting. At the other end of the spectrum are rituals that involve many people, including specialist healers, and that take place in settings removed from the familiar and rendered intentionally strange and distant.

Domestic settings with family members probably constitute the most common healing structure. Cross-culturally, mothers and grandmothers tend to be the first-line "expert" appealed to for healing. This domestic healing expertise takes both material and spiritual forms. We think here of the ritual chicken soup prepared by Jewish mothers and of the candles that Catholic mothers light in front of statues of saints on behalf of household members.

A healing structure found in many cultures is what I. M. Lewis has called a "cult of affliction." This refers to groups of people who share some sort of suffering or illness, and who gather together to seek solutions. The cults of affliction described by Lewis primarily involved women's ritual groups in Africa. The ritual action centered on spirit possession in which the afflicted women reached some sort of peaceful accommodation with their possessing spirits. In American society, the best-known instance of this structure is the variety of Twelve Step groups, such as Alcoholics Anonymous. The idea behind all of these groups is that people sharing afflictions, and those who already have overcome those same afflictions, can help one another heal.

Yet another context for ritual healing, which is larger than the family or the group of those who share in affliction, can be a religious group or congregation, which gathers to help its members heal. Good examples here are Pentecostal church services. In small-scale societies, the village or the tribe might gather for analogous purposes. The trance dancing of the !Kung is an excellent example of this sort.

According to how the particular affliction is defined, different healers come into play. Often, when one's own healing knowledge, or the greater expertise of one's mother and friends prove insufficient, healing specialists or practitioners are sought. Such healers are known by various titles: shaman, priest, doctor, midwife. We have found it useful to think about healers in terms of how large, significant, and powerful their roles are in specific contexts.

In some situations, the role of the healer is maximal; that is, the healer carries out specific actions that heal the patient, and the healing would not happen without the work of the healer. The maximum mode often is characterized by a hierarchical relationship between the healer and the one being healed. This hierarchy can be expressed in various ways: the healer is healthy, and the patient is sick;[3] the healer has inherent healing powers, and the patient does not; the healer has acquired specialized healing knowledge (in a variety of ways), and the lay person does not have this knowledge; the healer has a special ability to communicate with the gods or to channel divine energy, and the patient does not.

The high ritual status of the healer is made known through diplomas, lingo, insignia, special clothing, and honorific titles. Not surprisingly, perhaps, the maximum mode tends to be associated with greater elaboration of ritual performances: the performances show off the special knowledge, skills, or talents of the healer.

In many ways, the Western biomedical physician epitomizes this mode. Years of specialized training and apprenticeship induct her into the culture of biomedicine, in which she acquires the knowledge and skills related to her practice—how to "work up" a patient, formulate a case history, arrive at a differential diagnosis, manage a case, work within a medical team, and assume the mantel of authority conferred upon physicians, symbolized in the white coat. What differentiates the biomedical physician from some other types of healer is the careful distancing, on the part of biomedicine as a whole, from the notion that the physician taps into communication with the sacred. What takes its place is the power of scientific evidence, understood to hold sway even as it is susceptible to the surfacing of new and more compelling data. As a concept, however, evidence functions as a quasi-absolute.

A second mode for healers falls into a middle range in which the healer has a special ability to call on spiritual forces on the patient's behalf but does not have particular healing abilities. Good examples of this middle range come from cultures in which healing practitioners become possessed by spirits or deities who are the true healers; the practitioner is only a medium for the healing power. An example familiar to many of our students is Reiki healing in which the practitioner channels Reiki energy.

In many situations the role of the healer is minor in the sense that the healer is more of a facilitator of the patient's own healing powers than an "expert" who actually carries out the healing. A contemporary example of this mode comes from the world of hospices, hospital chaplains and congregational nurses, many of whom describe their work as a "ministry of presence"—as simply "being there" with the one who is ill. In this "minor" mode, the healer accompanies the patient, witnesses the patient's suffering, and supports the patient in his or her healing process. In contrast to the more hierarchical "maximum" model, in these instances the rituals tend to be relatively "understated."[4]

A final cluster of healing rituals do not involve a healer at all. We think here of group rituals in which everyone's actions function to, communally, heal the group. Twelve Step programs are a good example of this mode.

The role that played by the community in healing rituals is highly variable. Our previous example, Twelve Step Programs, is one in which the community is essential to the healing process. It is the very fact of the community gathering together that effects the healing. In this "maximal" mode, illness in the individual often is conceptualized as a reflection of illness in the social body, thus healing must occur at the communal level. The healing rituals that have developed with contemporary American spiritual feminist settings emphasize this approach with the declaration that the "personal is political and the political is personal." The notion that gathering in community is necessary for healing to take place has been well developed by Edith Turner and Victor Turner, who use the term "communitas" to describe the special emotional and spiritual emerges when people truly come together.

The fact that the community gathers together does not necessarily mean that the role of the community is to support the patient. On the one hand, we think of the many instances in which all family members gather around the bedside of one who is about to pass over into the next world. The family presence eases and enables that final healing. On the other hand, we think of the many instances in which the role of the community is accusative. (The extraction techniques described earlier may be particularly prominent in these instances.) Examples that come to mind here include various sorts of exorcisms, public punishment, exiling a sick individual, extracting confessions of sin, and so on. The contemporary Christian ex-gay movement, like other "deprogramming" efforts, falls within this category.

Finally, in many instances, illness and healing are understood to be individual matters. The popular jargon for this mode is "self-help rituals."

Beyond the role of individual and community, there is the role played by divine or sacred forces. Like the authority accorded different types of healers, the sacred takes on greater or lesser presence and action, depending on the type of ritual healing, and indeed shaping the nature of the ritual itself. Theologies enter the picture, articulating the nature of the sacred and its relation to humans and human affliction. At one end of the spectrum are rituals in which God, gods, or spirits *are* the healer, and humans the vessel or vehicle of healing. Ritual functions to invoke or invite that sacred presence. Christian laying on of hands, possession by the *orishas* in Santería or by the *lwa* in Vodou or the trance possession of the *zar* ritual all express the direct presence of the divine. The sacred shows up, and it is the direct force that brings about healing. At the other end of the spectrum are healing rituals defined as operating independent of the sacred altogether, as in the case of biomedical rituals. Although individual physicians may define their role within sacred frameworks provided by their own traditions, biomedicine itself does not. In the middle are healing rituals that express the role of the sacred as giving courage, comfort, and guidance.

The Process of Ritual Healing

Medical anthropologist Tom Csordas has argued that although the outcomes of ritual healing have been explored—a topic we shall address later in this chapter—less work has focused on the therapeutic process, "the nature of participants' experience with respect to encounters with the sacred, episodes of insight, or changes in thought, emotion, attitude, meaning, behavior" (1988: 121). Attention to process involves an inquiry into what could be called the action of the intervention, or how it is understood to bring about a change. This focus, Csordas argues (1983) is different from the question of how well a ritual intervention is thought to have worked.

In part, the process of ritual healing opens new transformative possibilities. As James Dow (1986) suggests, it provides new narratives into which the afflicted can enter and with which they can identify their own experience. This reframing of affliction is, as Csordas describes it, a rhetorical move that "redirects the supplicant's attention to new aspects of his actions and experiences, or persuades him to attend to accustomed features of action and experience from new perspectives" (1983: 346). It persuades the suffering individual or community to enter into the experience that is healing in its own right, that engages the afflicted in an experience of the sacred, and that has the potential to bring about the transformation sought in ways that the afflicted can identify and accept.

Particularly important in Csordas's interpretive framework is his emphasis on differentiating between two rather separate issues. The first is the process that brings about a disposition to engage in ritual transformation, the religious experience that ensues, the felt possibility of transformation, and the reality of incremental changes. The second is a focus on "the global role of psychological mechanisms such as suggestion, catharthis, placebo effect, or regression in service of the ego." Studies of these mechanisms, Csordas writes, "tend to discourage detailed analysis of therapeutic process in the experience of individual persons, since if healing can be accounted for by a nonspecific mechanism, all that need be specified is how that mechanism is triggered" (1988: 138).

This focus on process is congruent with understandings of ritual developed by Emile Durkheim and Victor Turner, not only in its making and remaking of the individual but also of the social (see Olaveson 2001). The symbolic repertoire explored over the course of the healing ritual not only communicates cultural meanings, but has its meanings reworked through performance by the collective (Schieffelin 1985), thereby introducing and redefining what healing means in the specific situation.

The Outcome of Ritual Healing—The Question of Efficacy

We suggest that the very presence of the question as to whether a healing ritual has worked helps to identify it *as* a healing ritual. Yet the question of working, as has frequently been observed, is a contextual one, related directly to how the affliction has been conceptualized and to what is recognized and accepted as a change or transformation. If we think about all the domains within which affliction can occur, we see immediately that efficacy will vary in relation to each one. It matters, for example, whether the illness is identified with the soul(s), spirit, emotions, psyche, *qi*, energy, anatomical physiology, genes, or some other culturally or religiously defined aspect of a person, or with some aspect of a collective social reality. Accordingly, the change sought and experienced may be observable; it may also be intangible, recognized in alternative ways.

With healing rituals, we deal with a particular constellation of circumstances. Unlike rituals that work because they tell a story in a particularly potent way, or celebrate group unity and cohesiveness effectively, or reinforce ethical teachings, healing rituals are usually expected to result in an empirically observable and relatively quick, transformation. According to ethnobotanist Nina Etkin, "Differences in medical ideologies notwithstanding, all human societies share a general understanding of medical efficacy as some combination of symptom reduction and other physical and behavioral transformations that indicate restoration of health. But this generalization obscures a wealth of meanings and expectations that are encoded within the complex patterns of medical behaviors that characterize different medical systems" (1988: 300). In contrast with a New Year's ritual, following which one can be reasonably certain the days will start getting longer (showing that the ritual worked), such is not the case in healing rituals. Unlike status-changing rituals (such as marriage or ordination) where the ritual effect (someone is now married) is in human hands, even the best healers cannot always heal their patients. Unlike the success of rituals that bring about subtle changes, the success (or failure) of healing rituals is pretty obvious—someone is or is not healed—so there's not a lot of room for ambiguity (on the face of it). Once we broaden the issue of efficacy to encompass the many dimensions of the person, it becomes possible to link even death and healing, particularly if the person is understood as having experienced the requisite transformation with which to enter death in the right state.

Efficacy may be partial and even temporary, and may be understood as occurring over time, through the repetition of the therapeutic ritual. It may occur at levels defined by ritual specialists and not recognized by the afflicted themselves; it may also be experienced on multiple levels by the afflicted, and assigned related layers of meaning, raising the question of who decides whether something has worked. Moreover, different kinds of effects may be intended, some more symbolic, others more tangible, and sometimes in different combinations. As Emily Martin Ahern (1979) suggests, the rhetoric of transformation must be taken into account. "Weak illocutionary acts" function along the lines of wishes, without the expectation that observable change will ensue, as opposed to "strong illocutionary acts," which are expected to yield results. She suggests that some healing rituals are only weakly associated with effects, bypassing the problem of efficacy.

Our students bring multiple ideas about efficacy to the table, and it can be productive to elicit these, encouraging the participants to specify how each aspect of efficacy traces back to specific views of affliction. Pre-med students steeped in the biological sciences may lean toward materially quantifiable definition, whereas those students who conceptualize their worldview as holistic may add in matters of soul, spirit, and mind. Encouraging a multifactor analysis will prompt students to think more precisely about each of these dimensions of ritual healing, and prepare them to arrive at better analyses of narratives and visual accounts of healing rituals.

Additional Teaching Notes

To the extent that students conceptualize ritual as stagnant and stultifying, it can be a useful exercise to invite discussion of their own healing systems. What cultural forms do they themselves assemble, whether biomedical or other, and how do these configurations shift circumstantially? What religious worldviews do they reflect, reinforce, or challenge? Such discussion can illustrate not only the pragmatic aspects of ritual healing, but also its fluid nature. To illustrate the ways in which ritual retains and reworks certain constants in the dialectic between the structured and the spontaneous, students can reflect on their own experience, and then engage in looking for these elements in examples of ritual healing. As another facet of the ways in which rituals are adapted to new times and places, it is important to review cases in which local realities from one site enter those of another, changing both in the process through the metamorphosis of globalization. The study of immigrant experience provides one such window (Barnes and Sered 2004). Comparisons between New Age ritual bricolage and such adaptations can prove illuminating.

NOTES

1. The typologies of etiological factors and of healing ritual techniques were developed by Sered over ten years of teaching in Israel and the United States.

2. For the differentiations among procedure, process, and outcome, we are indebted to Csordas (1988). Efficacy, it should be added, is a central issue in medical anthropology.

3. At the same time, the healer may have undergone grave affliction as part of the process of acquiring healing knowledge and authority.

4. In part, this role also reflects hierarchies in biomedicine, and degrees of participation in biomedical authority. In the sociology of nursing, for example, the subordination of nursing to biomedicine tends to persist, as opposed to a focus on what differentiates nursing. As Carl May and Christine Fleming (1997) observe, this stance reflects analytic stability and institutional inertia. It is not surprising, however, insofar as the physician has been used in the sociology of the professions as the exemplar of the process of acquiring professional status. (See Larson 1977, nuanced by Abbott 1988.)

USEFUL MATERIALS

In addition to our own *Religion and Healing in America* (see the reference list), the following works may prove useful to readers:

Turner, Edith. 2006. *Among the Healers: Stories of Spiritual and Ritual Healing around the World.* New York: Praeger Press.

Dudbish, Jill, and Michael Winkelman, eds. 2005. *Pilgrimage and Healing.* Tucson: University of Arizona Press.

Csordas, Thomas J. 2002. *Body/Meaning/Healing.* New York: Palgrave.

Hinnells, John R., and Roy Porter, eds. 1999. *Religion, Health, and Suffering.* New York: Kegan Paul International.

REFERENCES

Abbott, A. 1988. *The System of Professions: An Essay on the Division of Expert Labor.* Chicago: University of Chicago Press.

Ahern, Emily Martin. 1979. "The Problem of Efficacy: Strong and Weak Illocutionary Acts." *Man* 14, 1: 1–17.

Barnes, Linda L., and Susan S. Sered. 2004. *Religion and Healing in America.* New York: Oxford University Press.

Bastide, Roger. 1978. *The African Religions of Brazil.* Baltimore: Johns Hopkins University Press

Csordas, Thomas J. 1983. "Rhetoric of Transformation in Ritual Healing." *Culture, Medicine, and Psychiatry* 7, 4: 333–375.

———. 1988. "Elements of Charismatic Persuasion and Healing." *Medical Anthropology Quarterly* 2, 2: 121–142.

———. 1999. "Ritual Healing and the Politics of Identity in Contemporary Navajo Society." *American Ethnologist* 26, 1: 3–23.

Desjarlais, Robert R. 1996. "Presence." In *Performance of Healing*, ed. Carol Laderman and Marina Roseman, 143–164. New York: Routledge.

Dow, James. 1986. "Universal Aspects of Symbolic Healing: A Theoretical Synthesis." *American Anthropologist* 88, 1: 56–69.

Etkin, Nina. 1988. "Cultural Constructions of Efficacy." In *The Context of Medicines in Developing Countries*, ed. Sjaak van der Geest and Susan R. Whyte, 299–326. Dordrecht, The Netherlands: Kluwer Academic.

Kinsley, David. 1996. *Health, Healing, and Religion: A Cross-Cultural Perspective.* Englewood Cliffs, N.J. Prentice Hall.

Kraut, Alan M. 1995. *Silent Travelers: Germs, Genes, and the "Immigrant Menace."* Baltimore: Johns Hopkins University Press.

Larson, M. 1977. *The Rise of Professionalism.* Berkeley: University of California Press.

May, Carl, and Christine Fleming. 1997. "The Professional Imagination: Narrative and the Symbolic Boundaries between Medicine and Nursing." *Journal of Advanced Nursing* 25: 1094–1100.

Olaveson, Tim. 2001. "Collective Effervescence and Communitas: Processual Models of Ritual and Society in Emile Durkheim and Victor Turner." *Dialectical Anthropology* 26: 89–124.

Schieffelin, Edward. 1985. "Performance and the Cultural Construction of Reality." *American Ethnologist* 12, 4: 707–724.

Winkelman, Michael. 2000. *Shamanism: The Neural Ecology of Consciousness and Healing.* Westport, Conn.: Bergin and Garvey.

14

Reflections on Ritual in Noh and Kyōgen

Richard A. Gardner

Despite all the attention given to ritual in recent years, it is still not uncommon for religion to be treated more as a matter of faith, belief, or inner experience than as something people do. It thus bears reiterating, as many teachers do in introductory courses on religion, that religion inevitably involves ritual and is as much a matter of what people do as what they believe. These are valuable insights in and of themselves.

Such insights do not, however, completely clarify the relation of ritual and religion. As recent critical studies of the notion of ritual have shown, to accord ritual its proper place in the study of religion requires rethinking not only our notion of ritual but also our notions of religion and of seemingly every term and concept related to the study of religion. It also involves rethinking entrenched assumptions, largely derived from Western traditions, concerning distinctions such as thought and action, spirit and matter, body and mind, and belief and nonbelief (Bell 1992). In addition, critical studies of ritual theory are but part of an effort in recent years to critically reexamine seemingly every concept related to the conceptualization of religion from the Enlightenment onward.[1] Teaching about ritual thus involves, at least ideally, teaching about and rendering problematic seemingly every aspect of religion. This is a daunting challenge.

With these considerations in mind, I would like to propose here that noh and kyōgen plays, traditional Japanese performing arts that took shape in the fifteenth century, provide useful materials for teaching about ritual.[2] At the simplest of levels, the plays might be used to illustrate the central importance of ritual in religion. The plays might also be used, however, to teach and reflect on at least some of the broader issues concerning ritual and religion alluded to above. In addition, the plays provide some grounds for tempering the sense of hubris and seriousness that is involved in much academic theorizing about religion and, especially, the religions of others. I will attempt to unpack these observations through outlining the structure of a proposed course and the nature of the materials to be used.

There is seemingly no end to theories of religion and ritual. This poses a dilemma. Students need to be made aware that there is no given, evident understanding of what either ritual or religion is but competing and at times incompatible theories and approaches. Students need to be made aware, in other words, that we, as teachers and scholars, really have not quite figured out or agreed upon what it is we are talking about. At the same time, there is the danger of a course on ritual deteriorating into a rapid, perhaps even superficial, survey of theories of ritual and religion.

My solution to this dilemma is to radically, and at least somewhat misleadingly, simplify things with the following pronouncements. Theories of religion can be divided into two general types. The first focuses on congruity and understands religion and ritual as proclaiming, celebrating, or working to establish congruity, harmony, correspondence, or a fit between at least seemingly disparate things such as the acts of the gods and human acts, this world and other worlds, and human longings and the ineluctable realities of existence. Religion and ritual thus work to establish meaning, harmony, salvation, or the resolution of oppositions. A classic example of such an approach is to be found in the work of Mircea Eliade. Ritual is a repetition of the acts of the gods, renders the sacred present in this world through symbolic action, and thus realizes order, meaning, fertility, prosperity, salvation, redemption, or liberation.

The second type focuses more on incongruity rather than congruity. Though perhaps not as widespread as the first type, a concern with incongruity seems to be a growing theme in the study of religion and ritual. This orientation can be introduced through the work of Jonathan Z. Smith. For Smith, both religion and ritual are concerned not so much with establishing or celebrating congruities (such as between the action of the gods and the action of people) as with providing occasion to reflect on the incongruities or disparities between ideals and realities. Religion might be viewed here, indeed, as an ongoing effort to come to terms with and reflect on a wide range of incongruities.

Juxtaposing the approaches of Eliade and Smith has a number of advantages. The two can be introduced to students through rather brief readings. Eliade's understanding of ritual is presented in rather concise form in many of his writings (see, for example, Eliade 1954: 17–27, 51–62). Smith's approach can be introduced through his brief but important essay "The Bare Facts of Ritual" (Smith 1982: 53–65).[3] Eliade and Smith might also be used to illustrate a number of other oppositions in the study of religion. Eliade emphasizes general if not universal patterns, treats religious experience as dealing with the extraordinary, and presents religious symbols as multivalent and working transformations, such as rendering present the gods and mythic times of origin. Smith instead focuses on strategic action within historical context, treats religion as an ordinary category of human activity, and views religious language and symbols as ordinary, prosaic speech.[4]

Noh and kyōgen texts are useful for teaching ritual and testing theoretical approaches in a number of senses. Since the texts are relatively short (running from six to twenty or so pages in translation), they provide an economical means of using non-excerpted primary sources. Translations of the plays are also readily available, including many accompanied by introductions and annotations providing at least basic orientation to the historical, cultural, literary, and religious contexts of the plays.[5] Though short, the texts are rich and complex and thus provide occasion for extended discussion and close reading. In addition, students usually find the plays interesting in and of themselves. Most important, their use allows students to test ritual theory in relation to primary sources related to ritual rather than simply read other people's interpretations of ritual.

The texts are also useful for teaching ritual because noh plays frequently, if not characteristically, center on the performance of ritual actions by the characters portrayed within the plays. Though this is not so often the case in kyōgen, there are a considerable number of kyōgen that do involve ritual as a theme or event within the plays. One of the major preoccupations of noh plays (and of kyōgen to a lesser extent) is the relation of this world and other worlds. The plays are thus preoccupied with what might be termed the nature and efficacy of symbolic intermediaries—including sacred sites, temples, shrines, symbolic objects, ritual action, and performances of song and dance—that are presented as mediating between this world and other worlds (Gardner 1991). Many plays, in some senses at least, are preoccupied by what we would term questions concerning the nature and efficacy of ritual action. The plays thus offer evidence that at least some religious traditions are as much, if not more, concerned with questions of ritual, action, or practice than with questions concerning belief (Reader and Tanabe 1998: 1–8).

The plays are also useful in a course on ritual and religion because at least some people would question their appropriateness for teaching about either. Are not the plays theater, works of art? And are not religion and art, ritual and theater, and so on really different things that should not be confused? These questions, of course, reflect largely Enlightenment distinctions between religion and the arts, and they echo evolutionary theories about the relation of ritual and theater prominent at the beginning of the twentieth century. They thus provide a good occasion for thinking about these distinctions and how they are embedded in our approaches to religion and ritual.

As is well known, many traditional forms of theater and performance throughout the world had close ties with religion, were considered as offerings to the gods (religious ritual acts in and of themselves), and not infrequently centered on religious themes.[6] There is thus the possibility here of exploring whether Enlightenment and post-Enlightenment distinctions between religion and arts apply to pre-Enlightenment traditions and, of course, the vast variety of non-Western traditions. This is a particularly interesting question to consider in the case of noh and kyōgen. Many plays, as will be suggested below, seem to be struggling with a question that is at least roughly analogous to our question of the difference between religion and art or ritual and the performing arts.

It is also possible that performative genres such as noh and kyōgen, which seem to lie somewhat betwixt and between religious ritual and theater, might reveal aspects of religion not as readily discernable in more standard "religious texts." Victor Turner has extensively explored how liminal (or, in some formulations, "liminoid") phenomena, including a range of different types of performances and rituals, provide reflection and meta-commentary on various aspects of a culture and society. Noting the ways in which noh plays thematize artistic performances and religious rituals (the ways in which noh plays are performances about performances or rituals about rituals), Turner has characterized noh plays as highly reflexive and "hyperliminal" (Turner 1984). Noh plays (as well as many kyōgen) might be viewed as reflections on the nature of religious ritual, artistic performance, and the relation of the two. The plays might thus be viewed as forming what Lawrence Sullivan (1986) has termed an "indigenous hermeneutics" of ritual and performance.

This reflexive character of noh and kyōgen make the plays particularly well suited for our reflecting on at least some aspects of ritual theory. Almost all ritual theory, be it explicitly or implicitly, makes claims about how ritual is experienced by participants or about how ritual shapes participants. Though the plays do not offer direct evidence of how people have experienced or been shaped by ritual, they do provide good evidence for exploring one question: how have members of a religious community reflected on or imagined the nature, meaning, and efficacy of what we would call ritual action?

If we take seriously Turner's suggestion that noh contains reflections or meta-commentary on ritual or performance and Sullivan's suggestion that performances such as noh and kyōgen provide an indigenous hermeneutics, then perhaps we should consider these plays as providing more than data for testing and illustrating our theories and concepts. We might well consider, in other words, how others' reflections on ritual might provide insights, clues, and even "answers" concerning the theoretical questions we pose. In addition, we might well consider whether others' reflection on ritual, practice, and action might help us to reflect on our "practice" of doing the study of religion and ritual.

There is one additional way in which reflection on noh and kyōgen might well alter our understanding of both ritual and religion. Being often, if not characteristically, performed together as part of a single event, kyōgen (which always involves humor) and noh compel the viewer to confront a juxtaposition of the serious and the comic. Noh itself at times contains elements of humor. And the humor in both noh and kyōgen is often related to ritual. The plays thus suggest that serious matters such as religion and ritual have something to do with humor. The plays are representative of a tradition, indeed, in which humor is often intimately linked with religion, ritual, and the gods (Davis and Gardner 2005). As will be discussed below, humor plays a crucial role in one of the central myths in Shinto traditions, the myth of the heavenly cave. Cited as the origin of several Shinto ritual acts as well as of the performing arts, the myth suggests that humor and laughter play important roles in ritual and in the relations of gods and people. Perhaps if the study of religion had begun with reflections on texts such as this, we would have a very different understanding of both ritual and religion than we do today (Gardner 2005).

When making use of these materials in a class, I try to make the assignments as straightforward as possible. After reading Eliade, students are asked to apply his ideas to a play. They are usually able to make connections. Students are then asked to read and apply Smith, whose ideas considerably complicate matters. Eliade seems no longer to have all the answers. Along the way, the following questions arise: Do the theoretical readings somehow illuminate the plays? Do the plays provide evidence to support either or both of the theories? Does one theoretical orientation seem more helpful or applicable than the other?

To give a more concrete sense of how such a course might work, I will proceed by offering an introduction to some of the different types of plays that might be selected for use and suggesting some of the different types of issues that emerge or might be focused on. I will refrain from, as much as possible, offering detailed commentary of my own on the plays. The aim is simply to illustrate some of the types of connections that might be drawn between the plays and theoretical writings about religion and ritual.

Felicitous Congruities

As suggested, noh plays quite frequently present dramatizations of a variety of types of rituals. Included here are pilgrimages of various sorts, Buddhist rites for spirits of the dead, and performances of *kagura* (song and dance offered to Shinto deities). Many of these plays do seem to present symbolic, ritual activity as working transformations that bring about or establish congruities and correspondences of various sorts. Noh plays are often, indeed, described as inevitably ending with salvation, the attainment of enlightenment, or the establishment of order (see, for example, Plutschow 1990: 7, and his appeal to Frazer's theory of magic).

One of the most well known of noh plays in Japan, *Takasago*, provides an excellent means of illustrating or testing Eliade's understanding of ritual and the symbolism of the center (for a translation and commentary, see Gardner 1992). The play opens in Kyūshū with a Shinto priest at the Aso Shrine setting off on pilgrimage to Miyako (the present-day Kyoto), the capital and symbolic center of Japan. In Takasago (not far from present-day Osaka), the priest visits the famous Takasago Pine, where he meets an old man and woman (the woman is the god of Takasago and the man the god of Sumiyoshi) and asks them about the pine. In particular, he asks why the Takasago Pine and Sumiyoshi Pine, which are located in different provinces, are said to be "paired pines" (an expression usually referring to two pines joined at the root or base).

The old couple then explain to the priest the symbolism of the pines, the significance of song or poetry, the glories of the imperial tradition, and how the two seemingly separated pines are actually joined or paired. The old couple first point to a number of elements whose opposition or separation is taken as a source of human suffering: the unchanging (evergreen pines)/the changing (other plants, people), past/present, near/far, gods/people, husband/wife, sentient/insentient, and so on. As their explanation progresses, the old couple show how all of these seeming oppositions are symbolically joined in paradoxical unity in the pine which forms an image of the entire cosmos. Poetry or song, which is identified with the pines, is presented as the force uniting all of these seeming dualities or oppositions. The old couple also reveal that they are untroubled by all the signs of change and suffering marking the world because of their participation in the way of poetry. It is implied that people too, by participating in the way of poetry, might partake of the mode of being enjoyed by the gods.

In the second half of the play, the priest journeys to Sumiyoshi Shrine, where the god of Sumiyoshi appears in his youthful form and, following an invocation of his creation in mythic times by the god Izanagi, performs *kagura* along with the shrine maidens. This performance of ritual fits well with much that Eliade has said about ritual: it involves a return to the time of mythic origins and the presence of the gods. In the course of his performance, the god recites several poems, thus suggesting that *kagura* and the way of poetry or song are one and the same. The play thus imagines and presents *kagura* or ritual as having the power to unite or bring together all that is seemingly separate or opposed. The play ends with the suggestion that the two pines are also participating in the performance of *kagura*; the boughs of the pines join in the movement of the dance, and the sound of the wind in the pines is song. Suggested here is what is more clearly in other plays: the cosmos, if properly perceived, consists of ritual performance of song and dance in which the natural landscape participates along with people, gods, and Buddhas.

The power of ritual to work transformations that unite or bring together the human and divine realms is also envisioned, this time in a Buddhist idiom, in the play *Kakitsubata* (The Irises).[7] The play recounts the visit of a traveling Buddhist priest (who may or may not be on formal pilgrimage) to Yatsubashi, a place made famous as the site where Ariwara Narihira composed a poem about irises when he had been exiled from the capital. Arriving at the site, the priest meets a woman, and they fall into conversation about Narihira's life and the poem he composed about the irises at Yatsuhashi.

After a lengthy conversation, the woman excuses herself and then reappears wearing Narihira's hat and robe which he left as momentoes. Expressing surprise, the priest asks the woman who she is. She reveals that she is the spirit of the irises and that Narihira was a manifestation of the Buddha (a Bodhisattva of Song and Dance). His poems, she adds, should be understood as the preaching of the Buddha. The spirit and priest then exchange the following lines.

SPIRIT   Performing Buddhist rites,
          the Narihira of old portrayed in dance

PRIEST   is now the Bodhisattva of Song and Dance,
          temporarily made present as the living Narihira.

Having thus transformed herself into Narihira and rendered him present, the spirit then offers a performance of song and dance recounting Narihira's life. Ritual action is attributed the power to make present what it symbolically depicts and enacts.

Ritual is imagined as working such miraculous transformations, however, not only when performed by gods or spirits. In *Aoi no Ue* (The Lady Aoi), a seer is summoned to make a diagnosis when Aoi, the wife of Prince Genji, falls ill.[8] Though the seer is unable to cure Aoi, she does discover that Aoi is being tormented by the vengeful spirit of the still living Lady Rokujō, a former lover of Genji's. A holy man, Kohijiri, is then summoned to perform a healing rite that forms the climax of the play.

KOHIJIRI   The healing rites he now performs,
            wearing his cloak of hemp,
            in which, following the steps of En-no-Gyōja,
            he scaled the peak
            symbolic of the sacred spheres
            of Taizō and Kongō,
            brushing away the dew sparkling as Seven Jewels,

and a robe of meek endurance
to shield him from defilements,
and fingering his red-wood beads,
sasari, sasari—so he chants a prayer.

The vengeful spirit of Rokujō then attempts to frighten the holy man off.
Kohijiri, however, persists.

KOHIJIRI   However evil the evil spirit,
            The mystic power of holy men will never fail.
            With these words he fingers
            once again his sacred beads.

CHORUS   Gōzsanze Myōō of the East

ROKUJŌ   Gundari-yasha Myōō of the South

CHORUS   Daitoku Myōō of the West,

ROKUJŌ   Kongō-yasha Myōō

CHORUS   of the North,

ROKUJŌ   The most wise Fudō Myōō of the Centre.

As the holy man invokes manifestations of the Buddha Dainichi in the form of
a mandala, the chorus and Rokujō name the manifestations as they appear.
Through his ritual actions, Kohijiri has transformed himself into Fudō Myōō
and speaks to the vengeful spirit with the words of the Buddha. Confronted
with a manifestation of the Buddha, the vengeful spirit is appeased and lets go
of her anger.

Infelicitous Incongruities

As suggested, it is not uncommon to find noh plays described as uniformly
enacting a drama of redemption or salvation. When gods or Buddhas are
depicted as intervening in the world, the result is inevitably felicitous. When
Buddhist priests encounter spirits of the dead, they inevitably perform rites
leading to the release or enlightenment of the spirit (Plutschow 1990: 7; and
Turner 1984: 38). These characterizations testify, perhaps, to the pervasiveness
of the assumption that religion and ritual work to bring about order, meaning,
and salvation.

Many noh plays, however, do not so easily lend themselves to analysis in
terms of theories that view ritual as working to achieve congruities of various
sorts. Considered in relation to the plays discussed earlier, such plays suggest
that ritual performances are being evaluated in different ways in different
plays: sometimes they work miraculous transformations, other times they do

not. Introducing such plays to students can complicate their understanding of ritual and usually, but not inevitably, leads them to an appreciation of Smith's analysis of ritual in terms of incongruity.

To introduce the theme of incongruity, the play *Izutsu* (The Well Crib) is useful to use in juxtaposition with *Kakitsubata*.[9] In *Izutsu*, a wandering Buddhist priest visits the Ariwara Temple and encounters a woman who later reveals herself to be the spirit of one of Narihira's wives. The woman tells the priest that though Narihira is dead, he is still present in the world because of the many stories told of him.

Like the spirit of the iris in *Kakitsubata*, the spirit here also attempts to render Narihira more fully present in the world again. After putting on a robe left behind by Narihira, the spirit performs an *utsuri-mai* (dance of transformation) in an effort to transform herself into Narihira.

> WOMAN Donning the robe left as a memento
> by Narihira now passed out of this world,
> with a touch of shame I transform myself
> into Narihira and dance.

After she performs the dance and recites two of Narihira's poems, the chorus describes the spirit as having become Narihira. The spirit then looks into the well and sees her reflected image as being that of Narihira.

> CHORUS Just now there appears
> Narihira in his hat and robe.
> It is not a woman but a man.
> It is Narihira's image
>
> *(woman goes to the well crib and looks in)*
>
> WOMAN That I see and am filled with longing,
> filled with such longing
> that the spirit of the woman
> looks like a withered flower
> with the color gone,
> only the scent remaining.

The woman's success in rendering Narihira present, however, is fleeting. Filled with longing at the sight of Narihira, she sees, incongruously, not Narihira but only herself looking like a withered flower. Though the spirit of the iris in *Kakitsubata* was able to render Narihira present through a ritual performance of song and dance, the spirit here is left with only a sense of Narihira's absence.

The play *Senju* (Thousand Armed) enacts a similar case of failed transformation.[10] The performer here, however, is a living person rather than a spirit. The play is based on a story recorded in *Heike monogatari* (The Tale of the Heike), a narrative account of the defeat of the Heike clan by the Genji. Captured by the Genji at the battle of Ichinotani, Taira Shigehira is sent to Kamakura where he is sentenced to death by Minamoto Yoritomo. Yoritomo feels, however, a degree of pity for Shigehira and sends a female entertainer, Senju, to comfort him with song and dance before his execution.

After talking with Shigehira, Senju is moved to recount Shigehira's life in song and dance. While the performers in *Kakitsubata* and *Izutsu* seek to render the absent Narihira present, Senju's performance seeks to restore a happier past and climaxes with the following lines.

> CHORUS . . . and wondering how these dancing sleeves
> can possibly bring back the past,
> my feelings emerge as tears soaking the sleeves
> swirling like snow falling on the withered branches
> that bloomed again because of Senju Kannon's mercy.
> Since these are the sleeves of Senju,
> I will continue to wave them.

As these lines suggest, Senju takes her name from Senju Kannon, one manifestation of the Bodhisattva Kannon. The entire play, indeed, might be viewed as a comparison of Senju's coming to comfort Shigehira with Senju Kannon's coming to comfort and aid those suffering in this world. Making reference to a tale of Kannon's restoring a withered tree to bloom, Senju likens herself to Kannon and continues to dance with at least some hope that she will be able to save Shigehira from his present plight. The play ends, however, with no miraculous transformation having been worked and Shigehira being led off to his death. It is the difference, rather than the similarity, between Senju and Senju Kannon that is highlighted.

The play *Yamamba* (The Old Woman of the Mountains) also explores the incongruous relation between ritual performance and the object that it, at least in a sense, seeks to represent (Gardner 2004).[11] The play opens with a female entertainer setting out on pilgrimage to the distant temple Zenkōji. The performer takes her name, Yamamba, from the name of a song and dance that has made her famous and describes the life of an old woman of the mountains. While the party of pilgrims is making its final mountainous ascent to the temple, the real Yamamba suddenly appears and challenges the performer from the capital to perform her famous song and dance. The real Yamamba also complains that the performer has used the song and dance to gain fame rather than as part of religious rites to free her from the sufferings of samsara. The play thus seems to be reflecting on the differences between two types of ritual performance or between artistic performance and religious ritual.

When the performer Yamamba begins her song and dance, the real Yamamba appears in her true form and joins in the performance. There is, in at least one sense, a perfect congruity between the performance and what it represents; the object depicted by the song and dance is present. Incongruities, however, abound. As the play unfolds, it becomes clear that the performer Yamamba does not really know who the real Yamamba, the figure she represents in song and dance, is. Even as the real Yamamba performs the song and dance depicting herself, she fluctuates so quickly between identities, such as that of demon or simple old woman or enlightened being, that it is difficult to name the real Yamamba with any certainty. Reflecting the tendency to see noh plays (and perhaps religion in general) as leading to the resolution of oppositions or the attainment of salvation, some have understood Yamamba as an enlightened being expounding and manifesting the Buddhist doctrine of non-duality or the unity of samsara and nirvana (Brazell 1973). The play might be better read, however, as presenting and reflecting on two fundamental incongruities. Not only does the performer not know the object she claims to depict in her performance, the real Yamamba seems to be a being whose identity cannot be grasped or made to fit with any available concepts, ideas, or symbolic patterns.

Humor: Felicitous Incongruities

Both noh and kyōgen plays also present comic or humorous reflections on religion and ritual. Noh is frequently characterized as dealing with the tragic or serious dimension of things and kyōgen as dealing with the comic or humorous. To an extent, this is true. There are some noh plays, however, that make use of or even make a central theme of humor. While kyōgen inevitably have humorous moments, some plays have a decidedly dark if not tragic dimension (Golay 1973). Though distinct theatrical forms, noh and kyōgen are joined in important ways. The interlude in two-act noh plays are often of a comic nature, with kyōgen actors sometimes appearing. In addition, noh and kyōgen have traditionally alternated as a series of performances on a single day. Some kyōgen are even explicit farcical renditions of noh plays (Morley 1993).

The kyōgen *Jizō-mai* (The Jizō Dance) links humor and ritual performance and might be profitably juxtaposed with noh plays such as *Kakitsubata* or *Senju*.[12] The play opens with a traveling Buddhist priest arriving in a village and seeking shelter for the night. The villager he approaches, however, has firm rules against housing travelers. The priest, nevertheless, persists in his request for shelter and, through a series of comic subterfuges and plays on words, succeeds in gaining permission to stay the night. The priest is so comically charming that the master of the house even brings out some rice wine, and the two end up drinking together. After they have gotten a bit tipsy, the master requests that the priest perform a song and dance to repay the hospitality he has been shown.

The priest agrees and performs *Jizō-mai*, a song and dance in which he takes the role of the Bodhisattva Jizō and, perhaps, attempts to render Jizō present in some sense. With his hat in hand and dancing, the monk sings the following song.

(Monk stands before drums, hat in hand, and begins to dance.)
Monk:
Jizō, he lives in his realm of peace, on Karada Mountain. Hell,
Starving Ghosts, Beasts, Warring Demons, Humans, Angels,
the Yama Heaven, the Tosotsu Heaven, the Twenty-Five Stations,
he visits them all. And all beings, deep in sin, grasp aright the staff
he gives them: up he fishes them, drip, drip, drop, he hauls them up.
Long ago he rose on high to the Tōri Heaven of Shakyamuni the great
master, who, seated to preach, called to him our Jizō. The Nyorai,
in his goodness, lifted his own golden hand and thrice stroked our
Jizō's head. "Wondrous kind art thou Jizō, wondrous good art thou
Jizō," said he, "all beings, till the Latter Ages, I entrust to thee."'
And so empowered, ever since, he hurries all around. If anyone
heartlessly refuses him a cup of tea, poor Jizō, he's all worn out, but
when he happens by this very room, it's goblets ten and mugs
fourteen this feast day, two dozen drinks all guzzled down till scarlet
bloom his eyes. Wibble-wobble left he staggers, wibble-wobble right;
wibble-wobble weaving zigzag, he just can't hold in compassion's
tears, they overflow. Sleeves he presses to his face, sleeves he presses
to his face, Jizō of the Six Ways: see, see, he's drunk, he's crying! see,
see he's drunk, he's crying! Eeyah!

In *Kakitsubata*, the spirit of the irises rendered Narihira present through the performance of song and dance. In *Senju*, Senju fails to render the Bodhisattva Kannon present through song and dance and is thus unable save Shigehira from his tragic fate. In *Jizō-mai*, a Buddhist priest seemingly attempts to render the Bodhisattva Jizō present but only displays the humorous incongruity of a drunken, wobbling monk claiming to be the Bodhisattva Jizō (or perhaps this is an unexpected manifestation of a drunken Jizō?).

One of the most intriguing, perhaps even profound, treatments of ritual within noh is found in the play *Ema* (The Votive Plaque).[13] The play opens with an imperial messenger journeying to Ise Shrine to make offerings on behalf of the emperor. The messenger and his party arrive on the evening before the New Year when two gods of the shrine hang an *ema* as a sign of the weather in the coming year. An *ema* bearing the picture of a white horse foretells sunny weather; an *ema* with a black horse foretells rain. At the shrine, the messenger meets an old man (actually the goddess Amaterasu) and old woman (actually the god Tsukiyomi).

When asked by the messenger to explain the ritual of hanging the *ema*, the old man states that the ritual imitates people's foolishness. The sense of this remark is explained. Although the gods have pledged over and over to take care of people, people fear the gods will not fulfill their pledges and insist on having some sign or indication of the coming year's weather. People are foolish for not believing. The gods also suggest, however, that people are foolish for taking the color of a painted horse's hair as a sign of the coming weather. Here people seem to be deemed foolish for believing in the wrong way, for confusing a sign for the thing itself. The gods then enter into a dispute about which *ema* to hang this year. Linked with the sun, Amaterasu wishes to hang the white *ema*, whereas Tsukiyomi, linked with the moon and water, argues for hanging the black *ema*. They finally agree to hang both *ema*. The gods here are perhaps enacting people's foolishness in expecting a single sign. Both sun and rain, of course, are needed for bountiful crops in the coming year.

The two gods then embark on what might be read as a debate about the relation between a sign or symbol and what it refers to. They begin in opposite positions with one praising the powers of poetic language and the other claiming that poetic language is a form of deceit. They happily, however, end up in agreement with both recognizing the inevitable deception involved in the use of signs and symbols yet also the validity and efficacy of sign and symbol. At least implicitly admitting to the deception they have been involved in thus far, the two gods then reveal their true identities to the imperial messenger.

In the second half of the play, Amaterasu returns in her true forms and reenacts the events recorded in the myth of the heavenly cave. This myth recounts how Amaterasu, upset with her brother Susano-o's actions, shut herself up in a cave and thus threw the world into darkness and chaos.[14] The other gods, however, take action. They gather birds and induce them to crow, fashion a mirror and *magatama* jewels, perform divination with the shoulder bone of a deer, and uproot a *sakaki* tree and hang from its branches blue and white pieces of cloth, the mirror, and the *magatama* jewels. The goddess Ame no Uzume then performs a dance on top an overturned tub and ends her performance by exposing herself and thus provoking the other gods to laugh. Wondering what is going on, Amaterasu opens the door to the cave and asks why Ame no Uzume is singing and dancing and the other gods laughing. Told that another goddess more wonderful than herself is present, Amaterasu is shown the mirror and, fascinated by her reflection, is lured out of the cave.

The *Kojiki* account of this myth clearly portrays the gods as self-consciously tricking or deceiving Amaterasu by creating the illusion that another goddess is present. In addition, Ame no Uzume's performance is cited throughout the Japanese tradition as the origin of *kagura* (the song and dance

offered to the gods), *kamigakari* (rites of possession), and many forms of theater and performance. At least one version of the charter myth for much of
Shinto ritual thus suggests that deception, as well as humor, is a central part
of ritual action.

Though there is no mention of Ame no Uzume's exposing herself,
Amaterasu in *Ema* briefly recounts the myth and recalls how fascinated she
was by the song and dance performed by Ame no Uzume. There is no indication that Amaterasu is upset at having been deceived; she chooses rather to
reenact the deception again and responds with amusement, fascination, and
delight. In the myth as well as the play, there is a recognition that there is a
gap between symbolic and real presence and that deception is an inevitable
part of ritual. At the same time, deception is presented as a means of establishing presence: a performance creating the illusion of presence brings about
the presence of the goddess.

Conclusion: Leading Questions and Reflections

In presenting this overview of plays, I have tried to provide just enough of my
own commentary to make clear some of the ways the plays might be related to
theoretical issues in the study of ritual. When teaching with these materials,
I try to provide, at least initially, as little of my own commentary on the plays as
possible. After going over the theoretical readings with students in some detail
to make sure the general ideas and concepts are at least relatively clear, I then
ask students to write a series of brief essays relating the theoretical writings to a
number of different types of plays. I emphasize here close reading and what
might be termed "close writing." The assignment is: "Restate some point or
points from the theoretical writings and then relate them in detail to passages
from the plays. The plays may be used to either support or question the theoretical writings. Explain as clearly as possible the relation between the theoretical concepts and examples drawn from the plays."

I would like to say that the readings are so artfully arranged and the
writing assignments so carefully calculated that I simply sit back and wait
for the students to make their own discoveries, but this is not entirely true.
Though the students do quite well at relating the two sets of readings, I gradually and inevitably resort to hints, clues, leading questions, and finally outright explanations of various sorts. Here I would simply like to suggest some
of the questions I either directly or indirectly attempt to raise.

As should be clear by now, the plays present different evaluations of the
nature and power of performance or ritual. Some plays seem to provide
support for Eliade's understanding of ritual by presenting ritual as working,
through the repetition of the acts of the gods or past events, miraculous and

extraordinary transformations in which this world is brought into conformity with the past or the world of gods and Buddhas.

Other plays, however, seem to be extended reflections on the incongruities involved in performance or ritual and thus to provide support for Smith's understanding of ritual. Whether cast in a tragic or comic mode, such plays present performance and ritual as not working the sorts of transformations that other plays imagine. We thus have two seemingly opposed theories of ritual, yet we also have evidence that seems to support both theories. Which theory is correct? Or are both right? Might the theories be synthesized in some way? Or are they fundamentally incompatible?

Can we divide the plays as neatly, as I have done, into those focusing on congruity and those concerned with incongruity? If read closely, most plays form a complex reflection on the interplay of congruity and incongruity. Even *Takasago*, which might be read as celebrating the unity of all things, makes use of an incongruity, the separate but "paired" pines, to induce a vision of unity. In addition, there is the incongruity of the priest setting out on pilgrimage to the sacred center Miyako, but discovering a sacred center partway there on the periphery. Perhaps the center is not at the center?

I have also found it useful at this point, if not earlier, to introduce at least some aspects of Catherine Bell's notion of ritualization. Rejecting a universal definition of ritual, Bell argues that "ritual should be analyzed and understood in its real context, which is the full spectrum of ways of acting within any given culture, not as some a priori category of action totally independent of other forms of action. Only in this context can the theorist-observer attempt to understand how and why people choose to differentiate some activities from others. From this perspective, the focus is less a matter of clear and autonomous rites than the methods, traditions, and strategies of 'ritualization'" (1997: 80). Though noh and kyōgen plays do not reveal the "full spectrum" of ways of acting in medieval Japan, they do seem to offer an imaginative presentation of and reflection on the ways of acting available to people.

From this perspective, it might be asked what the presence of different evaluations of ritual and performance within the plays means within the context of medieval Japan. Do they reflect the opposed, conflicting understandings of different individuals or groups? Or do the different evaluations reflect the ongoing efforts of a community to understand the nature and power of performance or ritual? Perhaps there was no one certain view of just what performance and ritual are?

Perhaps the plays then might be viewed as-holding up for examination different strategies of ritualization? Are the plays contrasting artistic performance and religious ritual as different types of action? Or are they reflecting on the difference between successful and unsuccessful acts of ritualization?

Senju might be read, for instance, as suggesting that artistic performance does not have the same power as religious ritual. But does not the spirit in *Kakitsubata* seem to work a miraculous transformation through artistic performance? Maybe the plays are suggesting that the performances of gods, Buddhas, and spirits have the power to work transformations and that the performances of people do not? But some plays, directly or indirectly, do seem to imply that people can access such powers through performance and ritual. By questioning the power of ritual or performance, are some of the plays questioning or rejecting religion? Or are they simply reflecting on the limits of certain types of symbolic action? Perhaps the plays, in other words, are exploring the possibility that, even within a single culture, "ritual may not be a way of acting that is the same for all times and places" (Bell 1997: 82).

Bell suggests here that ritual (or ritualization) might be defined in culturally specific terms because cultures classify actions in distinctive ways (1997: 82). The following questions might be posed here. How do all of the terms we are using—"ritual," "performance," "art," and "religion"—relate to the language and concepts found in the plays? Are we and the plays really talking about the same thing? Is it possible that there are distinctive notions of ritual and performance in Japanese traditions that are obscured by our universal notions (see Hoff 1978 and 1985 for Japanese notions of performance)?

The use of noh and kyōgen plays also allows for, if not demands, raising questions about the relation of humor to religion and ritual. What is the significance and meaning of the humor to be found in kyōgen and in some noh plays? Is this a satirical sort of humor critiquing and rejecting religion? *Jizō-mai* and other plays certainly raise questions about holy men, and others portray the gods themselves in humorous light. But such kyōgen were often performed together with plays portraying the gods in a more reverent fashion. And as *Ema* suggests, at least some of the gods are imagined as having a sense of humor. What is to be made of the juxtaposition of "serious" and "humorous" presentations of the same subject matter? Perhaps the humor is part of a serious effort to reflect on the nature of the gods, religion, and ritual?

Following Bell's insights into the parallels between the practice of ritual and the practice of theory, I have suggested throughout that the reflections on ritual to be found in noh and kyōgen are analogous to scholarly reflections on ritual. Considered in this light, *Ema* as well as other plays might be viewed as explicitly holding up for consideration the insight that ritual and symbolic action involve a complex interplay of congruity and incongruity, presence and absence, deceit and truth, and seriousness and humor. In many ways, the debate between Amaterasu and Toyouke on the nature of symbolic language and action parallels the debate between Eliade and Smith. Perhaps not a few of our theoretical debates have already been discovered and reflected on by those we study. Such reflections might even be of use to us. In *Ema*, the two gods agree to hang both *ema* and end their debate agreeing, at least implicitly, that ritual action involves an interplay of congruous and incongruous frames of reference and, indeed, that its very efficacy hinges upon such an interplay. Perhaps the gods are right.

NOTES

1. See the essays collected in Taylor 1998. For a humorous review of the book that suggests that our theoretical efforts to clarify the mistaken assumptions, categories, and contradictions of past theory often land us in but new muddles, see Chidester 2000.

2. Throughout this essay I often draw on two of my previous publications: "Nō oyobi kyōgen ni okeru shūkyōteki shōchō no kōsatsu" (1991) and "Sacramento, follia, tragedia e umorismo: relessioni sul potere dell'arte dello spettacolo nel teatro giapponese" (2006).

3. A related essay developing some of Smith's ideas that might also be used here is Gill, 1987 (see pp. 58–75).

4. For a succinct comparison of the approaches of Eliade and Smith, see Bell 1997: 10–12. Discussions of some these fundamental oppositions can also be found in Smith 1982: xi–xiii, and Long 1985: 96.

5. Perhaps the best and most useful book of translations, with excellent introductory essays, is Tyler 1992.

6. Though both noh and kyōgen have been at times performed as offerings to kami and Buddhas, the question of their status as religious ritual in some performative contexts is complicated and not considered here. Helpful discussions of the complex relations in Japan between what we would distinguish as theater and religious ritual may be found in Raz 1983, Plutschow 1990, and Ortolani 1999. It should also be noted that the most famous of noh dramatists, Zeami Motokiyo (1363–1433), wrote extensively on the noh theater and the art of acting. An introduction to and translation of many of his essays may be found in Rimer and Yamazaki 1984.

7. A full translation of the play may be found in Shimazaki 1977 (71–104). The translations given here are my own.

8. The passages from the play given here are taken from the translation in Japan Classics 1959 (87–102).

9. A full translation may be found in Tyler 1992, 123–133. The translations here are my own.

10. An annotated translation of the play may be found in Shimazaki 1981: 64–101. The translation below is mine.

11. A full translation may be found in Tyler 1992: 309–328.

12. The translation of the play drawn on here may be found in Tyler 1978a: 130–140. In both this volume and in Tyler 1978b, Tyler presents noh and kyōgen plays alternately to accord with the traditional pattern of performance. Tyler's translations in these two volumes are the only translations of noh that give a sense of the often fragmented, elliptical, and condensed texture of the language of the plays.

13. A translation may be found in Shimazaki 1972: 240–269.

14. I follow here the Kojiki account of the myth that may be found in Philippi 1968 (81–86).

USEFUL MATERIALS

Readers may find a number of works in the reference list to be useful, especially Davis and Gardner 2005, Hoff 1985, Gardner 2005, and all the Tyler works. Additionally, the following works may prove helpful:

Brazell, Karen. 1988. *Twelve Plays of the Noh and Kyōgen Theaters*. Ithaca, N.Y.: Cornell East Asia Program.

Gardner, Richard A. 1992. "*Takasago*: The Symbolism of the Pine." *Monumenta Nipponica* 47: 203–240.

Keene, Donald. 1970. *Twenty Plays of the Nō Theatre*. New York: Columbia University Press.

Lafleur, William R. 1983.*The Karma of Words: Buddhism and the Literary Arts in Medieval Japan*. Berkeley: University of California Press.

Tyler, Royall. 1987. "Buddhism in Noh." *Japanese Journal of Religious Studies* 14: 19–52.

REFERENCES

Bell, Catherine. 1992. *Ritual Theory, Ritual Practice*. New York: Oxford University Press.

———. 1997. *Ritual: Perspectives and Dimensions*. New York: Oxford University Press.

Brazell, Karen. 1973. "In Search of Yamamba: A Critique of the Noh Play." In *Studies on Japanese Culture*, Vol. 2, ed. Saburō Ota and Rikutarō Fukuda, 495–498. Tokyo: Japan P.E.N. Club.

Chidester, David. 2000. "Material Terms for the Study of Religion." *Journal of the American Academy of Religion* 68: 367–80.

Davis, Scott, and Richard Gardner. 2005. "Humor and Religion: Humor and Religion in East Asian Contexts." In *The Encyclopedia of Religion*, Vol. 6, ed. Lindsay Jones, 4205–4210. New York: Elsevier.

Eliade. Mircea. 1954. *The Myth of the Eternal Return or, Cosmos and History*. Translated by Willard R. Trask. Princeton, N.J.: Princeton University Press.

———. 1959. *The Sacred and the Profane: The Nature of Religion*. Translated by Willard R. Trask. New York: Harcourt Brace Jovanovich.

Gardner, Richard A. 1991. "Nō oyobi kyōgen ni okeru shūkyōteki shōchō no kōsatsu." *Shūkyō kenkyū* 64: 139–159.

———. 1992. "*Takasago*: The Symbolism of the Pine." *Monumenta Nipponica* 47: 203–240.

———. 2004. "*Yamamba*: yasei to imizuki no hōkai." In *Sekai no minshū shūkyō*, ed. Araki Michio, 151–162. Tokyo: Minerva shobō.

———. 2005. "Humor and Religion: An Overview." In *The Encyclopedia of Religion*, Vol. 6, ed. Lindsay Jones, 4194–4205. New York: Elsevier.

———. 2006. "Sacramento, follia, tragedia e umorismo: relessioni sul potere dell'arte dello spettacolo nel teatro giapponese." In *Grandi Religioni e Culture Nell'Estremo Oriente: Giappone*, ed. Lawrence E. Sullivan, 284–304. Milan, Italy: Jaca.

Gill, Sam. 1987. *Native American Religious Action*. Columbia: University of South Carolina Press.

Golay, Jacqueline. 1973. "Pathos and Farce, *Zatō* Plays of the Kyōgen Repertoire." *Monumenta Nipponica* 28: 139–150.

Hoff, Frank. 1978. *Song, Dance, and Storytelling: Aspects of the Performing Arts in Japan*. Ithaca, N.Y.: Cornell East Asia Program.

———. 1985. "Killing the Self: How the Narrator Acts." *Asian Theater Journal* 2: 1–27.

Japan Classics Translation Committee, ed. 1959. *Japanese Noh Drama*, Vol. 2. Tokyo: Nippon gakujutsu shinkōkai.

Long, Charles H. 1985. "A Look at the Chicago Tradition in the History of Religions: Retrospect and Future." In *The History of Religions: Retrospect and Prospect*, ed. Joseph M. Kitagawa. New York: Macmillan.

Morley, Carolyn Anne. 1993. *Transformation, Miracles, and Mischief: The Mountain Priest Plays of Kyōgen*. Ithaca, N.Y.: Cornell University East Asia Program.

Ortolani, Benito. 1999. *The Japanese Theater: From Shamanistic Ritual to Contemporary Pluralism*. Princeton, N.J.: Princeton University Press.

Philippi, Donald L., trans. 1968. *Kojiki: Translated with an Introduction and Notes*. Tokyo: Princeton University Press and Tokyo University Press.

Plutschow, H. E. 1990. *Chaos and Cosmos: Ritual in Early and Medieval Japanese Literature*. Leiden: E. J. Brill.

Raz, Jacob. 1983. *Audience and Actors: A Study of Their Interaction in the Traditional Japanese Theater*. Leiden: E. J. Brill.

Reader, Ian, and George J. Tanabe, Jr. 1998. *Practically Religious: Worldly Benefits and the Common Religion of Japan*. Honolulu: University of Hawaii Press.

Rimer, Thomas J., and Masakazu Yamazaki. 1984. *On the Art of the Nō Drama: The Major Treatises of Zeami*. Princeton, N.J.: Princeton University Press.

Shimazaki, Chifumi. 1972. *God Noh*. Tokyo: Hinoki shoten.

———. 1977. *Woman Noh*. Vol. 2. Tokyo: Hinoki shoten.

———. 1981. *Woman Noh*. Vol. 3. Tokyo: Hinoki shoten.

Smith, Jonathan Z. 1982. *Imagining Religion: From Babylon to Jonestown*. Chicago: University of Chicago Press.

Sullivan, Lawrence E. 1986. "Sound and Senses: Toward a Hermeneutics of Performance." *History of Religions* 26: 1–33.

Taylor, Mark C., ed. 1998. *Critical Terms for Religious Studies*. Chicago: University of Chicago Press.

Turner, Victor. 1984. "Liminality and the Performative Genres." In *Rite, Drama, Festival, Spectacle: Rehearsals toward a Theory of Cultural Performance*, ed. John J. MacAloon, 19–41. Philadelphia: Institute for Human Issues.

Tyler, Royall. 1978a. *Granny Mountains: A Second Cycle of Nō Plays*. Ithaca, N.Y.: Cornell East Asia Program.

———. 1978b. *Pining Wind: A Cycle of Nō Plays*. Ithaca, N.Y.: Cornell East Asia Program.

———. 1992. *Japanese Nō Dramas*. London: Penguin Books.

15

Ritual Performance and Ritual Practice: Teaching the Multiple Forms and Dimensions of Ritual

Linda Ekstrom and Richard D. Hecht

For several years we have jointly taught a course on religion and contemporary art that has been developed from our respective disciplines, religious studies and studio art. This course enrolls students from various fields, especially from the social sciences, the humanities, and the fine arts. These students come to our course with partial understandings of what might constitute either religion or art. As teachers, we therefore face a challenge of how to develop a common language that allows students from various disciplines to explore and understand our subject. In this essay, we intend to reflect upon our experience teaching this course and how we seek to help our students understand the ritual dimensions of religion and contemporary art practice. Some religionists might not believe that the practice of contemporary artists is "authentic" ritual and may only wish to accord it a status of being "ritual like." Likewise, many contemporary artists would argue that the labor-intensive nature of their practice is neither religious nor ritualistic. Thus, the problem of ritual is not only a pedagogic problem in which we must expand the students' understanding of religion or art and the ritual component of both. Ritual is also for us and others engaged in interdisciplinary teaching and research an interpretive problem. As teachers, we confront a common problem, how to introduce students to the breadth of ritual.

One of the important dimensions that we hope to help our students understand is the powers of ritual and how these are conveyed in a variety of expressions and forms. All ritual powers, we suggest to our students and will argue here, are rooted in ritual's ability to hold together opposing orders of reality. Here, we will begin by considering two rituals, one from the celebration for the feast day of the Virgin of Guadalupe and the other a performance by two art students. We will attempt to understand these two very different ritual forms through a series of theoretical frames drawn from the study of religion and the interpretation of contemporary art. Last, we will discuss the ritual practices of three well-known contemporary artists, Guillermo Gómez-Peña, Liza Lou, and Marina Abramović. The works of these artists are strikingly different, but each holds together, in practice and form, the transcendence and immanence of the sacred, and their work expands the range and breadth of our understanding of ritual.

Two Rituals

One of the important powers of ritual is how it negotiates the contradictory dimensions of religious tradition, between the individual and community, between religious and social hierarchies and the participants, and between spatial and institutional centers and peripheries (Shils 1975: 3–16). Consider, for example, the ritual structures of the feast day of the Virgin of Guadalupe on December 12 in a small, almost entirely Latino parish where we have taken students. Las Mañanitas begins celebrations around 5 A.M. The devotional ritual celebrations begin with dancers in feathered Aztec costumes who wear shell-rattles around their ankles and wrists. These dancers perform on the sidewalk in front of the church accompanied by drums and surrounded by congregants. However, when the Mass, the formal celebration of the Virgin, begins, the dancers do not enter the church in their costumes. Their temporary Aztec identity is left behind and outside the church as a symbol of the past being shed for a new Christian identity. But as the first ritual element of the annual feast day, the dance is also a symbol of resistance that persists to that very same new identity.

These celebrations have increasingly attracted more and more people, so that in December 2002, the planners decided to make a change and to erect a huge tent in the parking lot behind the church with the idea that it would provide more room for the growing numbers of participants. It was not easy getting the parishioners to go along with this innovation. The traditional singing of Las Mañanitas to the Virgin of Guadalupe had taken place inside the church. But the change in venue was only a symptom of a larger issue that arises in the devotion to the Virgin—a tension that exists between the hierarchical and institutional structures of a religious tradition and the people's own popular ritual devotion. The popular ritual is most characterized by an informality that seems to run counter to the liturgical structure of the Church's hierarchy. When the ritual was performed in the church, the image of the

Virgin of Guadalupe was located in a position of prominence near the Mexican flag and close to the congregation. Her image was decorated for the celebration and surrounded with a thick blanket of roses, her symbolic flower.

But the move from the inside of the church to the tent was about something other than accommodating more people. The ritual of Las Mañanitas reflects two countervalent forces that emphasize very different understandings of the powers of ritual. The church would define this ritual as a devotion to the Virgin within a celebration of the Eucharistic liturgy and would insist that the Eucharist must have priority over the devotion to the Virgin. However, most attending would experience the ritual as a Mass within the devotion, clearly giving priority to the celebration of their mother, the Virgin of Guadalupe. The boundaries of the church have always been porous in matters of personal devotion, and the great strength of Catholicism has always been its ability to accommodate what the religious elite might consider superstition or, at best, narrow piety.

At the same time, this ritual provides an opportunity to understand how the church has sought to circumscribe the ritual traditions centered on the Virgin as a way of controlling what takes place or might take place. At this morning liturgy, the presiding priest reminded the people of Pope John Paul's call that the Virgin is the "patron of the Americas." But in the same breath, he cautioned his parishioners not to put the Virgin before Jesus. He told them: "This is an image. It doesn't have any power. You don't have to touch the image. It's just a photograph. The true devotion is to Jesus, the Son of God." His comments suggest that he knew that once the church acknowledges this ritual, it might prove difficult to control. Despite this, very few among the faithful paid much heed to his warning. The people continued to press forward to be as close as possible to touch the image of the Virgin.

However, the tent gave more formality to the celebration, and it seemed clear that there had been a conscious structuring and organizing of the ritual that would take place. We saw that morning another example of the management of *intense* conflicts present in ritual and mediated by ritual. The Virgin's image had been placed at the front of the tent near a temporary altar and lectern, the chairs for the priests and deacon, and area for the *mariachis*. The seating for the assembly was set back a distance from the Virgin's image and the altar, with the separation producing a formal environment. The Mexican flag was absent and had been replaced by a red, white, and green cloth liturgical banner which hung behind the altar and chairs.

The Mass began with the image of the Virgin carried in procession from the back of the tent. She then entered the congregation anew surrounded by the priests and altar servers. Four female dancers and drummers dressed in Aztec costume followed. One dancer carried a clay vase burning copal, much as this ritual had been enacted in Mexico over the past centuries. The dancers were no longer outside the church as they had been in years past. Now they danced in front of the seated clergy, within the tent. The ancient native tradition of Mexico and the Aztec may be recognized, but it is within the controlling gaze of the church's officials. A young man wearing the white, simple shirt and pants of the native peasant ran to the raised dais and altar, while the narrator recited portions of the Nahuatl narrative, which tells of the Virgin's manifestations to Juan Diego and his meeting with Mexico City's bishop. Following Communion, there was no invitation from the presider to venerate her image.

In the celebration of the Feast of the Virgin of Guadalupe we see two competing religious styles—the formal Eucharistic liturgy and the informal devotion. The Eucharistic liturgy refers to the doctrinal and ritual norm that is the center of the church's life. Devotion describes an informal, highly individualistic, and often powerfully emotional expression of ritual. We might be tempted to think that this distinction between Eucharistic liturgy and devotion is solely a temporal expression distinguishing between a premodern and a modern religiosity. And here is where we see how ritual tempers, domesticates, and mediates these two conflicting religious styles or forms. We should think of these religious styles as locative religious forms: they represent sites along the continuum between center and periphery. Devotion might suggest the locative periphery, whereas the Eucharistic liturgy represents the center.

In a ritual performance piece with obvious allusions to the Catholic Eucharist, two advanced undergraduate art students, Sher Zabaszkiewicz and Katrina Erickson, passed a single loaf of bread among their classmates. Standing in front of each student, they broke off a piece of the still warm bread and said, "Body of Bread." Both artists were dressed in plain, white institutional chef's aprons to which the dust of bread flour still clung. Their heads were covered in white triangular scarves that were tied at the back of their necks. Each student consumed the bread they were offered in silence.

This sharing of bread was the culmination of a complex ritual performance that had begun earlier in the day as a final project in our course on religion and contemporary art. That morning, the entire class had walked across the campus to the art department where they entered a stairwell which took them down to a room below the complex. Here, they were met by the two students as they entered the space. In a solemn entrance procession, each student was handed a pair of food-preparation gloves and was greeted by one of the performers with "Welcome to the Body of Bread." The space had been uniquely prepared for this performance. The artists had constructed a circular ring-table measuring approximately twenty-five feet across. This table was large enough for twenty-five people to have a place around the outside of the ring. The table was draped in a domestic blue-and-white gingham tablecloth. One of the artists was waiting in the center of the ring as the students gathered around the outside of the table. At each place was a laminated ritual card, approximately the size of a placemat. This card was titled "A Liturgical Recipe for the Body of Bread." Three stations, each marked by a large stainless-steel bowl, were set up equidistant from each other on the table. The students immediately sensed the solemnity of the space and what was about to take place. They were silent as they entered, and once all had found a space at the table, the "formal" ritual began. The students had been gathered together in that room as "one body" to make bread.

The artists had choreographed a series of intricate ritual moves that began even before we had arrived. First, they spent considerable time preparing the space and gathering the ritual elements—stainless-steel bowls, beautiful wicker baskets which had been lined in cloth, measuring spoons, vessels and containers to hold the ingredients—which had been chosen with care and contributed to the sacrality of the space. Each of these elements had been selected to emphasize the unifying aspect of the ritual. There was a small stand in the center of the ring-table which held these implements until they were used by the participants. One artist worked from within the ring-table, and the other worked around its perimeter as both guided the participants in each ritual action. There were ten essential steps to mixing the dough and this developed from each of the three stations. The artist in the center moved to each bowl and directed the participant to mix in the various ingredients. After each ingredient was added, the artist intoned, "The Body of Bread" to which the entire group responded the same in unison. After each response the bowl was passed to the person on their right. The next ingredient was added and once again the ritual leaders and participants would repeat the litany, "The Body of Bread." Eventually, the three rounds of bread dough were ready to be kneaded, and the ritual card was sprinkled with flour to serve as the bread-board. Each participant kneaded the dough and then passed it to the right, repeating the litany until the dough was ready to be turned out into a circular pan for rising and baking. Throughout the ritual, the students were engaged in a silent focus, participating directly as prompted, or were held in fascination by the series actions. There was no talking, and the students did not seem at all awkward. Rather, they directly participated in an act of focused attention. We were both struck by how forceful their voices were in the liturgical response. The artists concluded the ritual, and the students quietly left the space while the artists carried the bread to a nearby oven for baking.

This performance piece raised several interesting issues for our students. How should this performance, with its close affinity to a Communion ritual, be understood? Should it be described as a "ritual-like" activity, or is it an example of ritual behaviors outside the formal context of a religious institution? In some respects, their art performance ritual echoes what some describe as "paraliturgies," or authentic rituals that operate at the periphery or outside of mainstream religious tradition and liturgical practices. The performance actualizes a form of womanist rituals in which women who have been marginalized by male-dominated religious practices create alternative rituals in which their role is central, thus subverting or challenging religious hierarchies. The performance expresses how the bread for the "one body" of worshipers might also be prepared by various individuals united ritually as one body in the common action of making bread and consuming it.

Some Theoretical Frames of Ritual

In our course, we have tried to provide students with a number of interpretive and theoretical frames in which to understand ritual and to begin to think about both the similarities and differences between traditional religious rituals and the practices of contemporary artists. One very significant conceptual insight arises from considering a structural parallel between ritual experience and mystical experience. It should be recalled that Friedrich Heiler, in the one and only comparative study that we have on the omnipresent ritual of prayer (originally published in 1932), understood prayer as "ordinary mysticism." The ordinariness of ritual and mysticism diminishes neither. Ritual holds together binary oppositions without allowing one side to dominate the other or to resolve the opposition into a third, synthetic reality. For example, the sixteenth-century Jewish mystic Isaac Luria understood that the divine was at one and the same time *mesovev kol 'almin*, "surrounding all the worlds [of emanation]" and *memale kol 'almin*, "filling all the worlds [of emanation]"; God was both transcendent and immanent. Luria insisted that both were literally true. That God was immanent and transcendent at one and the same time. Later Jewish mystical traditions would not be able to hold the antinomy together. Thus, the early modern Hasidic teachers would argue that God is literally *memale kol 'almin* and metaphorically *mesovev kol 'almin*, while their opponents, the *mitnagdim* of Eastern Europe, would argue that God is literally and only *mesovev kol 'almin* and that *memale kol 'almin* must be understood metaphorically. The inability to hold the antinomy of transcendence and immanence together as an unresolved ontological reality then stands at the heart of one of the most important socioreligious cleavages in the course of modern Jewish history. The potency of mystical and ritual experiences is the tension between the antinomies. Among the many antinomies that students can see at work in ritual and contemporary art are immanence and transcendence, center and periphery, material and immaterial, temporality and eternality, and presence and absence. We can thus describe the dynamic of ritual as a sacramental action in which ordinary objects, substances, and behaviors are transformed from one reality to another while at the same time retaining their original state and their ordinariness.

We often overlook the ordinary in the study of religion because of the theological weight of the "sacred" which we continue to inherit from Rudolf Otto. Ritual tells us something about the ordinary and the importance of matter and substance as they pertain to their transformation. Aidan Kavanagh reminds us of the tensions that are explicit in rituals and that cannot be neatly overcome, especially, for him, the tension between "Eucharist as meal" and "Eucharist as sacrifice." "The tension calls one to remember," Kavanagh writes, "that however elegant the knowledge of the dinning room may be, it begins in the soil, in the barnyard, in the slaughter house; amid the quiet violence of the garden, strangled cries, and fat spitting in the pan. Table manners depend on something's having been grabbed by the throat. A knowledge that ignores these dark and murderous human *gestes* is losing its grip on the human condition" (1973: 160).

Michael Taussig has underscored the mimetic power of binary antinomies. The most fundamental antinomy, the sacred and profane, is not a static relationship. The sacred is what it is because it can be profaned, and the profane is what it is because it can be sacralized. He writes that sacred things "are defined in many western languages by their astonishing capacity for pollution, danger, and filth, the Latin root *sacer* meaning both accursed and holy. Defacement conspires with this fateful ambiguity, energizing it while accentuating the accursed share now flooding forth in all its loathsomeness of glory—this accursed share that was there all the time, latent, so to speak, hidden, so to speak, all the more effectively granting sacred or quasi-sacred status" (52). Here, Taussig is not only commenting and revising Georges Bataille's classic argument about the power of ritual, but is also offering the first substantive revision of the sacred since both Durkheim and Rudolf Otto. The profane and the sacred are constitutive of one another. Taussig concludes that "thanks to defacement, images may become real—how the perturbation between revelation and concealment involves an oscillation in deceptively lazy loopings between literalness and metaphor, presence and representation" (52–53). Binary oppositions thus become inseparable and the requirement of one another. Thus, there is no possibility of the sacred without the profane or the profane without the sacred.

The sacramental dynamic of ritual and its mimetic or constitutive powers draws the debate and interpretation of ritual into one of the most distinctive contemporary art forms. How are we to understand performance art, precisely the kind of art that our students created in their "Body of Bread"? Linda Montano interviewed more than one hundred performance artists between 1979 and 1989. Many of these artists described their performances as ritual. For example, Anna Mendieta told her that she rejected painting because "it wasn't real enough." She described how she moved to performance art in 1973 in a piece she did in an Aztec tomb covered in weeds and grasses. "That growth reminded me of time," she said. "I bought flowers at the market, lay in the tomb, lay on the tomb, and was covered with white flowers. The analogy was that I was covered by time and history." Mendieta acknowledged the strong influence of her Cuban Catholic heritage. "When I first started working this way, I felt a very strong Catholic connection, but as I continued to work I felt closer to the Neolithic. Now I believe in water, air, and earth. They are all deities." She further described her preparation for performances as a disciplined ritual in which she wore special clothing, worked alone, used special tools and equipment, and rejected any diversion, all as a ritual mechanism to claim territory, the space of her ritual performances. "Doing that *charges* the whole area for me" (2000: 395–396).

But it is not simply that performance artists like Mendieta use the term "ritual" to describe their practice. There is also the very long and complex historical relationship between art and ritual. This historical relationship has recently been developed by Thomas McEvilley, who points to one of the decisive issues in art theory as precisely art's relationship to religion. Art was traditionally the adjunct of religion, but one of the significant repercussions of Marcel Duchamp's work was to push art toward science. Some avant garde artists, such as the action painters, maintained a connection to religion and some form of transcendent inspiration. However, since then, other artists have followed in the line of Duchamp and moved increasingly away from religion. Performance art, McEvilley suggests, has gone both ways. He reminds us: "Recently the art audience has learned to expect humor and parody from its artists, but twenty-five years ago, when an artist seemed to putting his or her body and life on the line for art, the experience of beholding such commitment brought a sense of awe to the audience. One might leave the performance space either shaken or inspired. Now the site of such commitment often seems anachronistic and embarrassing." McEvilley describes three points of origin for performance art. First, performance art came out of theater, and the art gallery acts as a theater arena. Second, performance art developed out of painting, especially through the work of action painters Jackson Pollack and Mark Rothko, in which color and the raw act of painting itself became an experience of transformation for both the artist and the art audience. However, the third point understands performance, especially the tradition of body performance art, as originating from "a revival of ancient ritual practices within the fine arts setting." Here the gallery "becomes an ancient ritual arena, perhaps a grove in the woods or a dolmen circle or an outback *arroyo* with special associations." Unlike the first two views, which understand performance art as part of Western tradition, theater, and painting, the third view understands performance as a withdrawal from Western civilization (McEvilley 1988: 23–25). Anna Mendieta's performance work, which consciously sought to reclaim ritual, was of this third form. Indeed, many performance artists claim some relationship to shamanic ritual practices, and this is not a casual appropriation or a simple linguistic move. These artists understand the power of ritual from an innate sense that at the core of the impulse of their work is an ability to bring forth that is realized only in ritual.

One of the most accomplished ritual artists, and here we believe that it is vital to place our emphasis upon "ritual," is Guillermo Gómez-Peña, who along with his colleagues (among them Roberto Sifuentes) has for almost a quarter century been involved in ritual performances that have deconstructed racial and cultural identities and have constructed a variety of hybrid, borderland identities, including the *CyberVato, El Mad Mex, El Pre-Industrial Cannibal, Border Brujo,* and *El Naftaztec.* Gómez-Peña defines himself as "a migrant provocateur, an intercultural pirate, a "border brujo," a conceptual coyote (smuggler), and, more recently, a "web-back," zigzagging the ever-fluctuating borders of Western civilization. "My life as a border crosser has been an intricate part of my political and aesthetic praxis," he writes (2000: 9). Gómez-Peña understands, much as Walter Benjamin understood history as permanent crisis, that there is permanent crisis in culture which is most perfectly articulated by the artistic genre of performance, and he often describes his work as a shamanic ritual (109–111). His rituals are "counter-rituals," much like the ritual desecrations of the Spanish Civil War, described by Bruce Lincoln, that were intended to expose the powerlessness of seemingly fixed social, cultural, political, and geographic borders. All are swept aside by the crises of the late twentieth century in the Americas. Counter-rituals are as powerful as "counter-histories" in destabilizing existing structures of authority or hierarchy. In perhaps his most convincing demonstration of performance as a counter-ritual, he constructed in 1994 an installation space called the *Temple of Confessions* which combined the format of the pseudo-ethnographic diorama with the religious dioramas that are found in many Mexican colonial churches. Sifuentes and Gómez-Peña were completely unprepared for what would happen in this environment. He writes that partly "due to the profound spiritual and cultural crisis afflicting U.S. society, and partly perhaps due to America's obsession with public and private confession, on opening day people stormed into the Scottsdale Center for the Arts and expressed to our end-of-century *santos* their inner-most feelings, fantasies and memories of Mexico, Mexicans, Chicanos, and other people of color" (Gómez-Peña and Sifuentes 1996: 14). Visitors to the Temple of Confessions immediately understood the museum space as a ritual space and acted out their confessions. Among the many written confessions that were deposited in the ritual was "I wish all Mexicans would be deported!! . . . And take all this bad art with them!" Over Sifuentes's diorama titled *Pre-Columbian Vato* was a neon sign which said, "We Incarnate Your Desires."

A Kitchen, a Backyard, and a House with an Ocean View

Several years ago, we took the students in our religion and contemporary art course on a field trip to the Santa Monica Museum of Art. This was a pilgrimage of sorts with a primary destination—to behold the work of the artist Liza Lou. There in the center of the museum was her rendition of the typical

American kitchen, flanked by the typical American backyard, each installation created to the human scale. Upon first encounter, Liza Lou's works seems to be a glitzy, jittery, hyper-real construction of a fantastical world of domestic life. The colors are glaring and bright, and each element has been tweaked so that the familiar objects of the home and yard are presented in a three-dimensional cartoonlike version. It is common for one to wonder how anyone could possibly find the amount of time to create such a work. Every square inch of the surface of every form in *Kitchen* (1991–1995, 168 square feet) and *Backyard* (1995–1997, 528 square feet) has been covered with tiny, sparkling glass beads. Bright and glittering patterns have replaced the mundane colors of the commonplace surface of the forms, and ordinary domestic items are invested with new meaning as bead-covered versions of their former selves.

Liza Lou has spent a substantial portion of her formative years as a young artist to create *Kitchen* and *Backyard*. It took her more than seven years of continuous work to create what many in the world of art would see as a completely eccentric and zany work of art, perhaps the product of an artist with an extreme compulsive or peculiar nature. It is not surprising that Liza Lou would make the remark, "I hate the word 'obsessive'" (Schjeldahl and Tucker 1998: 11–13). In an interview with the *Los Angeles Times*, she told the reporter: "People assume I'm insane before they meet me—they expect me to show up in frizzy hair and dirty slippers. When they meet me, they're really disappointed" (McKenna 1998).

"Obsessive" is never a word we would use to describe Liza Lou or her art practice. Nor would we use such words as "fetishistic" or refer to her activity as "compulsive" or "labor intensive." We would agree with Kristine McKenna that "devotional is a better description for the artist's relationship with her work, which she perceives as an homage to the virtue of simple labor and the power of the human imagination" (1998). It is significant that Lou identifies this homage through a fragment of Emily Dickenson's poetry. On the end of a kitchen cabinet she has beaded the poem:

> She rose to his Requirement
> dropped the play things of her life
> To take the honorable work
> of Woman and of Wife

There is no sense of randomness or chaos to her actions. Her process is well thought out and framed within a temporal pattern using symbolic materials and symbolic experience. Peter Schjeldahl writes of her work:

> Lou's inspired choice of a ubiquitous, humble subject for the mag-
> nificent, frozen hosanna of this work fulfills Charles Baudelaire's
> definition of beauty as a fusion of the eternal and the fleeting, the
> exalted and the everyday, heaven and hell, the sacred and the profane,

and reason and squalor. Its effect is the opposite of obsession: liberation from closed circuits of the self, prying us open to pure wonder. It brings about a high holy day of the mind, when things always obscurely true stand revealed, clothed only in the lucid radiance of the self-evident. (1998)

The heart and impulse of Liza Lou's work belong to ritual. A most common, ordinary, and inexpensive material, glass beads, become become the matter for sanctification. And, Lou believes that even before she begins stringing the beads, others have contributed. "Each bead has been touched and labored over," she said. "There's power there before you even begin using them in work." Hers is a practice where through the working of the artist's hands and in the duration of her process, attaching millions of beads to the surface of objects and forms, her body becomes an agent for transformation.

Lou is explicit about the nature of her work. She claims ritual and religion when she speaks about what she accomplished in these two works. She describes *Backyard* as being "like a prayer involving community and process." Making such a work "demands some kind of spiritual reckoning, and I like the idea of making a piece that honors mindfulness." *Kitchen* was very much a product of individual ritual, but *Backyard* took a different form. To complete *Backyard*, she hosted a series of "lawn parties" in which an expanding community of volunteers were engaged in beading the blades of grass. Some came weekly for many months; a ritual society was created. *Backyard* thus provided a communal experience of ritual which served as a possible companion or outgrowth from her intensely individual ritual. As in communal ritual or religious practices, it is assumed that this society's members maintain a private or individual ritual practice.

Another intensely individualized ritual practice is seen in the recent performance of Marina Abramović. For twelve days in November of 2002, the Yugoslavian artist set herself on display in the Sean Kelly gallery in New York City. The idea for this performance, *The House with the Ocean View*, came from the artist's "desire to see if it is possible to use simple daily discipline, rules and restriction to purify myself." The artist wondered, "Can I change my energy field? Can this energy field change the energy field of the audience and the space?" (Gotzler 2003: 4).

Abramović created three cubicle rooms, or living spaces, that extended out from the wall and were approximately eight feet off the ground. Each space had only the barest of essentials. The first room, on the left, had a toilet and a shower. The room in the center had a table, on which was placed a metronome to mark the passing of time in seconds, and a chair with a quartz crystal cube imbedded in its high back so the artist could rest her head against it and receive energy. A central part of her ritual performances has been the use of semiprecious stones, which she believes can transmit energies locked within them. To the right of this was the third room. In it was placed a wooden plank for a bed raised on four legs and a wooden basin against the back wall with a spigot that supplied Abramović with drinking water—all the artist allowed herself to consume during the twelve-day performance. Each and every action the artist carried out was exposed. Sitting, standing, and sleeping, dressing and undressing, showering numerous times a day, drinking water, and using the toilet were all public acts before the eyes of the visitors who came to the gallery. The construction of the rooms and their furnishings provided Abramović with no cover. She was fully revealed, being watched and watching others, locking eyes with visitors, communicating only nonverbally.

To move between the rooms, Abramović had only to pass through doorways and step across the two-foot gap between the cubicles. Each of the three rooms had a ladder leaning against it, connecting the gallery floor to the cubicle floor. However, should she attempt to leave the space of the rooms for the gallery below she would have had a perilous challenge. The rungs of each ladder had been replaced by large and very sharp butcher knifes with the knife-edge of the blade angled up.

When we presented this work to our students, one was familiar with it. She recognized it from the popular HBO show *Sex in the City*. In one episode, "Carrie Bradshaw," played by Sarah Jessica Parker, goes with a friend to a gallery to see a woman artist who is living in the space and "not talking or eating for 12 days." The scene was shot at the Sean Kelly Gallery using the actual space created for *The House with the Ocean View*, though an actor took the place of Marina Abramović. Carrie, who has little if any exposure to contemporary art, laughs at the spectacle and boldly remarks how she is certain the artist comes down at night when the gallery is closed and walks around New York carrying on her normal activities after hours. Another character, played by Mikhail Baryshnikov, overhears Carrie's skepticism and later calls her to invite her on a late-night date. His invitation includes their returning to the gallery in the middle of the night to prove Carrie wrong. "Let's go see her at 3 A.M. to be sure."

Carrie Bradshaw is not alone in her skepticism. Many of our students share a version of her doubt when they see Marina Abramović's extensive body of work. She is an artist who has spent her career pushing her body to its limits by putting herself through arduous and extreme bodily practices. "Her art activities are," as Linda Weintraub and colleagues write, "often so grueling and perilous that they propel her to an altered plane of consciousness" where "earthbound sensibilities cease to function" (Weintraub, Danto, and McEvilley 1996: 59, 64). Much of her work must be experienced as it has no material methods or forms that can convey its dimensions. It is difficult for many to grasp the breadth of Abramović's feats. How is it possible for one to undergo such experiences as she does?

Abramović has said that she early on recognized that "the subject of my work must be the limits of my body." In solo performances such as *Lips of Thomas*, 1975, Marina Abramović put her body through extremely dangerous situations. In front of an audience she began by slowly eating a kilo of honey with a silver spoon, then drinking a liter of red wine out of a crystal glass that she later broke using only the force of her right hand. Next she cut a star on her stomach with a razor blade and violently whipped herself until she ceased to recognize or feel pain. Following this, she lay down on a cross of ice blocks with a heater suspended over the star on her stomach. The rest of her body began to freeze, slowing her body reactions until the audience interrupted the piece to remove the artist and spare her life.

From 1980 to 1985, Abramović and her creative partner and lover, the performance artist Ulay, spent extended periods of time in the Australian desert where they were vulnerable to extreme physical challenges. They relied only on their own resources, subsisting on plants, insects, and small animals, such as rats, for food, and drinking water gathered from morning dew, plants, and puddles. They would sit naked for extended hours in the grueling desert heat. "The lengthy time spent in depriving the body restores the spirit," Abramović said, adding that we must "strive as eagerly for deprivation as we strive for plenty" (quoted from interview with Abramović, McEvilley, 16). In 1988, Abramović and Ulay walked the Great Wall of China. Abramović began at the wet cold of the sea, and Ulay began in the dry heat of the desert. Each walked alone toward the center in a prolonged meditation with the sole purpose of achieving awareness.

The same boots she wore on this arduous ritual walk were a component of her daily uniform in *The House with the Ocean View*. The performance was marked by its physical demands. She fasted from food for twelve days, she endured long extended periods of eye contact with individuals in the audience, she remained silent throughout the duration of the entire ritual, and she exposed her body in extremely vulnerable ways, bearing all of its natural functions to observers. Abramović sought, through an intense individual ritual, to change the public space of the gallery and to transfer her energy to the audience in an act of communion. The audience would in turn energize and sustain her throughout the duration. This was a type of ritual symbiosis. Being fully exposed to their gaze afforded her private ritual its public expression. Thus, the ritual involved a series of transformations—the artist's experience, the audience's experience, and finally, the gallery's own transformation into a ritual space. Indeed, all of Abramović's rituals engage transformative power. For example in a series of performances called *Boat Emptying/Stream Entering* (1988–1996), Abramović underscored how in her work she strives to "develop a new consciousness and approach the idea of unity between body and soul, between body and soul and the cosmos.... I want to demonstrate the unbelievable construction of our planet, point out its sources of energy and how, with a new consciousness, we can learn to re-arrange our body and soul within this structure" (quoted from interview with Abramović, McEvilley, 19). If Liza Lou begins with the simple glass beads as the basis of her ritual and transforms the ordinary into the holy, Marina Abramović engages the body and cosmos and in her ritual transcends their limitations. She begins with the individual, reaches to her audience, and ultimately the cosmos.

Whether we teach our individual courses or our religion and contemporary art course, the issue is always the same. We want to introduce our students to the possibility that religion or art is something different from what they think it is or that religion and art are much larger phenomena than they think. Of course that is not just an issue for our students. It is an issue for both our disciplines and is at the very heart of all creative activities and the advance of knowledge. Both of us are committed to the value of comparative work, and thus we have sought in our teaching to draw ritual practices from a variety of sources, in large part to expand the students' and our own horizons and to break down the boundaries that would confine religion to its traditionally ascribed roles and places. Indeed, our effort to draw the performance artists into discussions of ritual reveals our shared perception that religion is always more than what is done in religious spaces and in structured religious times. It means also that we hold a common definition of what religion might be and that our definition might serve as a bridge between our disciplines and our interdisciplinary work. For us, religion is an elaborate symbol system that takes form in symbolic communication, in symbolic behavior, and finally in symbolic places, objects, and persons. We recognize the breadth of this definition, but it nevertheless allows us and our students to think both comparatively and in an interdisciplinary way about ritual.

We would hope also that our students would come to recognize through our comparative and interdisciplinary teaching that ritual is a very sophisticated phenomenon. Its power in some respects arises through its ability to hold together seeming opposites and contradictions, the antinomies that we have described above. Here, there is a structural parallel to mystical experience in its most ordinary forms, as Heiler called it nearly seventy years ago. It is anything but meaningless, repetitive or obsessive action and behavior, and that is why we continue to think of the important revolution that ritual studies have made to the general study of religion in the last decades. It is also the case that ritual is about political power. That political power may be organized and administered by institutions or individuals, but it is usually shaped by ritual. The rituals of the Guadalupanas, the creation of paraliturgies, Protestant and Catholic marchers in Northern Ireland, or the Women in Green's appropriation of rituals mourning the destruction of Jerusalem all reflect the powers of ritual. But the ritual practices of Liza Lou and Marina Abramović also contain a politic and power in which their work is intended to transform the human condition.

There is one last objective in our teaching of ritual and drawing together our disciplines in a single course. Considering the practice of artists as ritual, rather than thinking of it as an incomplete or inauthentic claimant to the mantle of true ritual, considerably expands the presence of ritual in human life. Thus, we would conclude that ritual is a fundamental component of human orientation. Humans might be defined as ritual beings. We need ritual. It is interesting to think for a moment of the implications of Mark C. Taylor's "denegation of God" in which he believes we are left after the philosophical critique of religion in the nineteenth and twentieth centuries with only the tracings of the sacred, the outlines of the presence of the divine (Taylor 1999: 32–34). We would add that the "tracings of the sacred" must also include ritual which has remained a significant component of modernity.

Central to Mircea Eliade's understanding of ritual was its ability to replicate the originary events of the cosmos. Through ritual, individuals and whole societies are able to return to the beginnings of the cosmos, to reexperience the events that constituted the world as humans know it, and to reenter the cosmic time which is narrated in myth. Eliade referred to that time as the "fabulous times of the beginning," the supremely creational time, in illo tempore. Ritual makes present mythical time. Eliade describes this as the "ontology" of archaic peoples, his homo religiosus. This ontology makes cyclical time the pattern of the cosmos and is reflected in the movement of the stars, the sun and moon, the changing, repeated patterns of nature, and the processes of birth, life, and death. This archaic ontology with its essential cyclical pattern of time is broken and ruptured by "history" with its linear time. For Eliade, that rupture took place either with the rise of the critical philosophies of ancient Greece or the prophetic tradition of the Hebrew Bible. Linear historical time is profane time, meaning that it is time without a predictable mythic pattern in which the world is returned to the events at the creation of the cosmos with all of its potency to renew the cosmos as it was in the beginning. Linear time cannot be reversed. The present is distinctive from the past, and the future will be different from the past and present.

Eliade argued that the subsequent histories of religious traditions are formed in large part in response to the "terror of history" and its sense of radical openness without direction and without the potentiality of renewal. Human beings cannot withstand the "terror of history" and consequently attempt to return to the cyclical pattern of time, to reengage the power of ritual, and to re-create the cosmos as it was in the beginning. He referred to these as the camouflages or the persistence of the religious ontology of his homo religiosus. The prophetic "new heavens and a new earth" offer the possibility of history's return to some modified form of the cycle. Religious structures like messianism and apocalypticism are responses to that terror provoked by history's *telos* being unknown, a radical sense of being powerless to know the end, to control it, and of course, to predict it. Indeed, he reads religious cultural phenomena as the persistence of nostalgias to return to the cyclical experience of time. Marxist history, for Eliade, recapitulates the return to the origins in its primordial communism which is the goal of the proletarian revolution. Similarly, the depth psychologies of Freud and Jung provide response to that same terror by taking the individual back to the moment when psychological identity was formed. And film, the visual arts, and literature become a cultural semiotics for elaborate nostalgias intended to return us to the primordial beginnings when the entire cosmos was powerful, complete, or perfect.

For Eliade, it is ritual that allows human beings to pass from the ordinary time of duration, from the linear time that conditions them, into the exceptional and eternal time of the sacred. Ritual allows time to be set in the frame of the mythical, a time when the events which established the world can be indefinitely recovered and repeated. In ritual, time and memory collapse, and past, present, and future are experienced simultaneously. For Eliade, ritual and myth provide the possibility of overcoming amnesia. Myth and ritual are the dynamics that produce knowledge and memory.

Though we suggest to our students that Eliade's work on myth and ritual sets the frame for an understanding of ritual, we also provide them with the insights and theoretical revisions from subsequent studies of ritual. Eliade was not very interested in how ritual provides systems of classification, beyond his insistence, like Otto and Durkheim, that the most fundamental dichotomy was that of the sacred and profane. Ritual's ability to provide systematic classification has been the subject of many studies. Perhaps most important is the work of Jonathan Z. Smith, which is both a critique of Eliade's paradigm and a substantial advance in our knowledge of how ritual works. Smith has argued in his well-known essays and books that ritual is a means of focusing attention. Smith concludes his study of hunting rituals by noting that *"ritual represents the creation of a controlled environment* where the variables (i.e., the accidents) of ordinary life may be displaced *precisely* because they are felt to be so overwhelmingly present and powerful. *Ritual is a means of performing the ways things ought to be in conscious tension to the way things are in such a way that this ritualized perfection is recollected in the ordinary, uncontrolled, course of things"* [italics in original] (1982: 65). Ritual is systematic, precise action rather than behavior which is diffused, fragmented, and unintentional. Ritual perfects an individual's world and erases the accidental. The world of ritual is the world as it *should be*. But it is not simply a static acting-out of a perfect series of action. That perfect world is held in tension with the way things are (Smith

1987: 103). The ritual order, with its uses of various forms of symbolic and gestural discourses, presents a framework from which spontaneity, transformation, and transcendence can occur. Indeed, ritual cannot be separate from the discursive matrixes that constitute lived experience and the world. In all religious traditions, there are moments when ritual is called into question, when it appears to oppositional groups to be mechanistic and meaningless. But at the same time and in the very same cultures, other orientations toward ritual render its power in its creativity, in its ability corrosively to overturn, to subvert, and ultimately to neutralize "central" rituals. Here, we draw examples from Bruce Lincoln's interpretation of the revolutionary exhumations by the Republican and anarchist forces in the Spanish Civil War; David Kertzer's reading of the assassination of Aldo Moro, the head of Italy's ruling Christian Democratic Party, in 1978 and the assassination of Indira Gandhi in 1984; and Jeffrey Alexander's case study of the Watergate scandal (Lincoln 1989: 103–127; Kertzer 1988: 125–150; Alexander 1988: 187–224).

Others have explored the experience of ritual, and here we introduce some of the important ideas advanced in Victor Turner's studies of ritual. Some, of course, have argued that Turner's ritual process is an old-style functionalist or neofunctionalist interpretation. But Turner's emphasis was squarely on the experience of ritual. Though there has been extensive criticism of Turner's liminality and *communitas*, they, like Eliade's work, nevertheless have pedagogical value in teaching about ritual. Turner tended to see these as experienced in similar ways by all who participate in a specific ritual process. Of course, John Eade, Michael Sallnow, and their colleagues have underscored that ritual fields contain multiple and different experiences of liminality and *communitas*. Eade and Sallnow note that in many of the critiques of Turner, the recurrent theme was not anti-structure, but its opposite—the maintenance and reinforcement of social boundaries and distinctions. They suggest that pilgrimage is not only a field of social relations, but also "a realm of competing discourses. Indeed, much of what Turner has to say could be seen as representative of a particular discourse about pilgrimage rather than as an empirical discussion of it, or which might well coexist or compete with alternative discourses. It is these varied discourses with their multiple meanings and understandings, brought to the shrine by different categories of pilgrims, by residents and by religious specialists that are constitutive of the cult itself"(Eade and Sallnow 1991: 5). And we might add, constitutive of the ritual also. Yet, Turner gave great emphasis, perhaps against the "Protestantization" of ritual by other anthropologists and scholars of religion, to what we would call the meanings of ritual action. Ritual for Turner and others is always about meaningful action. In many cases, that meaning is realized only in the experience of ritual. It is an experiential meaning or knowledge that is distinctive from other systems that produce meaning and knowledge, and some would argue that these cannot be acquired by any other means. The implication of this is not a psychological insight into human processes, individual or collective. Here, the experience of ritual underscores that humans are ritual beings who cannot do without ritual and its meanings, that ritual is a necessary ingredient or dynamic in how we orient ourselves to and in the world. This leads our students to reconsider ritual forms that take place beyond the boundaries of traditional religion and are often described as inauthentic and only "ritual-like." Turner's interpretation, expanded from his own fieldwork among the Ndembu and their healing rituals and his survey of pilgrimage rituals in Western Europe and the Americas, allows us to consider symbolic behaviors as ritual, rather than making the artificial distinction between real rituals and ritual-like activities. There is only ritual! After Turner, what students might learn is that we are surrounded or embedded in multiple ritual expressions and forms.

Meaning is much broader than ideas, and perhaps one of the singularly important powers of ritual is to position ideas in a series of actions which constitute or reconstitute a web of meanings that provide an orientation to the small and big questions of human existence. Ronald Grimes arrives at this same position when he concludes that one dimension of ritual is a "structured waiting upon an influx of whole-making [holy] power" (Grimes 1994: 43).

The "whole-making" power of ritual, as Grimes describes it, is located in and acts through the body. If we and our students have understood him correctly, in ritual, meaning flows into the individual and is experienced in the body. Ritual constructs the body and also embodies the epistemic dimension of the ritual experience. Ritual is as much epistemological as it is sensual. It is through the senses as well as the intellect that the body is formed and re-formed, and only the body makes ritual experience possible. This is not a tautology, but a necessary recognition of how the body is believed to mediate ritual and to be transformed by it. In ritual, humans are all experiential learners.

Rituals Take Place

When Pope John Paul II visited Mexico City in winter 1999, he commissioned a digital reproduction of the original image of the Virgin of Guadalupe to be made and sent north to California. As patroness of the Americas, she belonged as much north of the border as south of it. In September, the image was placed in a wooden frame and trucked to Tijuana and San Diego. There, unlike so many millions of her devotees who have made the same trip, she crossed the border amid a fanfare usually reserved for royalty, statesmen, and heads of state. The image was loaded onto a train bound for Los Angeles' Union Station. In Los Angeles, she would visit more than fifty parishes of the Los Angeles

Archdiocese, a peregrination which would culminate with a huge celebration at the Los Angeles Sports Arena on her feast day, December 12. Devotion to the Virgin of Guadalupe runs deep in the identity of Mexicans and Mexican Americans. However, the circuit of the replica of the miraculous image in the heart of Mexico City's Basilica of Our Lady of Guadalupe transformed her into a transnational goddess. Bishop Gabino Zavala, who celebrated the Mass in her honor in the Olvera Street Church, could look at her and say: "This is a Virgin for everyone. Not just for Mexicans, not just for Latinos. She is a Virgin for all of us. She is here to unite all cultures together" (quoted in Ramirez 1999). The replica was then installed in an outdoor chapel in the new Cathedral of Our Lady of the Angels in downtown LA, which was dedicated in September 2002, completing a classic ritual connecting and cementing the periphery to the center.

The peregrination of the replica had an unintended consequence which provided an additional venue for our students to observe another ritual of the Virgin of Guadalupe. In 2002, Catholics in many of the parishes of the Los Angeles archdiocese took their devotion to the Virgin into the streets. For at least two decades, there had been public festivals marking the feast day of the Virgin in several parochial high school football stadiums in East Los Angeles. These usually included processions with banners of the Virgin of Guadalupe and other images of her around the track and field. But in December 2002, many parishes organized processions through public space in honor of the Virgin on her feast day. In Santa Barbara, the procession began at sunset in De La Guerra Plaza, one of the city's historic landmarks. The major's office is adjacent to the plaza. The procession moved out of the plaza and up State Street, the city's central boulevard, to Our Lady of Sorrows Church, where there was a community Mass. The marchers carried lit candles, banners, roses, and crosses with images of the Virgin, and many were dressed in clothing bearing her image (Dunnington 1997; Cuadriello 1999). The Guadalupanas, who north of the U.S.-Mexico border had concentrated on organizing pilgrimages to Mexico City for the Virgin's national festival and developing her devotion within parish churches for much of the twentieth century, were now making a claim to the public space of Southern California.

The use of the De La Guerra Plaza as the starting point for the procession was highly symbolic. The site is doubly the governmental center of the city; it is where the mayor's office is located in the modern city and was the original Mexican center of government, two hundred years ago. The procession not only reveals the Virgin as the protector of the city, claims the space for her and her devotees, but equally presents the old-new citizens of California. Certainly, both rituals underscore the vitality of Jonathan Z. Smith's idea that ritual is a focusing of attention and a perfection of the world. In Santa Barbara, the ritual procession in honor of the Virgin of Guadalupe makes real the identity of her devotees as participants in public culture; they emerge from the shadows of history and domination to be equal citizens. The perfection of identity through ritualized control of space deepens the original insight of Smith, which was oriented to a world in which tribal and other identities may have been less conflictual and less complex.

USEFUL MATERIALS

There are a number of important general discussions on the relationships of ritual and contemporary art. Among them are the following: Alberta Arthurs and Glenn Wallach, eds., *Crossroads: Art and Religion in American Life* (New York: New Press, 2001); Eleanor Heartney, *Postmodern Heretics: Catholic Imagination in Contemporary Art* (New York: Midmarch Arts Press, 2004); Linda M. Montano, *Performance Artists Talking in the Eighties*, which contains lengthy interview materials from some of the most important performance artists; Tracey Warr and Amelia Jones, eds., *The Artist's Body* (London: Phaidon Press, 2000); Bruno Latour and Peter Weibel, eds., *Iconoclash: Beyond the Image Wars in Science, Religion, and Art* (Karlsruhe, Germany: ZKM/Center for Art and Media and Massachusetts Institute of Technology, 2002). One of the most interesting video documentaries on contemporary art is the PBS's *Arts 21* or *Art in the Twenty-first Century* (all three seasons' broadcasts are available in DVD format), and the Web site (www.pbs.org/art21/multimedia/index.html) contains many video clips from the original broadcasts and other materials related to the artists. The journal *Religion and the Arts* (1997), housed at Boston College and published by E. J. Brill, is an important journal in the field. Its Web site (www.relarts.bc.edu) contains many important links in the field.

REFERENCES

Alexander, Jeffrey C. 1988. "Culture and Political Crisis: 'Watergate' and Durkheimian Sociology." In *Durkheimian Sociology: Cultural Studies*, ed. Jeffrey C. Alexander, 187–224. New York: Cambridge University Press.

Cuadriello, Jaime, ed. 1999. *Visiones de Guadalup*, vol. 29 of *Artes de Mexico*, 2nd. edition.

Dunnington, Jacqueline Orsini. 1997. *Viva Guadalupe: The Virgin in New Mexican Popular Art*, with photographs by Charles Mann. Santa Fe: Museum of New Mexico Press.

Eade, John, and Sallnow, Michael J., eds. 1991. *Contesting the Sacred: The Anthropology of Christian Pilgrimage*. London: Routledge.

Eliade, Mircea. 1954. *The Myth of the Eternal Return*. Translated by Willard R. Trask. New York: Pantheon.

Gómez-Peña, Guillermo. 2000. *Dangerous Border-Crossers: The Artist Talks Back*. London: Routledge.

Gómez-Peña, Guillermo, and Sifuentes, Roberto. 1996. *Temple of Confessions: Mexican Beasts and Living Saints*. New York: Powerhouse Books.

Gotzler, Amy, ed. 2003. *Marina Abramović: The House with the Ocean View*. Milan: Edizioni Charta.

Grimes, Ronald. 1994. *Beginnings in Ritual Studies.* Columbia: University of South Carolina Press.

Kavanagh, Aidan. 1973. *The Roots of Ritual.* Grand Rapids, Mich.: Eerdmans.

Kertzer, David I. 1988. *Ritual, Politics, and Power.* New Haven, Conn.: Yale University Press.

Lincoln, Bruce. 1989. *Discourse and the Construction of Society: Comparative Studies of Myth, Ritual, and Classification.* Oxford: Oxford University Press.

McEvilley, Thomas. 1988. "Stages of Energy: Performance Art Ground Zero?" In *Marina Abramović Artist Body,* ed. Emanuela Belloni, 14–25. Milan: Edizioni Charta.

McKenna, Kristine. 1998. "Beads of Sweat: Liza Lou's Extraordinary Beaded Environments Are a Tribute to Simple Labor—and Imagination." *Los Angeles Times,* May 17, 1998.

Montano, Linda M. 2000. *Performance Artists Talking in the Eighties.* Berkeley: University of California Press.

Ramirez, Margaret. 1999. "A Day of Devotion Downtown." *Los Angeles Times,* September 15, 1999.

Schjeldahl, Peter, and Marcia Tucker, eds. 1998. *Liza Lou.* Santa Monica, Calif.: Smart Art Press and the Santa Monica Museum of Art.

Shils, Edward. 1975. *Center and Periphery: Essays in Macrosociology.* Chicago: University of Chicago Press.

Smith, Jonathan Z. 1982. *Imagining Religion: From Babylon to Jonestown.* Chicago: University of Chicago Press.

———. 1987. *To Take Place: Toward Theory in Ritual.* Chicago: University of Chicago Press.

Taussig, Michael. 1999. *Defacement: Public Secrecy and the Labor of the Negative.* Stanford, Calif.: Stanford University Press.

Taylor, Mark C. 1999. *About Religion: Economies of Faith in Virtual Culture.* Chicago: University of Chicago Press.

Weintraub, Linda, Arthur Danto, and Thomas McEvilley. 1996. "Self-Transcendence: Marina Abramovic." In *Art on the Edge and Over: Searching for Art's Meaning in Contemporary Society, 1970–1990s.* Litchfield, Conn.: Art Insights.

16

Eventfulness of Architecture: Teaching about Sacred Architecture *Is* Teaching about Ritual

Lindsay Jones

Architecture is definitely the most visible and arguably the most powerful means both for expressing and for stimulating religious sensibilities. Religious communities in all cultural contexts, so it seems, go to great pains to fashion built environments that are conducive both to their specific ceremonial activities and to otherwise meaningful daily lives. Where religion is concerned, architecture matters. But what does architecture, even explicitly religious architecture, have to do with ritual? Nothing? A little? Lots? Or perhaps everything?

There is, I suspect, little resistance to the claim that architecture plays an important role in forming the background ambience in which rituals are performed. Occasional open-air exceptions notwithstanding, the great majority of ceremonial occasions depend upon quite careful arrangements of the built environment. Just as the timing of rituals is an urgent matter, so too is the configuration of the space in which rituals are performed. In countless instances, then, architecture sets the stage for ritual. I would contend, however, that this stage-setting function hardly exhausts the connections between architecture and ritual. The interactivity between built forms and ritual activities is both more intimate and much more complex. Nuanced discussions of religious architecture or, for that matter, *any* architecture, at least in my experience, invariably lead one into explorations of ritual. In fact, if exploring the multifaceted connections between architecture *and* ritual is an important and productive line of inquiry, to take that next step—and to conceive of architecture *as* ritual—can prove even more rewarding. In short, teaching about sacred architecture *is*—or ought to be—teaching about ritual.

Appreciation of this inextricability of religious architecture and ritual is the driving concern of my *Hermeneutics of Sacred Architecture: Experience, Interpretation, Comparison* (Jones 2000a, 2000b). This essay closes a circle insofar as that two-volume study evolved in large part out of classroom teaching experiences, and now this discussion draws on that work to make suggestions for a course on religious architecture. Both written and classroom cogitations on this set of issues rely on the foundational concept of what I term a "ritual-architectural event." That concept (to which I will return midway through this chapter) arises as an alternative to those very widespread interpretations of art and architecture that presume to retrieve *the* meaning of this ancient sanctuary, *the* intention of that megalithic henge, or *the* significance of some iconographic image (Jones 2000a: 40ff.). By contrast, instead of imagining that sort of stability between built forms and their meanings, I venture that the architectural meanings, like those that arise in ritual, are situational or "eventful." That is to say, architectural meaning is not a condition or quality of the built form itself; works of architecture, and the meanings they evoke, are not once-and-for-all. Instead, the significances and meanings arise from situations, or "ritual-architectural events," wherein people engage works of art and architecture in a kind of dialogical exchange, and the circumstances in which these human-monument conversations most often transpire are precisely those occasions that are routinely designated as "rituals." Accordingly, proceeding on the basis of the so-termed eventfulness of architecture, a course that is ostensibly about religious architecture is no less an exploration of ritual.

The Pedagogical Merits of Comparison: Two Course Conceptions

The mixed merits of comparison, especially cross-cultural comparison, are, aptly enough, much debated. Nonetheless, where pedagogy is concerned, the virtues of comparison are, I've found, beyond question. Accordingly, comparison, actually comparison of several sorts, would play a central role in any course that I did on religious architecture and/or ritual. Regarding the overall conception of a comparative sacred architecture course, I have exercised this commitment to comparison in two quite different ways. Both depend upon students' completion of one major project, but one has proven much more successful than the other.

Option 1: Comparing the Ritual Uses and Apprehensions
of One Specific Site

The losing option, as it were, requires students to select one specific site or building on which they will concentrate for the whole term, and then to work to appreciate the diversity of ways in which that one work of architecture has been used or understood. In other words, the comparison at issue in this formulation of the course entails consideration of the similar and different means by which various audiences have used, understood, and interacted with the same place or building. In this scenario, then, students are encouraged to appreciate, and to take seriously, not only the standard or "orthodox" ways in which religious buildings are used and understood—say, the "official" interpretation of Christian doctrines and artistic symbolism that is intended by architects and then reinforced by Church authorities—but also the unplanned uses of works of religious architecture, which may be variously reverent, subversive, exploitative and/or eccentric.

A comparative sacred architecture course arranged to this end could carry the subtitle "New—and Unanticipated—Uses of Old Religious Buildings," in which case the comparative initiatives are of two sorts. At one (largely synchronic) level, students are encouraged to appreciate that consequential ceremonial occasions (e.g., parades, masses, initiations, or coronations) invariably involve numerous social constituencies, each of which will have a distinctive apprehension of the proceedings as well as the relevant architecture. In other words, instead of simply presuming homogeneous and generalized apprehensions of architecture, students are urged to appreciate much greater specificity— and diversity—in the ways in which a single ritual-architectural event is experienced by various audiences and participants. To invoke a very blunt example, certainly the victims of an Aztec human sacrifice, their families, their captors, the ruling elite, and the assembled onlookers each have quite different experiences of the occasion and the relevant built forms. Those discrepancies ought to be acknowledged rather than blurred into some generically idealized description of the (supposed) meaning of the ritual and architectural symbolism.

Alternatively, at a second (and more diachronic) level, students are challenged to chart and appreciate how the uses of a single place or building have changed over time. This sort of initiative works best via a focus on very prominent and long-standing architectural forms; among countless possibilities, Stonehenge, the Parthenon, Hagia Sophia, or the Buddhist monument of Borobudur in Java—all monuments that have endured very long and rich "histories of reception," as it were—provide promising case studies. The student assignment in this case is to fashion something like a "ritual-architectural reception history," which is, in a sense, like the biography of the "life" of a building (Jones 2000a: 187–208). In other words, again urged to focus on the situational and transient status of architectural meanings, students are charged to retrieve a timeline that begins with the "birth" or creation of the monument and then chronicles the career of the structure with special attention to the various sorts of ritual activities in which that structure has been involved. Another very blunt example: the infamously sturdy old church of Santa Cruz de Bravo in Yucatan endured stints first as a Spanish Catholic sanctuary, then as the headquarters for the brutal cult of the Santa Cruz (who took their name from this monument), and, finally, in revolutionary times, as a prison. Instead of simply dismissing those ancillary usages as eccentric and meaningless abuses or misuses, those unanticipated appropriations are appreciated as moments in the reception history of the structure—they did, after all, actually happen—which speak again to the complex interplay of buildings, meanings, and rituals.

Comparison undertaken in either of these ways—that is, trained on the different apprehensions of a single architectural form that emerge either (a) simultaneously among different constituencies or (b) over time—remains, to my mind, *in theory*, a viable and interesting undertaking. But, as a matter of practical pedagogy, I have to admit that it has not worked very well. It is simply too difficult for undergraduates in a single term to familiarize themselves adequately with a previously unfamiliar place in ways that enable them to undertake this sort of critically nuanced work. Also, this assignment requires a level of abstraction that only some students can master in such short order; it is one thing to convince students that women's architectural perceptions are different from men's, or that the "orthodox" perceptions of a learned elite are different from those of less educated, less enfranchised constituencies, but it is quite another to guide students in articulating those sorts of differences with respect to particular cases studies. Moreover—and this may actually be the greatest and most telling obstacle—it is highly revealing of how limited are most written treatments of standing architecture that the library resources at students' disposal very seldom attend to the diversity of uses that a building engenders; instead, most of those sources presume a kind of generic, idealized user who, in my view, does not really exist. That is to say, the great majority of scholarly treatments of sacred architecture commit exactly the theoretical error that this course conception encourages students to avoid. Ironically, then, the pervasiveness of this interpretive deficiency provides both an incentive for doing a course that focuses on subversive and unanticipated usages of religious buildings and, disappointingly, an explanation for why it is so difficult for such a course to succeed.

Option 2: Comparing the Ritual Usages of Two Works of Architecture

Alternatively, then, the conception of the course that has proven more fortuitous requires that early in the term students select not one, but two specific buildings or sites on which they will concentrate for the remainder of the course. This option entails, in other words, a somewhat more obviously comparative initiative. Regarding the selection of those two sites, positively they do *not* need to be historically related; to the contrary, that they are distant from each other both in location and time invariably proves to be an asset. (That is to say, the goal here is largely synchronic, nonhistorical comparison.) Often the juxtaposition of one site about which the student already knows quite a lot, preferably from a personal visit, with another place about which she has minimal familiarity eventuates in a happy combination. Likewise, based on the principle that every course in comparative religion ought to stretch students' awareness of other cultures, my inclination is to require that at least one of the cases be non-Western, but strict enforcement of that rule could at times be counterproductive.

Moreover, although students often feel an inclination to select two sites that bear some obvious resemblance, I urge them *not* to try to anticipate the play of similarities and differences; it is among the theoretical initiatives of the course to demonstrate that no two works of architecture are, in principle, beyond compare. The sole mandatory criterion of commonality is that the two cases share a roughly commensurate scale. That is to say, they could be two cities (e.g., Beijing and Teotihuacán), two pilgrimage centers (e.g., Lourdes and Benares), or two buildings (e.g., the Khandariya Mahedeva and the Baha'i House of Worship in Evanston, Illinois). Also as a strict rule, the two cases should be *specific* buildings or sites, not general types or classes of buildings; for example, Chartres Cathedral and the Temple of the Emerald Buddha are excellent choices, but the wider categories of French cathedrals or Thai Buddhist temples are not acceptable. (There are important theoretical as well as logistical reasons for that mandate [Jones 2000a: 190–192].) Furthermore, although the hermeneutics of sacred architecture that I have in mind is deliberately anti-elitist, and, in principle, modest and unrenowned works of architecture are fully deserving of serious consideration, there are strong practical advantages to choosing relative high-profile places, in large part because both the available materials and the issues of interest are liable to be more ample. Angkor Wat, the Dome of the Rock, and Ise Shrine may, in some respect, constitute the trite and overexposed in studies of sacred architecture; but their renown is well-founded, and for the purposes of a class like this, these sorts of five-star sacred sites provide excellent project topics.[1]

Foundations on Which to Build: Experience, Meaning, and "Eventfulness"

Presuming that one elects to proceed with this two-case project model, the program of study could unfold in three broad, if very uneven, segments. The first two or three weeks—before students choose their specific project topics— ought to be devoted to consciousness-raising about very large matters concerning space, place, architecture, and ritual. Issues that I regard as most salient in this regard are addressed in the first volume of *The Hermeneutics of*

Sacred Architecture, especially chapters 1–6. But many viable resources engage these large issues (e.g., Tuan 1974, 1977; Lane 1988; Harbison 1992; Gallagher 1993; and Lippard 1997), and what a teacher chooses to use is, of course, contingent on her goals for the remainder of the class. Be that as it may, if the basic concern is to appreciate the links between architecture and ritual, I recommend raising, in succession, three foundational sets of issues.

Architecture and Experience: Focusing on the Use and Apprehension of Buildings

First, work to shift the study of architecture from a focus on buildings per se to the *human experience* of buildings. We can anticipate that students enrolling in a course titled something like "Comparative Sacred Architecture" bring with them an expectation that they will be concentrating on built structures—temples, mosques, pyramids, and so on. Premonitions of dim-lit classrooms with countless slides of famous and not-so-famous monuments, coupled with expectations of having to digest ample terminology about column styles and cornice details are perhaps inevitable—but they ought to be resisted. The more of that technical and art historical information that one can master the better; for this course, however, the focus of concern (and the ground of comparison) are *not* what buildings look like but rather how they are used and experienced, especially in the context of ritual.

This shift of attention from "objects" to experience (which is the subject of the first three chapters of *The Hermeneutics of Sacred Architecture*) is the sort of move that one could associate with the philosophical hermeneutics of Hans Georg Gadamer or perhaps even with John Dewey's *Art as Experience*, though either of those dense works seems a poor vehicle to get a college course out of the gate. Alternatively, geographer Yi-Fu Tuan's *Space and Place: The Perspective of Experience*, although not new (and not explicitly concerned with religion or ritual), remains a very serviceable book for raising these issues. Much of what Tuan has to say, particularly his basic distinction between "space" and "place," resonates with students' own intuitive sensations of space but also challenges them to nuance their thoughts about interactions between people and the built environment. Open discussion of these issues can expand horizons, and, at this point, no firm conclusions are required.

Be that it is may, it is crucial to pose at the outset of the course the challenge of interpreting—and comparing—religious buildings *not* primarily on the basis of what they look like, *nor* what they are made of, *nor* their eras of construction or geographical locations, *nor* even on the basis of the respective religiocultural orientations of their builders. All of these are, of course, viable as well as very common means of organizing and comparing religious architectures. But for the purposes of this course—and for the purposes of holding in the fore the connections between architecture and ritual—the great challenge is to shift (actually *lift*) the frame of reference to the level of experience, especially experience in the context of ritualized action. Though this theoretical aspiration is decisive for this course, it is a goal that will be constantly undermined by more standard accounts of sacred architecture that are preoccupied with matters of physical appearance, style, structure, and materials. Again, although these are perfectly respectable ways to constitute the study of sacred architecture, they are *not* the means that will lead to an appreciation of a somewhat venturesome formulation like architecture *as* ritual. In short, convincing students of the crucial difference that this reformulation of the study of sacred architecture makes will be a term-long pedagogical challenge.

Architecture and Meaning: Appreciating the Superabundance and Autonomy of Religious Buildings

The second very broad set of concerns focuses on the not-so-obvious connections between works of architecture and meaning. That buildings have meaning, even many meanings, seems self-evident. But all too often, either among lay audiences or in academic writing, the working presumption is that "the real meaning" of a building is that which was intended by the original architect or builders; all other understandings, usages, and construals are dismissed as *mis*understandings or *mis*construals, therefore undeserving of serious attention. By contrast, students ought to be encouraged to take a more fully democratic—and more accurately empirical—stance based on the observation that virtually every built form of consequence operates like a multivalent symbol insofar as it evokes different meanings and responses from different audiences. Moreover, built forms, especially long-enduring monuments like cathedrals and pyramids, are, to a significant extent, "autonomous" insofar as they invariably exercise a kind of freedom that enables them variously to transcend and/or undermine the original intentions of their builders. Just as "the sense of a text in general reaches far beyond what its author originally intended" (Gadamer 1975: 335), so religious structures, like rebellious children coming into adulthood, embark on lives of their own and engage in conversations of their own, over which their creators can exercise little or no restraint. As architectural theorist Charles Moore contends, "A building itself has the power, by having been built right or wrong or mute or noisy, to be what it wants to be, to say what it wants to say" (quoted in Cook 1973: 242).

Again, viable classroom resources for raising this issue about the diverse and fluctuating meanings of buildings are abundant. Few, I think, are better than David Chidester and Edward Linenthal's introduction to their edited volume, *American Sacred Space*, in part because they provide a very articulate little summary of scholarly debate concerning the timeworn question of what makes a space sacred and in part because they accentuate the notions of "reinterpreted sites" and "contested sacred space" (1995: 1–42). Chidester and

Linenthal provide, in other words, both a theoretical basis and some tangible historical examples for helping students appreciate that, irrespective of the careful planning of architects and designers, long-lasting and large-scale religious buildings—for example, Hindu temples, Catholic cathedrals, Muslim mosques, and Maya pyramids—nearly always have complex, independent, and largely unpredicted careers. Moreover, in addition to specifically religious functions, enduring religious constructions often work as sites for the expression (and contestation) of political authority, as foci for national identity, as "data" for various academic theorists, as tourist attractions, and so on. In short, the meanings of religious buildings are never confined to the deliberate intentions of their builders and are virtually always "contested."

Thus, where the prevailing tendency is to dismiss unintended usages and apprehensions of a building as "corruptions" or mistaken abuses, an alternate stance would be to celebrate such departures from original design expectations as "creative revalorizations" of an old architectural form. But, in either case, those unanticipated engagements with architecture happen and they are, to that extent, not less—to my view, as a historian of religions, they are actually *more*— deserving of attention than the idealized expectations of architects and builders.

Architecture and Conversation: The Concept of a Ritual-Architectural Event

The third component of this introductory phase of the course entails the exposition of a concrete strategy whereby students can respect those two preceding principles—namely, (a) that the study of sacred architecture is best served by shifting attention from buildings per se to the experience of buildings, and (b) that the meanings of buildings are situational, contingent, and invariably contested. That is to say, if students are to do more than pay lip service to these alternative ways of conceiving of the relations between buildings, experience, meanings, and ritual, they will require a tangible means of operating—and this is where I contend that we benefit enormously by constituting the interpretation of religious architecture, not in terms of buildings or objects, but instead in terms of "ritual-architectural events."

It is possible, albeit tedious (and probably not necessary in a classroom context) to build an elaborate philosophical basis for the "eventfulness" of sacred architecture by calling into question the still widely operative modernist assumption that if one cultivates the proper intellectual disposition, presumably a neutral or disinterested stance that will guarantee a "certitude of vision," she can lay hold of the once-and-for-all (or "real") significance of a work (or "object") of art or architecture (Jones 2000a: 38–58). Scholars working in this mode (more often by default than by decision) endeavor to disengage themselves from the works of art under consideration, to wipe away all preconceptions (or by *epoché* hold them in abeyance) so that they might achieve, in

Husserl's terms, "pure seeing" and, thus, an untainted grasp of "the meaning of the absolutely given." Interpreters who persist in this positivistic tact—whether explicitly or, more often, implicitly—constitute buildings as "objects" of study with the hope and expectation of revealing the authoritative meanings of those buildings via thoughtful and self-conscious reflection.

Alternatively, I want to position students' interpretive inquiries more in that tradition of (postmodern) hermeneutical philosophy that mounts a radical challenge to this entrenched notion of Cartesian "seeing" and, in so doing, provides a foundation for a more flexible (and, I'd argue, decidedly more empirically accurate) approach to the historical use and apprehension of sacred architecture. Heidegger, then Gadamer, and now a host of other critical theorists have, for instance, convincingly refuted the claim that interpreters can ever thoroughly disconnect themselves from their particularistic "life-worlds" and, likewise, that the world can ever be adequately conceived as a realm of neutral things or objects. They claim instead that truth is always an opposition of revealment and concealment, and thus that interpreters are naïve, and perhaps even irresponsible, in believing that they ever really see the total disclosure of any phenomenon, works of architecture included. From this perspective, the locus of meaning resides neither in the building itself (that is, a physical object) nor in the mind of the beholder (that is, a human subject), but rather in the negotiation or the interactive relation that subsumes both building and beholder—that is, in the ritual-architectural event in which buildings and human participants alike are involved. Meaning is not a condition or quality of the building, of the thing itself; meaning arises from situations. The meaning of a building, then, must always be a meaning for some specific audience, at some specific time, on some specific occasion.

Persuasive as this sort of discursion into postmodern hermeneutical philosophy may be (at least for a few of us), a little of that can go far in the undergraduate classroom. Thus, as a more simple and serviceable alternative to this sort philosophical abstraction, I recommend raising the same basic issues by leaning very heavily on the metaphor of dialogue or conversation—and then applying that metaphor at two levels (Jones 2000a: 38–58). At the first level, argue that the *experience* of sacred architecture, especially in the context of ritual, can be conceived as a kind of conversational situation wherein people engage built features in a to-and-fro exchange, bringing to those occasions their own distinctive concerns and questions, and, therefore, deriving from those situations their own distinctive results and understandings. Instead of imagining Hindu devotees, for instance, silently watching, pondering, or even "reading" various elements of their temples, we are much better served by conceiving of those occasions as conversational exchanges in which those devotees, in a sense, interview and interrogate the built forms, peppering them with questions and then listening to the multiplicity of replies that the temple offers. That is to say, the very notion of a so-termed ritual-architectural event, which shifts attention from buildings to the experience of buildings, is best conceived as an occasion of conversation.

Moreover, if the metaphor of conversation works at one level to describe the (indigenous) *experience* of sacred architecture, it can be invoked again at a second level to describe the (academic) *interpretation* of sacred architecture in which the students are involved. In other words, if the productivity of devotees' experiences of religious architecture depends upon the fact that they bring to those situations not disinterested objectivity but, to the contrary, a host of very specific questions or concerns (in Gadamer's language, "preunderstandings"), then, by the same token, the prospect of rewarding academic interpretations of sacred architecture also depends upon students bringing a compelling set of issues and questions to the interpretive conversation. Thus, instead of encouraging students toward supposed objectivity—that is, to approach their project topics without preconceptions and expectations—we ought to be encouraging them to exhaustively question what might be going on in ritual-architectural situations. Of course, there is a danger in overdetermining the outcome of their interpretive analyses, and they must be prepared to admit that their preconceptions were wrong; but the far more serious obstacle is that students will embark upon their analyses with a limited set of possibilities in mind, which is certain to lead to similarly limited interpretive results. The next big block of the course is, therefore, primarily concerned to alleviate that problem by providing students the sort of sustained and strategic pattern of questioning that can indeed lead to productive interpretations with each of their project topics.

Interpretation and Comparison via Worksheets: A Strategic Pattern of Questioning

Once that foundation is laid, and once students have committed themselves to the two sites on which their individual projects will focus, the second and, by far, largest block of the class will be devoted to progress on that comparative project via the completion of a series of eleven so-termed worksheets (Jones 2000b). (The list at the end of this chapter outlines the eleven-part configuration of topics.) This component of the course plays, in other words, on that notion of interpretation as a kind of conversation—a questioning and listening for answers—wherein each of the worksheets outlines a fairly general cluster of questions that students will then bring to bear on their select cases. That is to say, each of the next eleven sessions will be devoted to some general theme, and, in each case, students will be charged with asking: How and to what extent is that theme relevant to their two respective sites?[2] Intimations of a kind of eleven-stage checklist, or maybe even a cookbook recipe, are not altogether unwarranted. But where students invariably enter the course with a quite limited oeuvre of ideas about how religious architecture can work, especially in relation to ritual, this extended slate of provocative questions and possibilities, in my experience, always substantially widens their interpretive horizons; it makes them, as it were, much stronger conversation partners in the analysis of architecture and ritual. Moreover, the cumulative results of students' participation in this eleven-stage interpretive exercise can serve as the basis of their final comparative papers. In fact, that students will, in an important sense, be composing that final paper from this phase of the course forward explains, I think, why this worksheet regiment has consistently issued in ambitious and well-considered papers (not something that I can say about every course that I teach).

This portion of the course is, in other words, an attempt to guide students through an initiative in morphological or synchronic comparison. As a rule, there will be no attempt whatever to link their two cases historically; nor will the resemblances and differences in the outward appearances of the two sites be of much consequence. Instead, the goal is to assist students in undertaking a comparison of their two respective sites that operates at the level of ritual-architectural events rather than that of buildings' structural or formal attributes. Via that focus on ritual occasions—or ritual-architectural events— the goal is, in one respect, to ascertain similarities and differences between two built forms; but, in another equally important respect, this is no less a comparison between the approaches to ritual that obtain at the two respective sites.

As regards the specific configuration of the subsequent pattern of questioning, I draw on the second volume of *The Hermeneutics of Sacred Architecture*, which outlines a so-termed morphology of ritual-architectural priorities (see list at end of chapter). In fact, that volume opens with an introduction that explains this notion of comparison via sustained and strategic interrogation, which is then followed by eleven chapters that precisely match the eleven topical worksheets that I have in mind here; synopses of each of those eleven worksheets appear, albeit in a somewhat over-elaborate form, in the appendix to that volume (Jones 2000b: 295–332). Relying throughout on the notion that ritual-architectural events have a dialogical character, the first three worksheet assignments deal with various means for initiating those sorts of conversational exchanges between people and built forms; the next four worksheets address the content or sorts of topics that are addressed in those exchanges; and the last four worksheets explore various modes of presentation that are used to choreograph such ritual-architectural exchanges. For the purposes of the present discussion, a brief comment on each of those three sets of assignments with have to suffice.

Architecture as Orientation: The Instigation
of Ritual-Architectural Events

This first set of three worksheets is dedicated to reflection on the alternative means whereby ritual-architectural events are instigated or initiated. In other words, though productive engagements with architecture operate in ritual circumstances, these sorts of transformative exchanges are nonetheless the exceptions rather than the norm; in most instances, people pay little explicit attention to their architectural surroundings. Consequently, to override indifference and get the conversation started, as it were, is often the architect's (and the ritual choreographer's) greatest challenge. Cross-cultural studies of sacred architecture demonstrate, however, that there are a myriad of ways in which designers of buildings and ceremonies can light that spark and summon the involvement of perhaps reticent onlookers. These first worksheets, then, are intended to explore the wide range of what I have termed "strategies of ritual-architectural allurement" whereby people are variously encouraged, enticed, and/or coerced into productive and transformative conversational exchanges with architecture by considering three quite distinct variations on the theme.

The first of the worksheet assignments in that vein—launched under the rubric of "homology (priority I-A)"—requires students to give serious consideration to Mircea Eliade's (in)famous model of sacred space (1957, 1976). Several aspects of that renowned scheme are especially germane to analyses of sacred architecture: the notion of hierophanies, which speaks to the possibility of architecture that is understood to mark the site of a manifestation or showing of "the sacred"; the concept of *imago mundis*, whereby Eliade draws attention to the very widespread notion of architectural configurations that are conceived as microcosmic replicas of the wider cosmos; and the idea of *axis mundis*, that is, architectural configurations that participate in the symbolism of the center, and thus mark privileged points of access between earthly and otherworldly realms. In some respects outdated and overworked, Eliade's celebrated terminology and commentaries on sacred space nonetheless continue to provide an exceptionally useful line of inquiry with respect to specific ritual-architectural configurations, especially for students not previously familiar with Eliade's work. For many undergraduates, these variations on homologized architecture raise provocative and challenging prospects that had never occurred to them before.

Thus, while no longer serviceable as a complete theory of religious architecture (as if it ever was), Eliade's timeworn formulations can be transformed into a set of heuristic questions whereby students are requested to ask, for instance, whether either of their selected architectural cases is located at the site of a supposed hierophany. Is either of their selected cases configured as an *imago mundi* or downscaled replica of the universe? Or is either of their cases understood to mark an *axis mundi* or sacred center? Moreover, where such questions eventuate in affirmative replies, I would wager that that those homologized architectural configurations are best conceived not as the full design agenda (as Eliade might imply), but rather as strategies of ritual-architectural allurement that work to persuade audiences of the legitimacy and seriousness of the context (Jones 2000b: 25–32). That is to say, this line of questioning—whether initiated via readings from Eliade or others (e.g., Wheatley 1967; Cohn 1981; or Eck 1981)—directs attention to a strategy of allurement wherein architectural configurations are depicted as synchronized with transhuman cosmic patterns and thus demanding of serious attention. In short, homologized architecture issues a persuasive invitation, perhaps impossible to refuse, to involve oneself in the subsequent ritual proceedings.

The second variation on this theme is a worksheet labeled "convention (priority II-B)," which raises the prospect of ritual-architectural circumstances that are made compelling and alluring because the relevant forms explicitly conform to standardized and/or conventionalized stipulations and rules (Jones 2000b: 47–65). Again, cross-cultural and cross-disciplinary surveys reveal numerous permutations—each of which can be transformed into a heuristic question. Students can be encouraged to consider, for instance, the possible relevance to their cases of: (a) the notion that there are certain universally applicable rhythms and proportions, observable in the workings of nature and mathematics, that are being replicated in architecture (e.g., in Italian Renaissance architecture that obeys the mathematical precise proportioning outlined in the rule books of Vitruvius or Alberti, or in Hindu temples that conform to the design stipulations articulated in the *Shilpa Shastras*); (b) the possibility that a god, variously conceived, has decreed certain ritual-architectural prescriptions that are being observed in architectural design (e.g., in Islamic design standards that are understood to have been delivered directly by Allah); and (c) the host of cases in which the claim to legitimacy, and thus serious attention, is based on the claim that prestigious forebears, "the Ancients" as it were, have established definitive patterns that are being replicated in the architectural design (e.g., in the abundance of Sikh temples that have been directly modeled after the Golden Temple in Amritsar).

Whereas virtually every ritual-architectural circumstance participates in one way or another in some version of this convention priority (I-B), the third worksheet—labeled "astronomy (priority I-C)"—raises a prospect that has far more limited application (Jones 2000b: 66–81). At this point, students are asked to consider whether either of their cases deploys a strategy of allurement wherein architectural configurations and/or ritual timing are correlated with respect to the movements of celestial bodies, e.g., a spring equinox, a helical rising of Venus, or an appearance of the moon on the horizon (Aveni 1982; Eddy 1977). Though in a few cases (e.g., arguably at Stonehenge or at numerous astronomically aligned Maya pyramids and monuments) these sorts of celestial cues can serve as crucial means of persuading audiences of the auspiciousness of a ritual-architectural event, in most cases, such sky phenomena are largely irrelevant. Be that as it may, it is worthwhile here—as with respect to all of the other worksheet assignments—to have students question their project topics in ways that lead to wholly negative replies. To give serious consideration to an interpretative possibility that is subsequently rejected is, to be sure, a fruitful exercise.

Architecture as Commemoration: The Content of Ritual-Architectural Events

Whereas the first three worksheets venture questions about the instigation of ritual-architectural events—that is, means to get the conversation started—the next four raise questions about the content of those subsequent ceremonial occasions. This block may provide somewhat smoother going not only because students ought by now to have caught on to the protocol of interrogation via worksheets and have become fairly familiar with their respective sites, but also because these are the most straightforward of the eleven worksheet topics. The first one—"divinity (priority II-A)"—asks students to search after ways in which either of their cases variously houses, commemorates, and/or represents a deity, divine presence, or conception of ultimate reality (Jones 2000b: 92–108). This set of prospects is complicated but also enlivened by the enormous diversity of culturally specific conceptions of gods and other supernatural entities and presences that emerge in various contexts (Mitchell 1988; Van der Leeuw 1963; Lane 1988: 103–124). Salient permutations on the divinity theme include: (a) circumstances in which built forms are actually identified as or equated with a deity (e.g., Cretan palaces, which are conceived as the body of the Minoan earth goddess and thus as "living organisms"); (b) the more obvious and prevalent notion of architectural configurations that are imagined as residences or houses of a god (e.g., oracle temples in ancient Greece or China); or (c) the more subtle notion of architecture that is conceived as a built expression of the *attributes* of a divinity (e.g., triangular or three-tired architectural allusions to the three elements of the Christian Trinity).

The second worksheet query in this group—"sacred history (priority II-B)"—requires interrogation of the many ways in which ritual-architectural events can be occasions to (re)tell a story or to commemorate an important mythical, mythicohistorical, or miraculous episode (Jones 2000b: 109–128). Of numerous overlapping variations on this theme, students should ask: (a) Does either of their cases constitute an architectural embodiment of a cosmogony (e.g., in the way that the moat-encircled Angkor Vat is a direct expression of a Southeast Asian creation story)? (b) Does either case commemorate a mythical narrative (e.g., in the way that the configuration of the Aztecs' Templo Mayor facilitates reenactment of the story of the birth of the war god Huitzilopochtli)? Or perhaps a miraculous episode (e.g., in the way that countless structures memorialize the apparition of a god, angel, or vir-

gin)? Or (c) is either of their sites largely preoccupied with the commemoration of a specific mythical or mythicohistorical individual (e.g., in the way in
which Sikh shrines or *Gurudwaras,* that is, doors or seats of the *guru,* are, in
almost every case, associated with some particular individual sage)?

The third worksheet of this set—"politics (priority II-C)"—demands consideration of the means whereby ritual-architectural events variously commemorate, legitimate, or challenge socioeconomic hierarchy and authority
(Jones 2000b: 129–152). With the current vogue for cultural studies, students
could, these days, get lots of messages suggesting that it is in these socioeconomic considerations that they will find "the real (political) meaning," which
resides behind the idealized (religious) meanings of their respective sites.
Though there is merit in that hermeneutic of suspicion, I would encourage
them instead to treat this political dimension as simply one, albeit an important one, among the numerous forces that are at work in most ritual-architectural choreography. Be that as it may, of the many permutations deserving
consideration, three stand out: (a) ritual-architectural configurations that, either subtly or unmistakably, reflect and perpetuate the prevailing social hierarchy (e.g., the relative heights of houses that denote various Hindu castes); (b)
architectural configurations that challenge, undermine, and (maybe) change
the prevailing social hierarchy (e.g., Muslim mosques inside which the social
distinctions that obtain in the outside world are erased); and (c) configurations
that serve functions that are more explicitly governmental (e.g., countless re-
ligion-civic structures that are designed to impress and/or intimidate as well as
to facilitate day-to-day decision-making).

The last worksheet in this group—"the dead (priority II-D)"—requires
students to search after ways in which their respective sites may commemorate revered ancestors and/or other deceased individuals or groups (Jones
2000b: 153–182). Insofar as commemorations of sacred history (priority II-B)
and politics (priority II-C) very often entail venerations of the honored dead,
here especially one can observe that there is considerable overlap between the
various categories in this framework; but instead of a liability, that seeming
imprecision can become an occasion to remind students of the heuristic and
contingent status of these categories. The goal of this patterned interrogation
is, after all, a nuanced comparison of their two specific sites, and what lands
under which heading is, in the end, not very important. In any event, at least
three variations on the commemoration of the dead deserve serious consideration: (a) ritual-architectural configurations that commemorate the dead
irrespective of any actual bodily remains (e.g., chapels, stadiums, hospitals or
public monuments that are dedicated to, and maybe named for, specific individuals); (b) the not-so-obvious prospect of built or carved forms that are
imagined as the actual embodiment or transmutation of the dead (e.g., British
megaliths that, according some interpretations, serve to keep ancestors alive

by embodying them in stone); and (c) the far more common, if spectacularly varied ways in which architectures are designed for the assiduous treatment and accommodation of the actual bodily remains of the deceased (e.g., cemetery and burial configurations of nearly endless variety).

Architecture as Ritual-Context: The Presentation of Ritual-Architectural Events

Whereas the first set of worksheets focuses on various means of initiating ritual-architectural events, and the second set concentrates on the content or subject matter of those ritual occasions, this third and final group explores the "modes of presentation" that are issue in various ritual-architectural situations. These last worksheets, in other words, organize and explore different ways in which architecture participates in concocting an efficacious context for ritual or, to phrase it somewhat differently, they present four alternative ways of describing the interactive relationship between human ritual participants and built ritual contexts (Jones 2000b: 183–187). By contrast to the quite direct line of questioning in the previous four assignments, this group again challenges students to engage fairly abstract ideas (ideas that are, I admit, difficult to summarize in the present context). One compensation is, however, that by this late stage in the course, students ought to be quite familiar with their two case studies; and, again, precision is less important than evoking serious reflection on possibilities not otherwise considered.

The first presentational option—"theater (priority III-A)"—uses that term in a distinctive way to direct attention to ritual-architectural configurations that serve as backdrops or stages for the performance and spectator viewing of ritual dramas (Jones 2000b: 188–212). The hallmark of this mode of ritual-architectural presentation, which might appropriately connote glitz and/or gore, is an incentive toward inclusiveness (as opposed to exclusiveness) insofar as the designer's aspiration is usually to invite, cajole, or sometimes force even reticent onlookers into involvement in the ritual proceedings. Students should entertain the possible relevance of at least three variations on this sort of aggressive solicitation of involvement: (a) configurations that facilitate the presentation of ceremonial performances on a fixed podium or stage for a similarly stationary assembly of onlookers (e.g., as in the case of spectacular pageant spaces or arenas as well as countless more modest church and classroom layouts wherein a seated audience faces a speaker, screen, or ensemble of singers, dancers, or actors); (b) configurations that facilitate ceremonial movement along processional ways or parade routes past a largely fixed audience or reviewing stand (e.g., outdoor civic or religious parade routes or indoor, longitudinal Christian basilicas like that which hosted the sumptuous liturgical processions at Cluny); and (c) configurations in which onlookers are compelled to become ritual actors insofar as they themselves also are moving along in promenade or parade (e.g., at a very large-scale pilgrimage, say to Mecca, wherein all participants are on the move, or, at a more modest scale, Christian liturgies that require people to walk to the altar space to receive the host).

The second option in this group—"contemplation (priority III-B)"—again deploys a somewhat distinctive use of a broad term, this time to encourage consideration of circumstances that involve the purposeful and direct (as opposed to *in*direct) reliance on architectural features as foci of meditation or concentration (Jones 2000b: 213–236). In other words, beyond the use of architecture to create an ambience or backdrop for ritual performance, which entails an indirect experience of the built forms, this option entails cases in which architectural features become the explicit objects of contemplation, broadly conceived. Of numerous variations on this theme, students should consider the possible applicability of two contrasting possibilities: (a) voluntary and somewhat esoteric ritual occasions wherein people enthusiastically elect to participate and focus their attention on architectural features because they perceive the occasion as an opportunity for spiritual growth (e.g., in the practice of Tibet monks who fix their attention on mandala diagrams or building layouts as guides and supports to their meditations); or (b) less rarified, more plainly didactic and probably more manipulative occasions wherein indifferent or even resistant participants are forced into contact with partisan symbols and images (e.g., Abbot Suger's famous architecturalization of the theory of "anagogical illumination" in the Gothic cathedral of St. Denis—that is, his confidence that concentrating directly on splendid architectural forms and stained glass could somehow transport worshipers from the material world into a blissful immaterial realm—also served the more prosaic function of educating unlettered devotees on the history and rules of the Christian faith).

The third component of this set relies on the rubric of "propitiation (priority III-C)" to raise the prospect of sacred architecture designed and built to please, appease, or manipulate "the sacred," however variously conceived (Jones 2000b: 237–263). Again, the manifold range of possibilities that deserve consideration can be arranged under two large categories: (a) propitiatory ritual uses of standing architecture, which could entail any number of architectural configurations that facilitate ritual negotiation and bargaining with deities (e.g., especially in relation to Abrahamic conceptions of a covenant or contract, a prime purpose of many sanctuaries is to provide a context in which to exercise a give-and-take relationship between human communities and a powerful but not entirely unreasonable God); or (b) architectural construction processes that are themselves conceived as propitiatory ritual (e.g., any number of Christian churches built in fulfillment of a promise made to a god or saint who helped one through a crisis or, from a more Asia frame of reference, the similar abundance of Buddhist, Jain, and especially Hindu temples that were built with the express intention of improving one's rebirth status).

The last entry to the framework returns to a perhaps more obvious set of possibilities under the heading of "sanctuary (priority III-D)." This mode of presentation stands in opposition to the inclusiveness of the so-termedtheater mode (priority III-A) insofar as the main incentive here is one of exclusive-ness or restricted access in the form of ritual-architectural configurations that provide refuges of purity, sacrality, and/or perfection (Jones 2000b: 264–293). This may, in cases, involve the appropriation of some sort of natural sanctuary space, most notably caves, or it may entail the (ritual) transforma-tion or sanctification of a seemingly ordinary place into one of special sanctity. Students should consider, among literally countless variations on the theme, the possible applicability of at least three possibilities: (a) sanctuaries that effect a complete rejection of society (e.g., in Anabaptist or Shaker commu-nities, or Hezychast or Cistercian monasteries, any of which may be conceived as fabricated "foretastes of heaven"); (b) sanctuaries that display an exemplary model of society (e.g., in experimental communities or long-established mo-nastic orders, which then serve as museum-like spaces for showcasing those alternative approaches to life); or (c) sanctuaries that provide a mechanism for hierarchical exclusion (e.g., as in the Jerusalem Temple's rigorously enforced separation of Jews from gentiles, clergy from laity, men from women, etc.).

Synthesizing Worksheets: Student Presentations and Final Comparative Papers

Forcing students through this eleven-stage gauntlet of questioning may seem variously tedious, baffling, and exhausting; and I concur that, when summa-rized in this staccato fashion, the scheme may appear inordinately elaborate. But this is a proven plan. When stretched out over a full term, the exercise virtually always leads students into deeper and more expansive interpretations of their respective project topics than would issue from more conventional, less programmatic research strategies. Moreover, one of the most exciting results is the way in which architectures that bear no obvious resemblances in appear-ance, geography, or religious tradition—say, Mexico City's Basilica of Guada-lupe and the Kasuga Shrine in Nara, Japan—emerge as both similar and different at the level of ritual-architectural events. That is to say, in addition to insights into architecture and ritual, this class has often served to convert students to the viability and merits of comparison, including the embattled prospect of nonhistorical cross-cultural comparison.

In any case, once students have completed the eleven pairs of worksheet assignments, the final stage of the process would be to synthesize those in-dividual assignments into a final comparative paper. This is where the notion of ritual-architectural priorities becomes salient. The rubric of priorities is intended to acknowledge that any ritual-architectural situation reflects a kind of competition, or a set of trade-offs, between various factors (or priorities). In some cases, for instance, the strategy of allurement via the synchronization of ritual timing with celestial phenomena such as equinoxes or moon risings (i.e., astronomy, priority II-C) is exceptionally important (that is to say, it is a high priority), while, in other cases, it is almost wholly irrelevant (which is to say, it is a very low priority). Or in some ritual-architectural situations, the principal incentive is to facilitate communication with a deity (i.e., divinity, II-A, is the dominant priority), while other configurations are focused almost wholly on the commemoration of a specific deceased individual (i.e., the dead, II-D, is the dominant priority). Therefore, at this point, students would be required to revisit their individual worksheets to ascertain which of the eleven ritual-architectural priorities have emerged as especially significant and which have proven considerably less important or perhaps even irrelevant. In fact, as one last heuristic exercise, it is worth having them assign numbers to each of the eleven priorities as a means of suggesting a relative order from most important to least important for each of their two cases.

Upon completing that ranking of the priorities, the composition of the actual paper very well might be a kind of narrative rehearsal of the student's consideration of each of the eleven possibilities, which is then complemented with assessments as to which of those priorities are most significant as well as observations about the similarities and differences between their two sites. There is, of course, the unhappy prospect of essays that resemble laundry lists, devoid of compelling conclusions; but it is also possible that perfectly capable papers may follow very closely the regiment of the worksheets. The best papers, however, will transcend the simply formulaic by adducing from the long heuristic exercise some more broad hypotheses as to the similarities and differences between their respective cases. In those somewhat more daring instances, the papers venture a strong thesis at the outset, and then the inventory of the respective priorities is undertaken—and shaped—in the service of advancing that thesis. Final essays of that sort have, in other words, greater unity and sharper edges, and thus issue in more rewarding, if perhaps more tentative, conclusions. In either case, though, as I noted earlier, no course with which I have been associated has issued in consistently stronger and more thoughtful student papers than this one.

As a very last step in the course, consider allowing each student the opportunity to present her comparative project in class. Class size, schedules, and teachers' feelings about the merits of student presentations would all figure in, and I concede that the quality of the class presentations will be as uneven as the students giving them. But, in my experience, allowing myself and others in the class a chance to talk to individual students about their projects has proven very rewarding. Thus, on balance, risking the prospect of an anti-climax, I am inclined to devote the final sessions of the term to student presentations. Give them the last word.

A MORPHOLOGY OF RITUAL-ARCHITECTURAL PRIORITIES

I. Architecture as Orientation: The Instigation of Ritual-Architectural Events
    A. Homology: Sacred architecture that presents a miniaturized replica of the universe.
    B. Convention: Sacred architecture that conforms to standardized rules and/or prestigious mythicohistorical precedents.
    C. Astronomy: Sacred architecture that is aligned or referenced with respect to celestial bodies (e.g., the sun, moon, planets, or stars).

II. Architecture as Commemoration: The Content of Ritual-Architectural Events
    A. Divinity: Sacred architecture that commemorates, houses, and/or represents a deity, divine presence, or conception of ultimate reality.
    B. Sacred History: Sacred architecture that commemorates an important mythical, mythicohistorical, or miraculous episode.
    C. Politics: Sacred architecture that commemorates and legitimates (or challenges) socioeconomic hierarchy and/or temporal authority.
    D. The Dead: Sacred architecture that commemorates revered ancestors and/or other deceased individuals or groups.

III. Architecture as Ritual Context: The Presentation of Ritual-Architectural Events
    A. Theater: Sacred architecture that provides a stage setting or backdrop for ritual performance.
    B. Contemplation: Sacred architecture that serves as a prop or focus for meditation or devotion.
    C. Propitiation: Sacred architecture and processes of construction designed to please, appease, and/or manipulate "the sacred," however variously conceived.
    D. Sanctuary: Sacred architecture that provides a refuge of purity or perfection.

NOTES

1. Three more words of caution concerning the selection of project topics: (1) In principle, it is compelling to endorse a very broad designation as to what constitutes "sacred" or "religious architecture" so that football stadiums and shopping malls are contenders, but for the purposes of this class, more plainly and explicitly religious works of architecture serve better. (2) Additionally, I would, in principle, endorse the

possibility of working with virtual or imaginary architecture (e.g., the steel and microchip jungle of *Blade Runner*), unbuilt architecture (e.g., St. Gall, which provided a kind of utopian model of an ideal Carolingian monastery but was never built), or strictly mythical architecture (e.g., Mt. Meru). But in practice, allowing students to focus on those sorts of imaginal cases creates a set of skews and challenges that, in the end, are counterproductive; it is better to have them working on tangible historical (or contemporary) places. (3) By the same token, while the so-termed architecture of nature (e.g., caves or maybe landscape features in Australian outback) could likewise qualify, in principle, as sacred architecture, more plainly constructed architectural forms (e.g., temples and mosques) will, in the end, provide more pedagogically beneficial project topics.

2. In other words, if students complete the eleven topical worksheets for each of their two selected sites, they will eventually complete a total of twenty-two worksheets. Note also that, if time permits, it would be even better to devote two sessions to each of these eleven themes. In that case, the first session could be devoted to a general (lecture) presentation of the respective topic at hand (i.e., this is the common concern of all of the students), and the second (discussion) session could be devoted to more individualized reflections on the ways in which that topic is or is not relevant to students' specific project topics.

USEFUL MATERIALS

Chidester, David, and Edward T. Linenthal, eds. 1995. *American Sacred Space.* Bloomington: Indiana University Press.

Gallagher, Winifred. 1993. *The Power of Place: How Our Surroundings Shape Our Thoughts, Emotions, and Actions.* New York: HarperPerennial.

Lane, Belden C. 1988. *Landscapes of the Sacred: Geography and Narrative in American Spirituality.* New York: Paulist Press.

Lippard, Lucy R. 1997. *The Lure of the Local: Senses of Place in a Multicentered Society.* New York: New York Press.

Oliver, Paul, ed. 1977. *Shelter, Sign, and Symbol: An Exploratory Work on Vernacular Architecture.* Woodstock, N.Y.: Overlook Press.

Tuan, Yi-Fu. 1977. *Space and Place: The Perspective of Experience.* Minneapolis: University of Minnesota Press.

REFERENCES

Aveni, Anthony. 1982. "Archaeoastronomy in the Maya Region: 1970–1980." In *Archaeoastronomy in the New World,* ed. Anthony Aveni. Cambridge: Cambridge University Press.

Chidester, David, and Edward T. Linenthal, eds. 1995. *American Sacred Space.* Bloomington: Indiana University Press.

Cohn, Robert L. 1981. *The Shape of Sacred Space: Four Biblical Studies.* Chico, Calif.: Scholars Press.

Cook, John, and Heinrich Klotz. 1973. *Conversations with Architects.* New York: Praeger.

Eck, Diana L. 1981. "India's Tirthas: 'Crossings' in Sacred Geography." *History of Religions* 20 (May 1981): 323–344.

Eddy, John A. 1977. "Medicine Wheels and Plains Indian Astronomy." In *Native American Astronomy*, ed. Anthony Aveni. Austin: University of Texas Press.

Eliade, Mircea. 1957. "Sacred Space and Making the World Sacred." Chap. 1 of *The Sacred and The Profane*, trans. Willard R. Trask. San Diego: Harcourt.

———. 1976. "The World, the City, the House." In *Occultism, Witchcraft, and Cultural Fashions*. Chicago: University of Chicago Press.

Gadamer, Hans-Georg. 1975. *Truth and Method*. Translated by W. Glen-Doepel. London: Sheed and Ward.

Gallagher, Winifred. 1993. *The Power of Place: How Our Surroundings Shape Our Thoughts, Emotions, and Actions*. New York: HarperPerennial.

Harbison, Robert. 1992. *The Built, the Unbuilt, and the Unbuildable: In Pursuit of Architectural Meaning*. Cambridge: M.I.T. Press.

Jones, Lindsay. 2000a. *The Hermeneutics of Sacred Architecture: Experience, Interpretation, Comparison*. Vol. 1: *Monumental Occasions: Reflections on the Eventfulness of Religious Architecture*. Cambridge, Mass.: Harvard University Press.

———. 2000b. *The Hermeneutics of Sacred Architecture: Experience, Interpretation, Comparison*. Vol. 2: *Hermeneutical Calisthenics: A Morphology of Ritual Architectural Priorities*. Cambridge, Mass.: Harvard University Press.

Lane, Belden C. 1988. *Landscapes of the Sacred: Geography and Narrative in American Spirituality*. New York: Paulist Press.

Lippard, Lucy R. 1997. *The Lure of the Local: Senses of Place in a Multicentered Society*. New York: New York Press.

Mitchell, George. 1988. "The Temple as a Link between the Gods and Man." In *The Hindu Temple: An Introduction to Its Meaning and Forms*. Chicago: University of Chicago Press.

Tuan, Yi-Fu. 1974. *Topophilia: A Study of Environmental Perception, Attitudes, and Values*. New York: Columbia University Press.

———. 1977. *Space and Place: The Perspective of Experience*. Minneapolis: University of Minnesota Press.

Van der Leeuw, Gerardus. 1963. "The House of Man and the House of God." In Gerardus van der Leeuw, *Sacred and Profane Beauty: The Holy in Art*. New York: Abingdon Press.

Wheatley, Paul. 1967. "City as Symbol." Inaugural Lecture delivered at the University College, London, November 20.

17

Ritual and the Writing Class

Christopher I. Lehrich

The teaching of writing, once almost exclusively the province of English departments, has increasingly become the task of professors from across the humanities and social sciences. In many cases, faculty, especially junior faculty, are asked to make their smaller seminar courses "writing-intensive" or the like, the idea being to improve writing by requiring more essays on a subject that presumably interests the students. Unfortunately, few of us learned to write in this fashion, and fewer still had any instruction in writing pedagogy. All too often, we associate learning to write with grammar or literature courses. How, then, can we teach writing in a course devoted to the study of ritual? Is good writing pedagogy consistent with our other goals, or must we sacrifice ritual on the altar of prose?

In this chapter, I sketch some ways to teach writing in a course on ritual. First, I discuss the objectives and principles that, for me, guide this process. Second, I offer some discussion of sample writing assignments and how they can help students improve both their writing and their understanding of ritual. In concluding, I reflect briefly on what we can learn from teaching such a course, not only about pedagogy but also about ritual.

Objectives and Principles

It is obvious enough that the primary objective of a writing course is to teach students to write well, or at least better. But it is not always clear what *sort* of writing they ought to do, or which particular skills matter most. In one common model, students read literary works, then write responses and analytical papers that discuss what they have read. In class, they examine facets of these literary works, from sentence structure to character, plot, theme, and historical context. In theory, they then synthesize all of this in their own writing. Because they find literature engaging in an emotional as well as intellectual sense, and they encounter great writers using language well, they are inspired to write powerfully, choosing words with care.

Setting aside the obvious point that my training is in religion rather than literature, I find this method problematic. Quite simply, the whole structure depends upon a notion of imitation that is not carried through into the desired product. If the students read a lot of Shakespeare and work toward mastering the intricacies of his styles, cadences, and forms, surely the obvious result is an improved ability to write like Shakespeare. But bluntly, the usual goal of a college writing course is to develop the ability to write not *like* Shakespeare but rather *about* Shakespeare. In short, this literary model of the writing course asks the students to invent literary criticism from whole cloth, focusing exclusively on primary sources.

Another part of the common model is the myth known as the "good college essay." There is no such thing—there are only essays by more or less informed writers, written more or less well, aimed at various audiences. Let me be straightforward: no purpose is served by teaching students to write like college students. They do that anyway! I prefer to teach students to write analytical essays in an academic style, on the notion that if students have the same ideals in their writing as do their professors, both will be pleased with the results.

These objections to writing pedagogy offer possibilities for teaching writing and ritual. For us, primary sources are a tricky matter. No one performance is definitive, no one description sufficient, no one perspective decisive. We necessarily ask students to read secondary sources, which is to say academic writing. If emulation is central to learning to write, as Robert Louis Stevenson claimed in "A College Magazine" (1887), then it makes sense to have students read what we want them to emulate: excellent academic prose.

This is not to say that to teach writing in a ritual course, one need merely follow one's inclinations as a scholar of ritual. I believe the process is somewhat simpler, as compared to that which our more literary-minded colleagues generally follow, but making the course work smoothly requires considerable effort nonetheless.

First, the selection of texts must balance analytical depth and quality against literary style and grace. You may find Kant intellectually stunning, but I do not imagine you want your students to hand in reams of pseudo-Kantian prose. Here, the scholar of ritual is singularly fortunate, in that many of the greatest scholars of ritual have also been great writers: the best writings of Durkheim, Radcliffe-Brown, Lévi-Strauss, Douglas, Turner, or Geertz can stand up with the best academic writing from any field (although, of course, this can depend somewhat on translations). If your students end up writing like *The Elementary Forms* or *Purity and Danger*, you have succeeded admirably.

Second, the teacher must tie examination of ideas and concepts to analysis of the prose in which they are couched. Here it can be useful to keep in mind a list of specific skills and writing structures and, when rereading the texts in preparation, to highlight particularly good examples. For instance, Durkheim's discussion of the a priori and empirical views on knowledge, in the introduction of *The Elementary Forms*, is a masterful example of summary and explication. Lévi-Strauss's analysis of Hidatsa eagle hunting in *The Savage Mind*, despite the execrable translation, beautifully demonstrates the principle of compression, of squeezing a great deal into a small space without sacrificing clarity. Douglas's winding-up of "The Abominations of Leviticus" with the remark that penguins ought to be *tref* elegantly demonstrates the use of humor and concreteness to make a point. Thus, when discussing these passages in class, the teacher of writing must guide discussion to focus on the *way* they are written, as well as on what they say. Fortunately, it is nearly axiomatic that the best writing happens in the most important passages, so that very close attention to the two views on knowledge actually helps immensely in understanding Durkheim's sociology of knowledge, just as close reading of the passage on Hidatsa eagle hunting will go a long way toward clarifying Lévi-Strauss's structural principles.

Third, the arc of assignments through the term must build particular skills as well as develop deeper understanding of concepts. I will return to this concretely in the next section.

Yet all is not sweetness and light. If students must analyze texts with the attention needed both to understand them and to unpack how they work rhetorically, they must also read slowly. In addition, students will mostly improve their writing through their own efforts, however guided, and this development does seem inversely proportional to the amount of class time spent on lecture. The practical upshot is that they cannot cover as much material. At the same time, they will come to understand what they do read relatively deeply.

To summarize, I believe that the central principles of college writing pedagogy should be *imitation* and *respect*. If you provide students with excellent models of academic writing and tell them *explicitly* that they should imitate, you will get results surprisingly readily. Do not waste time on sample college essays, even by previous students in your class, as these offer a low standard of excellence. This leads to the issue of respect: when we ask a lot of students and tell them why we do so, they respond positively to the challenge. If I give a class a great piece of writing, then follow it with a college essay example, I imply that the students cannot strive for excellence. Just so, if I give a class a watered-down version of Durkheim, I suggest that the students cannot understand Durkheim. Where the object is simply to ensure that the students have a working knowledge of concepts, this may be a functional model; where I want students to improve skills in writing and analysis, I must set the bar very high indeed.

Assignments and Skills

The central principle of assignments is that they be worth doing, and not just for college students.[1] Just as there is no point in learning to write a "college essay," or in fact learning to write a dissertation, there is no point in learning to do a specially designed college writing assignment. The skills gained are not worth the effort or time. Fortunately, an assignment worth doing is also comparatively enjoyable to read and thus grade.

When constructing an assignment, I imagine I will do the work myself, substituting texts as appropriate. For example, a very common summary assignment asks students to summarize a dramatic scene in five sentences. Without more to go on, this is not something I think valuable for myself, so why should I ask students to do it? Instead, I ask students to summarize an entire article—a rather difficult one—explaining that they will have to cut large portions of the argument and focus on what is important. Next, they must resummarize, this time in one sentence, the thrust of the whole article. Suppose you did this yourself for every text you read. You sit down with, let us say, Bourdieu's *The Logic of Practice*, and think you have more or less understood. So now, in a page or two, summarize the work cleanly, not as a book report or overview but as a brief explanation of the central points. Now do it again, this time in one brief paragraph. I submit that you would learn a good deal in the process. Furthermore, and this is essential from a writing-pedagogy perspective, such summaries are essential in your own writing. If you situate an analysis in a larger context, you must summarize the state of the field. If you challenge an argument, or build on it, you again summarize. Thus the kind of work we do every time we write must form the basis of what we ask of students. To make this clear, I suggest drawing students' attention to places in the texts at which the writers do, in essence, the assignment. This gives a model for emulation, as already noted, and also stresses that assignments are not "Mickey Mouse" busywork but central to scholarship.

In what follows, I sketch the outlines and concepts of several assignments I use, in the order I generally assign them. I certainly do not claim that all these are necessary, nor that they constitute an exclusive or exhaustive list. My hope is that teachers will find here some new ways of thinking about assignments and skills in the writing and ritual course.

Summary

When situating our analyses within the larger framework of scholarship, we refer to previous work. We may sketch an argument briefly, as a note; we may examine a theory in depth; we may present an approach as a springboard from which we will move. When a theory receives lengthy, close attention, we usually intend to challenge or disturb it, whereas a briefer treatment implies lesser engagement. This principle is one students commonly reverse: they think if they agree with an argument, they should write about it at length, whereas if they disagree, they should keep it quick and essentially submerged. Furthermore, when summarizing, we generally do not cover the entirety of an article or book, but rather focus on parts that both are relevant to our purposes and also form a cohesive whole. In the first assignment, then, I ask students to summarize a difficult article, and I explain (in less dense fashion) these principles.

I deliberately choose something very difficult for which they have no background, an article they cannot understand fully. I usually use "Fences and Neighbors," the first chapter of Jonathan Z. Smith's *Imagining Religion*. There are several pedagogical points here. First, a careful summarizer will find herself understanding better than she had previously, giving a feeling of accomplishment and a grasp of the text. Second, this shows that one can, from rhetoric and structure, discern the essential points of an argument. Third, the density and complexity of the article requires that the students cut a great deal, in fact the majority, to focus on one argument, contrary to their usual inclination to sacrifice depth and clarity for coverage.

The assignment has four small parts. First, outline the whole article, in detail, and highlight the important pieces. Next, summarize the gist of the article in one sentence; this focuses attention on which of the important pieces are essential. Third, summarize in two paragraphs, imagining that you will go on to challenge the argument; you must make the author's case as effectively as possible in order to give a strong basis for your own challenge. Finally, summarize again in one five-sentence paragraph, imagining in this instance that you will continue the argument or build from it; you must make the case briefly, but not waste time.

Explication

The explication continues from the longer summary, in that it goes on to explain exactly how the argument in question works, and raises questions and problems that require resolution. As you can see, we are building an essay introduction: after a description of the problem to be addressed, we choose a previous work that will situate our own analysis. We summarize carefully, then analyze in depth, and find ourselves with unresolved problems. In the next section of the essay, we present some data that will help with the problems, analyze, and conclude by using the data and analysis to resolve the problems discerned at the outset. In the explication, the point is to explain an argument in detail for two pages, pointing out difficulties.

For this purpose, I use selections from *The Golden Bough*, particularly the parts titled "The Magician's Progress," "Magic and Religion," and so forth. Frazer is trickier than he looks, but students challenge him readily because so much of his method and language seems so dated. An important point is to keep the explication from becoming a very long summary, and to emphasize that it should not *destroy* the argument but rather raise difficulties and questions that Frazer leaves unresolved. Whatever the text, a central goal here is to have students walk through the logic of an argument, step by step; I find this is the biggest hurdle for some students with analytical writing, in that many will simply isolate a single point and attack vehemently.

Lens Essay

The first long essay I assign, the lens essay, is so simple and obvious to students of ritual that it perhaps requires no explanation apart from the unfamiliar term; several other names for this assignment appear in writing manuals, but I find the "lens" image straightforward. Here you have a theory and an object (a description of a ritual), and you apply the former to the latter. We have all written papers like this; the only difficulty in composing the assignment is to choose material available to the students. By this point in my course, students have finished reading some Durkheim and are moving on to Radcliffe-Brown, Malinowski, and Homans; for an example, then, I generally suggest (but do not require) the Intichiuma, and ask students to present Durkheim's reading and then reconsider from the perspective of one of the functionalists.

Although the assignment is in a sense obvious, a number of complexities arise in the writing. First, I emphasize that Homans's "Anxiety and Ritual" (1941) is itself a masterful lens essay, playing off Radcliffe-Brown and Malinowski by reading the one through the other and vice versa. Though I emphasize that students need not do both simultaneously, as Homans does, I do impress upon them that he covers the whole ground in a few pages and furthermore proposes his own synthetic theory. This helps answer such questions as, "But how can I do all that in five pages?" Another excellent example is Durkheim's application of Robertson Smith's theory of sacrifice, in chapter 3.2 of *The Elementary Forms*, which answers the converse question, "How can I get five pages out of this?"

Second, many scholars will object to the method apparently espoused here. After all, such an assignment almost necessarily produces mechanical, turn-the-crank uses of theory. I agree, and indeed if this were the *final* assignment, I would object strenuously. As a preliminary exercise, however, the lens essay is useful because it demands an intellectual flexibility and precision in using models that helps enormously when dealing with more sophisticated ritual theories. If students can write rigorously and precisely, they can surely think that way; so long as theories remain pure abstractions without the possibility of application, the students will never really grasp what the study of ritual is about in the first place.

Finally, this assignment reveals an extraordinary division among students, one I cannot satisfactorily explain. When asked to choose a *specific* example of ritual, some students will choose broad topics like "sympathetic magic" or "childbirth." Some will discuss Intichiuma as though it were an abstract or even fictional notion—indeed, one student remarked that the problem with Durkheim is that he does not provide "real-world examples"! I have been known to harp on the necessity for concrete data and evidence for a class period, with no apparent effect. But the lens essay assignment will tell you which students have this problem, that is, which students think "specific" means "exceedingly general or universal." Given that we want them to understand what they read, and to progress toward understanding ritual, spotting students with this difficulty early rather than late is of real value on its own.

Imitation

This is another short assignment, a brief interlude between the first long paper and the later research papers. It is entirely focused on prose or analytical style and is, I think, the most readily eliminated or shifted part of this assignment sequence. The point is simple: to learn to write good prose, practice by imitating someone else's good prose slavishly.

For this assignment, I use the Hidatsa eagle-hunting example from *The Savage Mind*. I ask for three pages or so, and indeed the original passage is not much longer. The students are asked to be creative: they must invent a strange, exotic ritual, and then explain and dissect it and its equally odd context in precisely the same voice and method as Lévi-Strauss uses. Having done this, they must go on for a page or two and explain how they did it: what choices they made to change their own style and voice into his, using concrete examples.

For many, this assignment works wonderfully. They get excited about inventing strange rituals, and indeed the papers can be hilarious. Furthermore, there is no better way to figure out Lévi-Strauss than to try on the method, and some students emerge budding structuralists.

However, some students find this tedious, silly, or simply daunting. Grades on imitation can vary considerably from the general trends; that is, some strong students get C's, and some weak ones suddenly get A's.

I generally offer to drop the lowest grade on a short assignment, so that the occasional collapse on an imitation does no harm. On the other hand, those students whose grades suddenly jump up rarely drop all the way back down; the assignment appears to galvanize some confused students, helping them to understand the creative, dynamic nature of ritual and its analysis.

Comparison

The first true research paper takes the lens essay form and adds another component, either another ritual object or another analytical method. I offer both options, but pedagogically they have quite different purposes, which I will discuss separately. In any event, one ritual example (the only one if working with two theorists) must be found through research in the library.[2] At that stage of my course, I ask that one theorist be either Lévi-Strauss or Eliade, but this is hardly necessary. Depending on the students' research skills, they might be asked to provide more or less scholarly context for the ritual or the theoretical views.

When analyzing one ritual by means of two theorists, the student in effect situates the ritual within the bounds of scholarly discourse, and uses ritual data to resolve or clarify debate. Here one needs to push against students' natural inclination to write two separate lens essays and stick them back to back. Once again, Homans's "Anxiety and Ritual" provides an excellent example. Homans's interpretation of Andamanese teknonymy is really not the issue, nor does he go into great depth about the practice or its context; instead, he uses the ritual as a lens through which to examine a debate—really a squabble—between Malinowski and Radcliffe-Brown.

When analyzing two rituals from disparate cultures, the issue must be the grounds that permit the comparison. If we analyze two childbirth rituals, it is really childbirth that is at stake. By means of a mediating theoretical lens, the student views each ritual in the context of the other, and tries to provide a meaningful interpretation of the complex. Given the number of balls in the air, as it were, I find it helpful to guide students to choose a seemingly simple example and a relatively complex one, and use the former as an entree into the latter. This makes particularly good sense when the "simple" case is analyzed in depth by the theorist chosen; for example, a student who has read *The Sacred and the Profane* might look at baptism through Eliade's eyes, since he provides an extensive analysis, and then compare to another infant-initiation ritual.

Whichever way the papers go, the challenge of organizing a large and complex argument will be paramount. Again, I stress specific examples from the theoretical works read in class. By this stage, papers will be taking on a classically academic shape, and explicit parallels to previous work can provide strong models for organization and structure as well as style.

Research Synthesis

The final research paper is, of course, a synthesis of all that has come before. Pedagogically, I find it most efficient simply to explain how a complete research paper analyzing some ritual, theoretical problem, or complex is necessarily made up of all the building blocks we have already developed. In essence, there should be nothing new here: all I ask is that they use the tools they have honed.

One essential point, however, is that students receive no set topics whatever. They must go out and find interesting material, analyze it in light of any and all appropriate theorists, and compose a complete paper. This is purely pragmatic: having completed the writing requirement, students are supposed to know how to write research papers, and as a result, faculty teaching more advanced courses often provide little or no guidance.

I find that getting started is the most difficult part; many find it a daunting prospect to have to wander into the library and find something. Once forced to do so, however, students come up with a surprising range of topics, and often get deeply involved in their papers. Not surprisingly, perhaps, many papers are quite a bit longer than the eight to twelve pages I ask for, and some are of exceptional quality.

To recapitulate briefly: these assignments build up a series of essential components of a serious analytical paper on ritual. Students summarize and explain theories, apply them to specific ritual practices, and situate their work in the larger context of scholarly discourse. They learn how to find a topic *de novo* and select among theoretical approaches to achieve specific ends, and they develop a number of stylistic and analytical options from which to choose.

Conclusions: On Writing Ritual

Success in teaching writing through ritual depends upon all the usual elements of pedagogy: planning, patience, preparation—and of course grading, for which there are no shortcuts.[3] Indeed, in the weary drudgery of workaday grading, is it possible for the scholar to learn anything about ritual? To be sure, we always learn from our students, in class discussions, office hours, and papers, but that happens whether or not the course is focused on writing. What, if anything, does running a writing course on ritual teach us?

Writing takes practice, of course, but it is also *a* practice, in that writers manipulate the established structures of formal language in flexible, dynamic, creative ways. Just so, writing is performative: it has an audience, if only oneself or one's teacher, and it has a unique moment of definition and actuality, when it is published or handed in. Scholarly writing is distinctively marked off from other modes by any number of more or less explicit categories and indicators, and each discipline and field has its own emblemata. And writing is always analyzed from the outside, as an object different from the person examining it, although it is entirely composed and constituted of human thoughts and ideas. In short, scholarly writing is itself a ritual mode.

With that in mind, we must recognize in ourselves the instructors, the masters, in an initiatory process. This is not an intellectual game: I find that students often grasp Victor Turner's ideas on liminality best when they think of the class itself as liminal. We present the *sacra* for their examination, and while we claim to allow freedom of thought, we evaluate the degree to which they have correctly understood the riddles posed. The students are leveled, in that all have equal status when they enter, and they often form strong bonds over the span of a term—bonds that may well not last beyond exam week. And of course, the process is intended to be transformative in specific ways: they are graded upon how well they can walk the walk and talk the talk of the scholar of ritual.

To my mind, what is really striking about this not particularly novel idea is that a writing class seems to have a stronger initiatory character than an ordinary seminar of traditional form, at least partly because it is so obvious that we are teaching specific modes of behavior. But beyond this, I would argue that because scholarly writing itself is a ritual mode, we are in fact inducting novice priests into our order, elevating the ritual character of the whole process.

For scholars of ritual, reflection on the procedure can be enlightening, reminding us again not to keep ritual at a distance. Further, the fact that we actually teach theories of ritual enables students to reflect on the process too, creating a fascinating reflexivity in classroom discourse.

To take the best of many examples from my own classroom, I recall one student who had considerable social difficulties. A self-identified "science-fiction geek," she had no trouble expressing her ideas but a great struggle doing so in a manner congenial to her classmates. Finding herself largely outside the social arena, but unable to understand clearly why she had been excluded, she fell back on the only effective analytical tools at her disposal: theories of ritual. Quite suddenly, about halfway into the semester, she found herself applying every theory or concept she read in class to her own experience, seeing the classroom as a case study of ritual in society. When it came time to present her final paper project in a ten-minute lecture before the class, a required part of the course that she had been dreading, she defiantly analyzed the campus science-fiction community and its relations to other groups by referring to sci-fi gatherings and classroom meetings in ritual terms. I think she expected to be attacked, and to have the satisfaction of knowing that she understood what her classmates did not. In fact, her presentation led smoothly—without any assistance from me, I might add—into a lively debate about ways in which ritual practices can both form and be formed by their social contexts.

On a similar note, many students have told me, long after the semester's conclusion, that they find themselves thinking in terms of effervescence, liminality, and purity in their daily lives. Although this is largely a testimony to the power and persuasiveness of the texts they read, I suggest that it also arises from their having encountered these ideas in a class that necessarily bound together the constant college practice of writing papers to the terms and categories of ritual.

Students beginning a writing course sometimes ask, and clearly more often wonder, whether the conventions of scholarly writing are not mere elitism, conservatism, or exclusionary tactics. A partial response can be found in such works as *The Elementary Forms of the Religious Life*: it is not coincidental that Durkheim is both extraordinarily persuasive and also an amazingly good writer. But in a writing course on ritual, we can go further and ask students to answer the question for themselves in social-practical terms. Why does obedience to the conventions of a discourse best permit challenges to it, and to what extent does such obedience corrupt or subvert such challenges? Why is it that arguments are usually more effective when situated within the history of discussion? If we read the class as an initiatory process, what would be the effect (aside from a grade) if a student were to refuse the ritual entirely? In what ways would that be a worthwhile challenge, and in what ways would it undermine itself?

The potential rewards of a writing course on ritual are great, for both students and teachers. The more students reflect upon their own experience in ritual terms, and see writing as a mode of ritual behavior, the better they will understand what they read and, in my experience, the better they will write. Furthermore, the discussions they generate will spark ideas in the teacher's mind: by being forced constantly to think about writing as ritual performance, and about the class as an initiation into that practice, the teacher finds himself teaching, preparing, and grading in an increasingly intellectually productive fashion, with the little voice of the participant-observer constantly muttering over his shoulder.

If this brief discussion has accomplished anything, I hope it has provided practical ideas for how to teach writing and ritual without sacrificing either. I would emphasize above all that selection of texts worth imitating, in both prose and content, must be the central principle of any such course, as only by focusing closely on texts of such quality can good writing and good ritual studies happen together. Assignments should stress practical building blocks of scholarly writing and be couched in such terms that you yourself would benefit from doing the homework. Finally, by encouraging the class to see the writing and learning processes in ritual terms and by following their thinking, one can underscore the lessons learned while also developing one's own experiential and intellectual understandings of ritual.

NOTES

1. This sequence of assignments is adapted from the Boston University College of Arts and Sciences Writing Program curriculum for writing and research courses (WR150), originally designed by Michael B. Prince.

2. I recommend forbidding students to use any Internet sources, even ones like JSTOR, at least for the first research paper. If you have never done so, try asking a class of mostly sophomores how many of them have ever looked for a book in the campus library, or even darkened its doors. Simply forcing students to enter the library and find a book by call number is a worthwhile exercise. If you do allow Internet sources, you must devote considerable class time to guidance on evaluating such sources, as even quite sophisticated students often have a worrying tendency to assume that anything on the Internet that purports to be nonfictional is reliable.

3. With respect to grading and paper-marking methods, I have found nothing specific to ritual courses, and thus will not address the issue here. It is worth noting, however, that considerable evidence suggests that divided grades—one for content and one for writing—have a retarding effect on the improvement of writing skills. Debates about how much to mark, on what part of the paper, and in what color, are unending and inconclusive.

USEFUL MATERIALS

After reviewing some fifty college writing textbooks, I find few helpful for the sort of course described here. Most are weighty and expensive, packed with unnecessary drivel (e.g., how to compose Web pages), and usually full of errors. They provide mediocre college papers as examples, offer exercises rarely worth doing, and emphasize glitz over content. One of the most consistent student complaints about our hundreds of writing courses at Boston University, which have a wide range of topics and instructors, is that the writing manuals are useless.

More important, almost no such textbooks apparently recognize that there are modes of college writing other than literature papers, laboratory reports, and business memos. Worse, the discussions of argumentation and research usually presume that a researched argument will be a policy paper defending or proposing some social cause: why malpractice suits should or should not be capped, why ski resorts should or should not be liable when someone breaks a leg, and so on. Furthermore, the overwhelming majority of space devoted to "research methods" usually discusses ad nauseam how to search the Internet. So far as I can tell, in fact, few such textbooks are written by scholars outside of the education and English fraternities, and they offer almost nothing helpful to the teacher of a ritual course.

On the assumption that you would rather not take my word for it, there are three kinds of writing textbooks. There is the "quick reference," a relatively small volume presenting grammar and style rules in a compact fashion. Sadly, few of these seem aware that there are reference styles other than MLA, APA, and perhaps CBE; one announces that footnotes are "no longer used." If these come cheap, they can be handy, but they generally provide no exercises or guidance and cannot well serve pedagogical purposes for those needing assistance.

Next, there is the "writers handbook," usually a massive tome containing all the same material plus exercises and lots of extras. Unfortunately, these usually cost $50 or more, and are so jam-packed with extraneous tripe as to be difficult to use; in our experience at Boston University, students also complain if they have to carry these monsters around all day. Although these volumes usually claim to be all-inclusive references of lasting value to the student, nearly all are promptly sold back at textbook exchanges.

One exception, and it is hardly perfect, is Andrea A. Lunsford, *The St. Martin's Handbook*, 5th ed. (Boston and New York: Bedford/St. Martin's, 1993). It is well written, clearly organized, and quite obviously written by a scholar with a real knowledge of academic standards and ideals. Its weakness is grammar and mechanics, so it may be unsuitable for students with poor fundamentals. Some may also find its text-heavy presentation difficult to navigate. If you must adopt a manual, I recommend this, but you will certainly find it necessary to supplement.

Finally, there is the "argumentation manual," which comes under a number of labels. These provide more extensive discussion of argumentation styles and types, and then usually a lengthy reader of sample essays by more or less well-known writers. The introductory sections can be useful, but the sample essays are rarely valuable examples of academic prose: a Gloria Steinem op-ed piece may well be persuasive and elegantly written, but it is not an appropriate model for a research paper on ritual.

You will find, I suspect, that you fall back on old standards: Strunk and White, Fowler's, and the like. If you must teach grammar extensively, I suggest that you seek out a pure grammar textbook that provides a lot of exercises.

REFERENCES

Douglas, M. 1966. "The Abominations of Leviticus." Chap. 3 of *Purity and Danger*. London: Routledge.

Durkheim, E. 2001. *The Elementary Forms of Religious Life.* Translated by Carol Cosman. Oxford: Oxford University Press.

Eliade, M. 1959. *The Sacred and the Profane: The Nature of Religion.* Translated by Willard R. Trask. New York: Harvest.

Frazer, J. G. 1922. *The Golden Bough.* Abridged ed. (one vol.). London: Macmillan.

Homans, G. C. 1941. "Anxiety and Ritual: The Theories of Malinowski and Radcliffe-Brown." *American Anthropologist* 43: 164–172.

Lévi-Strauss, C. 1966. *The Savage Mind.* Chicago: University of Chicago Press.

Lunsford, A. A. 1993. *The St. Martin's Handbook.* 5th ed. Boston: Bedford/St. Martin's.

Malinowski, B. 1931. "Culture." In *Encyclopaedia of the Social Sciences*, ed. E. R. A. Seligman and A. Johnson, Vol. 4, 621–646. London: Macmillan.

Radcliffe-Brown, A. R. 1939. *Taboo.* The Frazer lecture, 1939. Cambridge: Cambridge University Press.

Smith, J. Z. 1988. *Imagining Religion: From Babylon to Jonestown*. Chicago: University of Chicago Press.

Stevenson, R. L. 1887. "A College Magazine." Chap. 4 of *Memories and Portraits*. London: Chatto and Windus.

Turner, V. W. 1967. "Betwixt and Between: The Liminal Period in *Rites de Passage*." In *The Forest of Symbols: Aspects of Ndembu Ritual*, 93–111. Ithaca, N.Y.: Cornell University Press.

Index